AF781617

Comparing Post-War Japanese and Finnish Economies and Societies

This book compares two countries with striking parallels in economic and political outcomes, yet with some distinct features in terms of institutional structures, relative size, and culture. Therefore, this book forms a fruitful platform for the study of the similarities and differences in the economic and societal development of Japan and Finland. Despite their geographic distance from one another and the aforementioned differences, both countries experienced rather similar economic and societal development patterns after the Second World War. The study of these societies both individually and through commonalities will provide a unique perspective on the emergence of modern economies and institutions.

The book provides comprehensive coverage on issues such as welfare state formation and society, security and military spending, education system, industrial development, international trade, governmental economic policies, energy solutions, and bubbles and their collapse; thus, issues typical for these countries, as well as for most modern states, are studied from a longitudinal perspective.

The book aims to answer a fundamental question in social science: Why do there seem to be common trends and developmental paths among countries differing in size, culture, and economic structure? This book will provide insights for those seeking to decipher how the developments in their own countries came about and where they may be headed.

Yasushi Tanaka is Professor of Economics in the Faculty of Economics at Kyoto Sangyo University. He is a labour economist with particular interests in human capital theory, OJT (On-the-Job Training), cooperative education, and economic inequality.

Toshiaki Tamaki is Professor of Economic History in the Faculty of Economics at Kyoto Sangyo University. He specializes in economic history of early modern Europe.

Jari Ojala is Professor of Comparative Business History at the University of Jyväskylä, Department of History and Ethnology. He specializes in maritime and business history.

Jari Eloranta is Professor of History at the Appalachian State University, United States, and Adjunct Professor (Docent) of Economic History at the University of Jyväskylä. He specializes in comparative economic and business history, especially nineteenth- and twentieth-century government and military spending and conflicts.

Routledge Studies in the Modern World Economy

1 **Interest Rates and Budget Deficits**
A study of the advanced economies
Kanhaya L Gupta and Bakhtiar Moazzami

2 **World Trade after the Uruguay Round**
Prospects and policy options for the twenty-first century
Edited by Harald Sander and András Inotai

3 **The Flow Analysis of Labour Markets**
Edited by Ronald Schettkat

4 **Inflation and Unemployment**
Contributions to a new macroeconomic approach
Edited by Alvaro Cencini and Mauro Baranzini

5 **Macroeconomic Dimensions of Public Finance**
Essays in honour of Vito Tanzi
Edited by Mario I. Blejer and Teresa M. Ter-Minassian

6 **Fiscal Policy and Economic Reforms**
Essays in honour of Vito Tanzi
Edited by Mario I. Blejer and Teresa M. Ter-Minassian

7 **Competition Policy in the Global Economy**
Modalities for co-operation
Edited by Leonard Waverman, William S. Comanor and Akira Goto

8 **Working in the Macro Economy**
A study of the US labor market
Martin F. J. Prachowny

9 **How Does Privatization Work?**
Edited by Anthony Bennett

10 **The Economics and Politics of International Trade**
Freedom and trade: volume II
Edited by Gary Cook

11 **The Legal and Moral Aspects of International Trade**
Freedom and trade: volume III
Edited by Asif Qureshi, Hillel Steiner and Geraint Parry

12 **Capital Markets and Corporate Governance in Japan, Germany and the United States**
Organizational response to market inefficiencies
Helmut M. Dietl

13 **Competition and Trade Policies**
Coherence or conflict
Edited by Einar Hope

14 **Rice**
The primary commodity
A.J.H. Latham

15 **Trade, Theory and Econometrics**
Essays in honour of John S. Chipman
Edited by James C. Moore, Raymond Riezman, James R. Melvin

16 **Who Benefits from Privatisation?**
Edited by Moazzem Hossain and Justin Malbon

17 **Towards a Fair Global Labour Market**
Avoiding the new slave trade
Ozay Mehmet, Errol Mendes and Robert Sinding

18 **Models of Futures Markets**
Edited by Barry Goss

19 **Venture Capital Investment**
An agency analysis of UK practice
Gavin C. Reid

20 **Macroeconomic Forecasting**
A sociological appraisal
Robert Evans

21 **Multimedia and Regional Economic Restructuring**
Edited by Hans-Joachim Braczyk, Gerhard Fuchs and Hans-Georg Wolf

22 **The New Industrial Geography**
Regions, regulation and institutions
Edited by Trevor J. Barnes and Meric S. Gertler

23 **The Employment Impact of Innovation**
Evidence and policy
Edited by Marco Vivarelli and Mario Pianta

24 **International Health Care Reform**
A legal, economic and political analysis
Colleen Flood

25 **Competition Policy Analysis**
Edited by Einar Hope

26 **Culture and Enterprise**
The development, representation and morality of business
Don Lavoie and Emily Chamlee-Wright

27 **Global Financial Crises and Reforms**
Cases and caveats
B.N. Ghosh

28 **Geography of Production and Economic Integration**
Miroslav N. Jovanović

29 **Technology, Trade and Growth in OECD Countries**
Does specialisation matter?
Valentina Meliciani

30 **Post-Industrial Labour Markets**
Profiles of North America and Scandinavia
Edited by Thomas P. Boje and Bengt Furaker

31 **Capital Flows without Crisis**
Reconciling capital mobility and economic stability
Edited by Dipak Dasgupta, Marc Uzan and Dominic Wilson

32 **International Trade and National Welfare**
Murray C. Kemp

33 **Global Trading Systems at Crossroads**
A post-Seattle perspective
Dilip K. Das

34 **The Economics and Management of Technological Diversification**
Edited by John Cantwell, Alfonso Gambardella and Ove Granstrand

35 **Before and Beyond EMU**
Historical lessons and future prospects
Edited by Patrick Crowley

36 **Fiscal Decentralization**
Ehtisham Ahmad and Vito Tanzi

37 **Regionalisation of Globalised Innovation**
Locations for advanced industrial development and disparities in participation
Edited by Ulrich Hilpert

38 **Gold and the Modern World Economy**
Edited by MoonJoong Tcha

39 **Global Economic Institutions**
Willem Molle

40 **Global Governance and Financial Crises**
Edited by Meghnad Desai and Yahia Said

41 **Linking Local and Global Economies**
The ties that bind
Edited by Carlo Pietrobelli and Arni Sverrisson

42 **Tax Systems and Tax Reforms in Europe**
Edited by Luigi Bernardi and Paola Profeta

43 **Trade Liberalization and APEC**
Edited by Jiro Okamoto

44 **Fiscal Deficits in the Pacific Region**
Edited by Akira Kohsaka

45 **Financial Globalization and the Emerging Market Economies**
Dilip K. Das

46 **International Labor Mobility**
Unemployment and increasing returns to scale
Bharati Basu

47 **Good Governance in the Era of Global Neoliberalism**
Conflict and depolitization in Latin America, Eastern Europe, Asia and Africa
Edited by Jolle Demmers, Alex E. Fernández Jilberto and Barbara Hogenboom

48 **The International Trade System**
Alice Landau

49 **International Perspectives on Temporary Work and Workers**
Edited by John Burgess and Julia Connell

50 **Working Time and Workers' Preferences in Industrialized Countries**
Finding the balance
Edited by Jon C. Messenger

51 **Tax Systems and Tax Reforms in New EU Members**
Edited by Luigi Bernardi, Mark Chandler and Luca Gandullia

52 **Globalization and the Nation State**
The impact of the IMF and the World Bank
Edited by Gustav Ranis, James Vreeland and Stephen Kosak

53 **Macroeconomic Policies and Poverty Reduction**
Edited by Ashoka Mody and Catherine Pattillo

54 **Regional Monetary Policy**
Carlos J. Rodríguez-Fuentez

55 **Trade and Migration in the Modern World**
Carl Mosk

56 **Globalisation and the Labour Market**
Trade, technology and less-skilled workers in Europe and the United States
Edited by Robert Anderton, Paul Brenton and John Whalley

57 **Financial Crises**
Socio-economic causes and institutional context
Brenda Spotton Visano

58 **Globalization and Self Determination**
Is the nation-state under siege?
Edited by David R. Cameron, Gustav Ranis and Annalisa Zinn

59 **Developing Countries and the Doha Development Round of the WTO**
Edited by Pitou van Dijck and Gerrit Faber

60 **Immigrant Enterprise in Europe and the USA**
Prodromos Panayiotopoulos

61 **Solving the Riddle of Globalization and Development**
Edited by Manuel Agosín, David Bloom, George Chapelier and Jagdish Saigal

62 **Foreign Direct Investment and the World Economy**
Ashoka Mody

63 **The World Economy**
A global analysis
Horst Siebert

64 **Production Organizations in Japanese Economic Development**
Edited by Tetsuji Okazaki

65 **The Economics of Language**
International analyses
Edited by Barry R. Chiswick and Paul W. Miller

66 **Street Entrepreneurs**
People, place and politics in local and global perspective
Edited by John Cross and Alfonso Morales

67 **Global Challenges and Local Responses**
The East Asian experience
Edited by Jang-Sup Shin

68 **Globalization and Regional Integration**
The origins, development and impact of the single european aviation market
Alan Dobson

69 **Russia Moves into the Global Economy**
Breaking out
John M. Letiche

70 **The European Economy in an American Mirror**
Barry Eichengreen, Michael Landesmann and Dieter Stiefel

71 **Working Time Around the World**
Trends in working hours, laws, and policies in a global comparative perspective
Jon C. Messenger, Sangheon Lee and Deidre McCann

72 **International Water Treaties**
Negotiation and cooperation along transboundary rivers
Shlomi Dinar

73 **Economic Integration in the Americas**
Edited by Joseph A. McKinney and H. Stephen Gardner

74 **Expanding Frontiers of Global Trade Rules**
The political economy dynamics of the international trading system
Nitya Nanda

75 **The Macroeconomics of Global Imbalances**
European and Asian perspectives
Edited by Marc Uzan

76 **China and Asia**
Economic and financial interactions
Edited by Yin-Wong Cheung and Kar-Yiu Wong

77 **Regional Inequality in China**
Trends, explanations and policy responses
Edited by Shenggen Fan, Ravi Kanbur and Xiaobo Zhang

78 **Governing Rapid Growth in China**
Equity and institutions
Edited by Ravi Kanbur and Xiaobo Zhang

79 **The Indonesian Labour Market**
Shafiq Dhanani, Iyanatul Islam and Anis Chowdhury

80 **Cost–Benefit Analysis in Multi-level Government in Europe and the USA**
The case of EU cohesion policy and of US federal investment policies
Alessandro Ferrara

81 **The Economic Geography of Air Transportation**
Space, time, and the freedom of the sky
John Bowen

82 **Cartelization, Antitrust and Globalization in the US and Europe**
Mark LeClair

83 **The Political Economy of Integration**
Jeffrey Cason

84 **Critical Issues in Air Transport Economics and Business**
Rosario Macario and Eddy Van de Voorde

85 **Financial Liberalisation and Economic Performance**
Luiz Fernando de Paula

86 **A General Theory of Institutional Change**
Shiping Tang

87 **The Dynamics of Asian Financial Integration**
Edited by Michael Devereux, Philip Lane, Park Cyn-young and Wei Shang-jin

88 **Innovative Fiscal Policy and Economic Development in Transition Economies**
Aleksandr Gevorkyan

89 **Foreign Direct Investments in Asia**
Edited by Chalongphob Sussangkarn, Yung Chul Park and Sung Jin Kang

90 **Time Zones, Communications Networks, and International Trade**
Toru Kikuchi

91 **Miraculous Growth and Stagnation in Post-War Japan**
Edited by Koichi Hamada, Keijiro Otsuka, Gustav Ranis, and Ken Togo

92 **Multilateralism and Regionalism in Global Economic Governance**
Trade, investment and finance
Edited by Junji Nakagawa

93 **Economic Growth and Income Inequality in China, India and Singapore**
Trends and policy implications
Pundarik Mukhopadhaya, G. Shantakumar and Bhanoji Rao

94 **Foreign Direct Investment in China**
Spillover effects on domestic enterprises
Deng Ziliang

95 **Enterprise Forms and Economic Efficiency**
Capitalist, cooperative and government firms
Kazuhiko Mikami

96 **Diversity and Transformations of Asian Capitalism**
Edited by Robert Boyer, Hiroyasu Uemura and Akinori Isogai

97 **Knowledge Transfer in the Automobile Industry**
Global-local production networks
Dessy Irawati

98 **Exchange Rates and Foreign Direct Investment in Emerging Asia**
Selected issues and policy options
Ramkishen S. Rajan

99 **Singapore, the Energy Economy**
From the first refinery to the end of cheap oil, 1960–2010
Ng Weng Hoong

100 **China-India Economics**
Challenges, competition and collaboration
Amitendu Palit

101 **Case Studies on Chinese Enterprises**
Edited by Donglin Xia

102 **Argentina's Economic Growth and Recovery**
Michael Cohen

103 **The Korean Labour Market After the 1997 Economic Crisis**
Edited by Joonmo Cho, Richard B. Freeman, Jaeho Keum and Sunwoong Kim

104 **China and India**
The quest for energy resources in the 21st century
Zhao Hong

105 **Beyond the Global Crisis**
Structural adjustments and regional integration in Europe and Latin America
Edited by Lionello Punzo, Carmen Aparecida Feio and Martin Putchet Anyui

106 **The Global Economic Crisis in Latin America**
Impacts and responses
Edited by Michael Cohen

107 **The Processes and Practices of Fair Trade**
Trust, ethics and governance
Edited by Brigitte Granville and Janet Dine

108 **Regional Development through Ecological Business**
Unique cases in Japanese rural regions
Makoto Hirano

109 **Aging and Economic Growth Potentials in the Pacific Region**
Edited by Akira Kohsaka

110 **Crises of Global Economies and the Future of Capitalism**
Reviving Marxian crisis theory
Edited by Kiichiro Yagi, Nobuharu Yokokawa, Shinjiro Hagiwara and Gary A. Dymski

111 **The Financial History of the Bank for International Settlements**
Kazuhiko YAGO

112 **Freight Transport and the Modern Economy**
Michel Savy and June Burnham

113 **Thoughts on Economic Development in China**
Edited by Ma Ying and Hans-Michael Trautwein

114 **China's Ethnic Minorities**
Social and economic indicators
Rongxing Guo

115 **Globalization, Outsourcing and Labour Development in ASEAN**
Shandre Thangavelu and Aekapol Chongvilaivan

116 **The Role of Informal Economies in the Post-Soviet World**
The end of transition?
Colin C. Williams, John Round and Peter Rodgers

117 **Demystifying the Chinese Miracle**
The rise and future of relational capitalism
Yongqin Wang

118 **Globalism and Regional Economy**
Edited by Susumu Egashira

119 **Russia's Changing Economic and Political Regimes**
The Putin years and afterwards
Andrey Makarychev and André Mommen

120 **Innovation and Regional Development in China**
Edited by Ingo Liefner and Yehua Dennis Wei

121 **International Trade Negotiations and Domestic Politics**
The intermestic politics of trade liberalization
Edited by Oluf Langhelle

122 **Emerging Knowledge Economies in Asia**
Current trends in ASEAN 5
Edited by Dessy Irawati and Roel Rutten

123 **The Internationalization of the Renminbi**
International Monetary Institute, Renmin University of China

124 **Financial Globalization and Regionalism in East Asia**
Edited by Takuji Kinkyo, Yoichi Matsubayashi and Shigeyuki Hamori

125 **Successful Business Dealings and Management with China Oil, Gas and Chemical Giants**
EurIng. Henry K. H. Wang

126 **State Building and Development**
Edited by Keijiro Otsuka and Takashi Shiraishi

127 **International Economic Development**
Leading issues and challenges
Edited by Fu Lai Tony Yu, Wai Kee Yuen and Diana S. Kwan

128 **Innovation, Globalization and Firm Dynamics**
Lessons for enterprise policy
Edited by Anna Ferragina, Erol Taymoz and Kamil Yilmaz

129 **International Remittance Payments and the Global Economy**
Bharati Basu with James T. Bang

130 **The Open Society and Its Enemies in East Asia**
The relevance of the Popperian framework
Edited by Gregory C. G. Moore

131 **The Economics of Knowledge Generation and Distribution**
The role of interactions in the system dynamics of innovation and growth
Edited by Pier Paolo Patrucco

132 **Japan's Aid**
Lessons for economic growth, development and political economy
Edward M. Feasel

133 **The Geographical Transformation of China**
Edited by Michael Dunford and Weidong Lui

134 **The Economics of Cooperative Education**
A practitioners' guide to the theoretical framework and empirical assessment of cooperative education
Yasushi Tanaka

135 **Comparing Post-War Japanese and Finnish Economies and Societies**
Longitudinal perspectives
Edited by Yasushi Tanaka, Toshiaki Tamaki, Jari Ojala, and Jari Eloranta

Comparing Post-War Japanese and Finnish Economies and Societies

Longitudinal perspectives

Edited by Yasushi Tanaka, Toshiaki Tamaki, Jari Ojala, and Jari Eloranta

Routledge
Taylor & Francis Group
LONDON AND NEW YORK

First published 2015
by Routledge
2 Park Square, Milton Park, Abingdon, Oxon OX14 4RN

and by Routledge
711 Third Avenue, New York, NY 10017

Routledge is an imprint of the Taylor & Francis Group, an informa business

© 2015 For editorial selection and matter, Yasushi Tanaka, Toshiaki Tamaki, Jari Ojala, and Jari Eloranta; for the individual chapters, the contributors.

The right of the editors to be identified as the authors of the editorial material, and of the authors for their individual chapters, has been asserted in accordance with sections 77 and 78 of the Copyright, Designs and Patents Act 1988.

All rights reserved. No part of this book may be reprinted or reproduced or utilised in any form or by any electronic, mechanical, or other means, now known or hereafter invented, including photocopying and recording, or in any information storage or retrieval system, without permission in writing from the publishers.

Trademark notice: Product or corporate names may be trademarks or registered trademarks, and are used only for identification and explanation without intent to infringe.

British Library Cataloguing in Publication Data
A catalogue record for this book is available from the British Library

Library of Congress Cataloging-in-Publication Data
Comparing post war Japanese and Finnish economies and societies / edited by Yasushi Tanaka, Toshiaki Tamaki, Jari Ojala, and Jari Eloranta.
pages cm. — (Routledge studies in the modern world economy ; 135)
Includes bibliographical references and index.
1. Finland—Economic conditions—20th century. 2. Japan—Economic conditions—20th century. 3. Finland—Social conditions—20th century. 4. Japan—Social conditions—20th century. 5. Finland—Politics and government—20th century. 6. Japan—Politics and government—20th century. I. Tanaka, Yasushi, editor of compilation.
HC340.2.C66 2015
330.94897'033—dc23
2014018208

ISBN: 978-0-415-65620-7 (hbk)
ISBN: 978-1-315-74620-3 (ebk)

Typeset in Galliard
by Apex CoVantage, LLC

MIX
Paper from responsible sources
FSC www.fsc.org FSC® C013604

Printed and bound by CPI Group (UK) Ltd, Croydon, CR0 4YY

Contents

Figures

Tables

Preface

This volume features comparative analyses of Japanese and Finnish economies and societies during the post-war era. Both Japanese and Finnish economies are quite interesting topics to study during the period in question, with many characteristics in common like fast pace of economic growth, ageing of population, advanced education system, and so on. Furthermore, both were on the losing side of the Second World War and, thus, bound to facilitate reconstruction in a challenging environment. But at the same, these countries are obviously rather different in terms of size, culture, nature, and geography.

Why, then, attempt to compare these two countries? The motivation for this volume is in fact based on this perceived 'incomparability'. Namely, our aim is also a methodological one: to try to find out how these comparisons can be made at a societal level. Of course, we also aim to bring out profoundly new information about these polities through comparisons.

In order to further enhance the comparative outcomes, all articles in this volume were done as a result of close collaboration by Japanese–Finnish research teams. This has enabled us to bring together in-depth knowledge from both countries – and to overcome the obvious cultural and linguistic barriers. The collaboration among researchers was developed via a series of workshops organized both in Japan and in Finland at the Kyoto Sangyo University and University of Jyväskylä, respectively. We hope that this volume will further serve to enhance this existing collaboration and broaden the research networks between the two countries. These meetings were supported by funding provided by JSPS (Japan Society for the Promotion of Science) and the Academy of Finland.[1] We thank these funding organizations for this support; without it, this work would have been impossible to carry out.

We would also like to thank Virginia Mattila for her language editing work, several research assistants that helped us get this book together (especially Jarmo Taskinen), and Yongling Lam from Taylor & Francis Asia Pasific for all their help during the process.

Finally, it is the researchers and their commitment that made this publication possible. Thus, we, the editors, would like to thank everybody that has been involved in this project. It was a long but surely a rewarding journey.

Editors
Kyoto, Jyväskylä, and Boone
April 2014

Note

1. This research was funded by the Academy of Finland's researcher mobility fund (decision numbers 140109, 140129, 140269, 140271, 140478, 252521, and 259776).

Contributors

Jari Eloranta is a Professor of History at the Appalachian State University, United States, and Adjunct Professor (Docent) of Economic History at the University of Jyväskylä. He specializes in comparative economic and business history, especially nineteenth- and twentieth-century government and military spending and conflicts.

Tadashi Fukui is a Professor of Economics in the Faculty of Economics at Kyoto Sangyo University. He specializes in public economics, especially analysis of social security.

Kari Heimonen is a Professor of Economics at the University of Jyväskylä, School of Business and Economics (JSBE). He specializes in international macrofinance.

Kazuhiro Igawa is a Professor at Kyoto Sangyo University, Faculty of Economics. He specializes in international macroeconomics and has a Ph.D. from Johns Hopkins University, United States.

Christopher Lloyd is Guest Professor, Finnish Centre of Excellence on Historical Research, Tampere and Jyväskylä Universities; and Emeritus Professor, School of Business, University of New England, Australia.

Shigeyoshi Miyagawa is a Professor of Economics, Kyoto Gakuen University, Faculty of Economics. He specializes in monetary policy.

Yoji Morita is a Professor of Econometrics, Kyoto Gakuen University, Faculty of Economics. He specializes in time series analysis.

Anu Ojala M.Sc. (Econ.) is a doctoral student in strategy and entrepreneurship at the University of Jyväskylä, School of Business and Economics (JSBE). She specializes in global competitive strategies of business schools.

Jari Ojala is a Professor of Comparative Business History at the University of Jyväskylä, Department of History and Ethnology. He specializes in maritime and business history.

Pavel Osinsky is an Associate Professor of Sociology at the Appalachian State University, United States. His research focuses on comparative history of revolutions and civil wars, as well as comparative methodology.

Maare Paloheimo is a postdoctoral fellow of the International Research Training Group 'Baltic Borderlands: Shifting Boundaries of Mind and Culture in the Borderlands of the Baltic Sea Region' at the Ernst Moritz Arndt University of Greifswald, Germany. Until spring 2014, she worked at the University of Jyväskylä, Department of History and Ethnology. She specializes in business–government relations and foreign influences in Finnish business life.

Park Seung-Joon is a Professor of Environmental Economics at the Kwansei Gakuin University, School of Policy Studies. He specializes in environmental policy.

Esa Ruuskanen works as an Academy Research Fellow at the Faculty of Humanities, University of Oulu. His current research focuses on human–nature relationships and the history of environmental concerns and protection in Central, Northern, and Western Europe from the seventeenth century to the present day.

Juha Sahi M.A. is a doctoral candidate in general history at the University of Oulu, Department of History. He specializes in business history with a special emphasis on networks of international trade. The working title of his ongoing doctoral dissertation: *Finland's Trade Relations with Japan, 1919–1974.*

Pasi Sajasalo is a Senior Assistant of Management at University of Jyväskylä School of Business and Economics and an Adjunct Professor of Corporate Strategy at Lappeenranta University of Technology. He specializes in strategy-related issues.

Kota Sugahara is a Professor of Public Finance at the Kyoto Sangyo University, Faculty of Economics. He specializes in local public finance.

Timo Särkkä is an Academy of Finland Postdoctoral Researcher at the University of Jyväskylä, Department of History and Ethnology. He specializes in history of economic thought and business history.

Toshiaki Tamaki is a Professor of Economic History at Kyoto Sangyo University, Faculty of Economics. He specializes in economic history of early modern Europe.

Yasushi Tanaka is a Professor of Economics in the Faculty of Economics at Kyoto Sangyo University. He is a labour economist with particular interests in human capital theory, OJT (On-the-Job Training), cooperative education, and economic inequality.

Olli Turunen M.A. is a doctoral student at the University of Jyväskylä, Department of History and Ethnology. Along with business and economic history, his research focuses on the history of economic thought, especially human and social capital and other intangible production factors.

Merja Uotila M.A. is a doctoral student at the University of Jyväskylä, Department of History and Ethnology. She specializes in the history of rural artisans.

Part I

Introduction

1 Comparing Japanese and Finnish economies and societies

Longitudinal perspectives

Jari Ojala, Yasushi Tanaka, Toshiaki Tamaki, and Jari Eloranta

Japan and Finland are not obvious countries to compare in terms of their historical experiences and the development of their respective societies during the twentieth century. They are located on almost opposite sides of the globe, the sizes of their populations and economies are vastly different, and culturally they seem to be quite dissimilar. Why then engage in such efforts? There are some precedents to this approach. In earlier comparisons between Japan and Finland, researchers have concentrated on contemporary issues, while longitudinal analyses have gained markedly little attention. (On Japan from a Finnish perspective, see Opas, 2007; Salomaa, 1999; Turkki, 2005; Vesterinen, 1995, 2001; see also Horiuchi, 2008; Momose & Ishino, 2008.) There are some examples of research comparing Japan and Finland, however, including analyses of management cultures (Koivisto, 1998), financial crisis (Miyagawa, Morita, & Sawada, 2008), labour markets (Räisänen & Heinonen, 2005), and welfare policies (Vuori & Merviö, 2007). However, only a few of these comparative analyses have been done in collaborative projects involving both Japanese and Finnish scholars, as was the case with studies on ageing of societies (EVA & Doyukai, 2006) and employment policies (Räisänen & Hori, 2008). The Swedish and Japanese economies, for example, have been compared in the context of welfare and demographic development (Mosk, 1983, 2000).

The analytical focus ties the volume and approach to the recent discussions, especially among global history scholars – that is, connections and comparisons between different areas, countries, and nationalities (McNeill, 1990; O'Brien, 2006; Pomeranz, 2000). From this perspective, this volume enables us also to discuss the theme of possible convergence between countries in different parts of the world – or whether the divergence that emerged several hundreds of years ago has remained between Asia and Europe, as Kenneth Pomeranz has argued (Pomeranz, 2000). The grand narrative both in Japanese and Finnish historical research has been one of modernization, Westernization, and integration to the world economy since the Second World War – and even earlier. The emerging speed of communication and transport plays a crucial role in this process of global convergence, enabling connections between different parts of the world. The direct political, societal, and economic connections between Finland and Japan might have been vague in world scale, but these two countries have been in constant interaction with each other nonetheless, with industrial production chains, international transfer of technology and knowledge, global political arenas, and cultural transmission. Furthermore, more direct contacts have occurred as well – as can be glimpsed, for example, from Chapter 10 of this volume, with a focus on trade relations between Japan and Finland during the twentieth century. Furthermore, direct flight routes between these two countries since the 1980s – the first ones between Europe and Japan – have further enhanced these connections.

Comparisons are the way to analyse these connections between different areas. Comparisons enable us, as implied by Fernand Braudel, to solve the key historical problems – or at least ask the right questions (Braudel, 1982). Comparisons, though, can be challenging, too, especially with historical material obtained from different kinds of sources with two rather distinctive languages – as has been the case with this volume. We are convinced, though, that the major obstacles in these efforts were overcome, following the guidelines stated in Chapter 2 regarding comparative methodology. Furthermore, the particular strength of the chapters in this volume is that they are all written by teams of Japanese and Finnish scholars, thereby enabling the authors to compile relevant data and previous literature from both countries in a representative fashion. The authors have met at two workshops organized in Kyoto, Japan (2010), and Jyväskylä, Finland (2011). In these meetings, the chapters were discussed in a scholarly manner to improve their quality and provide a consistent structure for the volume. These workshops were funded by the Japan Society for the Promotion of Science (JSPS) and the Academy of Finland. There are only a handful of previous research projects on which both the Japanese and the Finnish scholars have worked in such close collaboration. (On Japanese–Finnish comparisons see, for example, EVA & Doyukai, 2006; Koivisto, 1998; Miyagawa et al., 2008; Räisänen & Heinonen, 2005; Räisänen & Hori, 2008; Valaskivi, 2006; Vuori & Merviö, 2007.)

Moreover, Japan and Finland may not necessarily be that different after all. For example, this volume is motivated by the realization that economic growth in Finland and Japan has been among the fastest in the world throughout the past 130 years; the average growth rate in Finland was 2.4 per cent and in Japan 2.8 per cent during the period 1871 to 2003. These numbers are higher than, for example, in Sweden, the UK, or the United States. The growth figures for the post–Second World War period in particular are markedly similar in Finland and in Japan: fast growth and rebuilding of the economy and society from the 1940s to the 1960s; fast economic growth in the 1970s and the 1980s compared to the OECD average growth figures; and declining growth figures from the late 1980s onwards (see Table 1.1).

There are further similarities in terms of the overall economic development of these two countries: the gross domestic product (GDP) per capita figures are comparable (GDP in Finland in 2012 was 46,098 US $ and in Japan it was 46,736 US $); both countries have been successful in export-led industrialization; both are well known for their success in organizing higher education and promoting achievement, as indicated by the recent PISA tests; and both have been among the leading countries in developing high-technology industries.

Table 1.1 Annual average economic growth in Finland, Japan, and in certain other countries, 1871–2003 (%)

	Finland	*Sweden*	*UK*	*US*	*Japan*
1871–1899	1.2	1.4	1.3	1.8	1.7
1900–1914	1.5	1.3	0.5	1.3	1.1
1920–1938	4.8	3.1	1.4	0.6	1.7
1946–1969	**4.1**	3.3	1.7	1.3	**8.2**
1970–1989	**3.3**	1.9	2.3	2.1	**3.6**
1990–2003	1.4	1.5	1.9	1.7	1.2
1871–2003	2.4	2.0	1.5	2.0	2.8

Source: (Maddison, 2003, 2011)

The phrase that Finland is 'the Japan of the North' underlines these similarities between the Finnish and Japanese economies, but it can also refer to the cultural similarities between Finnish and Japanese people, for example, in their attitudes to life and work. There are, of course, significant dissimilarities as well. With a total population of 128 million, the Japanese economy is many times larger than that of Finland with its population of 5.3 million. The total GDP in Japan in 2010 was $5,458 billion US, while in Finland it was $239 billion US.

The aim of this book is, first, to provide readers high-quality scholarly perspectives and up-to-date comparative analyses on the economic and societal development of Japan and Finland by using certain illustrative cases. Moreover, our second aim is a more challenging one, namely, to try to make comparisons between countries that initially do not seem comparable; therefore, the aim of this volume is also to be a methodological test for longitudinal comparative analysis. This aim of the volume is developed further in Chapter 2, which aims to deliver a more structured approach to comparative, historical analysis. Comparisons between Japan and Finland offer a fruitful platform for the study of the similarities and differences in the economic and societal development after the Second World War, namely: "The main argument of this volume is that although Japanese and Finnish economies and societies might look today similar according to certain macro measures, the processes that have led to this are quite divergent – at least with the topics analyzed here. The future challenges, however, are quite similar for both countries."

Structure of volume

The themes selected for the volume represent areas that are typically linked with the development paths in both countries: welfare state challenges; export-led growth and internationalization of certain industrial sectors; education; labour market development; challenges in energy supply and regulation; and economic crises, together with the economic ideology and practical policies behind the societal development. Besides these country-specific chapters, the volume will also contribute to a more general discussion on comparative methodology in two chapters (Chapter 2 and the concluding chapter), both having authors with an outsider's view on the development in Japan and Finland.

The volume is structured into four parts and a conclusion. The introductory part includes, besides this chapter, also Chapter 2, which focuses on comparative analysis from a methodological angle. In their analysis of longitudinal comparative historical analysis, Pavel Osinsky and Jari Eloranta offer a comparative framework for this volume – namely, how historical comparative analysis has previously been utilised and what methodological solutions might be valuable in country comparisons such as presented here. Osinsky and Eloranta address the need for using various kinds of comparative methods, depending on the topics and questions stated. In this volume in particular, the rather long-run perspective together with the comparisons enable the authors to go beyond the traditional, national-historical narratives and to recognise, besides changes, continuities over time as well (Osinsky & Eloranta, 2015).

Part II analyses key societal developments in Japan and Finland by focusing on different aspects of the welfare society and state. The chapter on general welfare state development is complemented by analyses of higher education and military spending in Japan and in Finland. In their chapter 'Two Paths to Building a Welfare Society', Maare Paloheimo, Kota Sugaraha, Tadashi Fukui, and Merja Uotila argue that both countries have implemented various methods to address welfare policies and emerging social issues during the last decades of the twentieth century and early new millennium. Today, both countries are facing severe challenges with an aging of population and overall cost of the welfare state. By concentrating especially on issues related to family policies and reconciliation of family and working life, the authors stress the religious values that have influenced the way the emerging social issues were managed (Paloheimo, Sugahara, Fukui, & Uotila, 2015).

Higher education in Japan and Finland is compared in the chapter by Anu Ojala, Yasushi Tanaka, and Olli Turunen. Both Japan and Finland are today known for their well-developed and high-performing educational systems. By analysing the higher education systems in these two nations, the authors show that the structures of the two education systems have been rather different, though the outcomes have been equally impressive, as evidenced, for example, by the international studies on mathematics, science, and international student assessment studies (PISA). The most distinctive difference between the two countries is the fact that Japanese higher education is mostly based on private-sector solutions, whereas in Finland the focus has been on public institutions. The authors argue that despite this difference in the ways of financing higher education, both Japan and Finland display a strong adherence and commitment to maintaining high educational standards. By focusing on the educational policies in Japan and Finland, the authors show what kinds of institutional and organizational structures were created and how they performed over time. In both countries, higher education became a possibility for many during the past 100 years, whereas in the early twentieth century it was the privilege of a select few (Ojala, Tanaka, & Turunen, 2015).

The Second World War was a profound historical period for both Japan and Finland. Both countries were defeated in the war, partly devastated (especially Japan), large areas were lost, and Japan was even occupied by its former enemy. Military capacity was disarmed in both countries quite rapidly and new policies were implemented addressing the limited role of the military, and focus shifted to an expansion of the welfare policies. Thus, an interesting question is whether these processes were similar or different in these two countries. In their chapter, Jari Eloranta and Yasushi Tanaka analyse these processes of change from warfare to welfare state. Though both countries lost the war, they won the peace in a fashion with extraordinary economic growth until the turn of the 1990s. The authors argue that both Japan and Finland maintained fairly low levels of military spending after the Second World War while investing heavily in the welfare state. This process occurred, according to them, relatively quickly. Both countries exhibited trade-offs between social and military spending, with the former benefitting from the lower levels in the latter. Moreover, both countries have kept their military spending fairly low despite new security challenges in the twenty-first century. Both have also modernised their military establishments with the introduction of new technologies (Eloranta & Tanaka, 2015).

Part III of the volume, in turn, analyses macroeconomic developments and economic policies. These include an analysis of Keynesian economic policies, regulation in the energy sector, and a study of the 1990s' financial crises in Finland and Japan. The role played by the Keynesian macroeconomic theory in practical economic policymaking is stressed in the chapter by Toshiaki Tamaki and Timo Särkkä. This was identified in macroeconomic planning, in the rise of Social Democratic ideals, and the emergence of the welfare society. This regulation of capitalism was emphasised especially in order to maintain full employment. The authors show that the complex connections between economic theory and economic policies differed somewhat in these two countries: scale economies and cultural differences, together with social and institutional context, played crucial roles in these connections. Keynesian economic policies were rather unproblematic to implement, as the state has traditionally played a central role in the supply side of the economy in both Japan and Finland. However, the authors argue that the economic policies in these countries were never 'purely' Keynesian but rather conditioned by their economic and social surroundings (Tamaki & Särkkä, 2015).

Both Japan and Finland had energy-intensive industries and economies that were extremely dependent on the energy supply. Park Seung-Joon and Esa Ruuskanen emphasise in their chapter the role of the governmental policy making on securing a sustainable supply of energy. Both countries were reliant on energy imports, and especially after the oil crises of the 1970s invested heavily in nuclear power. The authors argue that this enthusiasm for nuclear power and suspicions regarding alternative energy sources determined the broad lines of energy policy in both countries up to the 2010s. Thus, there is a striking similarity in the type of power emphasised, though the organization of the energy system was rather different in Japan and Finland, as the chapter shows (Park & Ruuskanen, 2015).

The economic crises of the 1990s hit Japan and Finland particularly hard; both have been shown to be among the severest financial crises in recent economic history. The causes and consequences of these crises are analysed in depth by Kari Heimonen, Shigeyoshi Miyagawa, and Yoji Morita. The authors find similarities in these crises not only with each other but also when compared to other financial boom-bust cycles during the last decades. The authors emphasize financial deregulation and liberalization and banking crises as the background features for the crises. Both countries also experienced some exogenous shocks that deepened the downturns, as addressed by the authors in the chapter. Finland managed to survive and rebound from the crisis quite rapidly, while in Japan the economic downturn became prolonged. The rapid recovery of Finland from the crisis was caused, according to the authors, by the firm and active public intervention in the capital markets, especially to recapitalize the banking sector. In comparison, in Japan, there was a long delay in the commitment of public funds (Heimonen, Miyagawa, & Morita, 2015).

Part IV focuses on industries and trade and features two analytical chapters on the trade relations and industrial development in these two countries. The industrial development and export-led growth formed a basis for both the economic and societal development of both Japan and Finland during the period examined. The direct trade relations between Japan and Finland, examined by Juha Sahi and Kazuhiro Igawa, offer us, therefore, an example of how to better understand the importance of foreign trade for these countries. During the time period, the trade between Japan and Finland witnessed a massive growth in terms of both value and volume. Sahi and Igawa frame this development in conjunction with international changes from protectionism to free trade during the twentieth century. Though the trade with Finland was rather insignificant for Japan – but much more important to Finland – these trade relations have existed for almost a hundred years. Sahi and Igawa show that during certain time periods and with certain commodities, these contacts have been especially intensive. For example, Finland was the first European country to start regular imports of Datsun cars in the early 1960s. The trade has mainly been composed of industrial products, typically produced in both of the countries in question, like textiles and cars in Japan and forest industry products in Finland. Thus, this analysis can also provide more general insights on world trade and the position of Japan and Finland within it. This is further tested in the chapter on the face of new international trade theories. Sahi and Igawa suggest that trade between Japan and Finland is in a process of change from traditional interindustry towards intra-industry trade, with exchanges of products within the same industry. Thus, the chapter is also closely linked to a global history perspective: how international production chains have become more important in the global economy and trade, witnessed also in the case of trade relations between Japan and Finland (Sahi & Igawa, 2015).

As for industrial development, the paper industry is used as an example in the chapter by Pasi Sajasalo and Kazuhiro Igawa. The paper industry is a good example of industrial evolution in these countries, as they both were among the largest paper producers in the world throughout the period – though this product is usually more associated with the Finnish rather than the Japanese economy. The large-scale paper making has been similar in both countries, even though the markets and raw material base are strikingly different. Whilst the Finnish success in paper making has been based on domestic raw materials and international markets, the Japanese development has been the opposite: the markets are domestic, and the raw materials are mainly imported. The companies in both countries have also been among the dominant firms in their respective geographical areas, the Finnish ones in Northern Europe and the Japanese in the Southeast Asia. Sajasalo and Igawa concentrate especially on certain key institutional and organizational arrangements among the Finnish and Japanese paper industry firms during the post-war period, namely the Japanese Keiretsu and the Finnish sales associations (Sajasalo & Igawa, 2015).

The concluding chapter by professor Christopher Lloyd sums up the comparisons presented in the individual chapters and provides the topic a more general perspective on how to compare different countries over a long period of time.

2 Longitudinal comparative historical analysis

Challenges and possibilities

Pavel Osinsky and Jari Eloranta

Historical/longitudinal comparison as a methodology of research

Despite Cervantes's famous saying that 'all comparisons are odious', they are ubiquitous in contemporary social sciences and history (Slater & Ziblatt, 2013; Steinmetz, 2004). In reality, no social inquiry is possible without some sort of comparison. By examining individuals, families, organizations, or nations, we compare them, either deliberately or intuitively, with other individuals, families, organizations, or nations. While some comparisons may be random, indirect, or supplementary to other techniques, there exists a venerable tradition of social scientific research in which comparative inquiry is the primary method of exploration – that is, comparative historical analysis, a long-standing intellectual project oriented toward explanation of substantively important processes and outcomes by means of systematic and contextualized comparison (Mahoney & Villegas, 2007). Although such a method may be utilized at various levels of analysis, most frequently (and most fruitfully) it has been applied to the processes and outcomes among the nation-states, which is the approach of this book, varying from rather straightforward quantitative modelling (for example, the articles on the financial crises and military spending) to more qualitative narratives (such as the chapters on Keynesian policies and the welfare states). We would argue that both types of comparisons are appropriate and informative when used in conjunction with a consistent research design and application. Such comparisons, as done in this volume about Japan and Finland, inform us about their aggregate structures, as well as groups and institutions over time.

Historical comparison serves several purposes. According to Jürgen Kocka, heuristically, the comparative approach allows one to identify questions and problems that one might miss, neglect, or not invent otherwise. Descriptively, historical comparison helps to clarify the profiles of individual cases by contrasting them with other occasions. Analytically, the comparative approach is indispensable for asking and answering causal questions about important social/cultural/political processes and their outcomes. Pragmatically, comparison helps to distance oneself from the case one knows best. Because of this, comparison can have a deprovincializing and eye-opening impact on the analysis (Kocka,

2003). By comparing two different yet similar societies, the authors of this volume have sought to identify structures and processes that would be difficult to discern when analysing just one country or countries that are almost completely identical in many respects.

Comparative historical analysis encompasses a variety of methods and techniques. Charles Ragin (1987) identified two primary types of comparative studies: case-oriented comparative research and variable-oriented comparative research. Case-oriented research focuses at one or several instances (i.e., small N) of a certain phenomenon or an occurrence: a democratic transition, an outburst of ethnic violence, or adoption of neoliberal policies and the like (Ragin, 1987). By exploring various occasions of a certain event, scientists try to identify their commonalities and the underlying cause that produces such event. By examining different outcomes of processes in similar nations, they may wish to ascertain a cause of the divergence.[1] Either way, they treat each case as a whole unit and pay close attention to historical contexts of such occurrences. This, in essence, also applies to the chapters and the approach in this volume, that is, to do in-depth case studies of various issues and economic sectors to understand the twentieth-century development (and the challenges of the twenty-first century) better for two countries, Japan and Finland, that share some similar characteristics as well as many differing features in terms of their long-run historical development.

Variable-oriented research, on the other hand, involves study of large number of cases (large N) with a purpose of testing hypotheses derived from social scientific theories. Variable-oriented researchers do not study the cases they had selected in depth; instead, they identify several variables of interest and search for correlation between them. Such research does not pay as much attention to the contexts of historical processes and occurrences unless the approach utilizes long-run panel data. In variable-oriented research, parsimony and generality are generally given preference over historical complexity.

From the outset, case-oriented comparative-historical analysis emerged and evolved as a multidisciplinary endeavour with roots in sociology and political science, as well as in the disciplinary fields of history and developmental economics. Originally, historically grounded inquiries involving one or more societies were entwined with the explorations in European modernity and industrial capitalism. It is not surprising that elements of comparative historical research can be found in the writings of Alexis de Tocqueville, Karl Marx, Emile Durkheim, Max Weber, Thorstein Veblen, and other thinkers of the past. By examining massive historical transformations in the most advanced societies of the time, these scholars had constructed the influential interpretations of social change and had left a large number of the analytical building blocks for their intellectual successors (see e.g. Durkheim, 1912/2008; Marx, 1852/2008, 1867/1992, 1871/2012; Tocqueville, 1835/2003, 1856/2008; Weber, 1905/2002, 1922/1978; Veblen, 1899/2009, 1915/2006).

In the mid-twentieth century, comparative historical research receded due to the predominance of structural functionalism with its ahistorical and homogenizing vision of society. Confronted with the surge of political contention of the late

1950s and 1960s and dissatisfied with a functionalist discourse of modernization that had left little space for analyses of social inequality, conflicts, and revolutions, social scientists turned to the classical legacy of Karl Marx and Max Weber in search for answers to the intellectual challenges of the time. Critical engagement with classical legacy which had informed the new analyses of the social transformations resulted, in the 1960s and 1970s, in the publication of the path-breaking studies of Barrington Moore Jr. (1966), Reinhard Bendix (1964, 1978), Perry Anderson (1974a, 1974b), Immanuel Wallerstein (1974), Charles Tilly (1963, 1975), and Theda Skocpol (1979).

The distinct feature of the 'second wave' of the comparative historical analysis was its emphasis on the Neomarxist or Neoweberian structural explanations of social processes and outcomes at the macro and meso levels. Some of these theoretical fights are discussed indirectly in the chapter on Keynesianism, especially in Japan in the post-war years. In the 1980s and 1990s, however, predominance of structural political-economic determinism was challenged by the new approaches that emphasized the role of human agency, cultural interpretations, and identity politics. A lively and extensive dialogue with these perspectives resulted in incorporation of a variety of institutionalist, rational choice, culturalist, feminist, and colonial/postcolonial perspectives in comparative historical analysis and inaugurated the 'third wave' of comparative historical analysis (Adams, Clemens, & Orloff, 2005).[2]

This has also been the feature in many of the 'new' historical schools that have emerged since the 1950s and 1960s. For example, the study of military history has been changing ever since the Second World War, especially in the last four decades. Emphasis has been placed on a new set of problems, primarily concerning the ties between war – as well as the military establishment itself – and society (Eloranta, 2002; Howard, 1972). This so-called 'New Military History' was greatly influenced by such similar movements as the New Social History, New Economic History, and New Cultural History. The main idea behind the New Military History seems to be that there are numerous approaches available for a researcher of wars and conflicts that may not necessarily produce identical results. Another characteristic of this research orientation is that it has not become a dominant part of the field of military history rather than a complementary yet often vague set of interdisciplinary approaches. The viewpoints and methods involved have differed greatly, but this variety may prove vital in order to understand the different structures and elements of war and peace comprehensively (see e.g. Harrison, 1996; Iggers, 1984; McCloskey, 1987; Olábarri, 1995; Paret, 1992). In turn, the 'new economic historians', or cliometricians, have asked new kinds of questions and challenged long-held assumptions about historical events, such as the economic effects of slavery and the economic importance of railroads. They have brought modelling and quantification into the forefront of economic history analysis since the 1960s (Eloranta, Ojala, & Valtonen, 2010). While new methodological and empirical applications have been at the heart of these 'new' histories, most of them have also wholeheartedly embraced comparisons as a useful tool.

Rationale for and limits of historical case studies

The comparative analyses involving two or several nations have varied in their designs. Skocpol and Somers (1980) highlighted the three most common strategies of case-oriented comparative research (Skocpol & Somers, 1980). The first strategy involved engaging comparative history for the parallel demonstration of theory. In such research, social scientists selected a certain historical phenomenon and used several cases for examining how a phenomenon in question manifested itself in several nations. The second strategy used comparative history for the contrast of the contexts. Researchers examined how a certain institution could acquire different forms in different societies. The third strategy utilized comparative history for macro-causal analysis. This strategy used historical evidence to identify specific causal conjunctures leading to substantively important historical outcomes. Working along these lines, social scientists produced numerous historically and comparatively grounded analyses of state formation, democratization, ethnic conflicts, economic development, welfare policies, revolutions, nationalism, social movements, race relations, gender regimes, neoliberalism, and globalisation. Most of these fields of study are represented in this volume, with some aiming to answer broader theoretical questions and others focusing on particular aspects like state formation (see also Christopher Lloyd's concluding chapter).

What are the potential problems in making such comparisons? Despite the impressive contribution of comparative historical analysis to the contemporary social sciences, its theoretical and methodological principles were challenged from several academic quarters. A number of objections were raised by empirically oriented social scientists engaged in quantitative research. Goldthorpe (1991, 1997), for example, noted that most of the comparative historical research is based on secondary evidence (i.e. texts written by historians). He warned that primary data from the past ('the relics') uncovered by historians may be insufficient and that historians themselves differ in their interpretations of evidence. It is not clear, he noted, why historical sociologists preferred one historical interpretation in favor of another (also see Lustick, 2006). Lieberson (1991, 1994) has scrutinized Mill's methods of agreement and difference used by comparative historical scientists in a critical fashion. He concluded that such methods utilized a deterministic approach rather than probabilistic one, assumed no error in measurement, postulated existence of only one cause, and neglected interaction effects. These assumptions, he stated, were inappropriate since they contradicted a realistic appraisal of most social processes (Lieberson, 1991, 1994). We believe, however, that comparisons may enable scholars to solve some of the problems associated with interpretation of primary sources. Generalizations are always necessary to get to the 'big-picture' questions and answers (Skocpol, 1987; Stearns, 2003; Tilly, 1984). Recently this has led to the emergence of global history as a field, one that is heavily focused various types of transnational comparisons (see e.g. O'Brien, 2006).

Another set of criticisms was formulated by the practitioners of an increasingly influential interdisciplinary perspective in social sciences known as rational choice theory. Kiser and Hechter (1991, 1998) stated that that comparative historical analysis dispensed with general sociological theory and careful specification of social mechanisms in favor of ad hoc middle-range explanations prioritizing descriptive accuracy over scope and analytic power. By celebrating historical uniqueness of events and relying on vague 'explanatory principles', comparativists construct arguments that are essentially untestable. As a remedy to liabilities of historicism, they had suggested using an alternative, agent-based analytical framework with an arsenal of the universally applicable causal mechanisms developed within rational choice theory. Here in this chapter, we offer the perspectives from institutional economics to overcome some of those problems, to look beyond rational choice models towards historically interpreted rationality and bounded rationality.

Finally, some qualitatively oriented scholars had raised the issue of epistemological limits of comparative explorations that stem from the notion of incommensurability or impossibility of undistorted translation between texts and, correspondingly, cultures (Keane, 2005; Povinelli, 2001). If we assume that social practices are meaningful, contextualized, culturally constructed, and (wholly or partially) untranslatable, we may arrive to a natural inference that experiences and meanings of colonialism and postcolonialism, capitalism, democracy, and globalisation would be radically different to representatives of different cultures and cognitively inaccessible to outside observers. For example, the investigator who asks in rural India 'about equivalents of "individuals", "social structures", "kinship", "classes", "statuses", "rules", "oppositions", "solidarities", "hierarchies", "authority", "values", "ideology", "religion", "purity", etc., risks imposing an alien ontology and alien epistemology on those who attempt to answer' (Marriott, 1990: 1–2; for a detailed discussion of incommensurability, see Steinmetz, 2005). Historians in general tend to pose questions in a rather anachronistic fashion, to utilize sources compiled in the past with modern methodology and ideas. In this volume, however, the authors concentrate mostly on twentieth-century topics and history, with emphasis on recent phenomena, so such dichotomy is rarely present even if Japan and Finland seem to be culturally quite dissimilar.

In their responses to the criticisms, scholars who have practiced comparative historical research have followed two general strategies. Firstly, some analysts contested claims of evidence-related problems and methodological imprecision implicated in their studies. Mann (1994) argued that macrosociologists are well equipped to deal with secondary evidence because they are guided by social scientific theories and knowledge of more than one society. Many of them, he added, did collect primary data in their studies (Mann, 1994). Calhoun (1996) noted that some important sociological phenomena occurred only in small number of cases that made it impossible to study them by most statistical techniques. Savolainen (1994) pointed out that 'deterministic' case-oriented comparative research did not necessarily require the assumption that the outcome *had* to happen and, in contrast to quantitative research, allowed detailed contextualized examination of various causal configurations and interaction terms. George and Bennett (2005) identified a strategy of exploring social mechanisms known as 'process tracing'. Moreover, other scholars have gone beyond just countering criticisms. In order to formalize comparative analysis, Ragin (2000) elaborated on a fuzzy-set methodology, a promising strategy of research based on examining degrees of membership in well-defined sets of nations (see also Pajunen, 2008). All these scholars advocated methodologically rigorous comparative analysis meeting the standards of mainstream social science (also see Lange, 2013; Mahoney, 2006; Mahoney & Rueschemeyer, 2003; Mahoney & Villegas, 2007; Slater & Ziblatt, 2013).

Other comparativists chose a different strategy. Instead of trying to move their field closer to the mainstream, they decided to examine the epistemological foundations of the critics' claims. Reacting to Kiser and Hechter's (1991) rational choice theorizing, Somers (1998) noted that their dissatisfaction with the comparativists' alleged neglect of social mechanisms is rooted in their own peculiar understanding of reality composed of discrete agents, each endowed with the dispositional power of intentionality where causal mechanisms are seen as universalized patterns of decision making that are derived a priori from *their* version of theory. In reality, agental intentionality is a variable rather than a constant, whereas basic mechanisms of causality are in fact contingent and empirically variable situational arrangements that cannot be postulated a priori (also see Stinchcombe, 1991).

Responding to Lieberson's (1991, 1994) rejection of small-N comparisons as intrinsically inferior and unscientific, Steinmetz (2004, 2005) had exposed the precarious methodological foundations of positivism in social sciences. According to him, methodological positivism rejects invocation of unobservable entities, assumes constant causal conjunctures of events, and postulates that the social world can be studied in the same manner as the natural one. For Steinmetz, such assumptions are untenable. Comparative historical analysis insists on the variability of social-causal structures across time and space and thus rejects the assumption that social patterns are always universal. Shifting constellations of causal mechanisms rather than universal conjunctions, he contends, are the norm in open systems like society (also see Sewell, 1996).

As for incommensurability concerns, comparative historical analysis acknowledges (or at least should acknowledge) that social comparison necessarily involves interpretation and translation. Nonetheless, it should be wary with regard to both objectifying 'third-person' comparison and 'first-person' utterances. Claiming that studies of surface observables usually yield limited results, Steinmetz (2004) advocates comparison across theoretical mechanisms and underlying structural arrangements that may be utilized for juxtaposing events or societies that seem to have little in common at the empirical level.

Framework for effective historical comparisons

In this volume, the authors employ a wide range of methods and sources to make the comparisons between Japan and Finland meaningful and informative. They utilize both qualitative, historical comparisons of various institutions and policies as well as quantitative approaches to analysing the development of these two societies. Thus, the comparisons are strengthened by going beyond the historical narratives, even if the focus is still on small-N–type comparisons. In fact, the strength in these comparisons is the use of historical time series to reveal the longer-run dynamics of change and continuity. We would argue that good quantitative study of history is very similar to qualitative scholarship, and both methods can support one another if used properly. The basic principles in good historical comparisons include: (1) critical use of primary and secondary sources and systematic and transparent application of said sources; (2) framing the research with appropriate theoretical models and proper 'testing' of the models, whether quantitatively or qualitatively (or both); and (3) recognition of the historical contexts and limits of historical comparisons.

One theoretical approach that offers us a more nuanced take on history compared to the rational choice models is institutional economics. The various theoretical variants of neoclassical economics and history have often led economic history explanations towards many competing directions. Among the more recent attempts at a 'dynamic' and comprehensive theory, the institutional framework introduced by Douglass C. North – one of the key figures in the reemergence of institutional economics in recent decades (NIE, New Institutional Economics) – has proved persuasive in calling for a greater recognition among economists of the institutional features of historical events and time periods. The analysis of historical constraints has gained some momentum in economics in the 1980s and 1990s, especially in the context of reevaluating technological development and property rights (Lamberg, Ojala, & Eloranta, 1997; Liebowitz & Margolis, 1990; North, 1990). There are two important basic factors in North's institutional framework, namely increasing returns and inefficient markets (which embody large transaction costs). He assumes quite implicitly that institutions have no significance in economies in the absence of these factors. According to North, with these factors in effect, organizations develop and function in order to attempt to increase their gains within an institutional framework. Institutional economic history, as represented by North, offers us a chance of adopting a limited version of causality, as in path dependence, into economic explanations; within this framework, the interaction between organizations – be they a family, village, nation, corporation, and so on – defines the development of polities. The strength of the factors mentioned, combined with historical 'accidents', defines the historical development paths. While the authors in this volume do not explicitly utilize NIE as a theoretical approach, in many ways the chapters use these principles in the analysis. Accordingly, this approach enables the contributors to avoid the typical rational choice model caveats, since NIE does not embrace rationality in the same way. For example, North leans more toward the idea that rationality is determined by the circumstances (Denzau & North, 1994).

This volume represents a rare collaboration among the scholars in two countries not usually compared in such a fashion. The comparisons avoid needless juxtaposition of historical case studies and quantitative variable-based comparisons as opposites, thus often producing interesting and novel insights. As we have argued here, historical case studies can produce useful insights about societies and a small N is not necessarily a hindrance, as long as the case studies are done in a rigorous fashion. Here the comparative perspectives reinforce the results. Moreover, we would maintain that the ability to mesh various interdisciplinary approaches often leads to new results and increases the ability to reach broader approaches (see also Eloranta et al., 2010). It is not always necessary to compare nations of similar size, either, since the proper setup of the research can overcome the inherent problems in such comparisons – the scholars simply need to find relevant points of comparison, either similarities or differences or actual interactions.

The longer time period utilized in the volume, compared to the large-N comparisons over a shorter period, allows the authors to investigate structural changes over time and to observe both things that change as well as phenomena that stay the same. This approach is analogous with the NIE approach, that we should analyse both formal and informal institutions (as well as the organizations that play the game), especially since informal institutions change slowly over time. Finally, the longer time perspective allows the contributors to investigate the impact of exogenous and endogenous shocks for the two historical polities and their impact, thereby revealing societal structures better. While the perspectives offered in this book on the two countries have their limitations, we would argue that the strengths of such comparisons more than compensate for the limitations.

Notes

1. The former method is known as method of agreement and the latter method as method of difference, formulated initially by John Stuart Mill.
2. It is worth to mention that some analysts (e.g. Lange, 2013; Mahoney, 2006) resist calling this body of research the 'third wave', placing rational choice and culturalist and poststucturalist studies outside comparative historical analysis.

Part II

Welfare societies

3 Two paths to building a welfare society

The development of work- and family-related policies in post-war Finland and Japan

Maare Paloheimo, Kota Sugahara, Tadashi Fukui, and Merja Uotila

Introduction

Finland and Japan, having different historical, economic, political, and cultural backgrounds, created advanced welfare societies after the Second World War. As will become evident in this chapter, in the last few decades, both countries have implemented various methods to address welfare policies and emerging social issues. In addition, the present chapter will also consider the challenges that Finnish and Japanese societies will face in the future. Nowadays, for instance, ageing due to longer life expectancy, fewer children, and questions related to employment and labour supply have concerned preoccupied governments in both countries.

According to the literature, a welfare state system is characterized by the following five components: (1) a system of social security; (2) the roles of the central and local governments as the managerial core of the system; (3) social recognition and legislation to ensure fundamental human rights, which support the establishment of the system at the ideological level; (4) the justification of state intervention in the economic sphere to achieve full employment; and (5) the realization of extensive democracy based on the principle of parliamentary decision making in the political sphere (Fujimura, 2000: 3). Consequently, an increase in the need for more adequate functioning of the welfare state causes the size of government to increase via parliamentary elections[1] (Meltzer & Richard, 1981).

As Figure 3.1 shows, in Finland, the general government size measured by the ratios of government expenditure and revenue to GDP exceeded the OECD average, and the increases in costs were significant especially in the 1970s and 1980s. On the other hand, as we will demonstrate in the remainder of the text, since benefit cutting was implemented in the latter part of the 1990s, recently government size in Finland seems to have stabilized. In Finland, the role of the state has been emphasized, as the welfare system includes a large public sector.

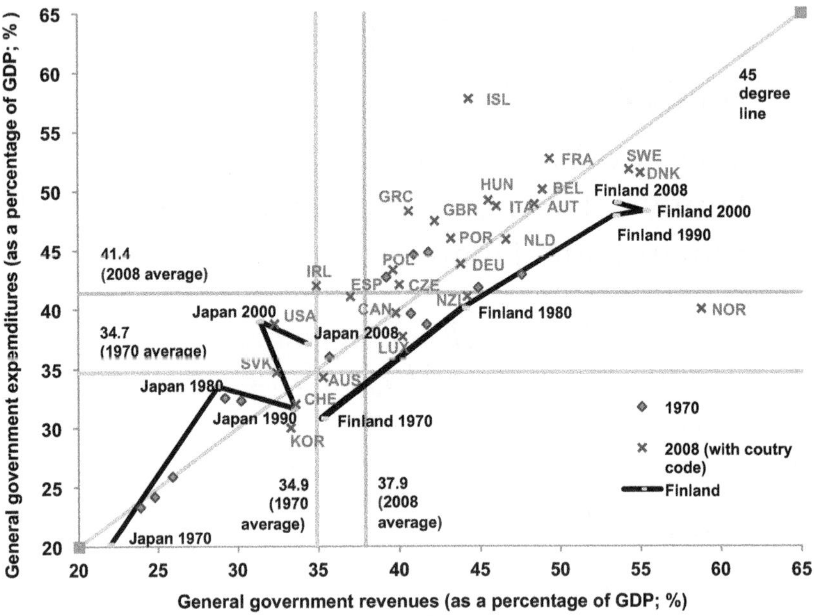

Figure 3.1 General government size as a percentage of GDP

Source: (OECD, 2010b)

Note: The general government sector consists mainly of central, state, and local government units together with social security funds controlled by those units. The main revenue of general government consists of taxes, social contributions, dividends, and other revenues. The main expenditure items consist of the salaries and other costs of civil servants, social benefits, interest on the public debt, subsidies, and gross fixed capital formation.

However, the Finnish welfare system has experienced challenges due, for example, to economic reasons, which has served to accentuate criticism about the nationally based welfare state. In the beginning of the twenty-first century, issues of great importance have been the expected changes in the age structure of the population and globalisation. (For further discussion, see e.g. Alestalo, 2000; Kiander & Lönnqvist, 2002; Sipilä, Anttonen, & Baldock, 2003.)

In contrast, the size of government in Japan has always been smaller than in other countries. This means that the priority of economic development had been higher than that of social security in the strategy of the Japanese government. The size has been increased in an unstable fashion, but expenditures have almost always exceeded revenues, contrary to the situation in Finland (Takegawa, 2009). Until quite recently, the role of the Japanese government has not been large in the social sector because the private sector, and in particular big corporations, offered generous welfare programmes of their own. In addition, families, in particular housewives, have informally provided almost all care for children and the elderly. However, facing rapid ageing and change in family structure, the reform of the social security system, particularly the pension system and long-term care as well as social support for families, has been discussed, but reaching a political consensus on the future policies has proved difficult (Bradshaw & Tokoro, 2013).

Regarding these different situations in Finland and Japan, in this chapter we compare the development of the welfare state in both countries from the mid-1940s to the present and discuss what welfare policies will be needed in the future. Despite the different backgrounds, a comparative study can reveal novel perspectives on the societies studied and their social systems as well as facilitate our understanding of the development of their respective welfare state structures. (For comparative studies concerning welfare state development in both Nordic countries and Asia, see e.g. Kettunen & Petersen, 2011; Kröger, Anttonen, & Sipilä, 2003; Lin & Rantalaiho, 2003; Vuori & Merviö, 2007.) Due the diversity and complexity of themes related to welfare state, we will particularly focus on family policies and questions related to the reconciliation of family and working life.

Women's opportunities to engage in salaried work combined with public services is often seen as one of the crucial features among works in the earlier research tradition of welfare state development in Nordic countries (Anttonen & Sipilä, 2011: 82–9; Christiansen & Markkola, 2006: 23–4; Melby, Ravn, & Carlsson Wetterberg, 2008: 1–4). On the other hand, women have contributed more in unpaid caring work in Japan, as noted. Thus, women's workforce participation and its prerequisites are highlighted in this chapter. Table 3.1 illustrates some differences in the situation of women's workforce participation in both countries according to the average values between 2007 and 2011. The Finnish situation

Table 3.1 Women's workforce participation (average of 2007–2011)

Age cohort	*Workforce participation rate (%)*			*Unemployment rate (%)*			*Ratio of part-time employment to total (%)*		
	Finland	*Japan*	*OECD*	*Finland*	*Japan*	*OECD*	*Finland*	*Japan*	*OECD*
15 to 24	51.7	44.3	43.7	17.8	7.4	14.1	42.5	29.4	35.2
25 to 34	78.6	71.1	69.7	7.1	5.5	8.2	12.7	19.9	18.6
35 to 44	87.1	68.4	71.6	5.6	4.4	6.2	8.7	34.6	24.7
45 to 54	89.1	73.8	71.1	5.0	3.3	5.2	7.9	35.6	23.3
55 to 64	59.6	53.3	47.0	5.6	2.9	4.6	19.9	39.9	29.2

Sources: OECD Statistics.

Note: In the statistics, part-time employment is defined as employment with less than 30 weekly hours of work in the main job. The definition of part-time employment varies across OECD members (OECD Glossary of statistical terms). In the Japanese definition, a part-time worker is defined as one working fewer scheduled hours per day or who works the same scheduled hours per day but fewer scheduled days per week than ordinary workers in the same establishment (Explanation of Surveys, the Ministry of Health, Labour and Welfare, www.mhlw.go.jp/english/database/db-yl/2011/dl/chousa.pdf).

is characterized by high workforce participation and relatively high unemployment, particularly among young women. The data on young women aged 15 to 24 include students, who reported working part time in addition to studying. Moreover, the group of women aged 55 to 64 includes those in work because they are semiretired[2] (see also Kauhanen, 2008: 109–11; Myrskylä, 2012). In Japan, on the other hand, women's workforce participation is lower in all age cohorts. However, it can be seen that many Japanese female employees, especially middle-aged women, are part-time workers generally engaged in unskilled work. Therefore, we should pay attention to the different meanings of women's workforce participation and welfare societies represented by specific welfare systems, such as family support, public care for the elderly, and policies on female employment in both countries.

To explore these themes, this chapter is divided into four parts. First, we will briefly review theoretical discussions on the welfare state as well as the economic and societal development in Finland and Japan. The following part compares the evidence and welfare policies related to women's participation in working life. Finally, we consider the need for future reforms in both countries as concluding in the last part of this chapter.

Theory and development of welfare policies

Theoretical insights

In the wide range of literature on the welfare state, there are several and even contradicting views regarding the definition of the focal concepts. According to the seminal argument by Robson (1976), the concepts of *welfare state* and *welfare society* are understood here in the following way:

> a welfare state is not simply a national regime based on a set of objective principles or precepts which after discussion have been embodied in public policies carried out by legislation, central departments and local authorities. Its real force and strength must come from widespread feelings, convictions and responses among the citizens transmitted to their many associations which are consistent with and complementary to those policies.
>
> (45–6)

This suggests that we must be conscious not only of institutional or statistical differences but also socioeconomic properties, morals, and teachings which are described as *welfare society* when we consider the development of *welfare state* or compare such systems between countries.

In the stream of literature on welfare state development, there are two basic theories investigating welfare state establishment: the convergence theory and the path dependence theory. The former pursues socioeconomic changes as important factors in the development of welfare state. As is well known, industrialization and urbanization played roles in the beginning of the Western welfare state by causing structural changes in the working life and family (Lindbeck, 2002; Piore, 1987). This theory therefore suggests that the regime of welfare state will be similar among countries faced with similar socioeconomic situations[3] (Wilensky, 1975). In contrast to the convergence theory, the path dependence theory focuses on the initial conditions, in particular the ideological sphere and policy-making activities in the development of welfare state, emphasizing contingency, individuality, and the particularity of history. The most notable work by Esping-Andersen (1990) classified the welfare state regime of developed countries into three worlds: social democratic, liberal, and conservative Catholic. While the majority of the researchers in this field had paid attention to the differences between Western countries, some of them began to turn their attention to the relationship between the development of welfare state and social atmosphere in East Asia from the mid-1980s onwards (Aspalter, 2001: 3; Esping-Andersen, 1990). As Peter Lindert has aptly summarized, theories on the growth of government can be divided into five categories: (1) those implying a monotonic rise of the government spending share; (2) those implying an end to the rise; (3) those implying an eventual reversal; (4) theories with more conditional predictions; and (5) and those suitable for history-dependent hypotheses testing (Lindert, 2004).

Moreover, many scholars have developed further the methods and viewpoints presented in earlier studies. For example, Huber and colleagues (1993) used multiple indicators to estimate welfare state effort, which means how much (or often) the state spends on welfare policies, while most quantitative studies rely only on a single indicator, usually expenditure measures in a single category of welfare policies, assuming all countries can be ranked on a single scale of welfare state (Huber, Ragin, & Stephens, 1993). Then they found that the result depends on the kinds of indicators of the welfare state effort. However, the effects of Christian democracy and social democracy on an independent variable are significant irrespective of the kind of indicators. Yet another example is the study by Takegawa (2009), which attempts to add international circumstances at the time when welfare state started in a certain country to the two earlier theories which mentioned only domestic socioeconomic or ideological factors and comprehensibly explained the difference in the developments of welfare state among the UK, Japan, and South Korea (Takegawa, 2009). Sainsbury (1994) criticizes the argument of Esping-Andersen (1990) for being based on the viewpoint of male paid workers and reconsiders the role of welfare state from the perspective of gender equality at various stages, such as education, work, and family care (Esping-Andersen, 1990; Sainsbury, 1994). To summarize, the existing body of research is characterized by heterogeneity, and it can be claimed that several traditions or approaches have not yet confronted each other. (For further discussion, see e.g. Kettunen & Petersen, 2011.)

Before we present a more detailed consideration of the evidence on Finland and Japan, it is beneficial to briefly compare the situations of these countries in light of the aforementioned theories. As described in the introductory chapter of this book, both countries are facing similar socioeconomic conditions: mature economy, ageing society, economic independence from large countries (in the case of Finland the former Soviet Union, and in the case of Japan the United States after the Second World War), and entry into new economic and political cooperation (EU, ASEAN+3). This means that, according to the convergence theory, the welfare states in these two countries may have some characteristics in common.

On the other hand, the backgrounds, particularly ideological ones, of the respective welfare states are very different in these countries. As mentioned in the literature, the Finnish welfare state is considered to rest on Lutheran traditions, like the other Nordic countries, all of whom have a common cultural and historical context (Anttonen & Sipilä, 2011: 42–3, 8–9; Markkola, 2011: 104–6; Markkola & Ojala, 2012). Contrary to Catholics and reformed Protestants, the states professing the Lutheran faith introduced welfare systems earlier; thus, the state took over the responsibility from the church for the poorest elements in society. Sigrun Kahl (2005) states that the approach to persistent poverty in Lutheranism can be expressed as 'persistent poverty is a societal responsibility'[4] (Kahl, 2005: 29; see also Markkola, 2011). In the Finnish society in particular, the local authorities assumed responsibility for poor relief from the mid-nineteenth century onwards. Needless to say, the recipients of poor relief were stigmatized. In the early twentieth century, philanthropic associations and nongovernmental organizations (NGOs) complemented the public services and provided, for example, child and maternity health clinics and home help services, especially in urban areas. The state assumed the main responsibility for these services after the Second World War (Anttonen & Sipilä, 2011: 48–9; Laurent, 2012: 316–20; Urponen, 1994: 184).

The Japanese system is cited as a kind of Oriental welfare state based on Confucian and Buddhist thinking. It is characterized by

> the family-oriented value system of Confucian tradition that defines the East Asia welfare model, in which the state devolves much of the social responsibility upon family and local or corporate community, adhering to Confucian particularism as regards the welfare state universalism based on individual social rights'.
>
> (Kim, 2010: 413)

Although some Japanese researchers seem to position the Japanese welfare state close to the liberal or conservative Catholic tradition, in Esping-Andersen's classification according to the measures which show small government size and so forth (Uzuhashi, 2002), we suggest that the Oriental welfare state differs from Christian welfare states in respect of the role of the third sector, in particular religious institutions, in a welfare society.

In addition to the ideological background, both countries can be considered to have been in different international circumstances at the inception of the welfare state. Finland is often seen as a latecomer among the Nordic countries, as it implemented social reforms later than others. Despite this, it has become one of the leaders among developed countries. On the other hand, the Japanese welfare state was built during worldwide stagflation in the 1970s and the 'crisis of the welfare state' (OECD, 1981). Thus, Japan was unable to introduce new taxes, in particular value-added tax, to build a Western-style welfare state in the 1980s because it was already in a period of low economic growth, while its introduction had been discussed ever since the early 1950s (Ishi, 2001, 2009; Takegawa, 2009).

Finnish and Japanese societies after the Second World War

After the Second World War, both Japan and Finland went through a phase of rapid economic growth. The rapid economic growth of Japan in particular has attracted international attention. In this period, a largely agrarian nation became the world leader in many important segments of the economy (see Tamaki & Särkkä, 2015). However, Japan's amazing economic transformation did not solve all the emerging social issues, although the standard of living made a quantum leap (Takahashi, 1995: 243). The changes in the social structure of Japan also began in the immediate post-war period, such as the expansion of the middle class, which affected the whole society. In addition, massive urbanization took place, simultaneously transforming the Japanese society, kinship, and family structures and indeed the way of life (Kingston, 2011: 3–4; Tokoro, 2003: 45).

The development in post-war Finland shares similar characteristics with that of Japan. In Finland, the industrial take-off occurred later than in the other Nordic countries, and thus the social structure remained predominantly agrarian and rural until the 1950s. The eventual transition of a rural society into an urbanized wage-work society, with public and private services as the dominant sector of employment, was sudden (Kettunen, 2001: 226; Niemelä & Salminen, 2006: 9–10). This transformation, which also included the migration of working-age people from the rural areas to the urban centers, modified or superseded the traditional social networks which the care of children and elderly people had relied on and increased the need for social services together with a change in family structure and the increased participation of women in working life (Julkunen, 1990: 142; Kröger et al., 2003: 26; Niemelä & Salminen, 2006: 16).

Both Finland and Japan experienced a post-war baby boom, which occasioned remarkable changes in the present age structures. In the immediate aftermath of the Second World War, the population was replenished in war-struck countries as shown in Figure 3.2. The decline in the birth rate was sharper in Japan than in Finland, where it bottomed out in the early 1970s. Recently there has been slight rise in the birth rate, but it is still below the threshold for population renewal.[5] In Japan, on the other hand, the birth rate seems to continue to decline. Accordingly, this is considered to cause low economic growth as a result of a decreasing workforce. Thus, the two countries are now facing similar circumstances due to the drop in fertility, the aging of the baby boomers, and the rise in life expectancies.

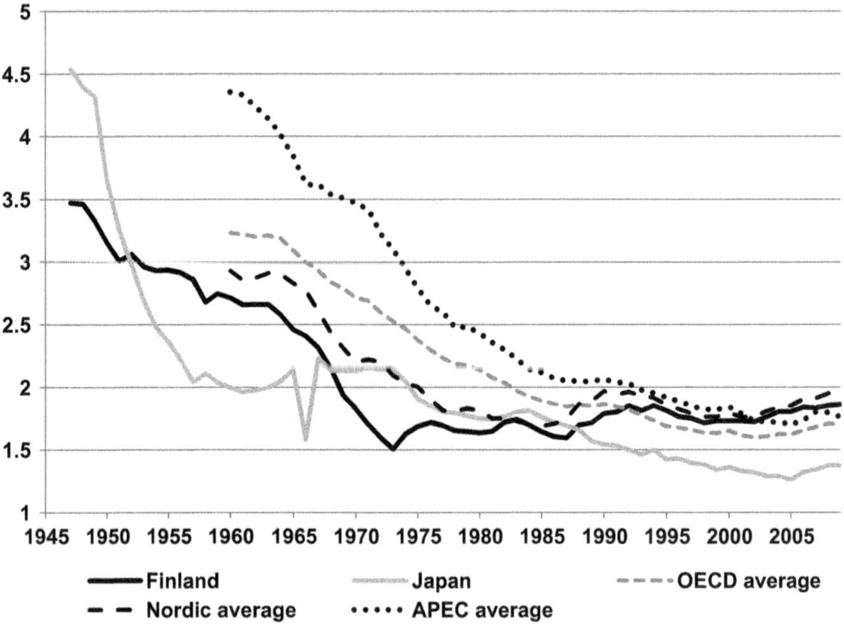

Figure 3.2 Total fertility rates (estimated number of children born to women aged 15 to 49)

Source: (OECD, 2010b)

The data from 1946 to 1959 are from the historical statistics compilations of the respective countries. The data from 1960 are from OECD Factbook 2010. The values of APEC (Asia-Pacific Economic Cooperation) average during the 1960s and 1970s were raised by Korea's (6.0; 1960) and Mexico's (7.25; 1960). The data after 2008 are estimated. Denmark, Finland, Iceland, Norway, and Sweden are members of the Nordic Council. APEC members include Australia, Canada, Japan, Korea, Mexico, New Zealand, and the United States. Since much data on Chile is unavailable, we exclude Chile from the calculation of the APEC average.

Both Finland and Japan were relatively late in taking their first major steps towards welfare state if compared with many leading industrialized countries. In the Finnish case, the development of social policy was slow in the prewar period due, for example, to meagre economic resources. Indeed, the public sector was not charged with vast social political tasks, and the overall development of social policies was gradual and characterized by conflicts and compromises between different political interests (Anttonen & Sipilä, 2011: 49; Bergholm, 2009: 32). In this situation, the role of voluntary, nonprofit organizations was emphasized, as they provided social assistance for the poorest members of society (Anttonen & Sipilä, 2011; Kröger et al., 2003: 28–9; Urponen, 1994: 184). In the post-war period, the discussion about social security and social rights gained new impetus and focused on making new social policy legislation. However, it must be mentioned that the way for large reforms was opened already before the war, when, for instance, the Maternity Grants Act (1938) was introduced (Anttonen & Sipilä, 2011: 32–3; Laurent, 2012: 319; Niemelä & Salminen, 2006: 10).

Finnish social thinking changed after the Second World War for several reasons. The Finnish nation, which had been socially and politically divided after the 1918 civil war that accompanied the attainment of national independence, became unified, and a new kind of uniformity was also perceptible in the political arena after 1945. In the wake of this wartime spirit, ideas of common responsibility, fairness, and social security were emphasized, which was connected to the ideology of universalism in social policy decision making. (On the development before the Second World War, see e.g. Alestalo, 2000: 62–3; Christiansen & Markkola, 2006: 10–1. On universalism, see e.g. Anttonen & Sipilä, 2011: 149–55; Kröger et al., 2003: 25–6.) National unification was one ideological basis for the evolution of social security schemes and also affected the emergence social security reforms. Several improvements were introduced, starting from a national pension scheme, health insurance, and improvement in the health care system. For example, a universal family allowance scheme, being the first expensive welfare reform, was created in 1948. The great economic transfers between the state and citizens and regions were a real novelty in Finland (Bergholm, 2009: 32–3; Niemelä & Salminen, 2006: 11).

The 1960s witnessed a new direction in social policy which was founded on ideas stressing national necessities and economic growth. Simultaneously, there was an increased tendency to use the Nordic region – and especially Sweden – as the frame of reference against which Finland was compared (Kettunen, 2006: 296–300). The Finnish welfare state matured in the late 1980s, and as a result, it developed into a universal, state-centred system with high female labour participation in full-time paid work (Alestalo, 2000: 65). However, the economic depression of the 1990s had profound impacts (Alestalo, 2000: 58–9; Huber & Stephens, 2001: 131–2; Niemelä & Salminen, 2006: 18), and major reductions in the social security system were introduced and eligibility for social benefits became more strictly controlled. Finland's EU membership[6] brought further changes due to the need to harmonize the Finnish legislation with those of the other EU Member States. (On EU membership and social policy, see e.g. Julkunen, 2001: 211–4; Kettunen, 2011: 33–4.) Since the depression of the 1990s, financing pressures have been acute questions for Finnish governments. Increased expenditure on pensions, health care, and social care services are constantly discussed in public. (On the concepts of health and social care, see e.g. Sipilä et al., 2003: 5–7.) Thus, improvements in the efficiency and effectiveness of social policies are called for by both politicians and social policy experts.

Similarly, the war occasioned major social and political reforms and dynamics in Japanese society. The reforms included changes in the social security system. Several new laws were also passed: the Trade Union Law of 1945 and the Labour Standard Law of 1947 safeguarded the rights of workers and improved conditions in the workplace. In 1951, the Social Welfare Enterprise Law was enacted. Until then, public assistance for people in need was considered to be the responsibility of families and philanthropic organizations (Laratta, 2009: 310–1). However, it was not until the late 1950s that more extensive reforms of the social security system were implemented (Takahashi, 1995).

It is argued that a new era of Japanese welfare state was experienced in the late 1970s. At this time, the rapid development and the strength of the Japanese economy commanded worldwide attention. Simultaneously, the Western countries faced a severe crisis (Laratta, 2009: 311; Miyamoto, 2003: 14). The theory of 'Japanese-style welfare society' was developed to contrast with the Western-style welfare state, in which the development was seen as increasing welfare dependency and undermining family relations. In the 1970s and 1980s, when the economy prospered, it was not deemed necessary for the public sector to play a major role in Japanese social policy. Basically, the Japanese model was based on the idea of the male breadwinner's secure working career and incomes and strong family support functions (Miyamoto, 2003: 14; Tokoro, 2012: 652).

However, the longer life expectancy and the changes towards smaller nuclear families resulted in a situation in which new policy initiatives were required, as families could not adequately support their oldest members. The social security system for the elderly has been somewhat reformed from the 1980s onwards in order to prepare for the super-aged society – for example, the reform of the National Pensions (1986), the Health Service System for the Elderly (HSSE), and the Long-Term Care (LTC) Insurance System established in 2000. Actually, these reforms, especially the LTC, are considered to have helped Japanese married women to be released from the care of their own or their husbands' parents (Campbell & Ikegami, 2000). However, the social security system for families has experienced few significant improvements, and the measures taken by the government have been criticized for failing to adequately meet the childcare needs of the families whose mothers were increasingly engaging in paid work (Tokoro, 2012: 652–3). Policy responses to the declining fertility rate were initiated from the 1990s onwards – for example the so-called Angel Plan to expand nursery schools and community centres for supporting childcare, as well as the Child Care and Family Care Leave Act enacted in 1995[7] (on the Angel Plan, see Takahashi, 2003: 83–4). Figure 3.2 suggests that such measures have not contributed to a rise in birth rate.

Financing the welfare state

Although the Finnish government was obliged to have a fiscal deficit due to the recession in the mid-1990s, its budget conditions recovered in the 2000s. On the other hand, the Japanese governmental expenditures, approximately 60 per cent (in the Finnish case) and 40 per cent (in the Japanese case) of central government spending is expenditure on social security.[8] However, such a policy is basically financed by the burden on present generations in Finland, while it seems to be postponed to future generations in Japan (see Figure 3.3).

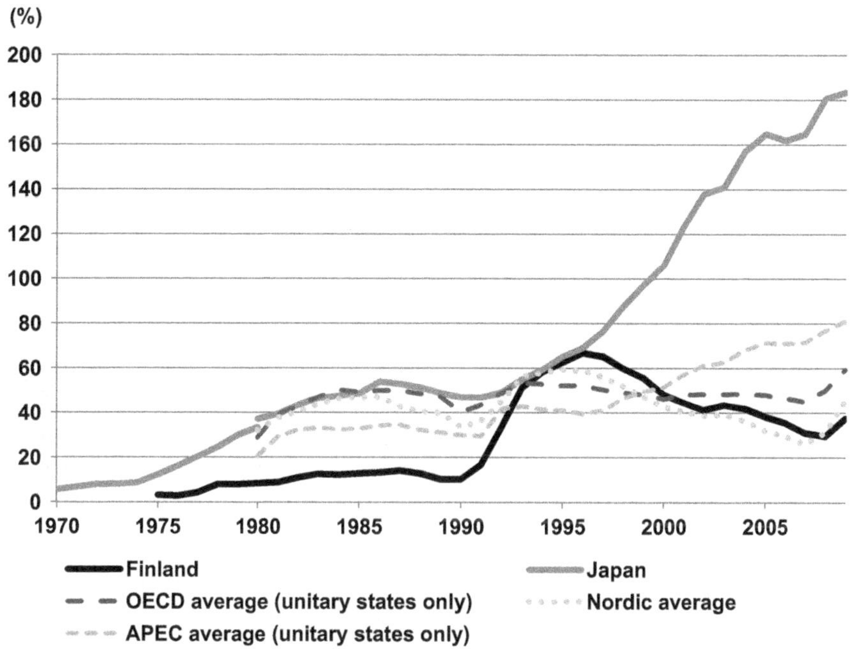

Figure 3.3 Central government debt (as a percentage of GDP)

Source: OECD National Accounts Statistics

Note: Federal states (Australia, Austria, Belgium, Canada, Germany, Mexico, Switzerland, and the United States) are excluded. Japan's data in 1970–1979 are from the Ministry of Finance. Finland's data in 1975–1989 are from Statistics Finland.

Judging from the data on taxes and social security contribution burdens, the Finnish population has to pay already, while the Japanese people have not. According to Figure 3.4, which shows governmental revenue from taxes and social security contributions as a percentage of GDP, the burden in Finland is 41.7 per cent, ranking alongside the other Nordic countries. On the other hand, it is 26.8 per cent in Japan, which is far below the OECD average (33.4 per cent). In addition, the share of personal income tax in the tax revenue of the respective countries is 31.3 per cent (Finland) and 20.4 per cent (Japan), while the revenue share of corporate income tax in Japan (13.5 per cent) is approximately double that of Finland (7.2 per cent). Thus, the public financing of the Japanese welfare state relies on companies, whereas the Finnish system, on the contrary, requires individuals to contribute to the welfare state.

However, the heavy burden on individual, particularly personal income tax has been criticized for reducing the incentive to work. Therefore, the reform of a combination of taxes – for instance, a decrease in the income tax rate and an increase in the VAT rate – is being considered in Finland (OECD, 2011: 92).

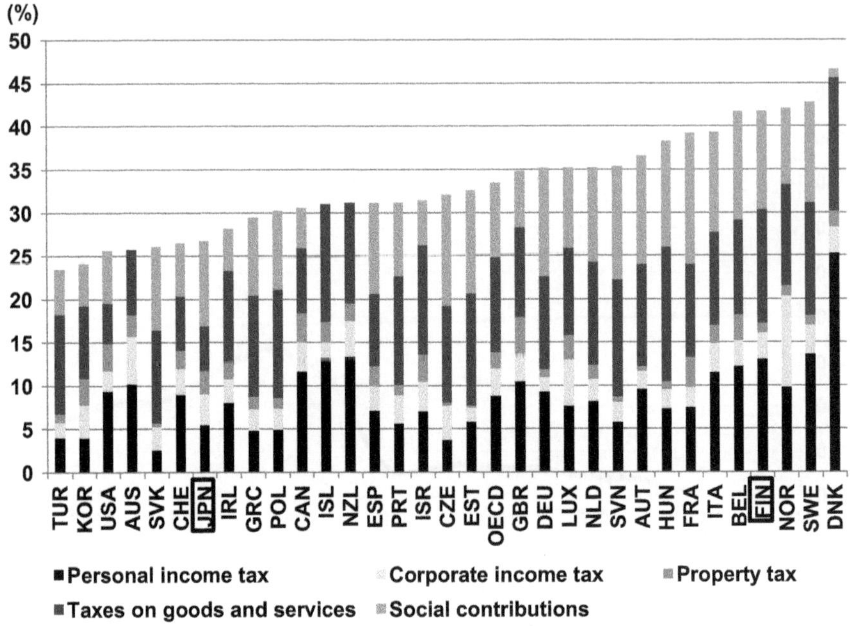

Figure 3.4 Public finance by taxes and social contribution (as a percentage of GDP, average of 2007–2010)

Source: OECD Revenue Statistics 1965–2011

As we mentioned, the implementation of new policies to reduce governmental debt is a significant problem for Japan. In this challenging situation, raising the burden on individuals could be one of the options.

Work and family in Finnish and Japanese societies

Employment and work culture

Before discussing the reconciliation of work and family in Finland and Japan, we first contemplate the work culture and employment situation as a whole. Historically, the fundamental difference between these two countries has been that Japan relies more on a single-male-provider model, while the dual-breadwinner model has been common in Finland. As a small, poor, and sparsely populated agrarian country, Finland could not afford to overlook the contribution of women in paid labour, but their participation was already needed in the prewar period (Anttonen & Sipilä, 2011: 259; Julkunen, 1990: 142–3, 51–52; Kröger et al., 2003: 43). Today the same model is still valid, and both spouses work in order to ensure that the family's finances are in order. Japanese society, on the one hand, has emphasized more patriarchal values and culture

(Kingston, 2004: 284–91). Finland, on the other hand, has followed the Nordic welfare ideology and has emphasized women's right to economic independence with the right to an income adequate for the support of self and family (Melby et al., 2008: 11–3).

In both countries, the culture emphasizes the meaning of work, although with different connotations (Christiansen & Markkola, 2006: 10). In Japanese work culture, a special employment custom used in large companies, called *lifetime employment*, is a genuine feature. This lifetime employment is not an employment contract but an employment custom that became widespread in the Japanese economy after the Second World War. Workers could be retained by the same company (or sometimes its subsidiary), which provided them with work from the beginning of their career until their retirement. In practice, the system provided benefits and provisions for the worker himself as well as his dependents through the main breadwinner's membership (Tokoro, 2012: 651). This custom, which was typical in core industrial and service sectors, can be considered to bring large benefits relating to economic production for both the employee and employer: a secure career and accumulation of knowledge about technology and the business model in the company. The employment custom has also contributed to the low unemployment rate, but this custom has faced serious challenges due to globalisation. Accordingly, the social security system is thought to be insufficiently prepared for the future. (Okamoto, 2011, finds a correlation between strong financial performance and ability to maintain lifetime employment, using the survey data.)

In many countries, the post-war era witnessed several changes in labour markets, employment, and labour policies, also in Finland and Japan. In post-war Japan, the high economic growth was conducive to high employment. The unemployment rate in Japan has been kept at a low level, but it has recently gradually increased (see Figure 3.5). In post-war Finland, the structural transformation was likewise remarkable (Alestalo, 2000: 63). Finland attempted to implement a full employment policy, but due to national and international factors, unemployment has fluctuated and increased, especially in the early 1990s. Government implemented several measures to lower the unemployment rate: for instance, it supports the mobility of labour. Nowadays the aim is specifically to help young people, long-term unemployed, and immigrants to enter the labour markets (see e.g. Myrskylä, 2012).

The change in the composition of labour support policy, using pecuniary implementation of unemployment allowance and expenditures on an active labour market programmes, are shown in Figure 3.6. According to the simple regression results, the world trend seems to be towards *welfare to work* – that is, an active labour market programme has been weighted against unemployment allowance more in 2007 than 1990. In Finland, the need for public support was obviously large due to a deep recession. At a later stage, benefit cuts, especially the unemployment allowances, have been implemented. Conversely, labour support by the Japanese government has been more modest in relative terms than that in Finland because of the aforementioned lifetime employment custom. Furthermore,

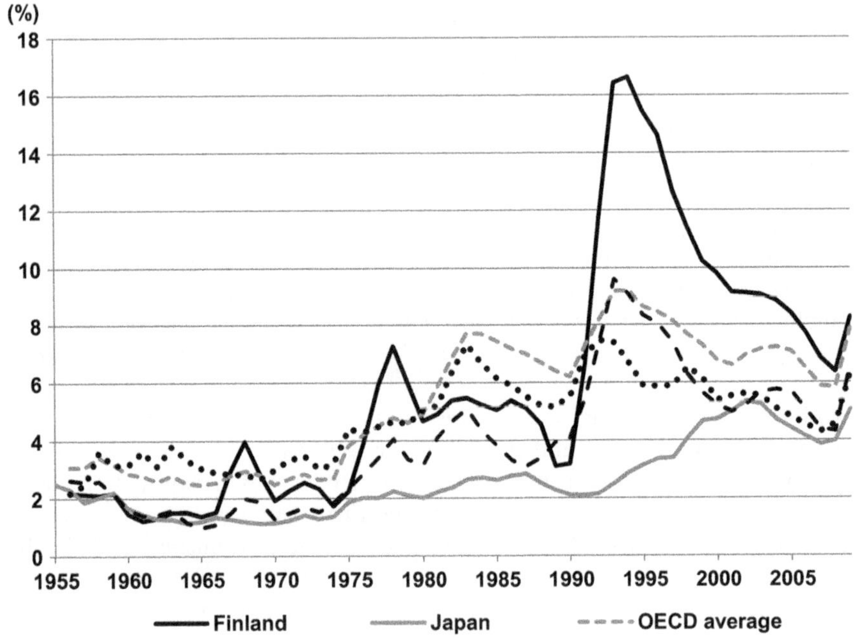

Figure 3.5 Unemployment rates (as a percentage of total labour force)

Source: OECD Labour force statistics 2010. Iceland's data start from 1961 and Korea's from 1963. Mexico's data are excluded from the APEC average due to lack of data.

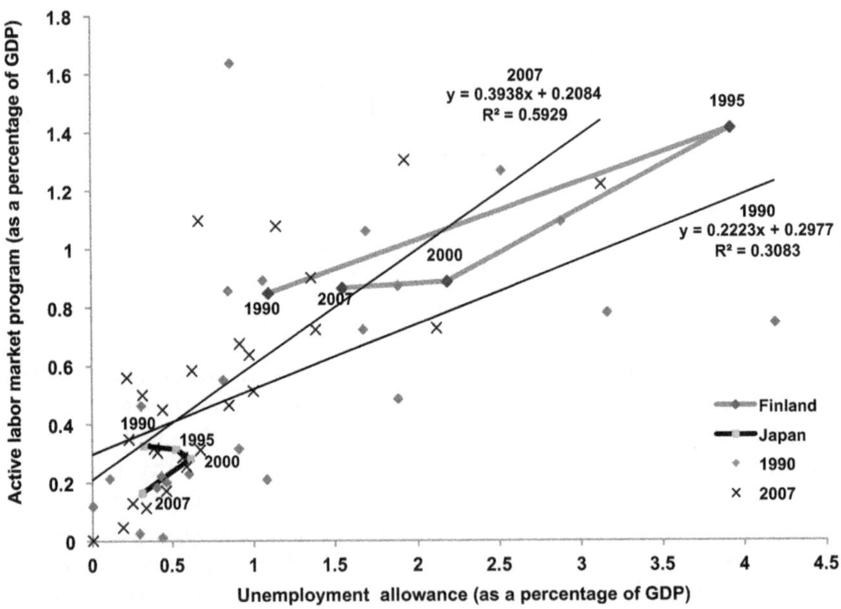

Figure 3.6 Composition of labour support (public and mandatory private)

Source: OECD Social expenditure statistics 2010.

expenditures on the labour market programme have been cut in Japan because vocational training schools, which are basically managed by local government, were closed due to the financial troubles of local governments in this period.[9]

Work and family

Several factors contribute to the differences between women's opportunities to participate in working life in Finland and Japan. To begin with, Japanese young women are typically expected to leave work on marriage; after that, it is more difficult for them to reenter the labour market than for Finnish women. The characteristic seems to be partly culture related and partly due to difficulties in arranging children's daycare. Japanese married women have been assumed to be full-time housewives, in particular throughout the modernization after the Second World War. For a long time, the proportion of the 'extended family', meaning three generations (grandparents, parents, and children) residing under the same roof was higher in Japan than in Western European countries. (On the change in traditional family in Western Europe, see Kautto, 1999: 63–72; Kersbergen, 2000: 21–2.) For example, it amounted to 17 per cent of all family types in 1975; now it is about 9 per cent. In this family setup, grandparents and parents, particularly the wives, took care of each other; grandparents supported childcare, and wives helped in grandparents' daily lives. Even if they lived separately, the care of children and grandparents has been considered the wife's task. Due to these reasons, Japan's social security, especially public care services, has relied on women's contributions. (For a further discussion, see Takahashi, 1995: 134–44; 2003; 2010: 45–6.) As the traditional assumption and social norm is that women take care of the children and close relatives after marrying, the labour participation ratio decreases among women in their late 20s and 30s. However, the traditional pattern is changing due, for example, to urbanization, the rising cost of living, changing patterns of marriage, and increasing numbers of single-parent families (Kingston, 2011: 43–4; Tokoro, 2003: 46–7; Vuori & Merviö, 2007: 16, 26–7, 52–7).

As in other Nordic countries, a Finnish family consists of two generations, parents and their children. The changes in family structure towards smaller nuclear families took place in the post-war period, meaning in practice that grandparents usually live independently and separately from their children and grandchildren. Indeed, according to the 1970 legislation, children are not obligated to provide for their parents (Kröger et al., 2003: 30; Niemelä & Salminen, 2006: 16). In addition, various kinds of family units have become more common and, for example, the numbers of unmarried couples and single parents have increased in recent decades. For these reasons, services and benefits are not directed at the family unit as such; family members are considered as individuals (Kautto, 1999: 64–9). In other words, the system aims to promote consistent equality and individual liberty. This is based on the state's responsibility for the general welfare. In this respect, the foundations of Finnish welfare ideology differ from those of Japan, where the meaning of family support functions and job security has been greatly emphasized (Tokoro, 2012: 652).

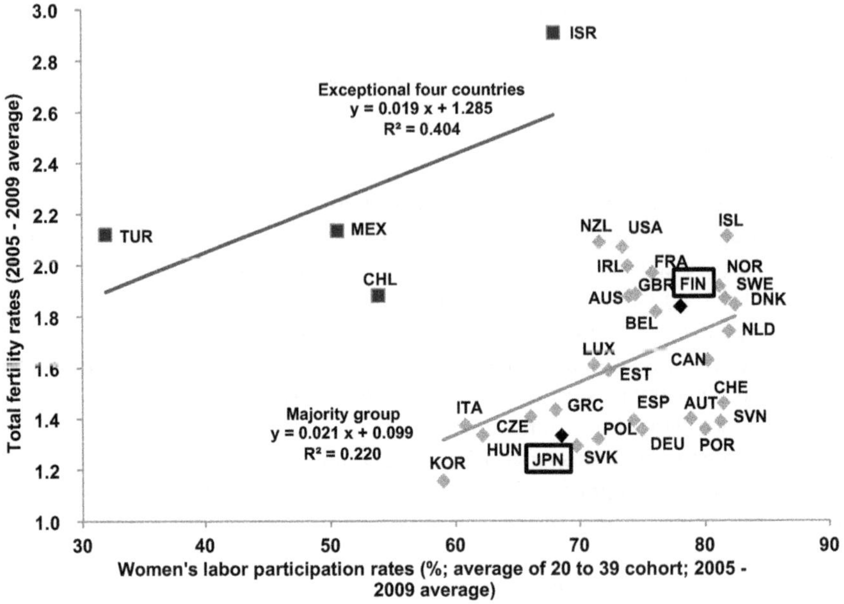

Figure 3.7 Correlation between birth rate and women's workforce participation
Source: OECD Social expenditure statistics 2010.

A closer look at the relationship between birth rate and women's labour participation in OECD member countries between 2005 and 2009 (see Figure 3.7) reveals considerable variation between the countries scrutinized here. First, there are four countries whose total fertility rates are relatively higher than those of other countries respective of the relationship with women's labour participation rates (Turkey, Mexico, Chile, and Israel). The whole trend indicates that birth rate tends to be higher by 0.2 points in the countries where the women's labour participation rate is 10 per cent higher than in other countries. In this trend, Finland is among the countries achieving high birth rate and high participation rate. By contrast, Japan remains below the trend.

A further comparison sheds more light on the development of female labour participation in Finland and Japan. Figure 3.8, displaying evidence for 1990 and 2010, shows that Finnish women engaged more often in paid work than Japanese women did. This is evident in almost all age cohorts. In addition, the use of flexible working time arrangements, such as part-time work and temporary jobs, applies especially to women employees (see also Table 3.1; Kauhanen, 2007: 109; 2008). Figure 3.8 also shows that a major upward change took place in the labour participation rate of young Japanese women aged 25 to 34 in 2010. One reason may be the introduction of childcare leave in 1992. Women's tendency to marry later than before could be another

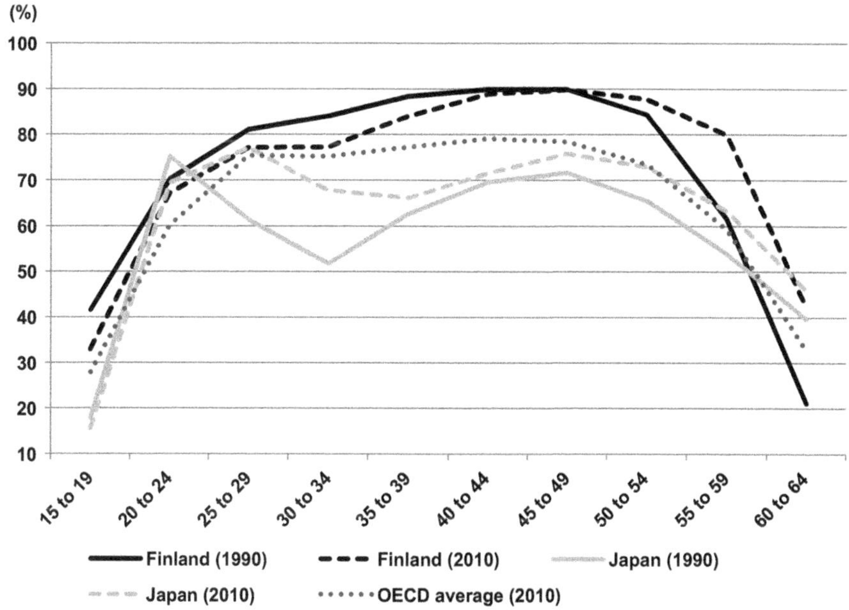

Figure 3.8 Women's workforce participation rates (as a percentage of total population of women)

Source: Labour Force Statistics 1988–2008, 2009 Edition, OECD.

explanation.[10] It seems that marriage and having children are still barriers to young women's labour participation in Japan. By contrast, the labour participation rates of Finnish women in their late 20s and 30s have declined from 1990 to 2010.

A closer look at employment rates among mothers from 2008, as demonstrated in Figure 3.9, explains the Finnish situation. As seen in this figure, the majority of Finnish women with children under 3 years old do not engage in paid work. The rate is lower in Finland than in other Nordic countries. An obvious reason for this is the Finnish family policy, which aims to improve the opportunities of parents to spend time with their children.[11] In Finland, access to public childcare services, the option for parental leaves, and various kinds of allowances or benefits contribute to the reconciliation of occupational and family responsibilities. Long-standing policy of subsidized daycare (since the early 1970s) and parental-leave programmes, which include also fathers, facilitate the reconciliation of parenthood and wage work (Niemelä & Salminen, 2006; Rønsen & Sundström, 2002).

There is a universal right to municipal day care in Finland, that is, children's day care is organized by municipal authorities and access to the services is provided for everyone, including children of families in which the parents are unemployed or are students. Furthermore, there are various allowances, such as home care allowance, for families whose children do not participate in

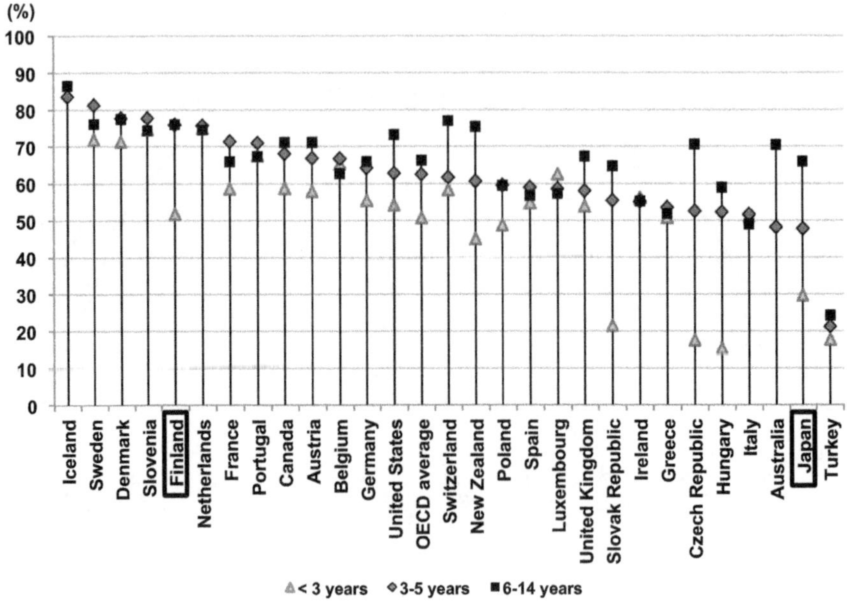

Figure 3.9 Employment rates among mothers with small children (by age of youngest child, 2008)

Source: OECD Family database.

municipal day care but are looked after by one of the guardians or another person such as a relative or a private daycare provider. This system is aimed at promoting gender equality and strengthening the mothers' position in the labour market (Rønsen & Sundström, 2002). However, young women's position in the labour market is weaker than that of young men, because women may need a temporary leave of absence due to childbearing and -rearing, and a portion of the costs of maternity leave will fall on employers (Kauhanen, 2007: 105).

Regarding the Japanese situation, mothers with children under 5 years old are seldom engaged in paid work. This may be related to the scarcity of authorized childcare centres, kindergartens, and other childcare services. The number of children on the waiting list for admission to nursery schools has been increasing and stands at approximately the 25,000 level currently.[12] Therefore, large numbers of applicants have to wait for vacancies or make other childcare arrangements (Kingston, 2004: 281–2; Takahashi, 2003: 83–8; Tokoro, 2003: 47). This question has remained unsolved since 1995, when the aforementioned Angel Plan was launched.

A possible reason for such findings in both countries is cultural: in both Finland and Japan, home care of small children is socially and culturally respected (Takahashi, 2003: 102). On the other hand, there is pressure to increase women's workforce participation in both countries. For example, there is a constant discussion in Finland concerning women's contribution to the labour market due to interruptions of as many as several years due to childcare at home, which in turn decreases women's pensions.

Differences in attitudes towards support for families also emerge in the analysis of the benefits in kind and cash available to families. Figure 3.10 illustrates the relationship between monetary size of public and mandatory private service for families and the workforce participation of young women, since not all the individual measures for families can be compared across countries due to their wide variety. In the figure, cash benefits denote subsidies to families with children, for example, childcare allowance, public income support payments during periods of parental leave, and income support for one-parent families. Benefits in kind include social expenditures on direct financing and subsidizing of providers of nursery schools, childcare services, and public spending on assistance for young people and residential facilities and so on. The trend lines in the figure suggest that more women are employed in countries where greater benefits in kind are provided. However, many OECD countries prefer cash benefits to benefits in kind.

Finland differs from the other Nordic countries in that it provides more benefits in cash; the popularity of the home care allowance contributes to this (see also Rønsen & Sundström, 2002). In Japan, on the other hand, cash benefits and benefits in kind are almost of the same size. However, they are at a lower level

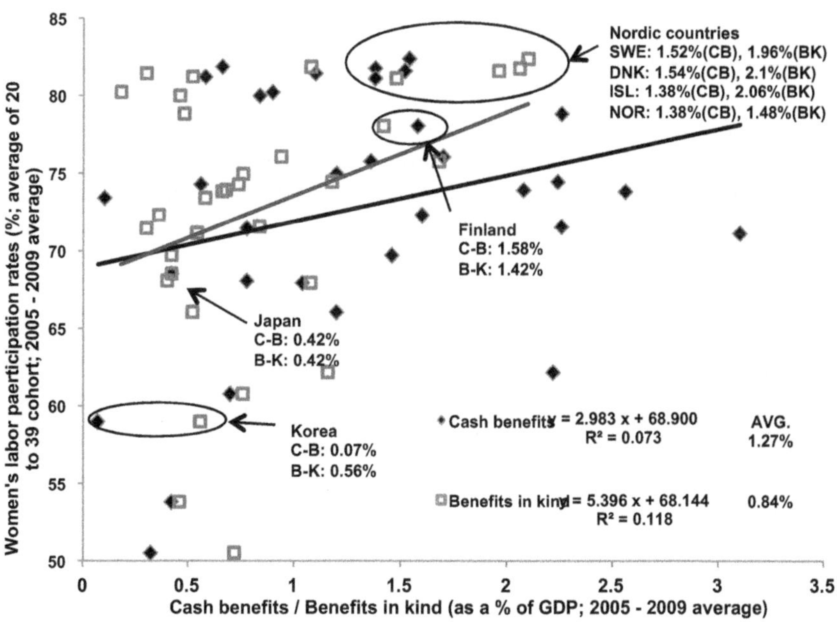

Figure 3.10 Public and mandatory private spending on families

Source: OECD Family database and OECD Social expenditure statistics 2012.

than in the Nordic countries. As mentioned, there is a shortage of children's daycare services in Japan. In addition, childcare allowance is the only financial support for the family, but it is low and depends on the family's income level.

In Japan, a new phase of social security reforms was started by the Democratic Party government in 2010. By this reform, the range of age which can receive the child allowance was expanded, and the amount of the allowance was increased substantially. Although the amounts of provision are scheduled to be reduced for several years in order to secure stable fiscal resources for the provision, it was an epoch-making challenge intended to enhance the social security of child-nurturing families. Another remarkable action was the start of the Comprehensive Reform of Social Security and Tax settled on under the Democratic Party government. The reform emphasizes that one of the pillars of measures is an improvement of childcare, which includes the solution of the aforementioned issue of children on the waiting lists. In addition, the reform specifically mentions how to finance the new policies by increasing social burdens and improving efficiency in government sectors in order to overcome the fiscal problem.[13]

To sum up, there are distinctive patterns of female workforce participation in both countries. For instance, notable differences can be found in female workforce participation rates and employment of various age cohorts, as well as the amount of part-time and full-time work. In Finland, female workforce participation has concentrated on the public sector, which has been connected to the expansion of the welfare state and the provision of public social services. The labour markets are gender segregated, as women tend to engage in care provision in the health sector, education, and social work. Furthermore, in Finland the reconciliation of work and parenthood has given rise to heated public discussion. For example, publicly provided daycare is one of the universal services intended to enable the full-time employment of parents. In Japan, on the other hand, women have continued to bear the major burden of work–family reconciliation. In addition, the rapid increase in single-parent families as a result of increased divorce rates has raised concerns, and the low income level of single mothers has been emphasized by some observers of social policy.

Conclusions

To conclude regarding the post-war development in Finland and Japan, it could be said that welfare policies have taken shape over a long time period and under various kinds of social and political climates. In both countries, the process has been influenced by economic, political, and societal as well as culture-specific factors. In the long run, religious values have influenced the way these two societies have evolved and how the emerging social issues are managed. More succinctly, there is a long-standing tradition in Japan, founded on a combination of Confucian and Buddhist moral teachings, that the family and the local community are the proper resources for the relief of distress. In Finland, Lutheranism has influenced the culture and mentality and has played a role in terms of social policy and welfare. Its influence is persistent, although the Finnish society is nowadays highly secular. In addition, voluntary organizations and associations – either religious or secular – have contributed actively to the welfare state project. Similarly, both countries have also followed and emulated foreign ideas and examples when developing their own models of welfare society. In many cases, the other Nordic countries have served as a frame of reference for Finland, while Japan has emulated the developments in other Asian countries (see descriptions by Kim, 2010; Lin & Rantalaiho, 2003).

As indicated in the preceding sections, Japan has emphasized in particular the meaning of economic growth. In Finland, economic growth and development have also been important, but in post-war Finland, issues such national uniformity, universal and equal social services, and also gender equality have been considered as important building blocks of a more modern society. In both countries, age, family, and employment structures are in a state of transformation, and these changes anticipate more or different kinds of social needs and risks in the future. In both countries, policymakers are challenged by the changes in the family structures (for example, increased divorce rates) and fertility decline, which partly relates to the fact that men and women are marrying later in life. Due the ageing of the population, ensuring welfare services for the elderly and the financing of pensions are among the main challenges for the Japanese policymakers. However, this focus has drawn criticism from some observers of social policy and social investment, and support for the current and future working population is called for despite the financial challenges posed by the prolonged economic recession as well as the consequences of the disastrous earthquake and tsunami in Japan's northeastern regions in March 2011. Finnish society is likewise trying to cope with the consequences of an ageing society in a situation of tightened state finances. For example, the public discussion has tackled issues related to the need to increase the workforce, which has put more pressure on female labour participation and employment-based immigration.

Notes

1. Meltzer and Richard simply describe the process of increasing in a general equilibrium model with voting.
2. In Finland, employees or self-employed persons who report they work part time in their main job are classified as part-time workers. This definition is not based on any limitations on hours worked but on the respondent's own idea of the work being part time (Statistics Finland, www.stat.fi/meta/kas/osa_aikatyo_en.html).
3. Wilensky determined in the basis of his empirical analysis that the consequences of economic development, demographic composition, and social organization are more important than political variables for the development of a welfare state in OECD countries.
4. According to Kahl's summary, persistent poverty is relieved in Catholicism, and it is an individual responsibility in Reformed Protestantism.
5. According to Statistics Finland's data on population changes, the slight rise in the birth rate continues. At the fertility rate prevailing in 2010, a woman would give birth

to an average of 1.87 children during her reproductive years. The birth rate had been rising for the past eight years in succession. For more information and Finnish statistics, see www.stat.fi/til/synt/2010/synt_2010_2011-04-15_tie_001_en.html.

6. Finland joined the European Economic Area in 1994, the European Union in 1995, and the European Economic and Monetary Union (EMU) in 1999.
7. *Annual Health, Labour and Welfare Report 2011–2012*, The Ministry of Health, Labour and Welfare, Japan.
8. See www.stat.fi/til/jmete/2011/jmete_2011_2013-01-31_tie_001_en.html (Statistics Finland); www.mof.go.jp/english/budget/budget/fy2013/01.pdf (Ministry of Finance, Japan). The share in the case of Japan is calculated without the expenditure for servicing the national debt.
9. The reports on the situation of public vocational training, the All-Japan Prefectural and Municipal Workers' Union, 2009 (in Japanese).
10. According to the report by the Ministry of Health, Labour and Welfare, a woman's age at first marriage has risen by 3 years from 25.9 years in 1990 to 28.6 years in 2009. In addition, a wife's age at the birth of the first child has also risen (from 27 years in 1990 to 29.7 years in 2009). Statistics on Birth (2012 version), the Ministry of Health, Labour and Welfare, Japan.
11. Child and family policy in Finland (2013), Ministry of Social Affairs and Health, Finland (www.stm.fi/c/document_library/get_file?folderId=6511570&name=DLFE-25916.pdf, retrieved 11 June, 2013).
12. Press release on the statistics of nursery school and children by the Ministry of Health, Labour and Welfare, Japan (September, 2012).
13. See the document 'Definite Plan for the Comprehensive Reform of Social Security and Tax' (July 1, 2011) by the Cabinet Secretariat, Japan (www.cas.go.jp/jp/seisaku/syakaihosyou/en/index.html, retrieved 11.6.2013).

4 Higher education systems and labour market outcomes in Japan and Finland, 1950–2010

Anu Ojala, Yasushi Tanaka, and Olli Turunen

Introduction

In recent decades, both Japan and Finland have drawn international attention to their education systems. Since the 1960s, Japan has been ranked among the top performers in the Trends in International Mathematics and Science Study (TIMSS), while Finland has received international acclaim for her outstanding performance in the Programme for International Student Assessment (PISA) by the OECD, and most recently both countries were ranked high in the OECD Skills Outlook 2013 Survey of Adult Skills (PIAAC). Both Japan and Finland were at the top of OECD countries in adult literacy and numeracy proficiency scores. There is no doubt that these outcomes are the results of the educational policies of the two countries. In particular, in both countries, belief in high educational standards as well as in the economic and intellectual benefits of education is firmly entrenched. This produces ready recruits for higher education, but the ways to organize higher education and how the students are catered for are quite different. According to UNESCO's Global Education Indicators (GEI) 2009, the percentages of enrolment in the private tertiary education sector in 2007 for Japan and Finland were 80 per cent and 11 per cent respectively, so while in Japan educational costs are mostly covered privately, Finnish higher education students receive considerable amounts of public financial support and study in a free, publicly funded system. Related to this issue is that, according to the GEI 2009, the enrolment ratios for tertiary education for Japan and Finland in 2007 were 58 per cent and 94 per cent respectively. They are almost at the bottom and the top of the enrolment rate ranking among the industrialized countries of East Asia, North America, and Western Europe. To explain these differences this chapter discusses the history of education in both countries, educational systems today, and trends in higher education. Furthermore, the chapter considers the costs and benefits of higher education in Japan and Finland in order to create a contextual setting for a later comparison of the post-war–era economic returns on higher education.

The aim of this chapter is to study educational policies in Japan and Finland, which formulate the systems and institutions of higher education. What are the economic implications of these policies for an individual going through the system and joining the labour force? Furthermore, what were the costs, private or public, of the wage premium attained via higher education? In short, our focus is on the human capital investment aspect of higher education, in which both the public and private economic costs as well as the private benefits of higher education are compared to ascertain the costs and benefits of higher education in Japan and Finland.

Broad trends in the history of Japanese education

Japan's encounter with Commodore Matthew C. Perry in 1853 prompted her to modernize when Perry led the American fleet to the Japanese port of Uraga near Tokyo to seek a trade treaty between the two countries. The Meiji Restoration soon followed in 1868 to modernize Japan, including her educational system. However, the importance of education had been recognized long before the encounter. During the feudalistic Tokugawa era, from 1600 right up to 1868, when the warrior class played the main social roles, schools were set up to educate the offspring of this class as the future ruling class. The Tokugawa government provided schools to teach Confucianism, literature, and medicine and, towards the end of the reign, even foreign languages.

Alongside the elite education system of the government, ordinary people developed their own system. The merchant class in particular felt a need to educate their offspring in practical subjects such as reading, writing, and arithmetic. Small-sized schools with no more than 20 pupils, called *Tera-goya* (or temple school), were set up to teach these subjects. This eventually spread to farming and fishing villages to help raise the literacy rate of the ordinary people and became the foundation of the development of primary education in modern Japan.

The history of the Japanese education system since the Meiji Restoration can be divided into two phases, with the Second World War as the dividing line. The first phase saw the introduction and diffusion of a Western education system. The Japanese government invited David Murray, professor of mathematics and astronomy from Rutgers University (known at that time as Rutgers College), United States, in 1874 to help create a modern and centralized education system for Japan. After half a century of reforms and restructuring, the new Japanese education system began to earn growing popularity and finally established itself with 8 years of primary education, 7 years of secondary education, and 3 years of higher education. Of the primary education, the first 4 (later extended to 6) years were deemed compulsory. The government employed a considerable number of teachers from the West to teach Japanese higher education students in subjects such as law, astronomy, medicine, mathematics, physics, chemistry, and engineering. At the same time, students were sent abroad in order to replace these foreign teachers in due course. Up to the Second World War, the education system in Japan was not insulated from the political climate and was used, to some extent, to support nationalism. The Imperial Rescript on Education (Kyoiku Chokugo) came into effect in 1890 as a guideline for the educational philosophy of Imperial Japan and lasted till the end of the Second World War. This promoted national unity based on the Imperial Throne.

The second phase was characterized by the democratization aims of the Allied Occupation Forces following the 1945 defeat of Japan in the Second World War. A new education policy was created with the guidance of the Civil Information and Education Section, with education experts from the United States to introduce a more democratic Fundamental Law of Education (Kyoiku Kihonho). Eventually, the old 8-7-3–year system with the first 4 years compulsory was changed to a system of 6-6-4 years of primary, secondary, and tertiary education with the first 9 years compulsory – or, as it is better known in Japan, the '6-3-3-4 system' for primary school, junior high school, senior high school, and university with primary and junior high school education as compulsory.

In sum, it is clear that the general level of education has greatly improved in Japan with the introduction of a Western-style education system after the Meiji Restoration and the reforms after the Second World War. A clear example of the improvements is the increase in the years of compulsory education. It was introduced with 4 years in the former period and then rose to 9 years during the latter period. The long-term trend in higher education also shows improvement. Since the foundation of the University of Tokyo, Japan's first university, in 1877, the number of students in higher education was about 100,000 in 1920 and then rose to 250,000 in 1940. More accurate figures are available after the Second World. Table 4.1 shows the trend in the number of university students from 1920 to 2000 in relation to the youth and total populations. It is clear that during the first half of the century, university students were the privileged few. The trend also suggests that higher education in Japan has changed from prewar elite education to post-war popular or mass education, even if the population growth is taken into consideration.

Table 4.1 Trend in number of university students in Japan, 1920–2000

Year	*No. of students in HE (A)*	*Population 15–24 years (B)*	*(A)/(B) %*	*Population Total (C)*	*(A)/(C) %*
1920	100,000	10,028,000	1.0%	55,963,000	0.2%
1940	250,000	12,710,000	2.0%	71,933,000	0.3%
1960	709,878	17,627,000	4.0%	93,419,000	0.8%
1980	2,206,436	16,123,000	13.7%	117,060,000	1.9%
2000	3,067,703	15,910,000	19.3%	126,926,000	2.4%

Source: (MEXT, 1962, 2009; Statistics Japan, 2006)

Note: A population census has been taken every 5 years since 1920. (A)/(B) should not be taken as the enrolment rate as it covers a wider age range but reflects the popularity of higher education.

Broad trends in the history of Finnish education

In order to comprehend the present situation and the structure of the Finnish education system, a historical overview of its early development is appropriate. The roots of the Finnish education system are in the European tradition. The foundations of the Finnish education system were laid long before Finland existed as an independent state. The education system evolved first under Swedish and after that under Russian domination.

During the Middle Ages, Finland, or more precisely the present geographical area of Finland, was under the rule of the Swedish Crown. Finland was part of the Kingdom of Sweden from the twelfth century to beginning of the nineteenth century, and education in Finland was related to European traditions through the education system of the Roman Catholic Church. The Church needed prelates and ministers, and the Diocese of Turku established a cathedral school in 1276 to meet these demands. In addition to offering instruction in Finland, the diocese sent students to European universities, the University of Paris being the main destination for Finnish students in the Middle Ages. However, at the end of the fifteenth century, the expansion of the university system to the German-speaking countries made it easier for Finns to study abroad, since the universities were geographically closer and the duration of the studies was shorter (Klinge, 2010; Kuikka, 2009). After Sweden departed from the Catholic tradition to adopt Protestant beliefs, the University of Turku, the first university in Finland, was established in 1640 as part of an integration policy of the Kingdom of Sweden. The aim was again to train clergymen, at this time for the Lutheran Church, and above all, civil servants to implement the development efforts of the state (Välimaa, 2001).

The main difference between the education systems in the Catholic and Lutheran eras was the role of the state. In the Catholic era, the Church was autonomous and separate from the state government. Knowledge and the Church were considered to be universal, above the state and nationality. Henceforth, education was connected to the Church. On the other hand, in the Lutheran system, the Church was a part of the state and the state began to govern both the Church and the education system (Klinge et al., 1987). The responsibility for educating people in the Lutheran system remained in the hands of the Church. The Lutheran Church focused more on the literacy of ordinary people, as, according to Lutheran beliefs, it was important for the people to be able to read the main teachings of the Bible (Laine & Laine, 2010).

Before the nineteenth century, the education of Finnish people was heavily dependent on their status at birth, meaning the social class into which a person was born. Formal education included mainly the education of clergymen and civil servants (Hanska, Vainio-Korhonen, & Rahikainen, 2010; Isosaari, 1973). Although the nobility and bourgeoisie might attend church and town schools, many of them were educated at home by governesses or relatives. The education of ordinary people, merchants, and craftsmen was more informal and based on learning by doing in their own living environment or in master, journeyman, and apprenticeship relationships. People were brought up and educated for the social class they were born into (Hanska & Vainio-Korhonen, 2010; Iisalo, 1988). In these years, education in Finland was fragmentary. Most of the schools were in towns and coastal areas and therefore did not reach people in the more remote rural areas (Joutsivuo, 2010). Education of the common people initially developed as a responsibility of the Church and its parishes. The education provided by the parishes concerned mainly religious instruction and learning to read the Bible. Although education before confirmation was made more or less compulsory in the 1740s, these parish schools did not reach all young Finnish people (Buchardt, Markkola, & Valtonen, 2013). It was not until the era of autonomy in the nineteenth century that the independence of the Finnish state and its educational system began to evolve. At that time, Finland was an autonomous part of imperial Russia, and efforts towards independence became stronger. The basic forms of Finnish institutions, such as the education system, were established (Lampinen, 1998/2000; Välimaa, 2013).

The nineteenth century witnessed the establishing of an education system for the common people (Isosaari, 1973). The Finnish education system evolved gradually from the education of clergymen to the education of civil servants and finally to the system of common education by the end of the nineteenth century. It has been claimed that it was not until then that the Church lost its authority over education (Ahola, 1995). The development of Finnish elementary schools started with the legislation of 1866. However, the act on compulsory education in Finland was not passed until 1921, which was relatively late in comparison to other Nordic countries (Buchardt et al., 2013).

The history of the Finnish education policy has been characterized by three ideological emphases. First, emphasis was placed on nation building, with education policy geared to foster nationalism. Secondly, emphasis was placed on the ideology of economic growth, with education seen as a means to improve the economic situation of society. The third idea was *social equality*, with education seen as a guarantee of social equality in society (Lampinen, 1998/2000). The period from the founding of the elementary school system in the 1860s to the beginning of the twentieth century was dominated by a policy of building and strengthening national identity connected to the idea of the civilizing effect of education. One of the key themes in this era was the strengthening of Finland as a nation by educating the population in their own language. These ideas were the basis on which the national system of education was created. The era from Finnish independence in 1917 to the middle of the 1960s was a somewhat hesitant and incoherent time in Finnish education policy (Lampinen, 1998/2000). The strongest national ideologies gradually lost their power. However, the ideas of education policy based on economic growth and social equality were not yet fully evolved or embraced. Education policy was overshadowed by the turbulent times between the world wars and reconstruction after the Second World War. It was not until the 1960s when the rapid change in economic structures yielded change in

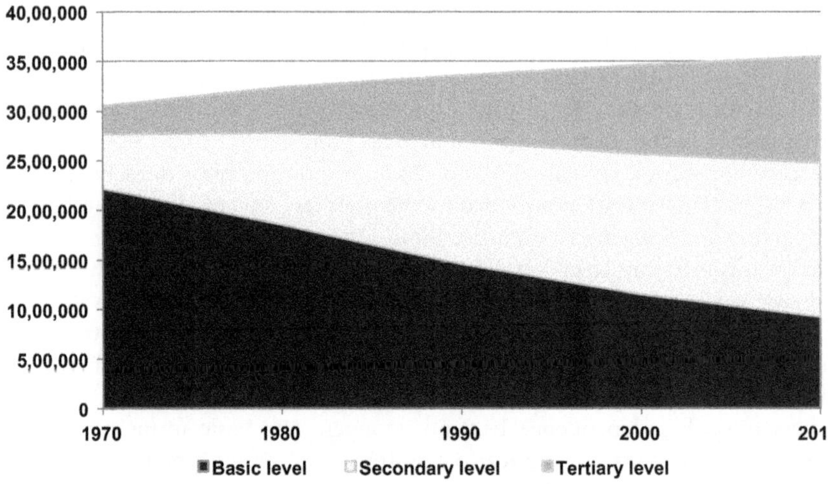

Figure 4.1 Development of education level of Finnish working-aged population (population 15–64 years)

Source: Statistics Finland, 2012a

education. In 1940, 64 per cent of the Finnish population earned their living from primary production, agriculture, or forestry, while in 1970 this same ratio had descended to 20 per cent (Hannikainen & Heikkinen, 2006; Hjerppe & Jalava, 2006; Iisalo, 1988). The increase in industrial work and the service sector meant a burgeoning demand for educated employees, causing a rise in the level of education in Finland. For example, the proportion of working-aged (15–64 years old) Finnish people with only basic education fell from 86 per cent in 1960 to 72 per cent in 1970 and further to 57 per cent in 1980 (Iisalo, 1988; Statistics Finland, 2012a). Figure 4.1 shows the development in the education levels of Finnish working-aged people 1970–2010.

The era between 1960s and 1990s was dominated by social change characterized by ideas of equality, both social and regional. Furthermore, the equality of educational opportunities was seen to create welfare for the whole society (Lampinen, 1998/2000; Valtonen, 2013). The structures of the Finnish welfare state evolved in the first decades of this era, and in particular the Finnish education system achieved its present form with equal education opportunities for all, the costs of education being met by taxation revenue (Buchardt et al., 2013). In the 1990s, the idea of economic growth via education and, furthermore, a strong belief in the benefits of education continued to be the main ideological themes of education policy. At the end of the twentieth century, education policy was adjusted to improve national competitiveness, as global competition increased and Finland became a member of the European Union (Lampinen, 1998/2000).

Table 4.2 Trend in number of university students in Finland, 1880–2010

Year	*University students (A)*	*Population 20–29 years (B)*	*(A)/(B) %*	*Population total (C)*	*(A)/(C) %*
1880	736	339,225	0.2	2,060,782	0.04
1890	1,863	357,100	0.5	2,380,100	0.08
1900	2,727	426,000	0.6	2,655,900	0.1
1910	3,238	471,400	0.7	2,943,400	0.1
1920	3,590	508,500	0.7	3,147,600	0.1
1930	7,411	640,800	1.2	3,462,700	0.2
1940	8,300	627,787	1.3	3,695,617	0.2
1950	13,851	635,632	2.2	4,029,803	0.3
1960	24,122	601,998	4.0	4,446,222	0.5
1970	57,871	776,130	7.5	4,598,336	1.3
1980	84,176	784,895	10.7	4,787,778	1.8
1990	112,921	720,429	15.7	4,998 478	2.3
2000	157,796	633,432	24.9	5,181,115	3.0
2010	169,404	673,843	25.1	5,375,276	3.2

Sources: Kokkinen, 2012; Statistics Finland, 2012a, 2012c

Finland has come a long way from a nation where once even basic education was a privilege of the few to a nation where a quarter of young people between the ages 20 and 29 are studying in universities. Table 4.2 shows a trend in the number of Finnish university students between 1880 and 2010. Similar to the development in Japan, higher education has changed from being the prerogative of the elite to equal opportunity in education.

The Japanese education system today

The education system in Japan is based on the '6–3–3–4' school year system, where the first 6 years of primary school and 3 years of junior high school are compulsory. These are followed by 3 years of senior high school and generally 4 years of university. Primary school starts at the age of 6 and university is completed at the age of 22 if studies are attended continually throughout the education system. Preprimary education in Japan includes kindergarten, which offers up to 3 years of preschool education prior to primary school. In higher education Japanese students can choose from two alternative paths, 2 years of college education or 4 or more years in universities. There are some variations in the length of the different degree programmes in higher education. For example, medicine and dentistry require 6 years of undergraduate studies. Japanese postgraduate programmes include 2 years of study for master's degrees

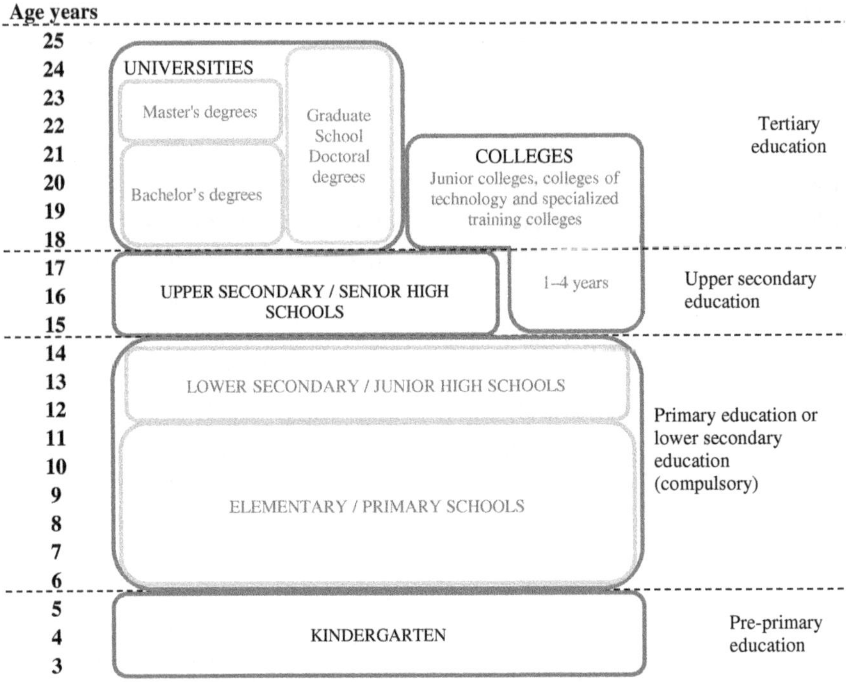

Figure 4.2 The main structure of the Japanese educational system

Sources: MEXT, 2013

and a minimum of 3 years for doctoral degrees. The Japanese academic year starts in April and ends in March.

Japanese primary and junior high schools, as part of compulsory education, are mostly public (see Table 4.3). The proportion of private institutions is higher among senior high schools, and the majority of the universities and junior colleges are private. Thus the Japanese system of higher education, unlike the Finnish system, is fundamentally private. The average number of students per year is quite stable throughout the junior and senior high schools at roughly 1,000,000 students. This suggests that the enrolment rate for senior high school is very high, although it is not a part of compulsory education. The enrolment rate for senior high school of those leaving junior high stood at 98 per cent in 2009.

The majority of university and junior college students in Japan study in private schools. There are considerably more male students than female students, which is the other fundamental difference between the higher education systems of Japan and Finland. Furthermore, very few students in Japan study in postgraduate programmes. There are more male students than female students in university, whereas students in junior colleges are mostly female. The largest group of university students in Japan, every third, studies social science subjects. This is

Table 4.3 Numbers of students and shares of public and private schools at different Levels of education in Japan in 2009

	Kindergarten	*Primary*	*Junior high*	*Senior high*	*University*	*College*
Students	1,630,336	7,063,606	3,600,323	3,347,311	2,845,908	160,976
Total number of schools	13,516	22,258	10,864	5,183	773	406
Public schools	5,255	22,048	10,119	3,862	178	28
Private schools	8,261	210	745	1,321	595	378
Share of private schools %	61.1	0.9	6.9	25.5	77.0	93.1

Source: Ministry of Education, Culture, Sports, Science and Technology in Japan (MEXT), 2009

followed by science and engineering, and the smallest is medicine and dentistry, which only every 40th university student studies.

The coexistence of public and private institutions at compulsory and non-compulsory levels implies a variation in the cost of education. Table 4.6 shows the variation according to Educational Statistics 2008 of the Ministry of Education. In order to more accurately compare household income to the costs of education at each educational level, households are divided into two separate categories: households with the head aged between 30 and 39 and 40 and 49, those typically having children in primary and secondary levels of education, respectively.

Although there are no tuition fees in public primary or junior high schools, studies in these schools are not free. School meals and extracurricular activities are subject to a charge in Japan. As seen in Table 4.6, the costs for public schools rise from kindergarten to senior high school. Private education is a considerable economic burden on families, particularly at the primary school level. According to the Household Survey, the Engel's coefficient, the proportion of family income spent on food in Japan since 2000, has been around 0.22. This figure is close to the proportions consumed by education (see Table 4.6), suggesting that education is a factor as important as or maybe even more important than food in household expenditure.

As seen in Tables 4.2 and 4.6, less than 1 per cent of the primary schools are private, and with their high costs, it is a luxury to have children educated in a private primary school. Despite the generally high cost of private education, there is a tendency to choose private schools because many private universities introduce their own high schools by either merging existing high schools or setting up new ones. These high schools are often provided with a certain quota for university entry, giving an easier path to their students. This is done in order to secure students in the face of a diminishing youth population. Private higher education is facing profitability challenges with the dwindling number of students

Table 4.4 Further breakdown of student numbers for universities and junior colleges in Japan in 2009

	Sector			*Gender*			*Degrees*		
	Public	*Private*	*%*[a]	*Male*	*Female*	*%*[b]	*Under-grad.*	*Post-grad.*	*%*[c]
University	758,713	2,087,195	73%	1,687,518	1,158,390	41%	2,527,319	318,589	11%
College	9,976	151,000	94%	17,478	143,498	89%	160,976	0	0%

[a]share of students in private schools;
[b]share of female students;
[c]share of postgraduate students

Source: MEXT, 2009

Table 4.5 Distribution of Japanese university students by field of study in 2009

Humanities	*Social Science*	*Science & Engineering*	*Medicine & Dentistry*	*Education*	*Others*
15.4%	35.3%	24.3%	2.5%	6.3%	13.6%

Source: MEXT, 2009

Table 4.6 Annual costs of education per student by school type in comparison to household income in Japan in 2006 (costs are presented in yen)

	Kindergarten	*Primary school*	*Junior high*	*Senior high*
Costs of public education	251,324	334,134	471,752	520,503
Costs of private education	538,406	1,373,184	1,269,391	1,045,234
Household income	4,886,508[a]	4,886,508[a]	5,847,600[b]	5,847,600[b]
Proportion of the costs of public education from the household income	0.05	0.07	0.08	0.09
Proportion of the costs of private education from the household income	0.11	0.28	0.22	0.18

[a] Average monthly disposable income of a household with the head aged between 30–39 years and [b] between 40–49 years

Source: Statistics Japan 2006a; Ministry of Education, Culture, Sports, Science and Technology in Japan (MEXT), 2008

paying tuition fees to cover school expenses, as the main source of revenue for private schools is tuition fees (Kinmonth, 2005).

Finnish education system today

The main theme in Finnish education policy is to provide equal opportunities for education. Education in Finland from the level of preschool to higher education is mostly free. The education system is publicly funded and there are no tuition fees. The key tendencies in the Finnish system are permeability and accessibility. The system is designed to allow variation in individual educational paths. In this system, higher levels of education can be reached through various paths (Finnish National Board of Education, 2013a). The first step in the Finnish education system is early childhood care and education, including

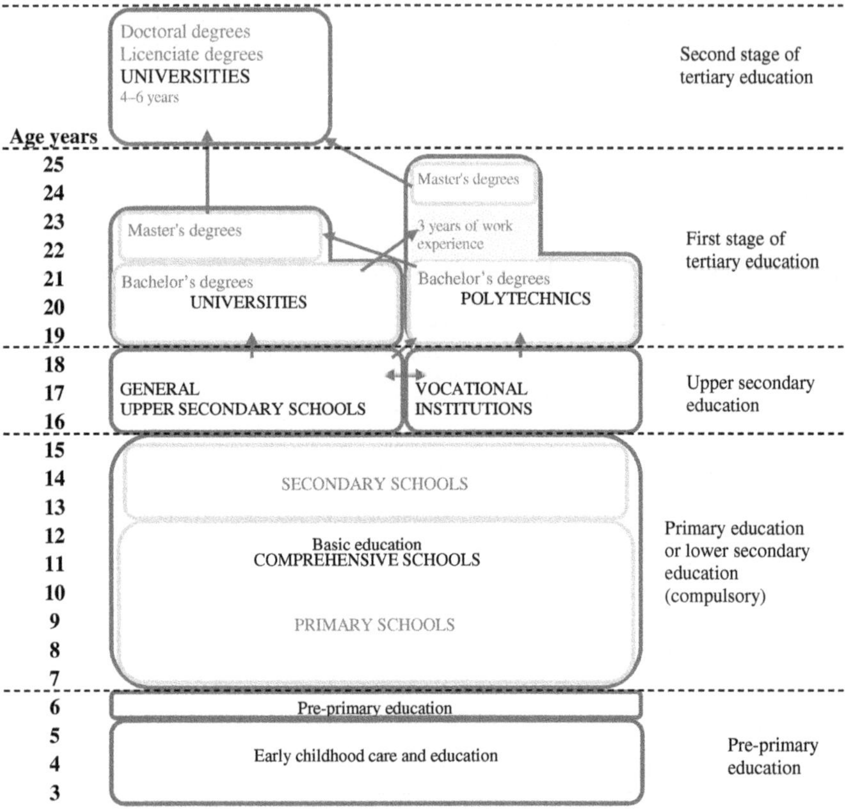

Figure 4.3 The main structure of the Finnish educational system

Source: Antikainen, Rinne, & Koski, 2006; Finnish Ministry of Education and Culture, 2013b

preprimary education. Preprimary education is a voluntary right for every 6-year-old child in Finland and provided mostly in preschools or public kindergartens or primary schools. There are some private preschools, but the number is limited. Studying costs in these private preschools is subsidized by the government. Therefore, preprimary education in Finland, both public and private, is free. Nevertheless, early childhood care, such as kindergartens, is subject to a government-subsidized charge depending on the income level and the number of children in the family. The organization of early childhood education and care in Finland is the responsibility of the municipalities. Finnish basic education consists of 9 years of compulsory comprehensive school, the first 6 in primary schools and 3 in secondary schools. Comprehensive schools in Finland are public, and pupils in basic education are allocated to the school nearest to their domicile (Finnish National Board of Education, 2013a). Comprehensive school is free, including studying materials, meals, and transportation. After 9 years of comprehensive school, pupils opt for general upper secondary schools or vocational institutions. In 2011, half of the young people completing comprehensive school continued in general upper secondary schools (high school) and 41 per cent in upper secondary–level vocational education (Statistics Finland, 2012b). At upper secondary level, there are no tuition fees, but students pay for their books and transportation. From the upper secondary level on, Finnish students have an opportunity to fund their studies with study grants and loans.

At the level of basic education, private schools are mainly schools providing teaching in other than official languages of Finland (namely Finnish and Swedish) and schools organized on a religious or Steiner pedagogic basis (Finnish Ministry of Education and Culture, 2013a). These schools are licensed, regulated, and coordinated by the government. As Table 4.7 shows, the number of privately owned schools is higher at the level of vocational institutes and polytechnics. From an educational point of view, private institutes do not differ much from their public counterparts, as they follow the national core curricula and qualification requirements. Both private and public institutes are provided with public funding. In Finland, education after basic level aiming for a degree is free of charge in both private and public institutes (Finnish Ministry of Education and Culture, 2013c). From the perspective of the students and their parents, there is no difference in the cost of education between private and public education providers. Vocational education may be provided by local and municipal authorities, government or state companies, or registered associations and foundations. Vocational education in Finland is regulated by government-set national objectives, and the educational aims of private polytechnics are authorized by the government (Finnish Ministry of Education and Culture, 2009a).

Table 4.7 Number of students and share of public and private schools at different levels of education in Finland in 2009

	Basic education	*Upper secondary education*		*Higher education*	
	Comprehensive schools	*General upper secondary schools*	*Vocational institutes*	*Polytechnics*	*Universities*
Students	553,329	112,088	250,200	135,033[a]	168,475[a]
Total number of schools	3,027	398	220	28	20
Public schools	2,989	390	140	17	20
Private schools	38	8	80	11	0
Share of private schools %	1.3	2.0	36.4	39.3	0.0

[a] Students in education leading to a qualification or degree.

Sources: Statistics Finland. 2012d; Statistics Finland, 2013

Table 4.8 Number of students in Finnish universities and polytechnics in 2009

			Gender			*Degrees*		
	Total	*%*	*Male*	*Female*	*%*[a]	*Undergrad.*	*Postgrad.*	*%*[b]
University	168,475	56	78,292	90,183	54	145,033	20,502	12
Polytechnics	135,033	44	61,816	73,217	54	135,033	0	0

[a]share of female students.
[b]share of postgraduate students.

Sources: Finnish Ministry of Education and Culture, 2013b; Statistics Finland, 2013

The Finnish system of higher education is a dual system consisting of universities and polytechnics. Polytechnics and universities, although regulated by the government, enjoy considerable autonomy in their operations, such as the design of their degree programmes, administration, and student admission (Finnish Ministry of Education and Culture, 2013d). The roles of these two higher education institutions are complementary. The universities promote independent research and scientific knowledge and provide the highest education based on their research, whereas polytechnics focus on diversified professional education designed to meet regional employment and R&D needs. The polytechnics carry out research and development serving polytechnic education and supporting working life, especially in engineering, business, and health care. The bachelor's and master's studies offered in the polytechnics are more vocationally oriented than those leading to university degrees. For example, master's degree studies in Finnish polytechnics require 3 years of relevant work experience (Hölttä, Jansson, & Kivistö, 2011). There are more female students in Finnish universities and polytechnics, whereas the situation is reversed in Japan, with 59 per cent being male in universities students in 2009 and a large majority (89 per cent) of junior college students being female.

Today the Finnish university system is in a transition initiated by the university reform of 2009. The Finnish universities have changed from being government offices to independent corporations under public law or foundations under private law. There have been mergers between universities, and today there are 16 universities in Finland, of which 9 are multifaculty institutions, 2 are schools of business and economics, 3 are art academies, and 2 are universities of technology. All of these offer bachelor-, master-, licentiate-, and doctoral-level degrees. The Finnish universities are all public, and their function is based on the legislation in the University Act (Finnish Ministry of Education and Culture, 2009a; Finnish National Board of Education, 2013b; Finnish Parliament, 2009).

The universities are mainly funded from the state budget; appropriations cover approximately 64 per cent of the budgets of universities. The rest of the funding consists of supplementary sources such as paid services, donations, and sponsoring (Finnish Ministry of Education and Culture, 2013d). The

Table 4.9 Distribution of Finnish higher education students by field of study in 2009

	University		*Polytechnics*	
	Students	*Share of female students*	*Students*	*Share of female students*
Humanities and Education	37,718	75.8%	1,496	79.5%
Social sciences, business and administration	37,247	55.6%	27,427	61.3%
Technology, communication and transport	36,536	22.8%	40,116	15.3%
Natural sciences	24,399	42.2%	6,039	25.1%
Social services, health and sport	15,225	69.5%	34,810	87.3%
Culture	13,744	70.1%	12,015	67.5%
Natural resources and the environment	3,253	54.8%	4,367	49.0%
Tourism, catering and domestic services	353	79.3%	8,684	79.7%
Other	0	0.0%	79	10.1%

Source: Statistics Finland, 2013

funding of polytechnics is divided between the local authorities and government. Central government is responsible for 42 per cent of the funding, and the share of local government is 58 per cent (Association of Finnish Local Authorities, 2013).

The figures for the costs of education in Table 4.10 are total expenditure on education and are not directly paid by households. Households pay the costs of the education through taxation. Due to differences between the Finnish and Japanese systems, these figures are not comparable with the cost figures for Japanese education presented in Table 4.6, which are the costs for private households. However, the figures in Table 4.10 will give an idea of the cost of education in relation to the disposable incomes of Finnish households.

Trends in higher education in both Japan and Finland

It has been mentioned earlier that university education in both Japan and Finland has transformed from education for the elite to education for the masses. In this section, we will look in more detail at the trends in higher education in

Table 4.10 Current expenditure on education by school type in comparison to household income in Finland in 2009

	Kindergarten	*Comprehensive schools*	*General upper secondary schools*	*Vocational institutes*
Current expenditure euros per student	5,300	7,300	5,400	9,900
Household income euros	36,020[a]	47,470[b]	48,650[c]	48,650[c]
Proportion of the costs of education from the household income	0.15	0.15	0.11	0.20

[a] Average monthly disposable income of households, where the person with the highest personal income is aged between 25–34 years,
[b] between 35–44 years, and
[c] between 35–44 years.

Source: Statistics Finland, 2011a; Statistics Finland, 2011b

Note: Current expenditure comprises of consumption expenditure of educational institutions.

both countries. As Figure 4.4 shows, both Japan and Finland have seen a considerable rise in participation in higher education. When compared with the figures in Table 4.11, it can be noted that these trends follow the development continuing from the 1950s.

In Japan, the male enrolment rate increased rapidly during the 1960s and 1970s. From the beginning of the 1980s, these rates declined so that at the start of the 1990s, they were lower than in 1980. Afterwards, the rate started to rise again, and the new rising trend in enrolment has continued. However, the overall trend shows a general rise in both countries. The rise in gross enrolment rate in Finland has been steeper, notably from the beginning of the 1980s to the 1990s. When growth in the 1990s started to level out, the hitherto relatively equal gross enrolment levels between males and females began to diverge, with female rates surpassing male rates in the late 1980s. In contrast to the Finnish development, in Japan, the difference between male and female gross enrolment rates has diminished from an approximate difference of 17 per cent in the 1970s and 1980s to an 8 per cent difference. It is worth noting that the gender disparity in Finland currently favours women by 24 per cent, whereas in Japan it favours men by 6 per cent (UNESCO, 2008). As will be seen later in Figure 4.7 and Table 4.13, this rate in favour of Finnish women is not reflected in their incomes.

Table 4.11 shows the trends in enrolment rates for higher education in Japan over the last half century obtained from the statistics of the Basic School Survey. Several trends are worth noting. First, despite a considerable gap in the enrolment rates between male and female students for university in 2005, in relative terms, the difference has been diminishing throughout the decades since the

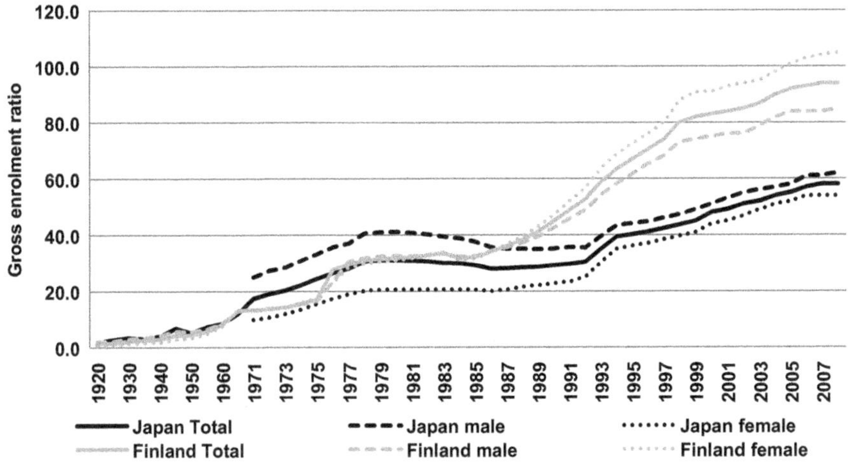

Figure 4.4 Gross enrolment ratios in tertiary education in Japan and Finland, 1920–2008

Sources: Nevala, 1999; UNESCO, 2013; Windolf, 1997

Note: Values 1993, 1996, and 1997 for Japan are averages of preceding and following years and for Finland values of 1976.

Table 4.11 Trends in enrolment rates for higher education in Japan

	1955	*1965*	*1975*	*1985*	*1995*	*2005*
Men						
University	13.1	20.7	41	38.6	40.7	51.3
College	1.9	1.7	2.6	2	2.1	1.8
Women						
University	2.4	4.6	12.7	13.7	22.9	36.8
College	2.6	6.7	20.2	20.8	24.6	13
	1956–1973		1974–1990		1991–2009	
Avg. rate of economic growth	9.1%		4.2%		0.8%	

Source: MEXT, 2005

Note: Figures include junior colleges.

Second World War. Whereas in 1955 only 15.4 per cent of university students were female, the figure was 23.6 per cent in 1975 and 41.8 per cent in 2005. Second, the steady rise in university enrolment for both men and women could be interpreted as a reflection of the rise in income with some time lag. Third, while junior college education for women gained in popularity until the 1990s, its importance is now waning. One way to interpret this trend is that at first, 2-year junior college degrees became popular as consumption goods among females, while from the 1970s onwards, they have been replaced by 4-year university degrees as investment goods. One explanation for this shift from junior colleges to universities may be in the differences in the wage distributions benefiting women with higher educational attainment. It is worth noting that education in junior colleges, tertiary type B education in Figures 4.6 and 4.7, raises 27 per cent of the females above the median wage in Japan, whereas in Finland this figure is 51 per cent. Furthermore, in Japan, 37 per cent of the women with tertiary type B degrees have no income from work, whereas in Finland, 13 per cent of the women with similar credentials are in such a position (see Table 4.13). Two-year junior colleges are becoming less popular and turning into a mere second choice for 4-year universities. In order to survive, they need some drastic changes in their curricula, such as offering more practically oriented courses with relevant qualifications.

Wage premium, labour market outcomes, and costs and benefits of higher education in both Japan and Finland

The Biannual Student Living Survey reveals the balance sheet of an average university student in Japan. Table 4.12 is an extract from the 2004 survey.

The main difference in finance between the university students in Japan and Finland is the tuition fees in Japanese universities. There are relatively high tuition fees in both public and private universities, which are financed by the families of students and students themselves through part-time jobs, whereas in Finland there are no tuition fees and the education system is financed through taxation. This means that the costs of education in Finland are a joint responsibility of all taxpayers. The relative proportion in Finland which taxpayers pay for the education is the same regardless of the usage of educational services. Although tuition fees in Japan for both public and private universities are high and burden individual students and households, the total expenditure on tertiary education as a percentage of GDP (see Figure 4.5) is higher in Finland than in Japan. Expenditure on education at all levels continued to rise in the OECD countries in 2008 to 2009 despite the economic crisis, and Finland was among the countries to share this trend, whereas in Japan, expenditure decreased (OECD, 2012).

Further examination of Figure 4.5 shows how the private share of expenditures on tertiary education in Japan has been constantly rising in the first decade of the twenty-first century. This trend is similar to that in the United States, where the price of private tuition relative to family income has doubled since the beginning of the 1980s to about 50 per cent of median family income, and public tuition has risen to about 10 per cent (Goldin & Katz, 2008). This is clearly different from the European countries, especially Finland. Many European Union member states offer government subsidies for tuition fees in order to keep the burden on students and their families lower. In Finland, in addition to the absence of tuition

Table 4.12 Annual income and expenditure of a university student in Japan 2004 (income and expenditure in yen)

	Income			*Expenditure*			
	Family	*Grants*	*Part time jobs*	*Fees*	*Living—costs*	*Accom-modation*	*Difference*
Public	1,410,000	280,000	288,000	624,000	1,191,000	548,000	–385,000
Private	1,976,000	374,000	314,000	1,312,000	1,181,000	537,000	–366,000

Source: MEXT, 2004

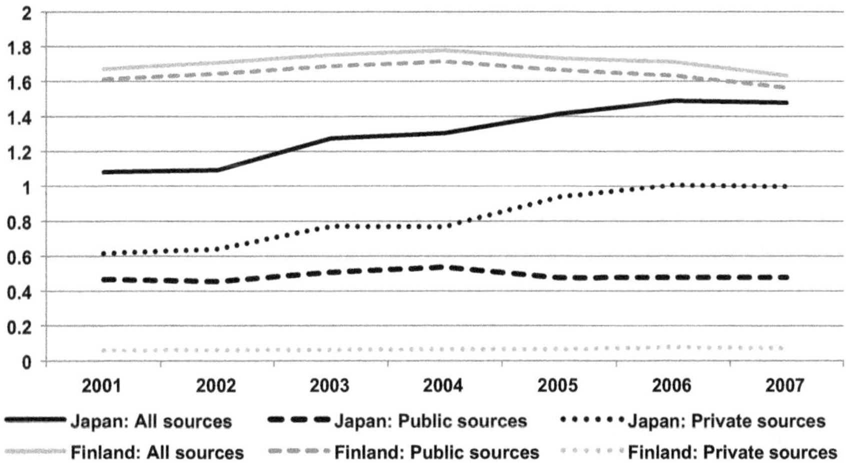

Figure 4.5 Total expenditure on tertiary educational institutions and administration as a percentage of Gross Domestic Product in Japan and Finland, 2001–2007

Source: UNESCO, 2010

fees, there is a generous student aid system that comprises a much larger share of public spending on tertiary education than the OECD average (Hölttä et al., 2011). Student aid includes a study grant, a housing supplement, and a state guarantee on student loans. Student loans are not very popular among Finnish students; according to Kela,[1] the number of students taking student loans is less than a half of those receiving student grants (Kela, 2011). In addition to these aforementioned support systems, Finnish students get financial support from their parents, and most students start working either in part-time jobs or in some cases full time while studying. For example, 61 per cent of Finnish university students in 2011 had a job alongside their studies (Statistics Finland, 2011a).

In contrast, student loans do exist in Japan, but it is effectively for the parents to pay for their children rather than for the students to invest in themselves. The Japan Student Support Organization (JASSO) is the largest financing board for students at higher education institutions and regularly publishes a report on the student loan situation in Japan. According to the 2007 report, 376,179 students have taken some type of student loan from either 2,766 organizations, from 724 local authorities, from 1,053 educational institutions, or from 874 NGOs. Sources of supply, therefore, are abundant. Apart from the JASSO, which also provides loans, the organizations use their financial resources for loans and grants at a ratio of roughly 2 to 1. The JASSO operates on a much larger scale than any of the other lenders – in terms of student numbers for universities and junior colleges, the JASSO lends to about 90 per cent of all the students, with a total amount of 800,000,000,000 yen (€5.7 billion; $7.8 billion). The actual monthly allowance for higher education ranges from around 20,000 to 65,000 yen ($200–500). This is hardly enough to pay for education and expenses. However, when we look at the effects of higher education in terms of income and labour force participation, the situation looks much better for the Japanese graduates, especially for men. Tertiary type A and advanced research programmes[2] generate more than twice the median income to 34.7 per cent of the graduates and raised the wage above the median for 74.7 per cent of people with such degrees (Figure 4.6). Only 12.4 per cent of those with a high school diploma reached twice the median wages, and only 43.4 per cent reached wages above the median. The wage profile of those with tertiary-type B education in Figure 4.7 illustrates how junior colleges in Japan, which are more popular among women, leave the graduates in a worse situation than those with only a high school diploma.

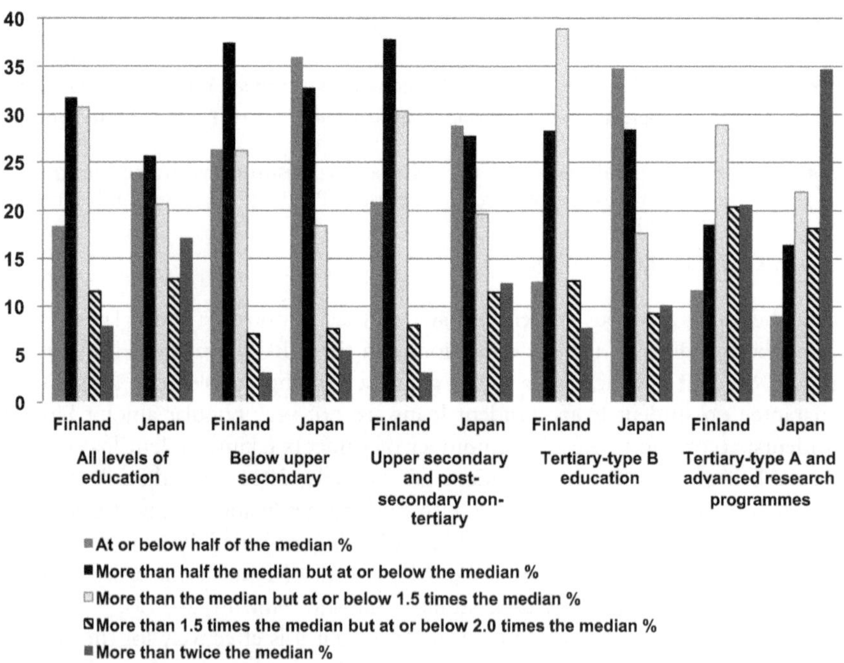

Figure 4.6 Distribution of the 25- to 64-year-old population in Japan and Finland by level of earnings and educational attainment in 2007

Source: OECD, 2010a

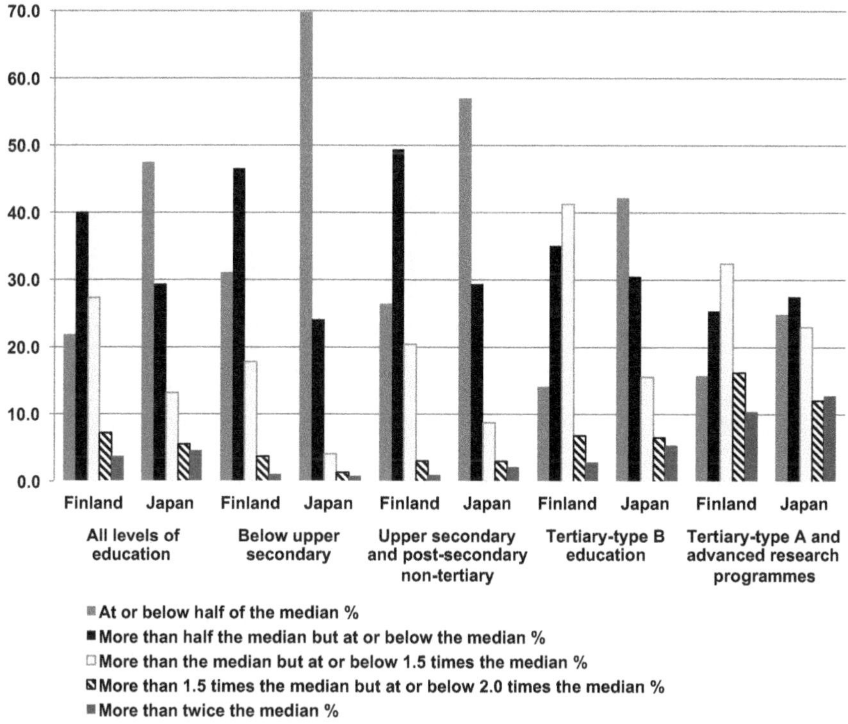

Figure 4.7 Distribution of the 25- to 64-year-old female population in Japan and Finland by level of earnings and educational attainment in 2007

Source: OECD, 2010a

Figure 4.7 illustrates the labour market situation of Japanese women in more detail, showing that 12.7 per cent of the women with A5 degrees earned more than twice the median and 47.7 per cent of them had wages above the median. However, no fewer than 29.9 per cent of the women with such degrees were without income from work. Of women with college education,[3] only 27.4 per cent reached wages above the median (Figure 4.7), and 36.7 per cent were without income from work (Table 4.13).

Indeed, as Kingston (2011) noted, women have long been shunted to the labour market periphery in Japan and borne the brunt of labour force adjustments. Women have had to serve as 'shock absorbers' against economic fluctuations, earning lower wages and lacking the job security common to their male colleagues. Part-time female workers have provided flexibility to the system of rigid lifetime employment and seniority wages. However, women are now disproportionately represented among part-time workers, who are the most vulnerable to the effects of downsizing (Kingston, 2011).

Wage distributions by educational attainment in Finland tend to be more equal than those in Japan. On all educational levels, both in total population and among women, the share of those earning more than half the median but at or below 1.5 times the median is greater in Finland. Furthermore, the share of those

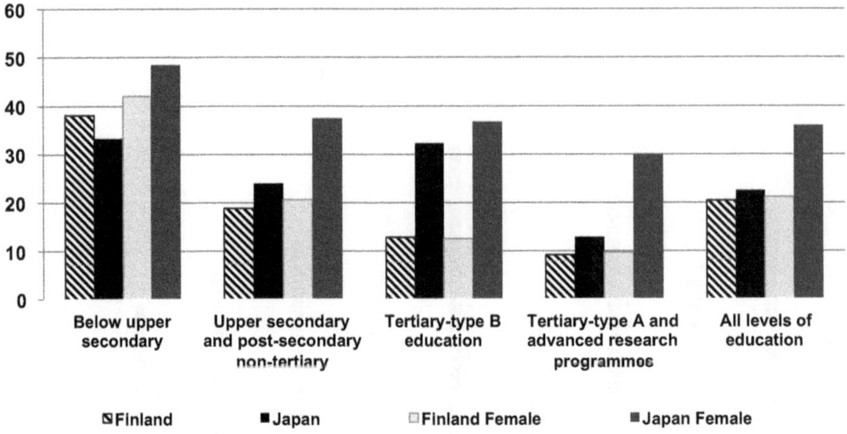

Figure 4.8 Persons with no earnings from work to population ratio by educational attainment in 2007

Source: OECD, 2010a

earning more than twice the median is lower in Finland on all levels for total population as well as for women. Figure 4.8 and the figures in Table 4.13 indicate that, except for those with no high school or vocational secondary degree (below upper secondary), the number of people with no income from work is lower in Finland than in Japan. Approximately 10 per cent of Finnish women with degrees from tertiary type A–level or advanced research programmes have no income from work, whereas in Japan the corresponding figure is almost 30 per cent.

When we look at the wage structure based on the level of education in Figure 4.6 and Table 4.13, the benefits of university education seem to be greater in Japan. No fewer than 74.7 per cent of those with tertiary type A degrees had above the median wage, while 34.7 per cent earned more than twice the median wage. For Finland, these figures are 69.8 and 20.6, respectively. It is important to mention, however, that education is not without cost. Further examination into the cost of education – both actual and opportunity costs – would be beneficial for the analysis of effectiveness of education. Some studies have been presented on these issues concerning both Finland and Japan. But as the approaches differ in terms of data and methods, an exhaustive comparison in this level would be a prospect for future research (For Finland, see Lilja & Mäkilä, 1996; Nygård, 1989a, 1989b; Uusitalo, 1999).

OECD statistics (Figure 4.9) show that Japanese women with tertiary type A and advanced research degrees have an earning premium of 90 per cent in comparison to the earnings of women with upper secondary or postsecondary nontertiary education, implying a significant level of return on higher education. When examined at the population level, Japan exceeds the OECD average in the earning premium of tertiary type A and advanced research degrees, whereas Finland is at the level of the OECD average.

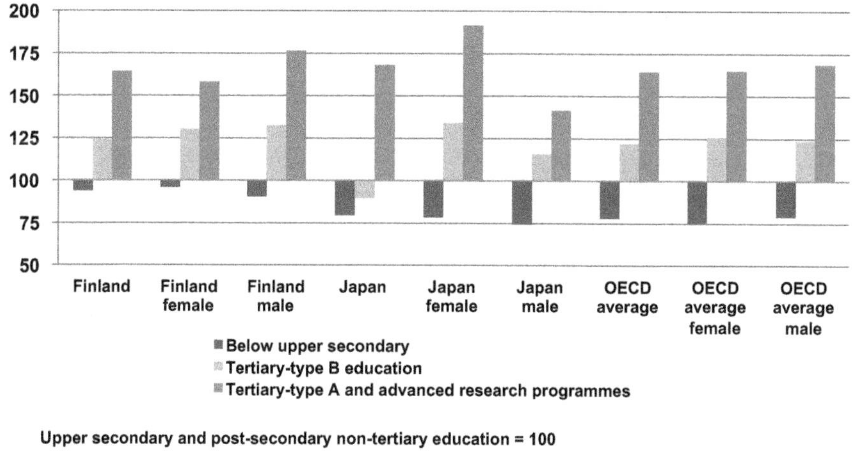

Figure 4.9 Relative earnings of the population with income from employment in 2007

Source: OECD, 2010a

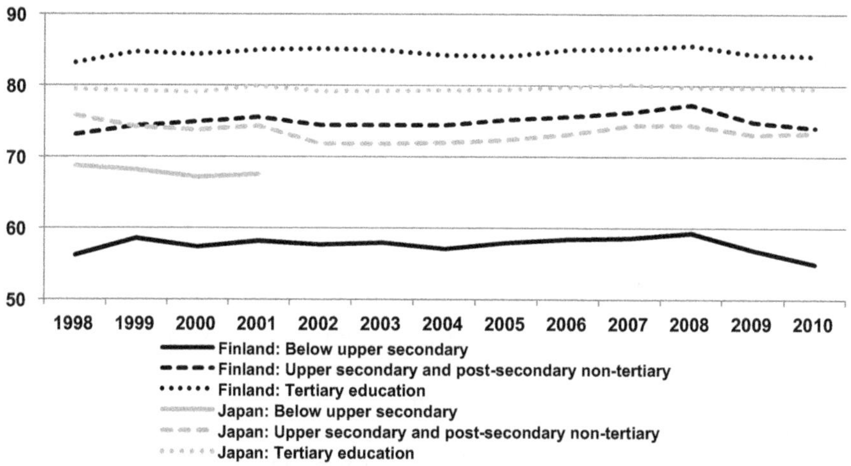

Figure 4.10 Trends in employment rates by educational attainment, number of 25- to 64-year-olds in employment as a percentage of the population aged 25 to 64

Source: OECD, 2012

Note: In OECD statistics figures for below upper secondary level of education in Japan are only available for the years 1998–2001.

Despite global economic slumps, higher education seems to remain a good guarantee against both unemployment and underemployment in the Finnish and Japanese job markets. The trends in Figure 4.10 show higher degrees in both Japan and Finland equal higher levels of employment.

Current issues in higher education in Japan and Finland

Since the bursting of the bubble in the late 1980s, the Japanese economic growth has not reached the levels of the earlier economic miracle. Indeed, the economy has stagnated with negative growth multiple times during the last two decades. The employment prospects for graduates are gloomy, and they are facing unparalleled upheaval in a job market marked by adverse structural changes. Until the 1990s, young people moved smoothly and swiftly from education into stable jobs, supported by the traditional Japanese employment system of lifetime employment and wage seniority. This system started to erode during the wave of restructuring and deregulation during the prolonged recession of the Lost Decade. This situation eased slightly from 2003 to 2007 during a modest economic recovery, but the problems returned in full force in 2009 with the Lehman shock (Kingston, 2011). These aforementioned issues caused a reduction in the return on investment in higher education for both the private and public sectors through lower wages and productivity.

In Japan, a skill gap between what companies expect from graduates and what the graduates are equipped with is taken for granted, and it has been the task of companies to provide on-the-job training for the graduates. However, with an economy no longer in healthy shape, companies are not willing to invest in a newly employed workforce. Instead, companies prefer to have the graduates with less skill gap, that is, with a sufficient level of 'generic skills', which includes communication skill and leadership. This concept is also referred as 'basic social skills' by the Ministry of Economy, Trade, and Industry (METI) and 'graduate skills' or 'employability skills' by MEXT. In order to alleviate these problems, Japan has introduced measures to ease the transition from studies to working life. Japanese higher education institutions are anxious to use various measures to bridge this gap by offering internships, placements, and work-integrated learning programmes. These 'career education' studies send students to companies for several weeks to build up their employability through connections and experience from the real working environment. However, as this is still a new trend, the graduates are still too often not ready 'off the rack', and career education may not be developed enough yet to achieve its goals with ease in a constantly changing and turbulent business environment (Kingston, 2011).

Similar issues concerning education and employment have raised discussion in Finland. The main concern is that university students are taking more years than required to complete their programmes. High labour force participation of the students has been considered as one of the causes, as 61 per cent of university students work alongside their studies (Statistics Finland, 2011a). In 2009, the Finnish government set up a committee to study the possibilities of reducing the time elapsing until graduation. As a result, changes were made to the university entrance and student aid systems, where progress in studies is more closely monitored than before. In addition to the swift transition of students to working life, cooperation and connections between the spheres of work and education are deemed important, and concerns about these issues are apparent in Finnish education policy discussions. The Finnish Ministry of Education and Culture has raised these issues as one of the key points in the future strategy of Finnish education. This strategy sees linkages between education and work as key tools in adapting to changing the economic structures and knowledge demands of the future (Finnish Ministry of Education and Culture, 2009b).

The other concerns are connected to the gender disparity of female graduates earning less than males with similar degrees and the employment rate of females with families being lower than that of males with families. The main concern behind all of these discussions is the age structure of Finland, with the fact that the working-age population in Finland is decreasing.

Conclusions

Education in Japan and Finland has come a long way from the systems in which even a basic education was a privilege of the few to systems with easily accessible higher education. In the 1920s, both Japan and Finland had only 1 per cent of the respective age group studying in universities, whereas in the 1960s, the corresponding figure was 4 per cent, and by the 2000s it had risen to 19.3 per cent in Japan and to 24.9 in Finland. The popularity of higher education has increased alongside the growing demand for highly educated workers and in spite of the diminishing age cohorts entering higher education.

The prolonged duration for graduation is seen as a current problem in Finland, which, alongside the diminishing working-aged population, is causing pressure for change on the Finnish education system. On the other hand, in Japan, questions have been raised about the adequacy of the academic qualifications to meet the demands of the future employers for the graduates. Swift and smooth transition from student life to working life is in the interests of both students and societies, and both the Japanese and Finnish governments have addressed these issues in their educational policies.

Finnish education policy is based on equality and accessibility of education at all levels. This policy has created an education system which is publicly funded all the way from primary education in kindergartens to doctoral studies in universities. In Japan, public schools concentrate largely on the compulsory level of education – primary schools. The number of private schools increases at the level of secondary education, ending up with three quarters of Japanese universities and 93 per cent of junior colleges as private institutions (Table 4.3). Both private and public universities in Japan charge tuition fees, whereas all the Finnish universities are public and charge no tuition fees. The cost of education in Finland is paid collectively through taxation. Therefore, the cost of higher education is more burdensome from the perspective of Japanese students and their families than for their Finnish counterparts. Yet the comparison of the total expenditure on tertiary education as a percentage of GDP shows (Figure 4.5) that burden on national level is higher in Finland.

Table 4.13 Distribution of 25- to 64-year-old total and female population by level of earnings and educational attainment in Japan, Finland, and OECD average

Country	Educational attainment	*Level of earnings*					*Persons with no earnings from work to population ratio*
		At or below half of the median	*More than half the median but at or below the median*	*More than the median but at or below 1.5 times the median*	*More than 1.5 times the median but at or below 2.0 times the median*	*More than twice the median*	
Country	*Educational attainment*	%	%	%	%	%	%
Finland Total	Below upper secondary	26.3	37.4	26.2	7.1	3.1	38.1
	Upper secondary and post-secondary nontertiary	20.8	37.7	30.3	8.0	3.1	18.8
	Tertiary-type B education	12.5	28.3	38.9	12.6	7.7	12.8
	Tertiary-type A and advanced research programmes	11.7	18.5	28.9	20.3	20.6	9.2
	All levels of education	18.3	31.7	30.7	11.5	7.9	20.4
Japan Total	Below upper secondary	36.0	32.7	18.4	7.6	5.4	33.1
	Upper secondary and post-secondary nontertiary	28.9	27.7	19.6	11.4	12.4	23.9
	Tertiary-type B education	34.7	28.4	17.6	9.2	10.1	32.2
	Tertiary-type A and advanced research programmes	8.9	16.4	21.9	18.1	34.7	12.9
	All levels of education	23.9	25.6	20.6	12.8	17.1	22.4

OECD Average	Below upper secondary	25.5	46.0	20.3	5.3	2.9	37.4
	Upper secondary and post-secondary nontertiary	15.8	37.7	28.5	10.5	7.6	20.0
	Tertiary-type B education	11.8	26.9	31.9	16.0	13.3	16.4
	Tertiary-type A and advanced research programmes	8.4	17.8	28.0	19.1	26.7	13.6
	All levels of education	15.6	34.6	27.2	11.6	11.0	22.4
Finland Female	Below upper secondary	31.0	46.5	17.8	3.7	1.0	42.1
	Upper secondary and post-secondary nontertiary	26.4	49.3	20.4	3.0	0.9	20.6
	Tertiary-type B education	14.1	35.1	41.3	6.8	2.8	12.5
	Tertiary-type A and advanced research programmes	15.7	25.3	32.5	16.2	10.4	9.7
	All levels of education	21.9	40.0	27.3	7.2	3.7	21.2
Japan Female	Below upper secondary	69.7	24.0	4.1	1.3	0.8	48.5
	Upper secondary and post-secondary nontertiary	57.0	29.3	8.7	3.0	2.1	37.4
	Tertiary-type B education	42.2	30.4	15.6	6.5	5.3	36.7
	Tertiary-type A and advanced research programmes	24.9	27.4	22.9	12.1	12.7	29.9
	All levels of education	47.5	29.3	13.2	5.5	4.5	35.9
OECD Average Female	Below upper secondary	38.8	48.7	10.0	1.7	0.9	44.1
	Upper secondary and post-secondary nontertiary	24.6	45.6	20.7	5.9	3.1	26.6
	Tertiary-type B education	17.3	35.7	30.1	10.8	6.1	20.2
	Tertiary-type A and advanced research programmes	12.0	24.2	32.5	16.5	14.8	18.3
	All levels of education	23.6	40.6	22.5	7.8	5.5	27.5

Source: OECD, 2010a

When examining the labour market outcomes of higher education, it is safe to state that in both countries, Japan and Finland, a higher level of education lowers the rate of unemployment and those out of the labour force. The demand for highly educated workers is rising, as the share of occupations with highly educated workers in the OECD countries has increased 19 per cent in the last two decades, whereas the share of occupations with medium- and low-educated workers has dropped 8 per cent at the medium level and 12 per cent at the lowest level (OECD, 2013). The wage distribution between men and women is more equal in Finland than in Japan, while wage differences between the education levels are smaller in Finland, which leaves Finns with degrees from tertiary type A or advanced research programmes below their Japanese counterparts in wage premiums of higher education. Although the gender disparity in wages and employment is notable in Japan, when comparing relative earnings of the employed population to education levels, Japanese women benefit most from higher education attainment. Relative wages of Japanese women with degrees from tertiary type A or advanced research programmes have an earning premium of 90 per cent over Japanese women with upper secondary and post-secondary nontertiary education (Figure 4.9). When the labour market outcomes of education in Finland are examined from the gender perspective, gender disparity in education favours women. They have a higher level of education than men, although this educational advantage is not reflected in their income levels.

Both Japan and Finland show a strong belief in and commitment to maintaining high educational standards. And it is worth emphasizing that such actions can be pursued with a heavy burden on the private sector as in Japan as well as on the public sector as in Finland. Either way, it seems to result in creating satisfactory economic and intellectual benefits guiding both countries in their aims to further improve higher education systems and the labour market outcomes of education.

Notes

1. Kela is a government office responsible for the student financial aid system in Finland.
2. Tertiary education type A includes bachelor's and master's degrees in universities. Level 5A in the UNESCO ISCED classification.
3. Level 5B in UNESCO ISCED classification.

5 Military spending in Japan and Finland

From warfare to welfare state

Jari Eloranta and Yasushi Tanaka

Introduction

Japan is a substantially larger polity and economy than Finland, and Japan's development towards modernity, by and large, began with the earlier Western colonial incursions and the Meiji Revolution (or Restoration) in the late 1860s. This series of political, economic, and social transformations changed Japan profoundly and created the basis for its industrial and military expansion prior to the First World War. Japan was not yet quite the superpower during this conflict or immediately after; however, with the rise of the military elite in the 1930s, it began to militarize and expand extensively. A defeat in the Second World War forced Japan to reorient completely once again, following an occupation by the Allies, towards low military spending and civilian economic expansion. Despite the fact that Japan lost the war, it seemed to 'win' the peace, namely by having extremely fast economic growth until the 1980s. The economic performance during the Golden Age of economic growth from the late 1940s to the 1980s was spectacular, making Japan the second-largest economy in the world. How much of this was due to the West imposing limitations on Japan's military capacity, beyond some small provisions, essentially forcing them to free ride on the United States? The answer is not entirely clear at this point. For example, the collapse of the bubble economy in the late 1980s eventually turned into a depression that still, up to a degree, hinders the Japanese economy, and the recent problems created by the Great East Japan Earthquake and the Fukushima disaster in 2011 are creating a lot of uncertainties. It seems that the economic performance, whether fast or slow, was driven by factors other than the absence of military spending, which is often called the peace dividend. However, there were some budgetary tradeoffs between social and military spending.

Finland's path was somewhat different from Japan's, driven by geographic and political realities. It emerged from being a relatively poor agricultural nation in the early twentieth century into a highly developed and versatile economy with an extensive welfare state in the beginning of the twenty-first century. There are significant insights to be learned from the Finnish 'story', as Peter Lindert has argued. It seems that the Nordic countries have found a way to combine extensive welfare states and high economic growth in the twentieth century (Lindert, 2004). There is no real initial evidence to suggest that economic development and military spending were interconnected. Finland's military spending rose strongly in the 1930s, prior to the Second World War, and the war ended up being a costly conflict for the country. Military spending levels after the war were conditioned, by and large, by the realities of the Cold War and the presence of a powerful neighbour in the East, the Soviet Union. Spending levels were higher, in relative terms, than in Japan but much lower than in countries involved in the Cold War alliances. There were some tradeoffs, like in the case of Japan, between military and social spending, yet no tradeoff between military spending and economic growth like the two typical forms of the 'guns versus butter' tradeoffs discussed in the literature. However, it seems that both Japan and Finland did maintain fairly low levels of military spending after the Second World War and invested more heavily in education and welfare state. It is unclear how much the absence of high military spending levels contributed to their economic expansion and/or transitioning to modern, service-based economies.

Both countries offer us a glimpse of quick transformation, both economically and politically, from a warfare to welfare state, especially due to the Second World War. As such, both countries participated extensively in this total war, dedicating massive resources to fight the war, and they were on the losing side, which imposed substantial constraints on their foreign and domestic policies. Niall Ferguson argues that warfare states before the twentieth century had fairly low spending-to-GDP ratios, with most of the central government budget being allocated for military purposes. The keys to the transformation toward a welfare state included the increasing cost of conflicts, along with the demands of twentieth-century total war, the spread of democracy, and growing bureaucratization of government services (Ferguson, 2001). Thus, while social transfers were relatively small in most states before the twentieth century, with Japan being one of the low-spending nations, they have come to dominate government finances in modern economies, Japan and Finland being no exceptions in this regard (Lindert, 1994). Here we want to focus on analysing the main features of that transformation as well as whether or how the so-called peace dividend manifested itself. First, however, we will review some of the theoretical approaches relevant for such a study.

Military spending and fiscal tradeoffs as a research challenge

There have been relatively few credible attempts to model the military spending behaviour of states based on their long-run historical/institutional characteristics. Based on a survey of the interdisciplinary literature, we are going briefly explore three perspectives: (1) the Webber-Wildawsky model of budgeting; (2) the Richard Bonney model of fiscal systems; and (3) the Niall Ferguson model of interaction between public debts and forms of government. First, Caroly Webber and Aaron Wildawsky have argued that each political culture generates its characteristic budgetary objectives – on the basis of these, Finland and Japan would differ somewhat, given the strong role social democracy has had in the former's political landscape in the twentieth century (Webber & Wildavsky, 1986). Their model, however, is essentially a static one and is not very useful in order to understand historical evolution of states in Europe, like the shifts experienced by these two countries after the Second World War. Richard Bonney has addressed this problem in his writings on mainly the early modern states. He has emphasized that the states' revenue and tax collection systems, the backbone of any militarily successful nation state, have evolved over time (Bonney, 1999; Eloranta, 2005; Eloranta & Kauppila, 2006). However, Bonney's work has exposed a gap in the research, namely the analysis of the transition of many European states toward the fiscal state and the alternative development paths in the nineteenth, let alone twentieth, centuries. Japan and Finland had both already matured into fiscal states by the Second World War, so the main change in their evolution as states came during and after this total war (Cameron & Neal, 2003; Lindert, 2004).

Furthermore, Niall Ferguson maintains that wars have shaped all the most relevant institutions of modern economic life: tax-collecting bureaucracies, central banks, bond markets, stock exchanges, and systems of public debt (Ferguson, 2001). Subsequently, we would argue that the model required to explain military spending in the long run such as in this chapter has to be evolutionary by nature, with regimes during different stages having different priorities and burdens imposed by the military spending and the international system. For example, a successful ascendancy to a leadership position in the post–Congress of Vienna European system in 1815 required higher expenditures and a substantial navy as well as fiscal and political structures conducive to increasing the availability of credit with recurring participation in international conflicts. While most nineteenth-century wars were not great power conflicts per se, they did have a substantial colonial component to them and profound consequences for future conflicts. In the twentieth century, many of the adverse consequences of the empire building and ruthless international competition resulted in massive great power conflicts, such as the Second World War (Broadberry & Harrison, 2005; Harrison, 1988, 1998).

We also need to discuss two key concepts to analyse Japan's and Finland's twentieth-century fiscal paths, namely the so-called peace dividend (= higher economic growth as a result of lower military spending) and 'guns versus butter' tradeoff (= budgetary tradeoff between social and military spending). Moreover, military spending (or any kind of government spending) is often argued to crowd out private investment, although the evidence on the economic impacts of military spending is conflicting. Overall, as argued by Todd Sandler and Keith Hartley (Sandler & Hartley, 1995), the supply-and-demand side effects seem to cancel each other out (or a slight negative growth effect might materialize). Moreover, the analysis of the conversion of military resources into civilian use, in order to achieve the peace dividend (implying a positive economic growth effect from the conversion of military production toward civilian uses; see e.g. Chan, 1995), seems to yield conflicting results as to whether this has any significant economic consequences.

The other conventional way of perceiving guns-versus-butter tradeoffs is to analyse the budgetary struggles between the proponents of military expenditures and social spending. These two categories of spending have been the primary functions of central (or federal) governments in the last 130 years. Of course, military spending was the primary spending category before the relatively slow emergence of social spending (see e.g. Ferguson, 2001; Lindert, 1994, 2004; Tanzi & Schuknecht, 2000). Since then, the emergence of the welfare state has challenged the primacy of the warfare state. And, although some studies have been conducted on such budgetary tradeoff effects (see e.g. Domke, Eichenberg, & Kelleher, 1983; Garand & Hendrick, 1991; Narizny, 2003; Palmer, 1990; on World War II, see especially Harrison, 1998), there have been no systematic efforts to investigate such possible budgetary tradeoffs in the long run, either with rich case studies or with large-panel data samples.

As William Berry and David Lowery (Berry & Lowery, 1990) have pointed out, often in the literature there is a common assumption (see e.g. Russett, 1982) of interdependence between the expenditure categories in the appropriations process, which may or may not hold. As they point out, there are three fundamental problems in this literature: (1) many studies have found little evidence of budgetary tradeoffs, perhaps due to the insistence of looking solely at the defence–welfare relationships; (2) the tradeoff literature has been characterized by a very limited form of empirical investigation, usually single-equation regression models or multi-equation causal models; and (3) there has been curiously little theoretical development of the concept of 'tradeoffs'. In fact, it may be that this expectation of perfect substitutability is flawed for several reasons: (1) the influence of interest groups and other persistent political structures (bureaucratic path dependence); (2) the dynamics of the legislatures; (3) regime type and responsiveness to various structural forces; and (4) the impact of spillovers and threats as equilibria-changing factors. Other problems to be investigated include the relevance of the time horizon, such as when and how this process might take place and for how long, as well as the identity of the winners and losers in the transition from one tradeoff regime to another (for more, see e.g. Eloranta, 2004).

Here we will investigate both the institutional/historical development of spending patterns for Japan and Finland and explore possible spending tradeoffs and a peace dividend. Most of the analysis is based on qualitative sources or relatively straightforward quantitative evidence, but we will also explore some more quantitative exercises to illustrate certain points. In general, however, our intention is not to get too technical in this chapter. In sum, our questions are as a follows: (1) How did the Second World War change the military spending of these two countries? (2) What were the institutional changes that explained the spending choices? (3) Were there budgetary or economic consequences for those choices? (4) What has happened in the post–Cold War period?

Growth of government and military spending in Japan and Finland

Both Japan and Finland were latecomers to industrialization in the late nineteenth century, when most Western countries were perfecting their fiscal models and transitioning towards warfare states capable of massive mobilization and wielding newest technologies. In fact, the nineteenth century introduced many such reforms: centralized public administration, reliance on balanced budgets, innovations in public debt management, and direct taxation. These reforms were also supported by the spread of industrialization and rising productivity. The nineteenth century, moreover, made possible the industrialization of war and armaments production, starting in the mid-century and gathering speed quickly. For most countries, the period leading to the First World War meant comparatively higher military burdens. In the First World War, this military potential was unleashed in Europe, with a total war of attrition causing, along with millions of casualties, economic dislocation and upheavals (Eloranta, 2005, 2007).

Finland benefitted obliquely from the war, as Russia devolved into uprisings and revolution, and ultimately became an independent state at the end of 1917. Independence was followed by a deadly civil war in 1917, which divided the nation. The victory by the Whites did not resolve many of the social tensions – it took time and reconciliation policies to make that happen by the end of the 1930s and after the Second World War. Japan in turn had westernized in the aftermath of the Meiji Revolution of 1868, resulting in a strong state and flourishing economy by the close of the nineteenth century. Japan had also emerged as a minor great power, with victorious wars against China in 1894 to 1895 and Russia in 1904 to 1905. Regardless, Japan gained very little from the First World War, despite loftier expectations. (On the impacts of the Meiji Revolution or Reconstruction, see e.g. Landes, 1999.)

In the interwar period, public spending by most advanced nations, especially in the 1920s, was very static by nature. New strains on spending were, however, imposed by the pension and healthcare concerns arising from the war, as well as reconstruction expenses. This meant that although in many countries, except the authoritarian regimes, budget shares of military expenditures dropped noticeably, the respective military burdens stayed either at similar levels or even increased. The mid-1930s marked the beginning of intense rearmament for the reluctant democracies, whereas many of the authoritarian regimes had begun earlier in the decade. For example, the Japanese rearmament drive (see Table 5.1), driven by a militaristic elite, was perhaps the most impressive, with a military burden as high as 23.2 per cent and a defence share of more than 45 per cent in 1939. For many countries, such as France and Russia, the rapid pace of technological change in the 1930s unfortunately rendered many of the earlier armaments obsolete only 2 or 3 years later (Eloranta, 2002; Webber & Wildavsky, 1986). Finland also rearmed heavily in the 1930s due to increasing tensions with the Soviet Union, with high relative spending levels in line with other European great powers, especially many East European states (see e.g. Eloranta & Kauppila, 2007).

Table 5.1 Military spending, military personnel, and central government spending in Japan and Finland, 1920–1938

	1920	*1925*	*1930*	*1935*	*1939*
Japan Military Burden	5.91	2.76	3.02	5.70	23.24
Finland Military Burden	2.96	2.82	2.92	3.18	11.39
Japan Defence Share	36.11	13.64	11.16	18.60	45.30
Finland Defence Share	23.09	19.96	19.88	19.09	56.54
Japan Military Personnel	0.55	0.51	0.45	0.59	1.34
Finland Military Personnel	1.05	0.96	0.78	0.86	1.00
Japan Central Government Spending	16.37	20.20	27.09	30.64	49.73
Finland Central Government Spending	12.83	14.11	14.68	16.65	20.14

Sources: See the sources in Eloranta, 2002; for the military and government spending figures and for the military personnel figures, see Singer & Small, 1993.

Note: Military burden = military expenditures as a percentage of GDP; defence share = military expenditures as a percentage of central government spending; military personnel = military personnel as a percentage of total population; central government spending = central government expenditures as a percentage of GDP.

The biggest total war that has ever taken place, the Second World War, had an initial phase from 1939 to early 1942 that favoured the Axis, which Japan was a part of ever since 1936, as far as strategic and economic resources and performance were concerned. After 1942, the demands of total war, especially in terms of absolute resources, turned the tide in favor of the Allies as the United States and the USSR joined the Allies. For example, the Allied total GDP was 2,223 billion international dollars in 1990 prices, whereas the Axis accounted for only 895 billion in 1943 (Eloranta, 2005, 2006b).

Finland's entry to the war occurred in November 1939. The coming of the world war had become more and more apparent in the 2 years preceding the start of the conflict. The beginning of the Winter War between Finland and the Soviet Union, taking place on 30 November 1939 to 13 March 1940, represented a time of stretching the small country's resources substantially without causing much civilian hardship; in general, there was no declining trend in economic activity due to the shift in employment from the main industries to military service (Hjerppe, 1988; Kronlund, 1989; Tervasmäki, Vuorenmaa, & Juutilainen, 1977). The Finnish military burden was slightly lower than those of the Great Powers, whereas its defence share was comparable. However, the military burden was not that atypical either. Comparatively, for example, Sweden's (a neutral state during the war) average military burden was 2.0 per cent and Canada's (Allied state) 21.5 per cent during the war years. Finland mobilized more of its male (and female, for various auxiliary functions) population for the fighting, in relative terms, than the Great Powers did and experienced fairly high levels of battle deaths, mostly during the most intense periods of fighting, namely in 1940 and 1944. Finland joined the ongoing World War again in June 1941, this time alongside the Germans with Operation Barbarossa against the Soviet Union. The Continuation War, according to the Finnish terminology, from 25 June 1941 to 19 September 1944, was the second of two wars fought between Finland and the Soviet Union during this period. Ultimately, the tide in the Eastern Front turned, also for the Finns. Despite a desperate and ultimately successful stand in the summer of 1944, stopping the Soviet major offensive, the Finnish troops ended the hostilities with a cease-fire on 4 September 1944, and the Soviet troops did the same 24 hours later. The Finns fought their former allies in the Lapland War from 1 October 1944 to 25 April 1945. The formal conclusion of the Continuation War was ratified by the Paris peace treaty in 1947 (Eloranta & Nummela, 2014).

Japan put its economy on a wartime footing in 1937 with the beginning of the war with China. Up until 1941, Japan was able to carry out foreign trade to a limited degree, although it was severely limited by the US embargo, and most of that came to a halt with the declaration of war against the US and some of the European nations. The Japanese GDP actually increased by 30 per cent during the war with China from 1937 to 1941, stayed at the same level during the war in the Pacific from 1942 to 1944, and collapsed after the war to about 70 per cent of the prewar level. Moreover, Japan was able to mobilize substantial material resources and troops for the war effort, including women and POWs. Living standards, in turn, declined precipitously (Hara, 2000; Harrison, 1988; Murray & Millett, 2009; Ránki, 1993; Taylor, 1961). Furthermore, Japan increased its military burden and the budgetary importance of military spending rapidly in the 1930s, especially towards the end of the decade (see Table 5.1). This trend continued during the war, possibly reaching the peak of 87 per cent of central government spending in 1944, mostly financed by debt. After the dropping of the atomic bombs and cessation of hostilities in 1945, Japan's economy was in shambles and wartime controls remained in place until 1950 (Green, 1995; Hara, 2000; Milward, 1977).

In the post-war period, both Finland and Japan joined Western nations in building up their welfare states, although their experiences and goals were different. The emergence of Western welfare states in the post-war period took place in increments. Between 1937 and 1960, the ratio of public expenditures to GDP as a percentage increased at a relatively slow pace in the OECD countries, often more related to increases in Cold War–induced defence spending (Tanzi & Schuknecht, 2000). The 1960 to 1980 period could be described as the golden age of public-sector intervention in the West. The fast public-sector growth in general slowed down in the 1970s with the economic crises as well as the arrival of more conservative governments in the 1980s. If we look at the development of general government expenditures as a percentage of GDP in the latter half of the twentieth century, we see that on average, this share increased steadily from circa 43 per cent in 1980 to circa 46 per cent in 1996 in the OECD. Therefore, no real reversal effect has taken place, as Peter Lindert has pointed out (Lindert, 2004).

In terms of security challenges, the end of the Second World War brought with it also a new hegemon, the United States, in the forefront of world politics, along with challengers from the East, namely the Soviet Union. NATO was established in 1949, which formed a formidable defence alliance among the major capitalist countries. The Soviet Union established the Warsaw Pact in 1955 to counter these efforts. Military spending levels, especially among the leading great powers, followed expansionary trends for social expenditures and peaked during the early Cold War. The American military burden climbed more than 10 per cent in 1952 to 1954, and the United States retained a high mean value for the post-war period of 6.7 per cent. Great Britain and France followed the American example after the Korean War (Eloranta, 2003).

The Cold War embodied a relentless armaments race, with nuclear weapons now as the main investment item, between the two superpowers and their respective blocs. Part of this armaments race was due to technological advances that led to increases in the cost per soldier – it has been estimated that technological increases produced a mean annual increase in real costs of circa 5.5 per cent in the post-war period. Nonetheless, spending on personnel and their maintenance remained the biggest spending item for most countries.

What about Japan's fiscal expansion in the long run? As seen in Figure 5.1, the Japanese debt-to-GDP levels were fairly cyclical in the long run, with peaks in the 1870s and early twentieth century and a strong growth trend from the 1970s onward. The Japanese central government spending levels were very low prior to the First World War and substantially higher in the interwar period – after the war, the spending levels were more stable, with a slight growth trend that was slowed down in the early twenty-first century. A dip in the spending share occurred in the 1980s due to strong GDP growth. Respectively, the military spending levels were fairly low throughout this period, with the exception of the Russo-Japanese war of 1904 to 1905, the 1930s, and the Second World War – military spending after the war has been consistently low all the way into the twenty-first century.

In the post-war period, Japanese foreign policy has relied heavily on the alliance with the United States, at least until the 1970s. The Americans also invested a lot in Japan's reconstruction in the immediate post-war period (Ferguson, 2001; Landes, 1999). Japan was disarmed after the defeat of the Second World War, and the armed force was reduced to a Japan Self-Defence Force 'Jieitai',

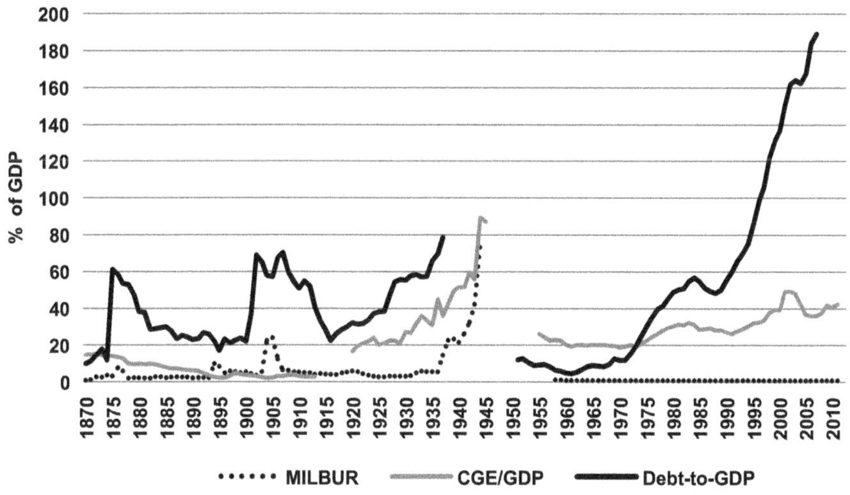

Figure 5.1 Japanese Central Government Spending (CGE), Military Spending (ME), and Central Government Debt (DEBT) (as Percentages of GDP), 1870–2011

Sources: For the period 1870–1944 (Eloranta, 2002, 2007; Hara, 2000; Hobson, 1993; Mitchell, 2003). For the post-war period: Historical Statistics of Japan (www.stat.go.jp/english/data/chouki/, accessed September 2013); SIPRI Military Expenditure Database 2013 (www.sipri.org/research/armaments/milex/milex_database, accessed September 2013); OECD Statistics (http://stats.oecd.org/, accessed October 2013). Public debt figures from (Reinhart & Rogoff, 2009; see also the website www.reinhartandrogoff.com/data/).

Note: The data are missing for the period 1945–1952 for a lot of these variables.

based on Article 9 of the Japanese Constitution of 1947, which outlaws wars (www.kantei.go.jp/foreign/constitution_and_government/frame_01.html). In the domestic policy sphere, vis-à-vis military spending decisions, Japan's choices were limited after 1952, when the occupation ended. The guiding principles were civilian control of the military, and antimilitarism started to erode slowly during the Cold War US–led fight against communism. Moreover, the introduction of Japan's first real post-war military doctrine, National Defence Program Outline (NDPO), in 1976 hastened an era of more active stance toward Japan's security policy and more aggressive military buildup. However, despite repeated US pressure to raise the military burden above 1 per cent, it did not happen, although many scholars have pointed out that even 1 percent of a large GDP is a lot in absolute terms (Hook, 1988).

In general, Japan has been a curious case among major states in the world. It has been able to create a very large economy and relatively large government as well while not suffering the adverse economic effects of such state formation (for more details, see esp. Calder, 1988; Estévez-Abe, 2008; Green, 1995; Kohno, 1997). Deficit financing has been commonplace after the 1970s Oil Crises and has helped increase the size of government debt substantially, without a penalty in the form of high interest rates (Ferguson, 2001). However, Japan's welfare state has always been more limited than the Nordic version, in fact resembling more the American or Australian model of market-driven welfare state. This has impacted both the revenue and the spending sides. Despite the efforts to keep the welfare state costs manageable, Japan is one of the countries facing an extreme pension crisis in the twenty-first century, especially since it has no real social security system in place (Lindert, 2004). Japan is thus an example of a country that has embraced the transition to a welfare state only in a limited sense.

In comparison, Finland provides an interesting example, somewhat similar to Japan, of the transition from warfare to welfare state. For Finland, the change from an agrarian society to rapid industrialization to a service society has been combined with a significant relative and absolute growth of government spending. This spending role, however, changed substantially from the early 1920s to the 1990s. Especially, the social spending role has changed from the early governments' efforts at attempting to keep social expenditure to a minimum to a welfare state with broad social safety net and increased government role. The welfare state building process was slower in Finland than in most Western nations, delayed by the divisive Civil War and its long shadow. The massive mobilization during the Second World War helped push forward an acceptance of stronger government role in the economy. In fact, the 1940s and the 1950s were a time of extending the measures already created in the 1930s, a process that was similar to Sweden and the other Nordic countries (Alestalo & Uusitalo, 1986; Eloranta & Kauppila, 2006; Hjerppe & Jalava, 2006; Kettunen, 2001; Paloheimo et al., 2015). Whereas the growth of social spending among Western states was very fast from the 1950s onwards, Finland was somewhat of a latecomer in this respect. For example, in the 1950s, the Finnish social spending share (of GDP) was only around a third of the Swedish share. But in 1970, the countries were almost at the same level. This pattern was very similar to other Western nations, in which the social transfer share grew even faster than in Finland in the period 1930 through 1960.

What about military spending pressures? The Cold War period induced countries to engage in extensive military spending, reminiscent of the late 1930s. Small countries had to manoeuvre between the two power blocs – for example, Finland maintained at least an appearance of neutrality while having to acknowledge the Soviets' security needs, whereas Sweden's neutrality was framed by high military spending and more advantageous geographic position. Nonetheless, the warfare state has remained an element, albeit a dwindling piece, of their spending basket up until the end of the twentieth century. Public spending on defence (17 countries, as a percentage of GDP) decreased from 3.4 per cent in 1960 to 2.0 per cent in 1995 (Tanzi & Schuknecht, 2000).

As seen in Figure 5.2, the Finnish central government spending share has increased in the twentieth century, most notably during and after the Second World War, although this growth trend has not been very precipitous. In comparison, for example, military spending had a much more substantial budgetary role in

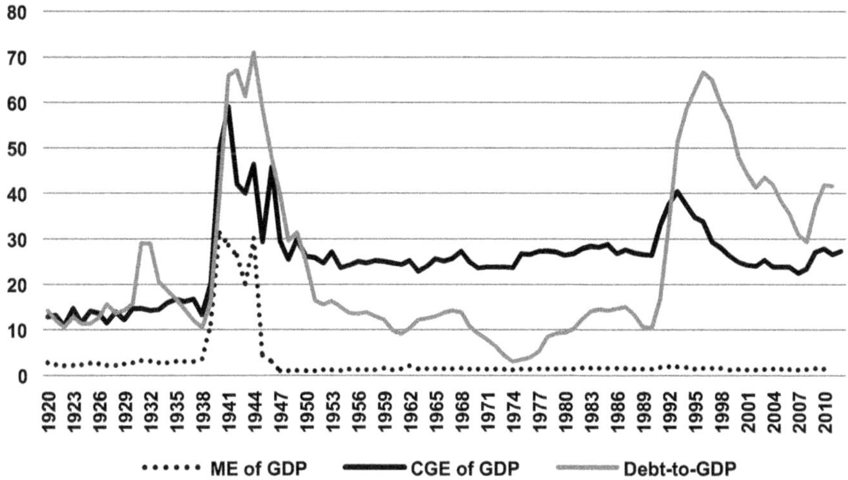

Figure 5.2 Finnish Central Government Spending (CGE), Military Spending (ME), and Central Government Debt (DEBT) (as Percentages of GDP), 1920–2012

Sources: Eloranta & Kauppila, 2006, 2007; Hjerppe, 1997. The figures have been updated using SIPRI Military Expenditure Database 2013 (www.sipri.org/research/armaments/milex/milex_database, accessed September 2013) and OECD Statistics (http://stats.oecd.org/, accessed October 2013). Public debt figures from Reinhart & Rogoff, 2009. See also the website www.reinhartandrogoff.com/data/.

the 1930s, whereas in the post–Second World War period, due to the limitations of the peace treaty, military spending has remained quite low, even by international standards. Central government debt increased dramatically in the 1920s and early 1930s, only to plummet during the depression decade. The war period again raised this share steeply, yet the Finnish post-war governments were able to cut indebtedness fast in the following decades, similar to other Western countries, in fact almost eliminating this debt by the 1970s. Since then, Finland has again had a growth trend and a steep rise in the 1990s (Eloranta & Kauppila, 2006; Hjerppe, 1997). The early-twenty-first-century trends are less clear.

While examination of general policy and spending trends is interesting and illuminating in its own right, we need to take a closer analytical look at military spending patterns and their fiscal implications for Japan and Finland. In particular, we want to examine the transition from warfare to welfare state more closely in the next section.

Quantitative perspectives on Japanese and Finnish military spending since the Second World War

Here in this section, we want to perform some quantitative analyses to see what determined the military spending patterns. However, instead of the typical defence economics analyses, which focus on the demand for military expenditures on the basis of certain key variables (usually income, prices, threats, and spill-overs), we want to first examine the impact of political economy variables on Finnish military spending. Then we want to investigate possible military versus social spending tradeoffs, such as whether the emergence of the welfare state led to a transition from the warfare to welfare state.

In general, it is difficult to find any evidence of budgetary tradeoffs in the case of Finnish post-war military spending. One has to remain a bit cautious, however, when interpreting these issues. Some of the caveats include possible problems with endogeneity and the need to take a closer look at the subcategories of central government spending, for example military spending, as well as institutional changes. For instance, have firms had an impact on the demand for particular types of spending in the Finnish case? In general, firms are usually interested in both limiting taxes and maximizing their share of public sector contracts. A preliminary way of gauging the importance of coalitions of firms is to assess the demand characteristics of military spending via various proxies; namely, we wish to investigate the political economy behind the spending choices.

Thus, we chose real military expenditures (ME) as our dependent variable, to be explained by the real GDP (GDP); the real value added of ships and shipyards (SHIP); the real value added of metal industries (MET); the real industrial value added of all industries (IND); ME_{t-1} represents lagged real military expenditures; D1 is an intercept dummy (0 before, 1975 and onwards 1); D1·SHIP is a slope dummy (D1 multiplied by the time trend of SHIP); D2 is a dummy variable representing the influence of the domestic Defence Committees (0 for other years except 1 for 1970–1972, 1975–1977, and 1979–1982, thus allowing 1 year after the completion to account for the impact); and GOV equals real central government spending. All of the variables, except the dummies, were utilized in logarithmic format for the period 1954 through 1985. The regression was estimated by ordinary least squares, both with and without an intercept (for further details, see Eloranta, 2006a).

The results of the regression indicated that the only variables, based on the *t*-tests (null hypothesis rejected at least at 10 per cent level of significance), that had an impact (both overwhelmingly rejected the null at 0 per cent level of significance) on the demand for ME were IND and GOV, in the following manner (with standard errors in parentheses):

$$\text{ME (log)} = -\,0.85\ \text{INDUSTRY (log)} + 1.82\ \text{GOV (log)}\quad \bar{R}^2 = 0.93\quad DW = 1.98$$
$$(0.0167)\quad (0.034)\quad F = 387.61\quad p = 0.00$$

where the 95 per cent confidence interval for ß4 (IND) was $-0.88 < ß4 < -0.82$, and respectively for ß8 (GOV) $1.75 < ß8 < 1.89$, both indicating that the coefficient signs and the sizes were fairly robust. Therefore, a 1 per cent decrease in industrial value added would result in a 0.85 per cent increase in military spending, and vice versa. Respectively, a 1 per cent increase in central government spending had a positive 1.82 per cent impact on military spending. The results suggest that (1) Finnish military spending increased in times of poor industrial performance, due to, for example, lobbying activities of the industries as a whole (as compared to just a single industrial branch such as shipbuilding) and reliance on government contracts during recessions; and (2) Finnish military spending has been highly sensitive to the development of post-war Finnish government spending and the budget bargaining in the political markets in general. Similar results have been found for the interwar period (Eloranta, 2002; Jalonen & Vesa, 1992).

What about the military versus social spending tradeoff (or lack of it in this case) variable – could it be instrumental in explaining Finnish central government or military spending patterns? As argued here, the growth of central government spending resulted, in addition to other explanatory forces, from the interaction dynamic (or, more likely, the 'stickiness' of this process) between military spending and social expenditures. The guns-versus-butter hypothesis in the context of central government budgets implies either that these two expenditure categories have no impact on the overall budget (i.e. there is an equal size tradeoff response between them) or that this interaction somehow drives central government growth tendencies. Another version of the tradeoff implies that a peace dividend occurs in the form of increased, more productive economic activity – namely, lower military spending should lead to economic growth, as in the case of the post–Second World War United States. However, it is likely that such a tradeoff occurs only in a handful of cases (Mintz & Stevenson, 1995; Ward & Davis, 1992). Moreover, it seems that on the whole, domestic and economic incentives involved in military acquisitions, as well as institutional constraints in changing, for example, conscription laws, tended to sustain military spending or at least limited its decline even under public pressure. In general, there seems to be little evidence of an automatic budgetary tradeoff between these two types of spending. For example, a military retrenchment may mean a smaller overall budget rather than more welfare programs, even if the preferences for defence spending are negatively related to preferences for social spending for the individual taxpayers and vice versa (Abelshauser, 2000; Eloranta & Kauppila, 2006; Grossman & Mendoza, 2003; Mintz, 1989; Mintz & Huang, 1991; Narizny, 2003; Norpoth, 1987). Thus, it seems more plausible that the influences shaping the demand for these two types of central government spending are interrelated yet moulded also by different factors.

Before we go further, we need to explore how to analyse the tradeoff between military and social spending. Estimating this tradeoff can be difficult, since there are several potential types of guns-versus-butter tradeoffs. First, 'guns' usually refers to military spending and the burden it causes for states. 'Butter', in turn, refers to either income or redistribution implications. Some have even extended the use of this term to cover tradeoffs between trade and security (Skaperdas & Syropoulos, 2001) or economic competition versus military competition (Grossman & Mendoza, 2003).

Here we propose two ways to initially measure the guns-versus-butter tradeoff. One way, here dubbed Method 1 (=MESETRADOFF1), would be to

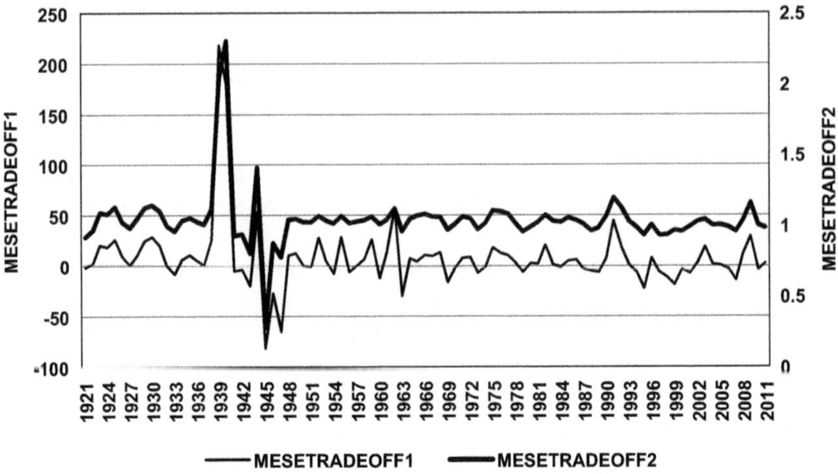

Figure 5.3 Finnish military expenditure vs. social expenditure tradeoffs, 1921–2011

Sources: For the period 1870–1944: Eloranta, 2002, 2007; Hara, 2000; Hobson, 1993; Mitchell, 2003. For the post-war period: Historical Statistics of Japan (www.stat.go.jp/english/data/chouki/, accessed September 2013); SIPRI Military Expenditure Database 2013 (www.sipri.org/research/armaments/milex/milex_database, accessed September 2013); OECD Statistics (http://stats.oecd.org/, accessed October 2013). Public debt figures from Reinhart & Rogoff, 2009. See also the website www.reinhartandrogoff.com/data/.

Note: The data are missing for the period 1945–1952 for a lot of these variables.

add up the change in military spending from the previous year to the current one with the change in social spending (= annual growth rate of ME + annual growth rate of SE: $(ME_t - ME_{t-1}) / ME_{t-1} + (SE_t - SE_{t-1})/SE_{t-1}$)). Method 1 occasionally produces negative numbers, which is problematic for a potential conversion into logarithms. If, however we utilize Method 2 and divide up the net changes in the subsequent years (= MESETRADEOFF2), we estimate the change in relative terms in the spending levels but with numbers greater than zero (= $(ME_t + SE_t)/(ME_{t-1} + SE_{t-1})$)).

As seen in Figure 5.3, in the case of Finland's military and social spending, the budgetary situation was more volatile from 1920 to the post–Second World War than after that period. The first indicator budgetary tradeoffs (MESETRADEOFF1) was fairly consistent and remained at a positive level throughout out the post–Second World War period, indicating lack of tradeoffs instead expansion of both. The second indicator (MESETRADEOFF2) varied more, above and below zero, implying some tradeoffs; thus, at other times one of the categories led into growth of government spending.

Some scholars emphasized that despite the low spending, Japan has experienced some small tradeoffs between defence spending and investment (Ward & Davis, 1992). As Mintz and Stevenson (1995) have discovered, there were links between post-war military spending and economic growth (Mintz &

Table 5.2 Granger Non-Causality Tests for Real GDP per Capita (GDPCAP), Military Burden (MILBUR), and Social Spending (SOCIAL) for Japan and Finland

JAPAN, 1958–2010	*FINLAND, 1950–2010*
GDPCAP ← (NONE)	GDPCAP ← (NONE)
MILBUR ← GDPCAP	MILBUR ← SOCIAL
SOCIAL ← MILBUR	SOCIAL ← MILBUR

Sources: See previous figures.

Note: Military burden = military spending as a percentage of GDP; social spending = social spending as a percentage of GDP. Note: Details on the ADF and cointegration tests are available from the authors.

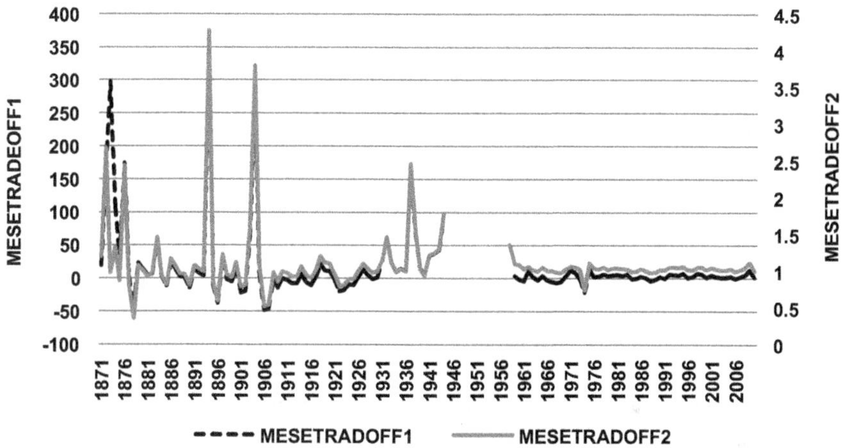

Figure 5.4 Japanese military expenditure vs. social expenditure tradeoffs, 1871–2010

Sources: see previous figures.

Stevenson, 1995). Their results also implied that nonmilitary spending had an impact on economic growth in the Finnish case (Cf. Table 5.2 in this chapter). In terms of the potential budgetary tradeoffs, as displayed in Figure 5.4, the Japanese spending patterns were rather different. As far as the military spending-versus-social spending tradeoff, there was a lot of volatility before the Second World War in terms of both of the indicators for Japan. In contrast, the post-war period exhibited a lot of stability. Moreover, after the war, the Japanese military spending levels were consistently fairly low, although some tradeoffs occurred. Based on the first indicator, the overall spending increased; based on the second one, the post-war period was mostly a story of budgetary tradeoffs.

We also attempted to verify the causal links between real GDP per capita, military burden, and social spending by applying Granger noncausality tests for the military spending and economic growth variables. This is a relatively simple way to test both forms of the tradeoffs, the budgetary one and the peace dividend.

Granger causality can be represented as:

$$X_t = \sum_{i=1}^{m} a_i X_{t-1} + \sum_{j=1}^{n} b_j Y_{t-j} + e_{1t} \tag{1}$$

$$Y_t = \sum_{i=1}^{k} c_i Y_{t-1} + \sum_{j=1}^{p} d_j X_{t-j} + e_{2t} \tag{2}$$

where the possible links between X and Y are verified by testing the following null hypotheses: $b_j = 0$ and $d_j = 0$, in addition to testing the validity of the lagged values of X and Y in predicting their performance. Granger causality can be understood as a weak (or predictive) causal link between variables. Due to potential problems of autocorrelation and nonstationarity, we chose to use the logarithmic forms of the variables. The ADF (Augmented Dickey Fuller) unit root tests revealed that at least Japanese social spending (as a share of GDP) exhibited a unit root, as did the Finnish real GDP per capita and social spending share. This is another indicator that in both countries, the military spending was very stable throughout the post-war period and that social spending exhibited a stochastic trend. Moreover, we performed the customary Johansen cointegration tests, which indicated at least one cointegration vector for Japan and two for Finland. Thus, we employed a vector error correction model (VECM) to assess the Granger noncausality relationships (up to t-2). Table 5.2 contains the results.

Based on this analysis, it seems that the Japanese military spending was determined by economic growth, which is a fairly typical result. This did not apply in the Finnish case. Neither case implied a peace dividend such that lower military spending led to economic growth, although that would have to be inspected further with more complicated macroeconomic models. Moreover, there seemed to be tradeoffs between military and social spending in both cases. For Japan, the military spending seemed to determine the social spending levels. For Finland, the relationships went in both directions. Therefore, based on the different representations of military versus social spending tradeoffs, both in the graphs and based on the Granger noncausality tests, budgetary tradeoffs occurred in both countries, but to a much greater extent in Finland. And in the Finnish case, the tradeoffs were particularly imperfect, thereby driving up public spending levels.

End of Cold War – what now?

Japan and Finland both have had major economic and security challenges in the last 30 years or so. Japan has had to endure persistent economic problems that began with the bursting of the bubble in 1989 and stagnation in the

1990s, the more recent earthquake and nuclear accident, China's and India's economic and military rise, and the unstable security situation in East Asia in general. Finland, in turn, has had to orient its foreign policy due to the Soviet Union's collapse in 1991, the loss of exports to the Soviet Union and a deep recession, joining the European Union and euro, and the impacts of globalisation. Both have shown tremendous aptitude for dealing with regional and global challenges – Japan from the perspective of a major economy and political player and Finland as a small nation in Northern Europe.

What has this meant for their military spending? In general, world military spending levels began a slow decline from the 1970s onwards, with the Reagan years being an exception for the United States. This was mostly the outcome of the reduction in tensions in the post–Cold War climate as well as the downfall of the USSR and the communist regimes in Eastern Europe. The USSR was spending almost as much on its armed forces as the United States was up until mid-1980s, and the Soviet military burden was still 12.3 per cent in 1990. Under the Russian Federation, with a declining GDP, this level dropped rapidly to 3.2 per cent in 1998. Similarly, other nations downscaled their military spending in the late 1980s and the 1990s (Eloranta, 2003).

Overall, according to the SIPRI figures, there was a reduction of circa one third in real terms in world military spending in 1989 through 1996, which shows how the end of the Cold War temporarily reduced tensions. In the global scheme, world military expenditure was still highly concentrated in the hands of a few countries at the end of the twentieth century, with the 15 major spenders accounting for 80 per cent of the world total in 1999. The newest military spending estimates display a growth trend in the world military expenditures once again due to new threats such as international terrorism and interstate rivalries in the twenty-first century. In terms of absolute figures, the United States still dominated the world military spending with a 39 per cent share of the world total in 2012. Nonetheless, the United States has entered the third millennium as the world's only real superpower – a role that it embraces sometimes awkwardly (SIPRI Military Expenditure Database 2013: www.sipri.org/research/armaments/milex/recent-trends).

In recent years, world military spending levels have decreased slightly but not uniformly due to the recent financial crisis. Most of the cuts occurred among the Western nations, and, for example, China increased its spending in 2012 by 7.8 per cent. Japan is among the group of nations that had cut its spending, a rarity among the Asian nations in general. However, in 2013, Japan indicated that it is going to increase its spending substantially as a response to the rising Chinese threat. A lot of the increases will go toward reversing previous cuts, with some gains in material purchases. (See esp. www.sipri.org/media/pressreleases/2013/milex_launch; world.time.com/2013/09/02/why-japans-first-defense-spend-hike-in-over-two-decades-isnt-going-to-buy-much/; on security threats, see also Christensen, 1999, 2006.)

As seen in Figure 5.5, the structure of Japanese military spending has not changed much from the 1970s to the early 2000s, which also reflects the

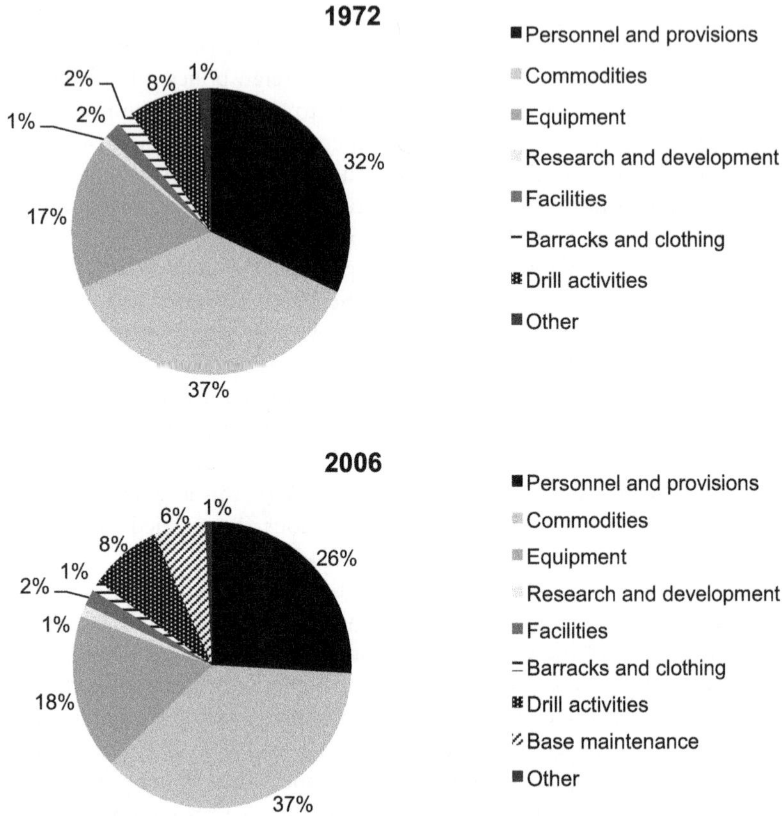

Figure 5.5 Structure of Japanese military spending, 1972 vs. 2006

Sources: Historical Statistics of Japan (www.stat.go.jp/english/data/chouki/, accessed September 2013).

stability of the spending levels (as a percentage of the GDP), usually around 1 per cent of GDP. Personnel costs have declined in this period and the cost of base maintenance has increased; those are the only notable changes. These changes are also reflected in Figure 5.6. The size of Japan's military force increased up until the 1970s, when it levelled off. In the early twenty-first century, Japan has reduced the size of its armed forces. In comparison, Finland's military force has remained at similar levels for most of the post-war period, with a steady, slowly declining trend.

Finland's security policies have always been tied to the existence of a powerful neighbour in the East, the Soviet Union/Russia. After the Second World War, Finland developed extensive commercial ties with the Soviet Union following the completion of the war reparations, most of which were in the form of metal goods. While the early Cold War years were a time of developing trade links,

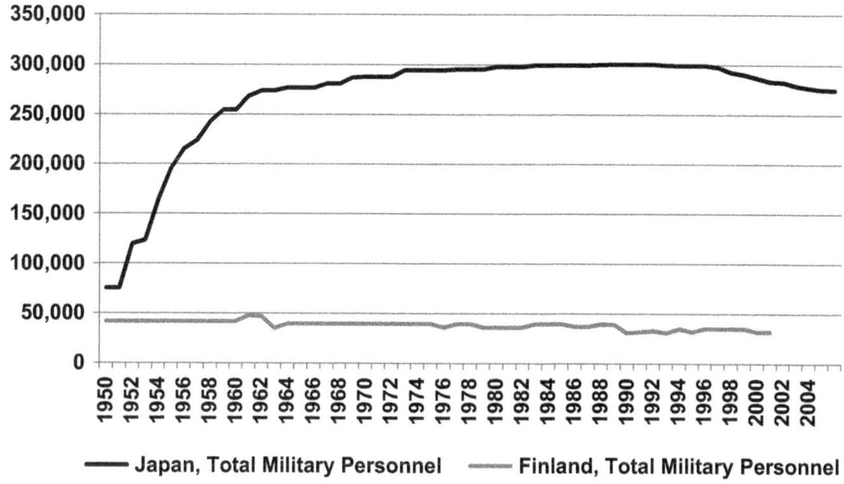

Figure 5.6 Total military personnel of Japan and Finland, 1950–2005

Sources: Historical Statistics of Japan (www.stat.go.jp/english/data/chouki/, accessed September 2013); Singer & Small, 1993.

Finnish trade with the Soviet Union grew, especially during the 1970s. This growth was related to the more hostile international economic environment and the new trade agreements. The role played by oil was central, forming an average of 74 per cent of the Soviet exports to Finland (Eloranta & Ojala, 2005).

The Soviet trade peaked during the Oil Crises: the clearing trade smoothed the problems caused by the oil prices. The trade with oil also opened up further possibilities for Finnish companies inside the Soviet Union. Subsequently, when the oil prices fell, this harmed the exports to the Soviet Union.

The Finnish foreign policy and business elites, however, were not keen on recognizing the downward spiral of the Soviet economy in the 1980s and usually tended to favor caution in their dealings with their powerful neighbour. Thus the Finns responded with caution in 1990 to 1991 to the decline and eventual collapse of the Soviet Union itself. Only then did they renounce the restrictions imposed by the 1947 and 1948 treaties and provide unofficial encouragement to Baltic independence. Similarly, many Finnish companies continued to hedge their bets on the Soviet markets in the late 1980s, which eventually disappointed them and contributed to the onset of a deep depression in Finland. The collapse of the Soviet Union brought with it other challenges besides the collapse of exports, including the emergence of remilitarized Russia, tensions between the EU nations and Russia, and availability of energy from the East.

Regardless of new and/or evolving threats, in Finland, the military burden has remained very steady in the early twenty-first century, between 1.2 and 1.6 per cent. The same applies to the budget share, which varied between 5.1 and

5.9 per cent of the central government budget in 2003 to 2014 (see www.defmin.fi/tehtavat_ja_toiminta/puolustushallinnon_voimavarat/talous/puolustusbudjetin_osuus_bruttokansantuotteesta; www.defmin.fi/tehtavat_ja_toiminta/puolustushallinnon_voimavarat/talous/puolustusmenojen_osuus_valtion_kokonaismenoista). In the 1920s and 1930s, the average Finnish military burden was 3.3 per cent and the mean budget share was 22.4 per cent. Obviously the modern Finnish military establishment is much less of a priority in fiscal decisions. Moreover, the share of purchases of military materiel of the overall defence budget was, on average, 27.1 per cent in the interwar period. That share, as seen in Table 5.3, is slightly lower in modern Finnish military budgets but not to a great extent. However, that share is projected to fall to 17.1 per cent in 2014, reflecting the new challenges facing the Finnish military establishment. In general terms, many military units are being combined or phased out, and the government has emphasized the need to make efficiency

Table 5.3 Structure of Finnish military spending, 2012–2014

	2012		*2013*		*2014*	
Expenditure Category	*Euros (Millions)*	*Percentage*	*Euros (Millions)*	*Percentage*	*Euros (Millions)*	*Percentage*
Purchase of Materiel	649.7	23.2	656.6	22.9	470.4	17.1
Wage Expenditures	815.3	29.1	832.7	29.0	844.3	30.7
Conscription Expenditures and Upkeep	160.9	5.7	170.5	5.9	158.7	5.8
Maintenance of Properties	238.4	8.5	242.9	8.5	254.6	9.3
Other Functional Expenditures	525.9	18.8	539.1	18.8	601.0	21.8
Military Crisis Management	52.7	1.9	61.5	2.1	60.1	2.2
Value Added Expenses	317.7	11.3	344.2	12.0	337.7	12.3
Other Expenditures	43.9	1.6	25.5	0.9	24.3	0.9
Total	2 804.5	100.0	2 873.0	100.0	2 751.1	100.0

Source: www.defmin.fi/tehtavat_ja_toiminta/puolustushallinnon_voimavarat/talous/puolustusmenojen_jakautuminen.

Note: The figures for 2013 and 2014 are estimates based on budget figures.

a priority in the reforms. However, Finnish military spending has not been cut drastically, despite the 2008 to 2009 financial crisis, a situation that is similar to some of the other EU countries. More than half of the EU nations have cut their real military spending by more than 10 per cent (see www.sadankomitea.fi/files/Finanssikriisin-vaikutus-Suomen-ja-Euroopan-unionin-jasenmaiden-puolustusmenoihin.pdf; www.sipri.org/media/pressreleases/2013/milex_launch).

Conclusions

In general, Japan and Finland both offer us a glimpse of a relatively quick transformation, both economically and politically, from pre–Second World War warfare state to post-war welfare state. In the case of Japan, the welfare state creation was more modest than in the case of Finland. Moreover, both countries maintained relatively low levels of military spending, and in both cases the spending levels were remarkably stable. The end of the Cold War has not changed that much, despite the new security challenges for each country: emergence of Russia and the European Union for Finland and China's and India's economic and political ascendancy for Japan.

Based on our findings on the post-war spending patterns, the Japanese military spending totals were determined by economic growth but not vice versa. In the Finnish case, we found no interaction between economic growth and military spending, thereby suggesting there was no peace dividend to be gained in this period. Furthermore, there seemed to be tradeoffs between military and social spending at the budgetary level in both cases. For Japan, the military spending seemed to have an impact on the social spending levels, whereas for Finland, the relationships went in both directions. Moreover, based on our analysis of the various possible forms of military versus social spending tradeoffs, budgetary tradeoffs occurred in both countries but to a much greater extent in Finland. And in the Finnish case, the tradeoffs were particularly imperfect, thereby driving up public spending levels.

Both states, even if they are very different in terms of size of the economy and location, indicate relatively rapid transformation to a modern welfare state. Military spending has taken a backseat in many ways for these states, despite some momentary changes in focus like in Japan in the 1970s and 1980s. Even the new security challenges have not changed the situation: military spending remains low in the second decade of the twenty-first century, and that is unlikely to change. Finland is in the middle of cutting certain types of military spending, especially certain garrisons, whereas Japan has introduced some new spending items, although many of those are related to the postearthquake policy considerations. The modern twenty-first-century fiscal state is much more complicated than the one that emerged out of the First World War, and both of these countries reflect that change.

Part III

Macroeconomic policies

Part III

6 Macroeconomic thinking and policymaking in post-war Japan and Finland

The role of Keynesian macroeconomics

Toshiaki Tamaki and Timo Särkkä[1]

Introduction

The period from the end of the Second World War to the oil shocks of the early 1970s was the age of Keynesianism, which became closely identified with macroeconomic planning. There were several reasons for the popularity of demand management after the war. The rise of Social Democratic ideals and the emergence of the welfare state created a call for demand management policies to maintain full employment, which for the welfare states was often a necessary condition for welfare to be affordable. It has been also maintained that demand management was one of the ways to demonstrate the superiority of capitalism over communism. Full employment, which the Soviet Union claimed to ensure through its system of central planning, could be achieved in the West through demand management. Although on the ideological front there could be no peaceful coexistence between socialism and capitalism, Keynes provided theoretical bases for the regulation of capitalism. The revolution of the policy defined by the use of demand management reached its climax in the 1960s, when Keynesianism was employed in many Western economies (Backhouse & Bateman, 2011, pp. 31–6, 9; Dostaler, 2012, p. 257; Linnamo, 1966, pp. 143–56).

The distinctive national traditions of pre-war economic thought survived into the post–1945 era, although they soon went into a rapid decline. Nevertheless, the globalisation of economics had not yet eradicated national idiosyncrasies. Keynesian ideas proved much more influential in some countries than in others (King, 2002, pp. 8, 140). Macroeconomic policies pursued along Keynesian lines in some countries did not necessarily imply a large and influential number of 'post Keynesians', a 'fundamentalist' Keynesian identity, working in the same country. For instance, Sweden is often regarded as a textbook example of a country that pursued social and economic policies along Keynesian lines right down to the 1990s, but there has never been a significant 'post-Keynesian' group in Sweden (Marshall, 1996, pp. 843–58).

As Pekkarinen (1988) has maintained, the relations among economic theory, economic policy, and economic development are complex: they are shaped by historical and institutional conditions and they are temporally and spatially conditioned. The Keynesian view maintains a unilateral chain of influence from economic theory through economic policy to the economy. The Keynesians were policy optimists, emphasizing the malleability of the economy by macroeconomic management. However, the existence of such a chain of influence is conditioned by a set of crucial economic-structural, institutional, ideological, and political intervening variables, which from the perspective of economic history cannot be ignored (Pekkarinen, 1988, pp. 1–9). These intervening variables, including the economic structures, institutions, and ideological and political traditions of Japan and Finland, display clear differences, as other contributions to this volume amply show. They also reflect differences in the sheer economies of scale and scope of Japan and Finland, which can be identified relatively clearly (see e.g. Maddison, 2001, and introduction of this volume). Instead of presenting a systematic picture of these variables, in this chapter we will concentrate on connections between economic theory and economic policies.

The analysis is nationally specific, which holds that despite the obvious differences and distinctive characteristics in Japanese and Finnish economic development, the style of argumentation about economic policy and the corresponding balance among policy measures still differ from one country to another. The national economic policy is created out of the broad economic-structural, cultural, ideological, social, and institutional frameworks of each country. This notion is in accordance with Keynes's own views about economic policies. On the one hand, he maintained that economic policies are related to particular conditions and times. On the other, he wanted subsequent generations to take his ideas and run with them in new directions (Backhouse & Bateman, 2011, pp. 94, 127).

Concerning the economic structures of Japan and Finland, particular attention will be paid to the industrial structure of the economies. Small, open economies such as Finland's usually differ from the kind of economic structure implicitly assumed by an aggregative, demand-oriented Keynesian framework such as that in Japan. Moreover, we will pay particular attention to the perception of the role of the state in the economy. Keynesianism represents a critique of the *laissez-faire* tradition, alien to countries such as Finland or Japan, where the state has traditionally played a more active role on the supply side of the economy.

During the post–1945 era, economic theory became increasingly global, but the nationally specific variables created tensions between largely imported macroeconomic theories and economic policies as well. In short, economists (Pekkarinen, 1988) have claimed that during stable economic conditions, when the existing course of economic and social development is not questioned, economic theories have little impact on economic policy decisions. The existing economic theory is used as a source of legitimatisation of the chosen policies. In contrast to stable conditions, during periods of economic and social crisis, the existing policy choices are questioned. In such conditions, economic theory may decisively affect policy thinking. It is notable that an economic crisis paved the way for the rise of Keynesian thinking in the 1930s similar to the way the Oil Crises of the 1970s facilitated he rise of the Monetarist counterrevolution.

While the prevailing policy views were in crisis, the early Keynesians were able to exercise a strong influence on the new orientation of economic policy during and after the war. During this process, the Keynesian theory model began to accommodate itself to economic and ideological conditions of the old economic policy. In the new economic conditions of the 1970s, its explanatory force deteriorated as new policy problems, like inflation and the balance of payments, emerged, after which Keynesian macroeconomics was attacked by a deflationary economic policy. As the economic policies backed by the Keynesian views were in crisis, it paved the way for the Monetarist counterrevolution, with Milton Friedman as its main theorist.

The internationalisation of economic theory and the neoclassical synthesis formed the core of Western economic thinking in the post–Second World War period macroeconomic theory. Economists have called the period between the end of the Second World War and the Oil Crisis of 1973 'the age of Keynes' or 'the age of Keynesian Revolution' (see, for example, Klein, 1966). The Keynesian economic model regards the central task of macroeconomic policy as the stabilisation of aggregate demand, utilizing the tools of fiscal and monetary policy. In this chapter, we investigate how this task was received in Japan and Finland, where Keynesian ideas and ideals were to a large extent imported, and how Keynesian macroeconomics fit into Japanese and Finnish economy and society.

Keynes and Keynesianism

The financial crisis of autumn 2008 and the almost unprecedented economic problems associated with it created a new call for the ideas and thoughts of John Maynard Keynes, who continues to attract the attention of researchers of the economy and economic history. (For recent studies, refer, for example, to Backhouse & Bateman, 2012; Cate, 2012; Clarke, 2009; Goodspeed, 2012.) In autumn 2008, people turned to Keynes in their search for tools to apply in the emergency situation. In this latest phase of Keynesianism, our view of Keynes differs markedly from that of the mid-twentieth century, the so-called 'age of Keynes' or 'age of Keynesian Revolution', when people regarded him as synonymous with stable economic growth (Backhouse & Bateman, 2012, pp. 1–5). That is to say that Keynes and Keynesianism have been reinterpreted time and time again because the world we live in has changed as well. Globalisation has transformed the world economy in such a profound way that the widespread confidence in government and planning of the post-war period seems, in the present-day atmosphere of skepticism, almost naive. Another reason for different perceptions of Keynes is that Keynes was a man with many facets. Besides being an important economic thinker, he was also a critic of capitalism, academic, journalist, businessman, government advisor, and much more. To concentrate on just his economic theories distorts the big picture and leaves our view unavoidably incomplete (on Keynes's many dimensions, refer to Clarke, 2009; Harrod, 1972 [1951]).

Keynes's posthumous fame is mainly based on his seminal work, *The General Theory of Employment, Interest and Money* (1936), in which he postulated that the level of economic activity was determined by what he called 'effective demand' for goods and services. Though very difficult to read, the book offers several versions of a simple macroeconomic model of the British interwar economy. In the context of the Great Depression of the 1930s and the sustained problem of unemployment in Britain in the interwar period, Keynes maintained that an increase in government spending or tax cuts, which in their turn increase private spending, would raise production and reduce unemployment. The basic reason for the labour market failure was that it was due to a deficiency in the aggregate demand, which was in turn the result of insufficient investment (on Keynes's definition of 'effective demand', refer to Keynes, 1957, p. 25).

Keynes challenged the previous attempts to conceptualise the problems of capitalism and adopted a new set of conceptual tools with which to analyse the economy in his study. In the process, he was able to build new conceptions of economic maladies that were not possible for his predecessors. However, Keynes did not overthrow all that had been presented before him but quite conversely built his theory largely on concepts and ideas developed during the 1920s and 1930s. He created his own theory that came to be the channel through which those previous ideas entered economics in the post–1945 era. The 'Keynesian revolution' in economic theory happened when a new generation of economists started to use Keynesian concepts to build new economic models of how capitalism worked. After the war, economists were increasingly turning to the use of mathematics in modelling. A new style of theorizing about the economy emerged as Keynesian concepts and mathematical modelling were combined, thus creating what is ultimately called 'the Keynesian revolution' in economic theory (Backhouse & Bateman, 2011, pp. 6–10; 2012, p. 210).

It is necessary to add that Keynes himself saw economics as a 'moral science', which explains his suspicion of econometrics. In other words, he believed that the interactions in the capitalist economy were not reducible to fixed numbers (Backhouse & Bateman, 2012, pp. 216–17). Furthermore, it is important to note that the models of the neoclassical synthesis are essentially not rooted in time, whereas Keynes was always conscious of time and process. While Keynes quite explicitly dealt with an economy with particular institutional characteristics, the neoclassical interpretation abstracts from institutional detail. As reinterpreted here, with his challenges of the dominance in economic thinking, Keynes opens a door to policy proposals addressing the 'what kind' and 'for whom' questions (Minsky, 1975, pp. viii–ix). It can be thus argued that the Keynes of our time is to a large extent a travesty. The popular conception of his ideas on economic policy, or what is commonly called as 'Keynesianism', should not be confused with Keynes's own thoughts. This difference between Keynesianism and Keynes's thoughts explains why his ideas have been useful for people living in different economic realities and have influenced often very different kinds of policy recommendations (Backhouse & Bateman, 2011, pp. 18–19).

Keynesianism in Japan

Marxism versus Keynesianism

For about two decades after the Second World War, the mainstream of economics in Japanese universities was arguably not dominated by Keynesianism but by Marxism. This is partly due to the fact that in the Second World War, the pervasive influence of Marxism in Japanese academia emerged; Japanese governments during or before war persecuted Marxists, and after the war was over, they returned to Japanese universities, becoming eminent figures or heroes freed from the right-wing governmental oppression, as was seen in the case of the economist Professor Hyoe Ohuchi (1888–1980) at the University of Tokyo.

The left wing exerted a major influence on both Japanese and European academics. Takuma Yasui (1909–95) was one of the most talented Japanese economists and an eminent mathematical economist. His articles used many mathematical techniques typically utilised by Marxists (Yasui, 1970–72). However, Japanese governments' economic policies were Keynesian. Marxism has not been accepted as a tool for economic policies, nor has Japanese society been Marxist.

As Keynesianism was not regarded as orthodox for economics and sometimes criticized as reactionary in the academic world, many or at least some eminent economists did not teach in universities. Some of them did not graduate from the Faculty of Economics (Saburo Okita, 1914–93; Toshihiko Yoshino, 1914–2005; and Hisao Kanamori, 1924–). Even if they graduated from the Faculty of Economics, the education they received was in many cases useless. This applies mainly to Osamu Shimomura (1910–89) here, because he contributed most to the Japanese age of high economic growth (*Kodo Keizai Seicho*). Without his contribution, *Kodo Keizai Seicho* might not have been possible.

Economic planning

According to Yukio Noguchi, the social, economic, and political structure for Japanese society after the Second World War was established as early as 1940. Noguchi regards this institution as the Economic System of 1940. This institution, Noguchi claims, became the social framework of Japan (Noguchi, 2010). The economic growth of Japan after the war was formulated not by the United States or GHQ (General Headquarter) but by the Japanese themselves. The economic growth in Japan was based on a military regime, which means the growth was more or less connected with a planned economy.

As is well known among specialists in Japanese economies, the Japanese economy has been guided by MITI (Ministry of International Trade and Industry) and METI (Ministry of Economy, Trade and Industry). Japanese banks have been firmly controlled and guided by MOF (Ministry of Finance). This is known as '*Goso-sendai hoshiki*', namely the convoy system. Japan has sometimes been considered 'the most successful communist country'. This system, Yukio

Noguchi maintains, was formulated during the course of the wars in Japan. For example, the Japanese direct tax system was born around 1940. The centralized tax system was created at the same time (Noguchi, 2010, pp. 55–62).

The Liberal Democratic Party has been the leading party and pro-American party in the post-war era. Nevertheless, their economic policy had been more or less socialist in terms of their attitude or orientation toward Japanese enterprises. As Gerschenkron suggested,, countries which are economically backward need strong orientation from their governments (Gerschenkron, 1962). The governments intervened in economic spheres and promoted economic growth. His thesis can be applied to Japanese economic growth after the war. It was possible, in essence, due to the institutions created during the war. Economic planning did support and encourage economic growth during the age of dominance by the Liberal Democratic Party. The Party was also able to intervene in Japanese business society by using bureaucratic systems, especially MITI, METI, and MOF.

In the course of the 1950s and 1960s, Japan experienced a dramatic transformation of its industrial structure; Japan changed from an agricultural to an industrial society. As is shown in Table 6.1, the ratio of labourers employed in agriculture, forestry industries, and fisheries declined from 19.2 to 5.3 per cent from 1955 to 1975. On the other hand, the main energy of Japan changed from coal to oil during the 1950s and 1960s (Park & Ruuskanen, 2014; Yoshikawa, 2012, pp. 94–6).

The main factors that contributed to the high level of Japanese growth were low energy prices, especially oil prices (1.8 dollars per barrel); cheap labourers with good education; and low exchange rate of the yen (1 dollar equal to 360 yen; fixed exchange rate system).

We should not forget that Keynesianism was appropriate for the Japanese economic structure from circa 1950 to 1970. Keynes's theory, especially of effective demand, is very useful for an industrial economy. Many young people

Table 6.1 The structure of Japanese industry (percentage of labourers)

	1955	*1975*	*1995*	*1998*
Agricultural forestry industries and fishers	19.2	5.3	1.9	1.7
Mining and building industry	6.3	9.8	10.2	9.1
Manufacturing (material type)	8.8	10.2	7.6	7.1
Manufacturing (process type)	18.7	18.8	16	15.5
Service	9.8	10.5	16.3	17.5
Other tertiary industry	28.9	35.3	38.2	38.7
Government and NPO	8.4	10	9.9	10.4
Total	100	100	100	100

Sources: http://www.cap.or.jp/~toukei/kandokoro/html/03/03_1migi.htm

moved from rural to urban areas, and some of them became factory workers. The more investment the Japanese had in manufacturing, the more profits they could expect. It was a happy time for the Japanese economy and Keynesianism. Many of the assumptions that Keynes adopted happened to exist in Japan for about 20 years after the war. In such a situation, an eminent economist and an important policy emerged: Osamu Shimomura and the 'Income Doubling Plan'.

Shimomura's theory

One of the most prominent Japanese Keynesians was Osamu Shimomura (1910–89), who entered into the Ministry of Finance in 1934 after graduating from the University of Tokyo. Apart from the translation of Keynes's *General Theory* by Tsukumo Shionoya in 1941 (Shionoya, 1941), several people were interested in this book in the Ministry of Finance, forming a research group. Shimomura was not a member of this group, but he showed a keen interest in Keynes.

In 1944, Shimomura received news about the Bretton Woods Agreements, and he pointed out the following important matters. First, he did not approve of the rebirth of a gold standard linked to the US dollar, because it would restrict each country's economic activities. Second, the International Monetary Fund (IMF) would become the most convenient means for the United States to control the world economy. Most likely he could not accept the dominance of financial market by the United States (Kamikubo, 2008, pp. 52–4).

He was also one of the writers of the First Economic White Paper (*Keizai Hakusho*). He contributed to this paper, but it is said that as his idea was very different from that of the chief editor Shigeto Tsuru (he was called an emperor), many of his contributions were ignored (Kamikubo, 2008, pp. 31–44). Shimomura perhaps maintained that the low productivity in Japan was the main reason Japan was seeing a decline in the standard of living and an increase in prices. Tsuru did not take note of this point. Tsuru graduated from Harvard University and acquired advanced tools for economic analyses, but on this point he was inferior to Shimomura. The First Economic White Paper has often been referred to as the best Economic Paper, and many of its merits were attributed to Tsuru. However, if Shimomura's contribution had been printed, it would likely have been much better.

In 1946, Shimomura contracted tuberculosis, partly as a result of overwork and malnutrition. However, during his recuperation, he read Keynes's *General Theory* many times, and so he developed his *own* theory, criticising *General Theory*. He published his book *Keizai Hendo no Josu Bunseki* (*Multiple Analysis of Economic Fluctuations*: Shimomura, 1952). He received his Ph.D. for this book from Takuma Yasui, who was and is one of the most eminent economists in Japan, as we have already mentioned. Yasui gave Shimomura's doctoral thesis a high grade. Although he was not trained as a specialist in modern economics, Shimomura's expertise in theoretical economics reached a very high level. In this book, he criticised Keynes's theory of macroeconomics.

He thought that the theory of *effective demand* could not explain the real mechanism of economic fluctuations very well.

The most important of Keynes's contributions in his *General Theory* was without doubt his theory of multiple effects. Keynes thought that depressions occur because of a lack of demand. He insisted that we should create demand by ourselves, leading to effective demand. While he knew also the importance of investment for economic growth, he was mostly preoccupied with effective demand. That is, his interest lay in investment as effective demand. If companies bought equipment and built factories, he claimed it would push up aggregate demand. On the contrary, Shimomura thought Keynes ignored that investment would increase the production of factories after a certain period of time (Mizuki, 1999, p. 29). As Keynes dealt with the short term in his *General Theory*, he did not need to pay attention to long-term effects.

Keynes's multiplier can be illustrated as a unilateral flow. Indeed, the connections between investment and effective demand are not unilateral but a feedback system. According to Shimomura, the feedback responds to savings. If the difference between investment and savings is not equal to zero, investment will fluctuate according to the rate of savings.

Keynes was interested in topics such as unemployment caused by a lack of effective demand or imperfect use of manufacturing resources. He insisted, therefore, that increasing effective demand would bring about an increase of production. Shimomura maintains that Keynes's theory is not sufficient as a theory of economic fluctuations in general.

Since effective demand cannot explain economic fluctuations comprehensively, we need a theory of effective *production*. Although researchers regard the essence of Keynesian 'effective production' as a savings-investment theory of interest-ratio determination, Keynes did not explain the meaning of this theory in detail. Namely, he did not deal with the following points: investment means an added accumulation of capital; accumulation of capital increases as a result of investment; and an increase of investment brings about an increase of capital as a rule.

Shimomura argued that 'effective production is determined in practice by regression investment'. Regression investment means investment which is expected to be retrieved: investment for the renewal of durable capital goods; investment in raw materials; and investment for maintaining the labour force (Shimomura, 1952, pp. 9–12).

Shimomura was a Keynesian, yet he was not a mere follower of Keynes's theory. He realized the significance of the equilibrium of total investment and aggregate savings and need for effective demand, but he also insisted that exhaustion and equilibrium would be needed for the supplementation for the determination of aggregate demand and that it is this process that determines the process of the output multiplier (Shimomura, 1952 passim). This theory became the backbone of Japanese economic growth during the term in office of the Ikeda cabinet.

The Japanese 'Income Doubling Plan'

The Liberal Democratic Party was founded in 1955. It was born through the amalgamation of the Liberal Party and the Japan Democratic Party. The first prime minister of the Liberal Democratic Party was Ichiro Hatoyama (1955–56), the second was Tanzan Ishibashi (1956), and the third was Nobusuke Kishi (1957–60). Kishi was forced to resign because he signed the new Japan-US Security Treaty despite the fierce criticism of the Japanese public.

In 1960, the Ikeda (Hayato Ikeda, the prime minister) cabinet (1960–64) published a plan titled 'Japanese Income Doubling Plan' (Fujii, 2012, p. 236), partly because Ikeda wanted to distract the party's attention from political to economic matters. Shimomura became the most important intellect of the Ikeda cabinet. They planned to double the average income from 1961 to 1970. Both Ikeda and Shimomura understood the importance of capital investment as an engine of economic growth. Shimomura estimated the average economic growth at around 11 per cent (Kamikubo, 2008, p. 126–31). He was most optimistic about the potential of the Japanese economy. His thinking attracted Ikeda. The rate of increase was set as 7.2 per cent annually, thereby leading to the doubling of the real national income. However, it was the Economic Planning Agency that decided on this rate, because they needed the catchphrase 'Income Doubling'.

Before this plan was published, the participation of women in the labour force declined, because most of them did not need to work, owing to an increase in their husbands' salaries. The Japanese average income levels likewise increased. Such a plan had already been discussed under the Kishi cabinet (Okita, 1981, p. 86). This plan accelerated this trend.

The money that Japanese companies needed was borrowed from the key banks. In Japan, saving was considered a virtue. In this period, Japanese workers saved about 20 to 25 per cent of their income. Some of them went to banks and others went to the Japanese post office to deposit their savings. Such considerable savings enabled the technological innovations in many enterprises. Moreover, Japanese companies used indirect finance. The government adopted protective policies in order to hinder imports from foreign countries and to support and encourage Japanese secondary industry.

Before the adoption of Shimomura's plan, there had been a heated debate concerning Japanese economic growth. Shimomura was most optimistic. He thought Japan would succeed in sustaining high economic growth of more than 10 per cent; on the other hand, others maintained it would be less, about 6.5 per cent. If economic growth made it possible for the labourers to shift from low-productivity to higher-productivity sectors, namely if the labourers moved from the agricultural to the industrial sector, it should have contributed to economic growth and the dissolution of dual structure (Okita, 1981, p. 86). Subsequently, Ikeda cabinet's policy of 'Japanese Income Doubling Plan' aimed at:

1. The improvement of social capital
2. A higher level of industrial structure

3. The promotion of trade and international cooperation
4. A higher level of human abilities and the promotion of technology
5. The relaxation of the double structure and the securing of social stability

These objectives were reminiscent of 5-year plans in some more or less socialist countries. In order to achieve these aims, the government offered cheap finance, restrained the imports for nascent industries, adopted a taxation system for nurturing industries important for Japanese economic strategies, and voted for subsidies (see Kamikubo, 2008, p. 135–41).

The Ikeda cabinet wanted especially to promote the secondary sector, industry. Japan was still a rural society after the war, but it went through a dramatic change from a rural to an urbanized society in just a few decades. Huge capital investments were made in steel and the chemical, automobile, shipbuilding, and computer sectors. Foreign technologies were also introduced. The results were impressive. The economic growth rate in Japan from 1955 to 1973 was 10 per cent (yearly average), and Japan had the second-biggest GNP in the world in 1968. During this period, the infrastructure consisting of roads, ports, and cities was greatly improved, and the period saw a rapid transition from agriculture to industry in terms of the labour force.

Shimomura recognised the absurdity of a controlled economy because of the experiences during the war. It was impossible to control the prices of all goods (Shimomura, 1981a, p. 83–4). Thus, he understood the inefficiency of a Marxist economy and already thought that Marxism failed to explain the real economy (Shimomura, 1981a, p. 81). He emphasized the importance of private equipment investment instead of gross fixed investment and attached great importance to innovation triggered by private equipment investment. Gross fixed investment was less suited to an innovative society. Demand control is not sufficient to realize economic development, Shimomura maintained.

Despite the fact that the Japanese economy experienced high economic growth, it was still poor. The dual structure – the differences in the wages paid by big and small enterprises – was large and needed to be corrected. Japanese economic development before the war was based on military, heavy industry, and the chemicals industry. But the standard of consumption did not rise sufficiently to generate increased demand for consumer goods.

In 1959, Ichiro Nakayama (1898–1978), who was a professor at Hitotsubashi University, advocated for 'Doubling of Wages' (Ito, 1981, p. 88). This was the first step in Ikeda's new economic plan. Shimomura's idea suited Ikeda's economic policy, because Ikeda needed to make the Japanese focus more on economic than on political issues and to think more positively. Shimomura's ideas may have differed somewhat from those of Ikeda, but he had to develop a concrete plan for the Ikeda cabinet. Shimomura was forced to fight against the Economic Planning Agency, for the latter insisted on the importance of maintaining a *plan*; but for Shimomura, it was sometimes impossible to adhere to the original plan. Shimomura maintained that the 'Income Doubling Plan' was only a plan, thus calling for more flexibility about the schedule (Shimomura, 1981c, p. 84).

During the age of the 'Income Doubling Plan' and until 1973, Japan experienced dramatic economic growth. The Japanese bought many consumer durables. Televisions, refrigerators, cars, air conditioners, and washing machines could now be found in many Japanese households, and this would have been impossible without the Income Doubling Plan. The standard of living in Japan rose dramatically. It is true that Japan had industrialized already in the Meiji period, but the production of durables did not increase as much as that of the heavy and chemicals industries, because Japan became a military society. After the Second World War, however, Japan abandoned its military regime, and the Japanese were now keen to acquire consumer durables.

Keynesianism in Finland

Macroeconomic theory in post-war Finland

Political choices with regard to economics can rarely be categorized as pure macroeconomic theories or one single economic policy. Finnish economic political thinking from 1948 to 1973 has often been termed by Finnish economists as 'traditional', which refers to the idea that the needs of major industries were regarded as essential for the well-being of the national economy. Capital-intensive industries such as the forestry industry required large investments, which were secured with foreign investment loans, with an active monetary policy, and by controlling wages and consumption (Sajasalo & Igawa, 2015).

In post-war Finland, the rationale was that the level of investment needed to be high and the wage level low in order to increase productivity and to survive in international competition. It has been maintained by Kosonen and colleagues (1978) that these political choices kept the structure of industry one-sided and industry oriented to produce basic commodities and raw materials (Kosonen, 1978). This one-sidedness made the Finnish economy vulnerable to outside economic turbulence. Finland competed with the high productivity of its forestry industry and with low employment costs rather than with specialized labour and products, science, or labour-intensive fields of industry. This led to a trade imbalance and also to a rise in foreign debt, as the more refined industrial goods were more likely to be imported from Sweden, West Germany, the United States, and Japan rather than being produced domestically. Only export-led shipbuilding, metalworking, and the textile industries diversified the Finnish industrial structure into new products.

Another significant feature of the post-war Finnish economy was the prominent role of state-owned industries. The share of the public sector in GDP fluctuated between 35 per cent and 50 per cent in post-war Finland. During the war, the government had a considerable role in the economy and companies, and the situation continued like this until the early 1950s due to rationing and war reparations paid to the Soviet Union. Furthermore, after the war, the forestry industry requested state intervention, as it needed to secure its infrastructure and energy supply. The government also encouraged the creation of large firms and offered incentives, subsidies, loans, and tax exemptions for the companies so that they would be better able to compete with the large North American and European firms. The phrase 'active economic regulation' (in Finnish *aktiivinen taloussäätely*) came to refer to the state's involvement in the post-war Finnish economy, which in turn led to a situation in which industries needed support from the political parties to back up their interests. Can the aforementioned development defined by Kosonen and colleagues (1978) be seen as the rise of Keynesianism in Finland?

Finland's post-war macroeconomic theory relied on econometrics and growth (Linnamo, 1957, pp. 277–9; Paunio, 1959a; 1959b, pp. 129–32). Socio-political thinking especially followed Keynesian premises, as it was maintained that social equality would not impede economic growth but actually foster it (Kuusi, 1961: 34). Full employment was the objective, which was to be achieved through active economic and fiscal policies (Kivinen, 1952, pp. 171–201; Tamminen, 1951, pp. 17–30).

During the period from 1948 to 1956, Finnish production returned to its pre-war level. The first Fagerholm cabinet (1948–50) put emphasis on the needs of the export industries and particularly the forestry industry. To boost export industries, the Finnish Mark was devalued twice in 1949. The Korean War led to an economic boom in Finland in the early 1950s. The economy also recovered with the aid of the first 5-year trade agreement between Finland and the Soviet Union, which was signed in June 1950. A favourable market situation and a combination of active monetary and trade policies led to economic growth from 1953 to 1956, during which agrarian people were recruited in increasing numbers to work in the industries. However, the wages were kept low. Even after the General Strike of 1956, the state was still able to control wages, proving that the employers managed to gain considerable victories over organized labour. By 1956, Finland's economy had entered a steep downturn, and active monetary policies were introduced to overcome this. The Finnish Mark was devalued again in 1957 (Kosonen, 1978, pp. 37–9; Waris, 1958, pp. 98–111).

Finland's entry into the European Free Trade Association in 1961 intensified Finland's integration into Europe, yet the forestry industry was wholly unprepared for integration, leading to a negative balance of trade (Sajasalo & Igawa, 2015). Furthermore, there were other structural changes in the economy in which the state-owned companies such as Neste (founded 1948) and Rautaruukki (founded 1960) had a significant role. From 1957 to 1965, the state continued to actively regulate the economy. It reduced company taxes, provided loans to companies, and advanced exports. The importance of education and scientific research was also understood, but decisions on these were postponed. By the late 1960s, customs between EFTA (European Free Trade Area) countries had been removed, which led to a diminishing competitiveness in the European context, although investments, especially in the forestry industry, were significant. From 1966 to 1975, the government's economic policies to meet the new economic challenges were similar to those of the post-war years. Rafael Paasio's Left-Centre government devalued the Mark in 1967. Moreover, significant tax reductions were extended to corporations. However, the structural problems of the economy were revealed by the increasing immigration to Sweden. The state also introduced new funding instruments to advance imports and scientific research. Following these decisions, public spending increased dramatically. (For a more detailed analysis of the Finnish economy, see, for example, Kosonen, 1978, pp. 29–45.)

The role of Keynesianism in the post-war Finnish economy

The period from the end of the war to the early 1970s brought about profound changes in the Finnish economy. But what was the role of Keynesianism in this development? Keynes's own ideas and the neoclassical synthesis they inspired reflect certain economic, institutional, and ideological circumstances that were characteristic of mature capitalist economies like that of the UK. In terms of economics, these countries had already passed through their industrialisation process and possessed a settled production structure fuelled by domestic demand, which occupied a decisive share of the economy. In terms of ideology, countries like the UK had strong liberal and relatively weak socialist traditions. The society had come into being on its own without much state involvement. The economic, social, and ideological structures of Finland stood in sharp contrast to this picture.

As far as the economic structure was concerned, post-war Finland was still in the process of industrialisation. The share of investment in the GDP was high, growth was export led, and the economy was heavily dependent on foreign trade. It is also noteworthy that exports were mainly concentrated in a few branches, mostly raw-materials processing such as the forestry industry, which was highly cyclical by nature. In an export-led economy like post-war Finland's, what was most significant to major firms was the domestic cost of production as a decisive factor contributing to the profitability of exports (Pekkarinen, 1988, pp. 7–8).

Moreover, the ideological and political features of the post-war Finland were dissimilar to those associated with Keynesianism. In Finland, both the employee and employer organisations exercised substantial control over policy. Export industries formed an active and coherent interest group, and labour was also well organized, as the union density was high and decision making in the trade unions was centralized. Such corporatist forms of collective decision making reflected ideas similar to those of the German Historical School rather than the Anglo-Saxon liberal *laissez-faire* tradition. Taken together, these characteristics of the economy and society shifted attention from the demand side of the economy to the supply side (Pekkarinen, 1984, pp. 11–39). Other aspects of Finnish intellectual history relevant to the understanding of economic policy are determinism and the way the role and nature of the state have been conceived. In the Finnish tradition, the state operates within the economy. The state has, from the beginning of capitalism, been pivotal to growth and industrialisation, thus playing a more active role than merely providing the basic legal framework for *laissez-faire* capitalism (Pekkarinen, 1986, pp. 36–7).

General Theory was for the first time introduced to the Finnish audience by Pauli Korpisaari and Lauri O. af Heurlin in 1940 (Heurlin & Korpisaari, 1940, pp. 190–201). This early interest in Keynes, however, waned, as the former author, Pauli Korpisaari, died in the Continuation War in 1941 (Suviranta, 1951, p. 17). In 1946, in the obituary of Keynes, the latter, Lauri O. af Heurlin, reminded the readers of the impact *General Theory* had had in macroeconomic theory not only internationally but also in Finland (Heurlin, 1946, p. 321). It was not, however, until the translation of *General Theory* into Finnish in 1951 by Ahti Karjalainen and Pentti Kivinen that Keynes's economic premises were fully appreciated in Finland (Heurlin, 1952, pp. 61–2; Keynes, 1951). The subsequent Keynesian milestones, such as, for instance, Lawrence Klein's *The Keynesian Revolution* (1949; Kivinen, 1949, pp. 94–7), Seymour E. Harris's *The New Economics. Keynes' Influence on Theory and Policy* (2nd impr., 1949; Kivinen, 1950, pp. 94–7), R. F. Harrods's *The Life of John Maynard Keynes* (1951; von Fieandt, 1951, pp. 240–4), Philip Ch. Newman's *The Development in Economic Thought* (Karjalainen, 1954, pp. 58–61), and Kenneth Kurihara's *The Keynesian Theory of Economic Development* (1959; Paunio, 1959a, pp. 274–6) were widely discussed by Finnish economists.

Thus, by the end of the 1950s, Finnish economic theory was in line with Keynesian thought. It has been maintained that Finland's economic policies with non-Keynesian characteristics provide a good example of loose interaction between economic theory and economic policy. The Finnish post-war economic policies have displayed rather one-sided emphasis on supply, cost, and competitiveness aspects. The policies stemmed from the interwar period and sustained their dominance despite the wartime and post-war political instability. The Second World War meant an extensive governmental intervention in the Finnish economy. As in many other wartime economies, rationing and planning were adopted in Finland. Further, the state organised the resettlement of war refugees from Karelia, which was occupied by the Soviet forces during the war. State-owned companies were established, and the metal industry was created mainly through state initiatives designed to cover the war reparations. As a consequence, the public sector was large, and both economic and social policies were interventionist (Pekkarinen, 1986, pp. 22–6; 1988, p. 15–17).

A significant institutional feature behind the post-war Finnish economic policies was a strong and independent central bank. The Bank of Finland was subject to parliamentary control, yet the legislation stressed the independence of the central bank in its relations to the government. The exchange rate policy was one of the key policies in Finland in which the central bank played an important role. Typically, when periods of economic prosperity have given way to downturns, deflationary fiscal and monetary policies have been utilised, often side by side with devaluation. The Finnish Mark experienced major devaluations at roughly 10-year intervals, typically towards the end of downturns, as in 1957 and 1967. Although the post-war Finnish economy was unstable, it grew rapidly (Pekkarinen, 1988, pp. 20–4).

To clarify the non-Keynesian features of Finnish post-war policies, Finnish economists have considered both structural and political factors. At the political level, the national policies exercised a degree of authority across most lines of political division. The bourgeois idea that the political and economic spheres should remain separate remained unquestioned by the Left, which was internally divided into Social Democrats on the one hand and Communists on the other. In Finland, the Social Democrats never integrated Keynesian stabilisation policy into their strategic goals, as was the case in Sweden. The Communists were influenced more by Marxism than by Keynesian ideas. The Right distrusted all reforms in its fear of the influence of the Soviet Union. The Agrarian Centre Party's ideology was based on thriftiness, but in its politics it shared the interests of the export-led forestry industry (Pekkarinen, 1986, pp. 34–5; 1988, pp. 24–5).

It can be concluded that the post-war Finnish economy bore little resemblance to the basic Keynesian premises. In terms of industrialisation, Finland was a latecomer compared to the early industrialized Western European economies. But after the war, the Finnish economy industrialized very rapidly. Between 1950 and 1970, the share of workforce in agriculture dropped from 46 per cent to 20 per cent, which was still high by Western European standards (Kosonen, 1978). Further, as described by Finnish economists, the financial sector too bore little resemblance to the basic Keynesian premises. That is due to the fact that unlike in mature capitalist economies such as that of the UK, the speculative use of investments had little impact on the Finnish economy, as companies invested in machines but little in stock.

Comparative perspectives of Keynes's influence on Japanese and Finnish economic policies

The economies of both Japan and Finland paved the way for economic growth not by *laissez-faire* but by state-planning policies, the extent of which was not, needless to say, as extreme as in socialist countries. In Japan, Shimomura was one of the most important nonacademic economists. Although the mainstream of Japanese academic economics was rooted in Marxism, Japanese governments adopted Keynes's theory because nonacademic economists, who were basically Keynesian, created economic policies. In some cases, they did not graduate from any faculty of economics. But after joining the Ministry of Finance, the Bank of Japan, or the Economic Planning Agency, they received OJT (on-the-job training) and became good nonacademic economists. The system was very similar to the Japanese employment system. Osamu Shimomura was one of those nonacademic economists.

Japan was very poor immediately after the war, and the islands were overpopulated. As noted in the First Economic White Paper, 'In Japan, governments, enterprises and households all are in deficit' (Economic White Paper, 1947). Japan began to recover from this miserable economic situation partly through hard work and partly due to the huge demand arising from the Korean Wars (1950–53). Partly because of the advantageous exchange rates, Japan could export goods – ships, automobiles, iron and steel, chemicals, electrical goods, and so forth – to foreign countries. Moreover, Japan aspired to export-led economic growth. In this process, the Japanese began to need more and more consumer durables, which they had not acquired much before and during the Second World War. Fortunately, these are visible and tangible goods. The consumers noticed an improvement in their standard of living. The factories in urban areas wanted young, hardworking labourers to increase their production.

The long-term economic growth from the 1950s to approximately 1970 in Japan was based on the development of secondary industry. The Income Doubling Plan was extremely useful in this period and improved the quality of life for most Japanese. Furthermore, Keynes dealt mostly with the demand side, and his interest in the supply side was superficial. Keynes's theory, as is well known, was based on the Great Depression of the 1930s. In this period, states had sufficient supply but lacked consumer demand. Thus, he hit upon 'effective demand' as the focus of analysis. From the period from 1950 to 1970, Japan lacked supply, too. Moreover, innovation was indispensable for the Japanese economy. It was a Schumpeterian economy. Shimomura's theory surpassed Keynes's in a way. Ikeda, who adopted his theory, succeeded in promoting and encouraging economic growth on a large scale.

The power of MITI and MOF was so strong that they controlled economic development in Japan. Subsequently, the Japanese companies adopted an indirect financing system, and corporate finance became centralized in Japan. MOF exercised control over Japanese banks. In other words, Japan was not a free economy per se, and the government exercised considerable influence. Especially, the Income Doubling Plan focused attention on the development of secondary sectors, and it had a considerable ripple effect on the Japanese economy. The impact of Hayato Ikeda and Osamu Shimomura on the economic policy for supporting and promoting Japanese economic growth after the Second World War was substantial.

Keynes dealt with the economic system as a whole and analysed the global economy. In the subsequent translations of the *General Theory*, he felt that he needed to explain his economic premises, his assault on the *laissez-faire* tradition, and endorsement of the state's active role in macroeconomic management to readers to whom these seemed mere common sense. In the Japanese edition, he admitted that 'Japanese readers, however, will neither require nor resist my assaults against the English tradition' (quoted in Clarke, 2009, pp. 160–1). In turn, Bruno Suviranta, who wrote the preface to the Finnish translation that was postponed due to the war until 1951, pointed out the obsolescence of the pre-war theoretical disagreements in the post-war economic reality (Suviranta, 1951, pp. 12–14).

Keynes attacked the neoclassical theory of distribution, since a freely competitive industrial society, it suggested, simply did not exist. In Finland, Keynesianism could not have been a reaction against *laissez-faire* economic policy because the state already had an active role in macroeconomic management. Furthermore, economic problems of oversaving and unequal accumulation of capital were insignificant in a country where the lack of capital was a more serious problem. In Japan, the percentage of savings was so high that Japanese companies could use indirect finance.

A further difficulty in estimating Keynes's impact on the Japanese or Finnish post-war economy is that Keynes concentrated on diagnosing economic phenomena and offered less comprehensive solutions. Thus, the meaning of the phrase 'Keynesian economic policy' is rather vague. At the level of the global economy, one of the significant outcomes of the recent economic crisis has been the question about the nature of capitalism that has come to dominate the world economy. Thus one might ask what relevance Keynes has in light of today's economic problems. One of the economic history arguments of this chapter is that macroeconomic thinking has its past, and macroeconomists would have a better understanding of what they are doing if they knew more about what macroeconomists have done in the past. It seems that, contrary to what Keynes proposed, in Japan and Finland, government spending and fiscal deficits are the real problem, not the solution. Attention has moved away from reforming the financial system to the problem of government debt (Backhouse & Bateman, 2011, pp. 141–3, 153).

In Finland, the economic and political elite has claimed that budget balance is to be achieved through austerity and through dismantling unaffordable social benefits, although dissenting views have been expressed by those who urge that instead of concentrating on budget deficit, the government should concentrate on creating growth. In Japan, the ratio of government bonds to national income has risen from 180 per cent in 2007 to 215 per cent per cent in 2012, and it threatens to rise even further if measures are not taken to reduce the annual government deficit. The size of the deficit implies that this cannot be done through small adjustments in taxes or government spending. In Finland, a generous welfare state controlled by democratically elected representative government is considered as important to economic success as free markets. For the most of the 1950s and 1960s, capitalism appeared to be working well. However, the crisis has also called into question the affordability of the welfare state in Finland.

Japan and Finland have been profoundly influenced by Keynesian macroeconomic theory, but their economic policies were not purely Keynesian but rather conditioned by their economic and social surroundings. The Japanese governments understood the importance of innovation in the long run, and the Finnish governments have also paid attention to the supply side. The Japanese governments' influence over companies was not as direct as was the case in Finland, but something like the use of guidance by the government as a tool. In general, Japanese governments wielded considerable power over the Japanese economy and Japanese companies.

Note

1. Timo Särkkä was a visiting researcher at Kyoto Sangyo University (KSU), Faculty of Economics, in 2011 and 2012. The visits were hosted by Professor Toshiaki Tamaki. Dr. Särkkä wishes to thank the funding bodies, the Academy of Finland, and the Research and Innovation Office of the University of Jyväskylä (JY) and the members of the research team for the faith placed in his research.

7 Energy supply and regulation

Park Seung-Joon and Esa Ruuskanen

Introduction

Energy has been essential for the economic growth of Japan and Finland after the Second World War as well as for the major changes people's lifestyles. Energy issues became major political and media issues at the time of the Oil Crises of the 1970s – and they are likely to remain so since the globe's natural resources are becoming scarce, population growth is accelerating energy demand, and the amounts of GHG (greenhouse gas) emissions that result from fossil fuel burning continue to grow in the early twenty-first century (see e.g. IEA, 2010; Monstadt, 2004).

A growing number of studies have offered cross-national comparisons on the regulatory trajectories of climate and energy policies since the 1990s (see e.g. Albrecht & Arts, 2005; Brossard, Shanahan, & McComas, 2004; Busch & Jörgens, 2005; Höhne, den Elzen, & Weiss, 2006; Monstadt, 2004; Ringius, Torvanger, & Underdal, 2002; Wickering, 2004), but only limited research has been carried out on the long-term developments in these matters. In this chapter, we trace the changes and, at the same time, continuities in regards to the Japanese and Finnish energy systems and energy policies in the post-war era. Both Japan and Finland have been used as examples in studies on the nuclear energy policy in the OECD countries between the 1970s and 2000s (see e.g. Högselius, 2009; Jahn, 1998), but these studies do not offer in-depth analyses arising from either nation, not to mention perform extensive comparisons between them.

Our main goal is to shed light on the energy policy trends of two catch-up economies which became extremely reliant on energy imports, tried to remedy their weak energy self-sufficiency, and, after the Oil Crises of the 1970s, struggled between two far-reaching options, namely nuclear power and alternative energy sources, such as biomass energy, geothermal energy, solar power, and wind power. We argue that enthusiasm for nuclear power and suspicions regarding the alternative energy sources determined the broad lines of energy policy in both Japan and Finland between the 1970s and the early 2010s.

Theoretically, the abovementioned issues are inextricably linked to the scientific debate on the convergence, divergence, and persistence of cultures, economies, and policies, which has been a subject of growing interest in social sciences since the 1980s (see e.g. Bennett, 1991; Jenkins, 2006; Jordan & Liefferink,

Table 7.1 Main energy indicators of Japan and Finland

Year	*Per capita energy (TPES toe per capita)*		*Energy intensity (TPES/GDP toe over thousand 2000 US$ ppp)*		*Energy self-sufficiency rate (% without nuclear)*		*Share of oil in TPES (%)*		*World crude oil price (nominal US$/ barrel)*
	Japan	*Finland*	*Japan*	*Finland*	*Japan*	*Finland*	*Japan*	*Finland*	
1960	0.87	2.20	0.17	0.27	58.1	54.3	38.9	23.7	
1965	1.37	2.89	0.19	0.29	35.7	41.2	59.6	42.6	1.97
1970	2.48	3.88	0.20	0.32	14.8	27.9	71.9	60.3	1.83
1975	2.75	4.21	0.20	0.28	7.6	22	73.4	62.4	12.05
1980	2.96	5.18	0.18	0.31	6.3	20.5	66.1	50.9	34.63
1985	3.02	5.30	0.16	0.28	6.9	20.8	56.3	39.0	27.21
1990	3.60	5.76	0.15	0.26	5.1	24.6	58.3	36.0	22.76
1995	3.99	5.72	0.16	0.28	4.5	27.9	55.8	30.9	18.34
2000	4.15	6.27	0.16	0.24	4.2	28.4	50.2	29.3	28.37
2005	4.14	6.56	0.15	0.23	3.9	30.4	47.9	29.4	56.01

Source: EDMC, 2012; OECD, 2010b

2004; Lévy, 1999; Pieterse, 2009; Pomeranz, 2000; Wiener, 2011). We take part in this debate by asking whether convergence, divergence, or persistence defined the developments of the Japanese and Finnish energy systems and energy policies after the late 1940s and, moreover, if it is even possible to examine these matters between such different countries given their cultural backgrounds and populations and the sizes of their economies.

Among different forms of energy, we focus on heat and electricity. It is essential to keep in mind that the oil and natural gas resources of Japan and Finland are negligible, which underlines the importance of fuel imports as long as energy production is heavily based on the use of fossil fuels. Thus, both domestic and foreign energy sources must be related to energy regulation.

Japan's and Finland's heavy dependence on energy imports, being respectively more than 90 per cent and circa 70 per cent without the inclusion of nuclear power in the early 2000s (see Table 7.1), could be seen as a consequence of their meagre fossil fuel resources. Weak energy self-sufficiency, nonetheless, is also due to political choices. Therefore, it is crucial to examine why Japan and Finland became so reliant on oil, coal, natural gas, LNG (liquefied natural gas), and uranium fuel imports and, furthermore, why domestic renewable energy sources, except industrial wood residues in Finland, were used so little in the late twentieth century (see Figures 7.1 and 7.2).

Choices between different energy technologies and primary energy sources, and, moreover, the whole question of the balance between supply and demand

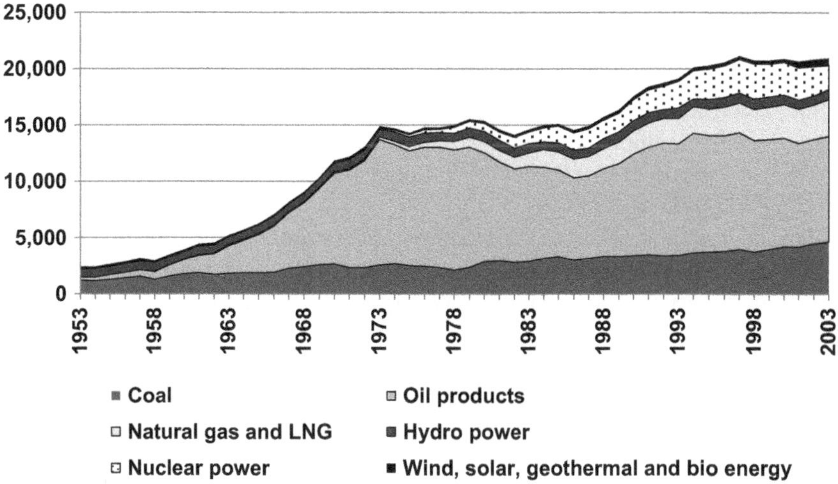

Figure 7.1 Supply of Military Personnel in Japan, 1953–2003

Source: Historical Statistics of Japan, www.stat.go.jp/english/data/chouki/index.htm

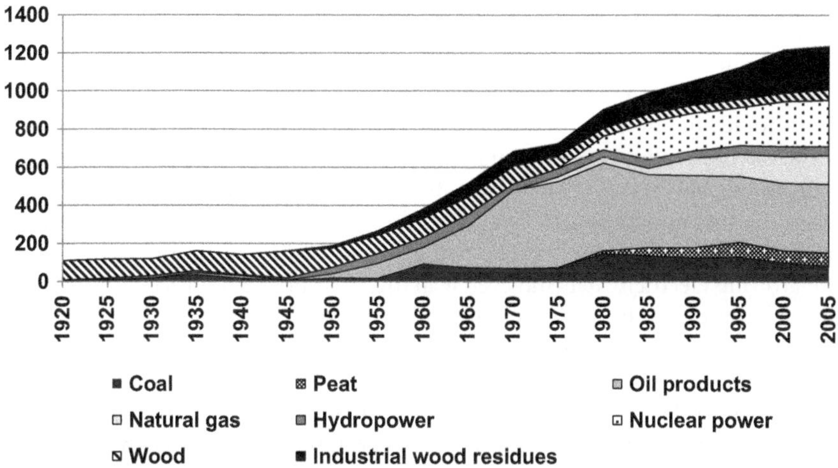

Figure 7.2 Supply of Military Personnel in Finland, 1920–2005

Source: Luukkanen, Vehmas, Karjalainen, & Panula-Ontto, 2009: 20 (from 1920 to 1965); Statistics Finland's PX-Web Databases, http://pxweb2.stat.fi/database/StatFin/ene/ehk/ehk_en.asp (from 1970 to 2005)

relate to public regulation. Simply put, energy systems are like intersections where public regulation, utilities' self-regulation, and markets meet. We investigate whether common principles can be identified, such as convergence, or clearly distinguishable characteristics in some periods as to the regulatory trajectories in Japan and Finland in the post-war era.

Politicians have a range of policies at their disposal, including command-and-control measures and incentive-based measures (Cato, 2011, p. 119). Although conventional textbooks often divide these measures – and in legal and administrative terms, these measures may have to be separated – in this chapter, incentives, for example taxation, feed-in tariffs (FITs), investment aid, and, with some reservations, even public R&D funding are considered as part of the broad concept of public regulation.

Finally, it is appropriate to ask whether it is meaningful to compare the evolution and spillovers of energy policies and public regulation between such different and distant cultures and economies. We argue that comparisons between countries other than just adjacent countries can be meaningful and definitely fruitful. In fact, Japan and Finland pursued the same goals after the Second World War: fast economic growth and equal geographical distribution of wealth and welfare. In spite of many differences, they also had much in common, including the long-term and special relationship with the Allied Powers (Japan with the United States and Finland with the USSR), the great importance of the energy-intensive industries, and the record economic growth in the second half of the twentieth century.

This chapter is divided into five sections. We have distinguished three periods, which creates the basis for the chronological order used in the study. Although certain turning points determine the beginning and ending of a period, interconnections are characteristic of the periods. Thus, what started in one period could continue in the next period(s), even relatively unchanged. Our periodization should, in any case, be considered as a useful tool to render the changes visible to the reader, not as an inflexible and strict dividing line.

In the second section, we analyse the period which began in the late 1940s, when the fuel import restrictions were lifted. Both Japan and Finland faced the fact that the existing power-producing capacity would not be enough to satisfy the growing electricity demand even if all the hydropower resources were utilized in the near future. In addition, conventional energy sources, coal in Japan and wood in Finland, began to lose their price competitiveness against oil, which had significant implications for a very long time. In this chapter, we address the fuel policies of Japan and Finland in the 1950s and 1960s and the consequences of the increasing dependence on oil for energy security. During this period, a novel electricity generation technology, nuclear power plants, arrived on the energy policy scene. We elucidate why the Japanese and Finnish energy policy decision makers promoted nuclear power and how it affected conceptions of cost-effective energy production.

The period analysed in the second section ended at the beginning of the 1970s, when the first Oil Crisis hit the Japanese and Finnish economies. In the third section, we scrutinise the energy policy changes after the Oil Crises of the 1970s, which had far-reaching consequences pertaining to energy self-sufficiency and energy efficiency. This period, which ended in the early 1990s as a result of the tightening of environmental regulations and the restructuring of the energy markets, was characterised by a more comprehensive energy policy, more diverse energy systems, the environmental awakening, and nascent deregulation processes. This period was also defined by significant political and financial support for nuclear power.

In the fourth section, our focus is on the period of big energy policy shifts from the early 1990s to the present day. We examine whether the convergence in climate policy led to convergence in energy policy and, altogether, how Japan and Finland adapted to the changes in the global energy and climate policy context.

Our research is based on the methods of comparative and contextual analysis. In addition, we use quantitative methods for tracing the evolution of energy supply and demand, energy self-sufficiency, energy efficiency, oil and electricity dependency, energy intensity, and CO_2 intensity. As sources, we use energy statistics, public primary source documents, and research literature. This chapter attempts no comprehensive study of the developments of the Japanese and Finnish energy policies and energy systems from the 1940s to the beginning of the 2010s. Rather than concentrating on details, we wish to elucidate the general developments in these matters.

From the reconstruction to the first oil crisis, 1945–1973

From the 1940s to the 1970s, both the Japanese and Finnish energy consumption and production structures underwent remarkable changes, after which the whole energy system became more complex and also vulnerable. The growth in energy consumption continued apace, especially in the 1960s: in 1960, total primary energy supply (TPES) per population (ton of oil equivalent [toe] per capita) was 0.87 and 2.20 in Japan and Finland, respectively, and in 1972 it was as much as 2.70 and 4.20 in Japan and Finland, respectively. (The calculations were made on the basis of the OECD's Energy Balances.) Most of the energy demand was met by imported oil, at a price of around 2 to 3 US$ per barrel in those days (see Table 7.1). In Finland, oil was mostly imported from the USSR, and its price was based on the clearing trade and payment system.

Industry accounted for the majority of the energy consumption from the 1940s to the 1970s. Generally speaking, there were barriers to improvements in energy efficiency in all sectors, including low oil prices from the mid-1950s to the late 1960s, limited knowledge about the environmental impacts of energy production, and the overall notions of the energy as a fuel for economic success and increasing welfare. The correlation between economic growth and the growth of energy consumption seemed obvious and natural in the 1950s and the 1960s, affecting the ways in which energy was interpreted, valued, and discussed.

In this context, it was essential for the energy policy makers to contemplate measures which would keep the wheels of business turning and secure the supply of fuels and electricity for industries, households, and transportation. The energy issue was something of a concoction of economic, industrial, and security policies and adaptation to the rapid growth in energy demand. Environmental concerns did not really fit into this picture, although they gained importance as of the late 1960s as a consequence of the emergence of the environmental movements and the increasing knowledge about the environmental impacts of the use of fossil fuels.

Public regulation was targeted at maintaining a cheap fuel and power supply, since dependence on imports increased dramatically from the mid-1950s in both Japan and Finland (see Table 7.1). Most importantly for the future, imported oil became the main source of energy. Even before that, the use of solid domestic fuels had declined sharply. This was a result not only of the low prices of imported energy but also of a lack of incentive-based measures and the mistrust of investors regarding domestic fuel production.

In Japan, the coal mining industry was heavily subsidised in the early post–1945 period, but since it became clear in the late 1940s that the country's weakness in export competitiveness was due to the high cost of domestic coal and steel, it was in those sectors that rationalisation plans were first laid (IEEJ, 1986). Reduced demand for coal and fierce competition from oil forced the closure of 140 coal mines between 1952 and 1954. In the late 1950s, the Japanese governments decided to make oil the country's primary source of fuel (Garside, 2005, pp. 187–91). In Finland, the state's price guarantee scheme for sod peat, which was used as a fuel for railway engines and small boilers, ended in Finland in 1953. Most peat-producing companies did not survive, and the use of peat as a fuel declined in the 1950s and 1960s (Ruuskanen, 2010, pp. 35, 88–9).

Although the growing dependence on oil imports perturbed Japanese and Finnish authorities in the late 1950s and the 1960s, influential policies to reduce oil dependency were not implemented before the shock of the Arab oil embargo of 1973. When the dependence on oil imports increased, the authorities' main aim was to secure the supply of oil and petroleum products through long-term contracts with the key suppliers, stockpiling regulations, and, on the other hand, by controlling the downstream oil market. Both the Japanese and Finnish oil refining regulations from the late 1950s to the early 1990s could be seen as protectionist. In Japan, only domestic oil companies were allowed to build and own oil refineries, which prevented Western oil companies from entering the Japanese petrochemical business (R. Clarke & Edwards, 1998, pp. 129–30). In Finland, only a state-owned oil company, Neste Oy (established in 1948), was granted licences to import crude oil and thus obtained a monopoly in the petrochemical business (Kuisma, 1997, pp. 451–60). The Japanese and Finnish downstream oil and natural gas markets remained strictly regulated until the beginning of the 1990s.

In addition to the oil and petroleum products supply, the supply security of electricity was among the state's major strategic areas. Reliance on electricity constantly increased in the industrial, service, and household sectors, underlining the importance of sufficient power-generating capacity.

Although the Japanese and Finnish electricity sectors differed, there were clear similarities as to the policies on the security of electricity supply. In both countries, the degree of governmental control over the power utilities was extensive from the 1940s to the early 1990s. In Japan, where the electricity industry was reorganised in 1951 and based on the state-regulated, privately owned monopoly utilities, thereby consisting of nine regional utilities, the Ministry of International Trade and Industry (in those days MITI) had to approve the utilities' tariffs on the basis of rate of return regulation. In addition, the government decided to establish a state-owned power utility, the Electric Power Development Company (also known as J-Power) in 1952 to augment electricity supplies nationwide at a time when the regional utilities did not have sufficient financial capacity to meet the electricity demand. J-Power built transmission lines as well as power stations and operated more than 50 power stations. The regional power utilities, however, accounted for more than 80 per cent of Japan's electricity-generating capacity and owned almost all the transmission lines. Transmission links between the utilities were quite poorly developed, which was due in part to the originality of the Japanese grid, being divided into two grids – that is, a 50-hertz German-model system in the East and a 60-hertz US–model system in the West. (Kibune & Kudo, 1996, pp. 93–4).

The Electric Utility Industry Law (1964) regulated the Japanese power utilities so that it became difficult for a newcomer to enter the electricity market. The law favoured big actors by requiring that a licenced power company should own enough capacity to meet the demand in its area. This essentially prevented the establishment of competing utilities in the regional electricity market. Joint research projects and grid cooperation among regional utilities also strengthened monopolistic tendencies in the Japanese electricity markets (Kibune & Kudo, 1996, pp. 94–5).

The US influence was quite significant in the formation of the post-war Japanese electricity sector, while the Finnish electricity sector converged with those of Sweden and Norway, and, with some reservations, the Austrian electricity sector. In Finland, the 'Three Big Ones', that is, the state-owned power companies, the industry's power companies, and the municipally owned utilities, comprised the electricity sector after the 1940s. The state's role strengthened at the same time as massive capital was needed to pursue the harnessing of the Northern rapids and, as a prerequisite for this, erect 220 kV and 400 kV transmission lines from the sparsely populated North to the industrialised and more densely populated South and West. The leading state-owned power utilities Imatran Voima Oy, Oulujoki Oy, and Kemijoki Oy in the 1950s and 1960s obtained an advantage over their privately owned competitors regarding the hydropower plans for the River Oulujoki and the River Kemijoki. In addition, Imatran Voima Oy had a monopoly in 400 kV transmission lines and in electricity imports and exports. The utility also set wholesale tariffs for electricity and charged transfer fees for the electricity fed into its grid by other suppliers.

As for the question of the similarities and differences of the Japanese and Finnish energy policies from the 1940s to the early 1970s, at any rate, the main trends in public regulation were defined by the convergence. On the whole, the state's control over the energy system increased. This nevertheless can be seen as a global trend in the industrialised capitalist countries (Hausman,

Hertner, & Wilkins, 2008). Import and production quotas, politically motivated licences, price tariffs approved by the key ministries, restrictions on foreign direct investments, limited access to the grid, and state control over the downstream oil and natural gas market characterised the developments in Japan and Finland until the 1970s.

From the first oil crisis to the threshold of the restructuring of the energy and climate policies

Four major social, economic, and environmental issues complicated the status quo of the energy policy in Japan and Finland from the beginning of the 1970s. In the first half of the decade, the most topical of these issues was the Arab oil embargo of 1973 and 1974 and its drastic impact on oil prices. Since the Japanese and Finnish societies were so heavily reliant on oil imports, the rising oil price affected the industry's competitiveness and general price level and seemed to fuel the economic recession.

The second major energy policy issue was poor energy efficiency, which was approached from different perspectives in Japan and Finland. In Japan, the undesirable correlation between the increasing energy consumption and environmental pollution likewise gave rise to this debate (see Table 7.2).

The following major energy policy issue, nuclear power, was also linked to the notions about the industry's and economy's competitiveness, although it also became a question which was involved with several concerns. At the time of the first oil crisis, however, nuclear energy represented a solution to air pollution problems, particularly in Japan, where the air quality in the major cities was poor. Yet it is important to note that the Japanese nuclear power plans

Table 7.2 Energy elasticity in Japan and Finland, 1960–2007

	Japan	*Finland*
1960–1973	1.16	1.26
1973–1979	0.46	0.80
1979–1985	0.16	0.48
1985–1990	0.84	0.60
1990–2000	1.38	0.63
2000–2007	–0.07	0.63

E > 1 More energy growth than GDP growth, efficiency decline

0 < E < 1 less energy growth than GDP growth, efficiency improvement

E < 0 negative energy growth

Source: Authors' own calculations based on the following databases: EDMC, 2012; OECD, 2010b

Note: Energy elasticity is defined as the quotient of the growth rate of energy consumption divided by the GDP growth rate.

were already accelerated in the late 1960s, resulting in 20 nuclear power plant construction orders between 1965 and 1972 (see e.g. JAIF, 2006).

The latest issue was the rising environmental concern. It was first associated with local problems arising from the environmental impacts of reservoirs and oil refineries, but from the early 1980s, it took a new twist as awareness of the acidifying emissions and climate impacts of the energy production increased. In Japan, the most important epoch as regards air pollution related to the Yokkaichi disease caused by the petrochemical processing facilities and refineries from 1960 to 1972 (see e.g. De Vos, 1984).

The oil price spike in the early 1970s was not exactly a complete surprise for the authorities in the OECD countries. Indeed, Japanese and Finnish authorities had already sought alternatives to oil before the first Oil Crisis, but plans were hardly implemented except for starting construction on the first nuclear power plants. Far-reaching plans to cut down dependence on oil in the generation of power and heat were more thoroughly debated and executed after 1973. As for the measures, Japanese and Finnish energy policy trajectories began to diverge due to different ways of approaching the arduous task. As regards the end, being less dependent on oil fuels, energy policy convergence between Japan and Finland continued, however. In particular, the policy convergence occurred in relation to nuclear power, which was regarded and promoted as a safe, modern, and profitable way of generating electricity.

The oil crises of the 1970s and the awareness of the risks inherent in import dependence stimulated the use of domestic primary energy sources. In Japan, the governmental Sunshine Project (1974–1990) was planned to develop the utilisation of renewable energy, coal gasification, and hydrogen energy. This programme already achieved success in the 1980s. Nevertheless, in large-scale electricity generation, renewable energy sources could not replace fossil fuels and nuclear energy (Kurokawa & Ikki, 2001, pp. 457–9; Watanabe, 1995, pp. 238, 40–8).

In Finland, the governments also allocated R&D funds and devised policies to address the threat of oil dependence and weakening energy self-sufficiency. The use of milled peat was fostered as early as 1971 by a governmental plan for peat fuel production, aiming at an annual production of 10 million m^3 by 1980 by the state-owned State Fuel Office (established in 1945). In 1974, the State Fuel Office's peat production target was doubled. Consequently, numerous inland combined heat and power plants and district heating plants shifted from the use of heavy oil or coal to the use of milled or sod peat. The share of peat in primary energy consumption rose from almost zero to almost 6 per cent by the early 1990s. The use of peat as a fuel enjoyed large governmental and also industrial support until the mid-1990s, when it was reassessed because of its high CO_2 emissions (Ruuskanen, 2010, pp. 36, 112–13, 85).

In Finland, biomass energy, on the contrary, did not easily achieve the same level of public support and investors' attention as peat. Actually, this was only achieved in the 1990s, when the GHG emission-mitigation schemes boosted the bioenergy plans, the economic and political significance of the pulp and paper industry decreased, and the governments devised incentives to foster the use of wood-based fuels in heat and power generation.

Even though alternative energy sources and technologies received more governmental attention after the early 1970s, power and heat generation merely switched from oil to other fossil fuels (see Figures 7.3 and 7.4). Furthermore,

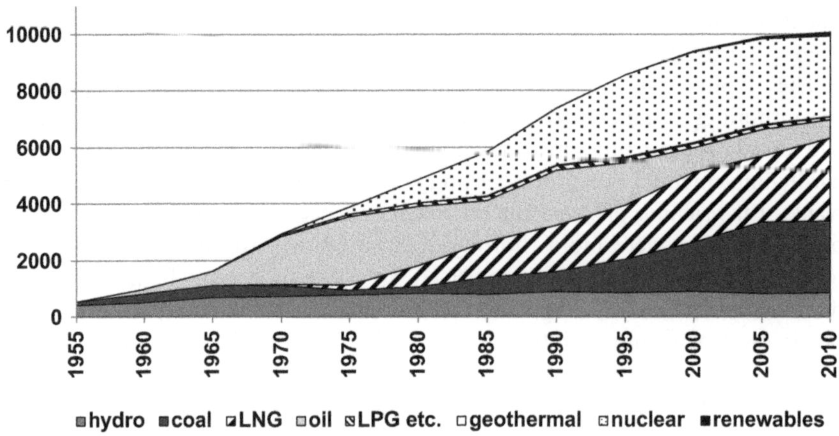

Figure 7.3 Distribution of electricity sources in Japan from 1955 to 2010 (Unit: 0.1 billion kWh)

Source: FEPC, 2011

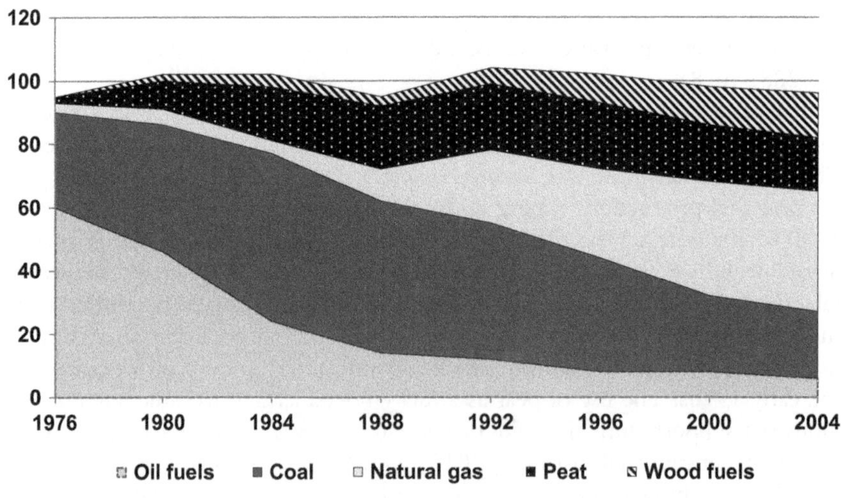

Figure 7.4. Fuels used in combined heat and power production in Finland 1976 to 2004

Source: Tarjanne & Kivistö, 2006, p. 8

in the 1970s, big power companies and industrial financiers favoured nuclear power due to the wide fluctuation in the variable costs of conventional condensing power plants. Investments in wind turbines, solar power plants, and geothermal power plants in Japan and in wind turbines in Finland were almost negligible before the 1990s.

In the long term, oil began to rule itself out of the primary power plant fuel market, owing to its price fluctuations. Nonetheless, petroleum products, that is kerosene in Japan and light oil fuel in Finland, maintained their position for longer in domestic heating as a result of relatively mild taxation of these fuels. As for the major trends, the energy self-sufficiency rate in Finland improved, while in Japan it continuously declined (see Table 7.1).

In addition to energy self-sufficiency, energy efficiency was also at a low level as a result of the developments in the 1950s and 1960s. Nonetheless, clear differences in the energy efficiency policies between Japan and Finland can be found. Japanese governments made energy efficiency a priority of the energy policy in the 1970s, aiming at reducing energy imports, air pollution mitigation, and innovations in energy-efficient technologies, whereas the Finnish governments registered the importance of these but did not impose stringent regulations or vigorous incentives before the late 1990s. In Finland, a large part of the energy-efficiency improvements in the 1990s was achieved through the industrial sector's far-reaching voluntary agreements.

In Japan, a governmental plan called the Moonlight Program was launched in 1978 to develop technologies which would conserve energy. This rather technology-oriented programme concentrated on innovations and their commercialisation. In regards to regulatory measures, the Law Concerning the Rational Use of Energy (1979) required more exacting energy efficiency standards in all sectors (see e.g. Zhang, Song, & Hamori, 2011). In many ways, Japan became a forerunner in energy efficiency, whereas Finland faced big challenges in this issue (see Table 7.2).

Even if Finland was not as ambitious as Japan concerning energy-efficiency policy in the 1970s and 1980s, its policies for promoting combined heat and power (CHP) generation through investment aid and low-cost public loans had salient indirect effects on energy efficiency. Naturally, not only energy policy measures and voluntary agreements in industry lifted the energy efficiency to a higher level. The whole issue needed to be reviewed in the context of the economic and industrial structures.

Nuclear energy became a strategic priority of both the Japanese and Finnish energy policies in the early 1970s in order to enhance independence from fossil fuels and capacity to produce affordable energy. The national nuclear energy programmes, however, dated back to the mid-1950s, when 'Atoms for Peace' raised worldwide expectations of limitless and inexpensive power generation (see e.g. Michelsen & Särkikoski, 2005; Shibata & Tomokiyo, 1999). In Japan, nuclear energy could also be considered to reduce reliance on energy imports owing to the commitment to a closed nuclear fuel (or plutonium) cycle (Pickett, 2002, p. 1338). Besides, it also related to the ambition of the post-war governments to have the potential to make an atomic bomb (Fujita, 2009). Finland, on the other hand, was totally dependent on imported nuclear fuel and nuclear technology.

Japanese and Finnish power companies invested heavily in nuclear power in the 1970s and 1980s. In 1970, Japan had only one commercial and two experimental reactors in operation; in 1993, there were 46 reactors accounting for 30 per cent of electricity production. Most of these reactors were constructed by privately owned monopolistic regional power utilities.

In Finland, the first nuclear power plant unit was connected to the grid in 1977 (Loviisa I), the second in 1978 (Olkiluoto I), and the third (Olkiluoto II) and the fourth (Loviisa II) in 1980. The Loviisa nuclear power plant was built by the state-owned power company Imatran Voima Oy, whereas the Olkiluoto nuclear power plant was erected by TVO Oy (1969), a nuclear power company owned by big forest industry companies, Imatran Voima Oy, and municipal electric utilities. By 1993, nuclear energy accounted for 32 per cent of the electricity production in Finland.

In both Japan and Finland, nuclear energy was promoted by various policies, including significant state R&D funds (in Japan and Finland), guaranteed regional monopoly (in Japan), and governmental subsidies for local governments in exchange for hosting a nuclear power plant (in Japan). In Japan, the constructions of the nuclear power plants were indirectly promoted through an electricity tax (Tax for Promotion of Power Resources), for about two thirds of the revenues from this tax have been spent on nuclear energy (Oshima, 2010). In Finland, the investment risk was alleviated through the Mankala principle. According to this principle, the owners of the so-called Mankala companies gain electricity in proportion to their ownership at a price lower than the price of electricity sold on the wholesale electricity market (Puikkonen, 2010).

Regarding the fourth major issue, environmental regulation became a salient force for change in the energy industry, at the latest in the 1980s. Before the 1970s, there were no effective flue-gas or water load regulations, but these were debated and implemented throughout the 1970s when more was known about the environmental impacts of energy production. The Japanese Basic Act for Environmental Pollution Control (1967), and especially its amendment in 1970, launched the beginning of real and serious antipollution policy. Effective transportation emissions regulations, however, were not implemented before the early 1990s. These policies had nothing to do with climate change but were measures which tackled the air pollution in the biggest Japanese cities.

In Finland in the 1970s and 1980s, the most intensive debate on the environmental impacts of energy production related to energy peat production and unharnessed rapids in Northern Finland. Environmentalists finally won the long struggle concerning the protection of free rapids when the Act on the Protection of Rapids was passed in 1987. This ended the power companies' plans to build new reservoirs in Northern rivers.

The restructuring of the electricity market and climate change mitigation in focus

While the Japanese and Finnish policy makers from the 1950s to the 1970s often looked for the cheapest possible way to secure the availability of the energy, the decision makers of the 1980s, 1990s, and 2000s had to contemplate the energy issue from a broader perspective. As of the early 1990s, the issues of the restructuring of the energy sector and CO_2 emissions reduction leapt to the top of the energy policy agenda worldwide. Despite the global convergence in relation with the jointly set GHG emission reduction targets and adaptation to the widespread economic trends in the liberalisation of the energy markets, the measures were often determined nationally.

Deregulation plans of the energy sector were already discussed in Japan and Finland in the 1980s, but they were not implemented before the 1990s and 2000s. Finland was among the forerunners in Europe in relation with the liberalisation of the retail and wholesale electricity markets, which took place in 1997. On the wholesale side, Finland, Norway, Sweden, and Denmark formed a single Nordic market area with a common power exchange system. As a part of the restructuring, the monopoly of Imatran Voima Oy in high-tension transmission lines and in electricity imports was ended in the early 1990s, and in 1995 a listed transmission system operator, Suomen Kantaverkko Oyj (since 1999, Fingrid Oyj), was established (on the liberalisation of the Finnish electricity market, see e.g. Glachant & Finon, 2003).

In Japan, the situation was quite different due to that country's special isolated geographic location. Japan was much more cautious about adopting the deregulation models in its own energy markets. The political pressure towards the restructuring of the power monopoly resulted from the appreciation of the yen in the 1990s, which impaired the competitiveness of the industry. In 1995, the wholesale generation market was opened to the Independent Power Producers (IPP), and in 1999, retail liberalisation was extended to cover extra-high-voltage customers. As a result of the amendments to the Electricity Business Act from 2003 to 2005, about 60 per cent of the electricity market was opened to competition, and a regulated third-party access to the networks as well as Japan Electric Power Exchange (JEPX) was established (Yamaguchi, 2009). The electricity transmission lines, however, remained in the ownership of the vertically integrated regional power utilities. Overall, the debate on further restructuring and unbundling settled after the California electricity crisis (2001), since the Japanese authorities wanted to avoid the risks of blackouts and to protect the economic interests of the power monopolies (on the restructuring of the Japanese electricity market, see e.g. Goto & Sueyoshi, 2009). The Japanese electricity sector remained highly concentrated, for in 2007, about 85 per cent of the country's installed generating capacity was owned by the monopolistic regional electric utilities. In Finland, the partly state-owned listed company Fortum Oyj and the industry-owned PVO Oy accounted in 2009 for about 65 per cent of the installed generating capacity.

Quite simultaneously with the restructuring of the electricity market, another challenge emerged and forced the policy makers to devise policies to tackle the question. This question was, of course, climate change. In 2008, Japan was the world's fifth-biggest emitter of CO_2, but considering per capita CO_2 emissions, it was under the OECD average. The per-capita CO_2 emissions of Finland in 2008 were slightly above the OECD average and clearly higher than in the other Scandinavian countries (see Table 7.3).

In the 2000s, approximately 90 per cent of Japan's GHG emissions were energy-related carbon dioxide. The emissions from the commercial and residential sectors increased from 1990 to 2005, while there were no major changes in the emissions from the industrial sector (Kyoto Protocol, 2008). In the 2000s, around 80 per cent of Finland's GHG emissions were energy related (Tilastokeskus, 2009). Historically, GHG emissions peaked especially in the 1960s and 1970s, after which they remained at a very high level (see Figure 7.5).

The Kyoto Protocol marked an epoch-making change in climate policy cooperation and coordination worldwide. Nonetheless, even if there were jointly set

Table 7.3 Per capita CO_2 emissions in selected OECD countries, 2008

Japan	Australia	Germany	France	Korea	Netherlands	UK
9.02	18.48	9.79	5.74	10.32	10.82	8.32
Finland	Denmark	Iceland	Norway	Sweden	USA	OECD Average
10.65	8.82	6.89	7.89	4.96	18.38	10.61

Source: IEA, 2010

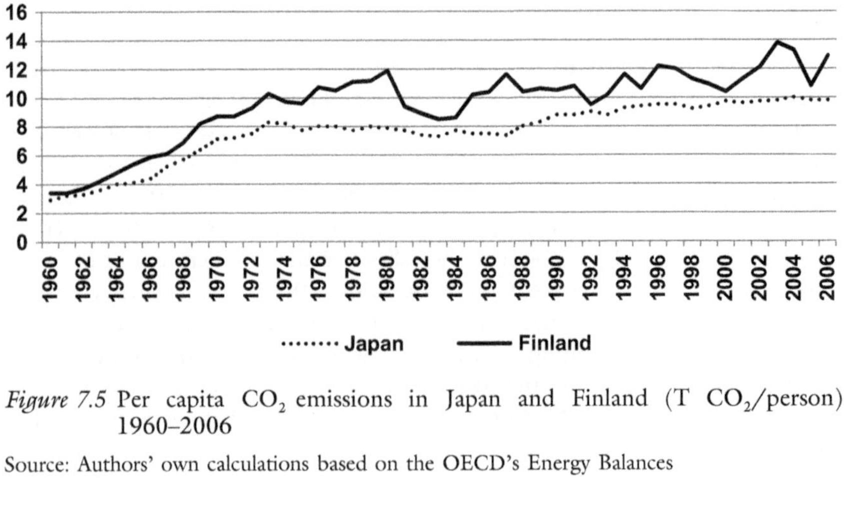

Figure 7.5 Per capita CO_2 emissions in Japan and Finland (T CO_2/person) 1960–2006

Source: Authors' own calculations based on the OECD's Energy Balances

policy goals on stabilizing GHG emissions, there was not necessarily convergence in energy policies owing to the contradictory policies and expectations in various countries and diverse historical realities in each country's energy systems (Kyoto Protocol, 2008).

Finland ratified the Protocol in 2002 and had a target to stabilize its emissions at 1990 levels (Kansallinen ilmastostrategia, 2001). As a member of the European Union (since 1995), Finland was bound to follow the Union's common climate policy, which was very ambitious in pursuit of a low-carbon economy.

Japan ratified the Kyoto Protocol in 2002 and was thus obligated to 6 per cent GHG emission reduction during the first commitment period. However, Japan did not succeed in implementing effective market-based energy policy instruments for climate change mitigation in the 2000s. Carbon surtaxes were discussed at the academic level, but they were not realised. As an example of the Japanese climate policy instruments, an emission trading scheme known as JVETS was launched in 2005, but it was not effective, as the scheme was voluntary and did not cover the major emitting industries. Plans for carbon taxes or a cap-and-trade scheme were shelved mostly due to opposition from the heavy industries. On the other hand, Japanese governments of the 2000s relied more on the industry's voluntary action plans and the promotion of nuclear energy in reducing air pollution and CO_2 emissions.

In the late 2000s, both the EU and Japan set even stricter targets in pursuit of a low-carbon economy. To meet their new GHG reduction targets and to enhance the competitive advantage of renewable energy, Finnish and Japanese governments followed the international trend to introduce feed-in tariffs, albeit quite slowly. So far, Japan had relied on subsidies and the voluntary net metering schemes of utility companies. A market-based Renewable Portfolio Standard Law (RPS law) was enacted in 2003, which imposed an annual obligation on electricity retailers to take a certain amount of their retail electricity from renewable sources. In fact, it limited the potential of renewables in Japan because the annual targets were very modest, around 1.3 to 1.6 per cent of the total electricity production excluding large-scale hydropower. METI (Ministry of Trade, Economy and Industry) did not want to introduce German-style feed-in tariffs, since these were opposed by the monopolistic utility companies. However, declining competitiveness of Japan's photovoltaic industry finally forced METI to introduce a feed-in tariff for solar energy in 2009. Moreover, the Japanese government decided to expand the feed-in tariff scheme to cover electricity from wind, biomass, small-scale hydro, and geothermal sources in August 2011 as a consequence of the energy policy redirection after the Fukushima Dai-ichi meltdown.

In Finland, feed-in tariffs for electricity produced from wind power, biogas, and wood-based fuels were introduced in 2011. Finnish governments had previously relied on fiscal instruments and investment aid schemes which were supported by the industry. In point of fact, the industry interest groups criticised the feed-in tariffs quite harshly until the late 2000s.

In Japan in the 2000s, the fastest-growing renewable energy sector was photovoltaic, in which the energy capacity was 3,618 MW in 2010 (third place worldwide). Installed wind power capacity was 2,304 MW in 2010 (twelfth place worldwide; GWEC, 2010; IEA-PVPS, 2010). In Finland, the greatest expectations were on biomass energy, which already accounted for about 22 per cent of total energy consumption in 2008.

In Japan and Finland, the Kyoto targets also hastened plans to increase the share of nuclear energy in power generation. A decade earlier (1991), the Finnish parliament had decided to exclude the construction of additional nuclear power plant units from the national energy strategy as a result of the growing antinuclear movement. Nonetheless, in the 2000s, both Japanese and Finnish energy and climate strategies on emissions reduction largely relied on the prospect of increasing the use of nuclear energy. In addition, nuclear energy was considered a way to lessen the reliance on the fuel imports and, as to Finland, the dependence on electricity imports from Russia (around 10 TWh per year in the 2000s).

In 2005, the Finnish government granted TVO Oy a construction licence for a fifth nuclear power plant in Finland. In Japan, the government's Basic National Energy Plan 2010 introduced a vision to significantly increase the share of nuclear energy. Fourteen new reactors were to be built, and the share of nuclear power generation was designed to cover 53 per cent of electricity production by 2030. The METI classified nuclear power as a sort of 'zero-emission power source' along with renewable energy sources. Nevertheless, after the Fukushima Dai-ichi meltdown, this plan was revealed to be completely utopian, and Prime Minister Yoshihiko Noda announced that it would be terminated.

Both the Japanese and Finnish nuclear energy plans in the 2000s were based on inaccurate estimates of the real costs and time spent on a nuclear power plant design and construction in the 2000s. Once the estimates had been proved incorrect, the price of electricity from nuclear power would be something entirely different from what was presented as a basis for the decision making.

The third unit of Olkiluoto in Finland, being the first unit in Western Europe under construction at the time of the liberalised electricity market, can be seen as an example of a 'nuclear dream' which became almost an economic fiasco with multiplied costs and delayed completion. At the time when the turnkey contract between Areva and TVO Oy was signed, the total costs were estimated to be 3.2 billion euros, but in 2013 the cost estimate was between 8 and 8.5 billion euros in total (*Aamulehti* 2013). The power plant should have been completed in 2009, but according to the estimates, it will not be connected to the grid before 2016 (*YLE Uutiset* 2013; *Talouselämä* 2013). Moreover, in 2010, the Finnish government decided to take a decision-in-principle for two new reactors, which was approved by parliament in the same year. The decisions-in-principle concerned TVO Oy and Fennovoima Oy.

The decisions of the Finnish and Japanese governments in the 2000s reflected the widespread institutionalised notions that nuclear power would be reliable and the most cost-effective way to generate power and the fastest way to reduce GHG emissions. These notions have been proved debatable. It has been calculated that in Japan, historically, the total cost of the electricity from nuclear power plants was higher than the price of the electricity from thermal power plants (Oshima, 2010). Furthermore, investments in nuclear power in the 2000s did not reduce the import dependence or GHG emissions as was expected. In fact, the Japanese electricity appetite was met by increasing consumption of coal in the 2000s.

Naturally, the Fukushima Dai-ichi meltdown has caused an intense debate in Japan concerning the future of its nuclear dependence and the political power of the 'Nuclear Village', the pro-nuclear camp inside society. At least it is known that the social and economic bill of the Fukushima disaster will be huge.

Conclusion

The post-war history of the Japanese and Finnish energy systems can be divided into three ostensibly different yet interrelated phases. The first of these was an era ruled by the ever-increasing use of liquid oil fuels, having an obviously detrimental effect on energy self-sufficiency. The growing dependence on oil imports was allowed to continue as long as an abundant supply of cheap oil epitomised the world's energy markets. The second phase began as a consequence of an external shock which was, predictably, connected to the growing oil appetite worldwide. The first Oil Crisis of 1973 made way for plans for reducing oil dependence and enhancing energy efficiency. Whereas Japanese governments relied on energy-efficiency plans, Finnish governments initiated incentives to promote the use of domestic solid fuels, thereby raising the level of energy self-sufficiency.

Despite the aforementioned differences, both countries committed to the increasing use of nuclear power. In a way, nuclear power represented a solution to reduce the use of oil in power generation, but first and foremost, it related to the older plans to be at the forefront in the peaceful uses of the atom and its attractive prospects for finding a limitless source of power.

In Japan and Finland, the energy system became more diverse, but nevertheless the market concentration remained unchanged. The Japanese wholesale and retail electricity markets were dominated by the regional monopolies, while in Finland the retail electricity market was a natural monopoly of the regional power and heating utilities, and the wholesale electricity market was dominated by both state-backed and industry-backed power companies until the mid-1990s.

The third phase took shape in the early 1990s, when the conventional practices were replaced by new objectives. Environmental protection became an increasingly binding policy, climate change mitigation goals were adopted for the first time, and the popularity of the deregulation theories grew among the decision makers. In Japan, the major changes were the ratification of the Kyoto Protocol and the partial restructuring of the electricity market in the 2000s. In Finland, the electricity market had been fully liberalised and opened to foreign companies since the mid-1990s; the wholesale electricity market became common with those of the other Nordic countries at the end of the 1990s; and climate policy and the Kyoto targets were steered by the EU and its ETS scheme in the 2000s. Both the Japanese and the Finnish governments planned to scale up the share of nuclear power in electricity production in the 2000s and relied on the rhetoric which repeated the notions of the security, affordability, and necessity of nuclear power to meet the challenges of a warming climate and unsteady economic competitiveness.

To answer the questions posed at the beginning of this chapter, we now contemplate how the events introduced in the previous chapters apply to the themes of the convergence, divergence, and persistence of cultures. Firstly, several convergence mechanisms can be traced, related for example to the harmonisation of domestic practices by means of international legal agreements and commitments, the interdependent but uncoordinated diffusion of practices by means of cross-national imitation, emulation or learning (Busch & Jörgens, 2005), or the adaptation to external crises. In this context, it is uncertain whether one can draw a conclusion on convergence between Japan and Finland, since the changes were often supranational. On the face of it, Japanese and Finnish oil policies between the 1950s and 1960s and soon after the first Oil Crisis seemed to converge, but in fact both countries just followed the paths that were typical in other capitalistic industrial nations. In addition, the monopolistic tendency and increasing state control did not characterise only the Japanese and Finnish energy sectors from the late 1940s to the 1980s. Such transnational common practices can be found elsewhere: tight control of the downstream oil sector, FDI restrictions, and state price regulation, among others.

It is thus of the utmost importance to scrutinise the question of convergence in a context in which specifically Japan and Finland converged despite the trends among the industrialised capitalistic nations (see Table 7.4). This underlines their cultural characteristics and cultural persistence.

Having scrutinised the selected energy policy issues, the two countries may be considered to differ from other nations in terms of (1) commitment to

Table 7.4 Comparison of Japanese and Finnish energy policy issues

Selected energy policy issues	*Japan*	*Finland*
Power monopolies, 1950–1990	Prevalent	Prevalent
Oil dependence, 1950–1970	High	High
Nuclear dependence, 1970–2010	High	High
Energy efficiency targets, 1970–2000	Extensive	Moderate
Contribution of renewables in TPES	Low	Moderate
Energy self-sufficiency, 1970–2010	Low	Moderate
Deregulation of energy sector, 1990–2010	Moderate	Extensive
ETS schemes	National	Supranational
Implementation of FIT before 2010	Negligible	Negligible

nuclear power in the long run and (2) weak commitment to FIT schemes in the 1990s and the 2000s.

A particularly interesting period regarding these issues was the one between the 1990s and 2000s. In the 2000s, there were actually no new initiated nuclear power programmes or plausible political plans to introduce new reactors among the OECD countries except in Japan, Finland, the Czech Republic, France, Korea, Poland, Turkey, and the UK (Schneider, Froggatt, & Thomas, 2011). The 'nuclear renaissance', a misleading catchphrase coined by the supporters of nuclear power, was to come true mostly in China, Russia, India, and Eastern Europe, where the wholesale electricity markets were defined by state-backed power monopolies or a single-buyer model. Having taken into account the countries with liberalised or partly restructured wholesale electricity markets in the 2000s, Finland and Japan were very rare exceptions among the nations committed so strongly to nuclear power. Beyond that, they were also rare exceptions of market economies without binding commitments to feed-in tariff (FIT) or renewable energy certificate (REC) schemes before the end of the 2000s.

Certain economic, legal, and political support mechanisms benefiting nuclear power can be traced in Japan and Finland. In Japan, enormous sums of money were allocated for subsidising the communes that approved and permitted the nuclear power plants in their areas, and electricity tax revenues were likewise targeted largely at the nuclear power industry in order to maintain the existing infrastructure. In Finland, it can be assumed that large-scale willingness for nuclear power investments in industry and the municipal power companies would not have occurred in the 2000s without the existence of the so-called 'Mankala principle', which created a way to bypass seasonal electricity price fluctuations that are typical in the conditions of the Nordic Power Exchange. Beyond that, antinuclear opposition was historically relatively weak in Japan and Finland. As a consequence of the economic benefit achieved through nuclear power siting permits, peripheral municipalities were actually eager to commit to the construction of plants.

It is a matter of debate, albeit an essential one, whether one can describe the aforementioned nuclear-driven paths as convergence or the cultural persistence. We tend to consider that the issue is more one of cultural persistence, so that the enthusiasm for nuclear power in Japan and Finland in a sense reflected enduring cultural structures, such as the notion about the manufacturing industries as a source of prosperity, the ideal of the pursuit of fast economic growth, faith in technology, trust in authorities and the technical sciences, and the influence of so-called clientela relationships in society (Averyt, 1975). Instead of emphasising the issue of convergence, it may be more fruitful to discuss why both Japan and Finland made very similar decisions in relation to nuclear power and FIT schemes. This issue provides an excellent case for in-depth comparison between the Japanese and Finnish cultures and societies. The causes of Japan's and Finland's high nuclear dependence, its economic, political, and societal ramifications, and rhetorical premises form a relevant subject for further research.

8 The financial crisis of the 1990s in Finland and Japan

Kari Heimonen, Shigeyoshi Miyagawa, and Yoji Morita

Introduction[1]

Financial bubbles have plagued most countries around the world in the past century, including the United States, the United Kingdom, Germany, Australia, Japan, and the Nordic countries, as well as the emerging economies in Latin America and Asia. Irrespective of the geographic location of the country, the boom-bust cycles have traditionally followed a rather similar path: expansion of bank lending following financial market deregulation, major inflows of foreign capital during the boom, positive international business-cycle developments, a sharp turn in the economic development, a rapid turn in the capital flows from inflow to outflow, speculative currency attacks, and finally major banking crises. Typically the crises were in part triggered by an external shock, but bad institutions and bad economic policies also played an important role in the emergence of the boom-bust cycle. Moreover, the boom-bust cycles were not related solely to the financial market of the economy; the actual economic conditions played an important role in the sequence and severity of the events in the boom-bust cycle.

This chapter focuses on the Japanese and Finnish crises of 1992 and 1991, respectively, both of which appear on the list of severest financial crises in recent economic history. Reinhart and Rogoff (2008) placed them in the group of the Big Five financial crises in the industrialized countries (Reinhart & Rogoff, 2008). The Japanese crisis of 1992 marked the beginning of the severe and long-lasting decrease in Japanese output, known as the lost decade. Finland experienced a crisis which was the most severe in an industrialized country since the 1930s, and it was more serious than those in the other Nordic countries (Jonung, Kiander, & Vartia, 2009; Jonung, Söderström, & Stymne, 1996; Kindleberger & Aliber, 2011). Irrespective of certain differences between these two crises in Japan and Finland, they shared many features and sequences typical of boom-bust cycles.

The financial crises in Japan and Finland can both be attributed to banking crises. Typical factors behind the banking crises were explicit deposit insurance and financial liberalization (moral hazard problem; see e.g. Demirgüc-Kunt & Detragiache, 1998; Hutchinson & McDill, 1999a; Kaminsky & Reinhart, 1996).

Banking crises were affected by macroeconomic factors such as a sharp fall in GDP growth and a fall in stock prices (see e.g. Hutchison & McDill, 1999a). All these factors were behind both the Japanese and Finnish crises.

These two crises are also very similar in many other ways. Financial market deregulation played a major role in both countries, marking the opening of an economic boom. During the financial deregulation, credit expanded significantly and resulted in bank lending reaching record highs (Cargill, Hutchison, & Itō, 2000; Shigemi, 1995; Tarkka, 1988). There is a sharp contrast to the situation before the deregulation. In Finland, the credit market was highly regulated and there was a continuous excess demand for loans. In both Finland and Japan, banks dominated the financial system. The company bond and the stock market had a relatively small role to play in the financial intermediation. Household savings were mostly channelled through the banks to finance business investments. The lending and borrowing interest rates were relatively low and inflation was moderate. Especially in Finland, real interest rates were occasionally even negative, which increased the excess demand for loans and overinvestments (Pohjola, 1996). Both in Japan and in Finland, the birth of the vibrant bond markets both at home and abroad was one of the key issues in the liberalization process. It is noteworthy that in both countries, the options for bank borrowers opened up much faster than the options for savers.

The deregulation of the financial market enabled bank lending to increase and meet the demand. In Finland, before the deregulation, the problem was an excess demand for loans. In Japan, the lending was increased, since due to the deregulation, the banks got into trouble while losing many of their best borrowers, the large companies. The Japanese banks had to find new customers. There was an increase in small-business lending and in lending to the real estate industry (Hoshi & Kashyap, 2000). As a result, the total bank lending increased and asset and property prices soared.

One important factor behind the Japanese and Finnish bubbles is the financial accelerator process. The key factor behind the mechanism is the price of the collateral (Bernanke, Gertler, & Gilchrist, 1999). The mechanism started to operate to an extent not previously experienced in the Nordic countries or Japan. In effect, this process enhanced the capability of firms and households to borrow more and more funds. Together with the credit expansion, asset prices started to increase. Higher asset prices increased the value of the collateral, which further boosted the demand for loans and investments. The leverage cycle came into effect (Geanakoplos, 2010). In Finland, this process was further accelerated due to the tax policy. Among others, interest rate payments on mortgages were tax deductible. During the boom, the leverage became too high. In Japan, the tax on land holding is relatively lighter than on land transaction. The distortion of the tax system on land worked to promote the increase of land prices.

Eventually, the boom came to an end. Now the leverage cycle and financial accelerator process worked the other way round. The value of collateral decreased, causing serious problems for indebted firms and households. Banks and creditors required even higher collateral as a result of the unstable economic conditions and falling asset prices. The leverage was too low during the recession and after the bubble burst.

The leverage cycle was especially severe in Japan and in Finland. Among the bubble-bust advanced economies, Finland and Japan experienced record high fluctuation in asset prices, house, land, and stock prices. The Finnish figures were the highest among the Nordic countries. Japan had 275.6 per cent stock price increase from August 1982 to August 1987. Finland experienced a 291 per cent increase of its stock price index from September 1982 to September 1987.

The booms of the Japanese and Finnish economies were strong, and the busts had serious consequences. The negative effects of the leverage cycle were accentuated in Finland due to a currency mismatch in assets and liabilities. Due to the deregulation of the foreign exchange market, firms were able to borrow in foreign currency. Foreign currency loans had a lower nominal interest rate than loans in domestic currency but were subject to an exchange rate risk. Small firms in the domestic sector did not fully understand the consequences of the exchange rate risk, since the Bank of Finland was committed to a fixed exchange rate, a target zone exchange rate with a fixed band. Finally, the Bank of Finland was forced to realign the currency band. The large realignment of the target-zone exchange rate caused a devaluation of the Finnish *markka*. This increased the value of foreign currency–denominated loans, whereas the value of the collateral remained the same and furthermore decreased gradually due to the domestic economic downturn. The currency mismatch in loans and assets further deteriorated the creditors' financial position. As a result, the bursting of the bubble caused an increase in the number of nonperforming loans in the banking system. This hampered the banking system and impaired its ability for financial intermediation. Problems in financial intermediation also had serious negative effects on the economy as a whole. As a result, the Finnish economic crisis in 1991 was the most severe peacetime recession in Finnish history: Finland's GDP dropped about 14 per cent from its peak in 1990 through 1993. In 1993, investments fell to 55 per cent of their 1990 level. Value added in the private sector fell about 20 per cent below trend. At the same time, the stock market lost about 60 per cent of its value, and in 1994, unemployment rose from 3 to 20 per cent.

In part, the bubble-bust pattern of the Finnish economy was related to the developments in the aggregate economy. However, the most common factor behind the bubble-bust episodes was the instability of the financial sector. Eventually the performance of the economy started to gradually improve as the realignment of the exchange rate evaluation restored the price competitiveness of the tradable sector of the Finnish economy. Subsequently, the economy as a whole started to recover.

The Japanese economy was on the verge of a financial panic, especially in 1997 and 1998, when major financial institutions failed. The Nordic countries and Finland experienced the same financial distress around 1990. On the other hand, the Nordic countries successfully achieved renewed economic growth, while in Japan the recession was prolonged. The crisis hit the Finnish economy particularly hard, yet the recovery from the slump was particularly rapid. In Japan, the banks' return on assets continued to decline. The banks fell into a spiral, and even after the crises, the number of nonperforming loans remained persistently high.

This chapter focuses on the background factors behind the boom-bust cycles in Japan and Finland. We review the major economic developments before and after the bursting of the financial bubble in both countries chronologically. Moreover, we survey the determinants of the economic bubble, evaluate the reasons for the bursting of the bubble, and describe the post-bubble events in these economies. In addition, we discuss both the similarities as well as differences between the Japanese and Finnish boom-bust cycles. Finally, we ponder on the lessons to be learned from these two crises.

The Nordic economies in crisis: the case of Finland

All the Nordic countries experienced a rapid increase in credit from 1985 onwards due to financial deregulation. An increase in credit generated an asset market boom in Finland, Sweden, and Norway. Finally the bubble burst and those countries experienced a fall in asset prices in the years around 1990. However, not all the Nordic countries experienced a boom and bust in asset prices. The boom in asset prices was much less severe in Denmark than in the other Nordic countries.

Finland serves as an instructive and extreme example of the Nordic crises. The seeds of the Finnish crisis lay deep in the structure of the Finnish economy. A fixed but adjustable exchange rate regime and a highly restricted capital market before the deregulation both created the framework for the Finnish macroeconomic policy until the 1980s. The Finnish inflation-devaluation cycle prevailing before the 1990s is often characterized using the Scandinavian inflation model, such as the EFO model (Edgren, Faxén, & Odhner, 1969). The inflation-devaluation spiral featured in the EFO model had its effects on both the real and financial side of the economy. Typically, the Scandinavian inflation model had its roots in the centralized wage bargaining system and the prominent role of the open sector in the economy. The increase in productivity in the open sector far exceeded the increase in productivity in the closed economy sector. As a result of the central wage-setting procedure, real wages also increased in the closed economy sector following the export sector. This depreciated the real exchange rate. The prices of domestic goods increased relative to those of foreign goods. This process also known as a Balassa–Samuelson effect (Balassa, 1964; Samuelson, 1964). Gradually the country ran repeatedly into current account deficits and lost its foreign exchange reserves and price competitiveness. The unemployment rate started to increase and government balance went into deficit. As a result of this (kind of) process, Finland ended up with successive devaluations (García-Iglesias & Kilponen, 2006). The strategy was possible since the exchange rate regime was fixed but adjustable, and Finnish interest rates, credit markets, and capital flows were strictly regulated. This left hardly any room for speculative attacks. Moreover, a relatively rapid inflation, a regulated interest rate, and lending enabled a negative interest rate. This favoured the creditors.

Due to the higher inflation, eventually devaluations became inevitable. However, speculative attacks were quite rare, mainly because of the highly restricted capital markets. Finland ended up devaluing simply because of the depletion of foreign exchange reserves via the current account deficits. The country was unable to finance its balance of payments via restricted capital inflows. Expectations of devaluation had hardly any impact on the interest rate differential between the domestic and foreign interest rates. The role of the regulated capital market emerged via the behaviour of the forward exchange rate dynamics. The forward rate was policy determined and not by the forward foreign exchange market. Forward rates were allowed to be freely determined in the markets only from April 1980 onwards. However, the capital flows and credit markets were still highly restricted and the threat of speculative attacks remained relatively low irrespective of the existing devaluation expectations. The deregulation of the Finnish financial market started relatively late, but it was fast. It started in April 1980 when the banks were allowed to cover their commercial forward positions and ended within 10 years, in 1991, when free foreign borrowing was allowed (Vihriälä, 1997). The unsuccessful deregulation of the Finnish financial market was the cause of the Finnish financial boom-bust cycle.[2]

Macroeconomic impacts on the Finnish economy

The Finnish economy experienced a severe recession in the 1990s. The size and the consequences of the recession were substantial in comparison with the economic history of the industrialized Western world. Real GDP decreased rapidly from 1990 to 1993. The GDP growth rate fell more than 14 per cent in 4 years. It reached a peak in 1990 and then declined sharply toward the end of 1992, as shown in Figure 8.1. At the same time, the Finnish unemployment rate rose from 3 per cent in 1990 to almost 20 per cent at the beginning of 1994. The depression was caused by the financial liberalization at first, but there were also other factors involved.

During the years 1986 to 1987, the economic growth in Finland accelerated significantly and the economy started to overheat. One reason for the boom was a sharp increase in the terms of trade. The price of energy decreased, and there was a rise in the world market of forest products, and the Finnish terms of trade increased by 15 to 20 per cent. In addition, the economic policy was not restrictive concerning the boom in the economy. Clearly, fiscal policy was not used as a countercyclical instrument. The boom ended in 1990, while the GDP growth declined from +5.4 per cent (1989) to –6.5 per cent (1991). Private investment, consumption, and net export of goods and services declined sharply. The decline of the real sector of the economy continued until the autumn of 1993.

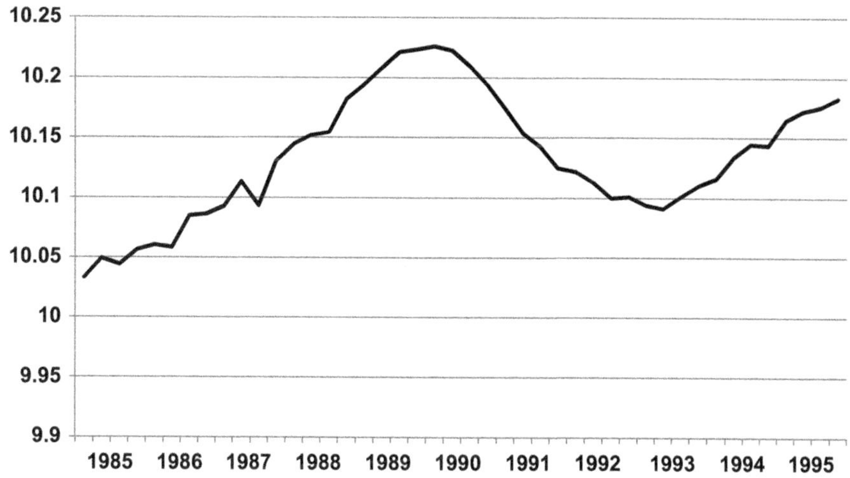

Figure 8.1 Finnish real GDP (in Logs)
Source: OECD database

Gorodnichenko and colleagues (2012) propose that the major cause of the Finnish Great Depression was the cost restructuring of the manufacturing sector and a sharp increase in the cost of energy rather than deregulation of the financial sector (Gorodnichenko et al., 2012). That is, the major catalyst for the Finnish recession was the collapse of trade with the former Soviet Union. The collapse of the barter-type Soviet trade had a negative impact on the price of energy in the Finnish economy. The rise in the energy prices was facilitated via its impacts on the production structure of the Finnish economy. The barter-type trade skewed Finnish manufacturing production and investment in a way which effectively allowed Finland to export to the Soviet Union products which were not competitive in the Western goods markets (Kajaste, 1992). Many of the goods produced were specialized for the Soviet market only. In the barter-type trade, Finland exported those specialized goods at an overvalued exchange rate to the USSR in exchange for energy imports. In fact, the barter trade with the Soviet Union had been very beneficial for Finland while it successfully insulated the Finnish economy from the most negative impacts of several energy crises. During the 1980s, the Soviet trade accounted for roughly 20 per cent of Finnish exports. Accordingly, no sector was totally immune to the collapse of the Soviet trade. In fact, the impact of the collapse of this trade on the Finnish economy resembles the impacts of the collapse of the Soviet trade on other transition economies (Gorodnichenko et al., 2012).

Hence the collapse of the Soviet Union, and with it, the barter-type trade itself inflicted a major negative shock to the economy. The goods that Finland had exported to Russia had no alternative market because they were produced to Soviet specifications. As a result, the price of energy surged in Finland. In effect, Finland experienced simultaneously both the collapse of a major export market and an increase in the price of the energy. All the natural gas and 90 per cent of imported oil came from the USSR. The price of oil was based on the dollar price of oil, yet over time, the barter price of oil favoured the Finnish exports. Moreover, many of the sectors booming due to the Soviet trade became noncompetitive in the Western markets. The collapse of exports to the Soviet Union increased unemployment and the demand for nontraded goods, which further amplified the impact of the negative economic shock from the collapse of the trade with the Soviet Union. Notably, Sweden experienced a rather similar economic downturn, including currency and banking crises, during the 1990s. However, the Swedish economic relationships with the former Soviet Union were much weaker. This may in part explain why the consequences of the financial distress were particularly severe in Finland compared to those in Sweden (see e.g. Gorodnichenko et al., 2012; Jonung et al., 1996).

One important factor postponing the Finnish economic crisis was the rigid wage-setting procedure in Finland. Collective agreements were made about the wage levels at different levels of job complexity in a given industry, and the system also allowed upward wage drifts. The trade union membership rates were traditionally high in Finland. Almost 40 per cent of workers were covered by collective wage arrangements, and 85 per cent of the workers belonged to unions (Böckerman & Uusitalo, 2006). Moreover, the union contracts largely determined the wage increases of some 95 per cent of the workforce due to the extension of the union contracts to nonmembers. In the Finnish centralized wage-setting procedure, the government played an active role. Government mediated negotiations and occasionally, for example, changed the employers' costs or changed the tax parameters in order to reach an agreement in the labour market. Even though the Finnish recession was at its deepest during the years 1992 to 1993, the trade unions rejected wage cuts. Simultaneously, unemployment increased. After the recession, union membership declined. Union density declined by more than 10 percentage points in less than 10 years. Finally, the price competitiveness of the Finnish export sector was retained via massive devaluations. However, the devaluations had marked negative impacts on firms and households indebted in foreign currency.

Deregulation of the Finnish financial market

The boom-bust cycle would not have happened without the deregulation of the Finnish financial market (Honkapohja & Koskela, 1999; Honkapohja, Koskela, & Paunio, 1996). The deregulation generated an asset market boom working through the banking sector. Finally, a twin-type currency-banking crisis pushed the Finnish economy into a crisis.

The deregulation was started in the 1980s and ended at the beginning of the 1990s, (Vihriälä, 1997). It was problematic in many respects (Honkapohja & Koskela, 1999). First, the deregulation of the capital flows was continued although the Finnish exchange rate regime was kept relatively fixed. Gradually, monetary policy ceased to be effective. The Bank of Finland held the exchange rate on a relatively narrow band. The target-zone regime was connected to the European Monetary System (EMS) and ECU (European Currency Unit). Finland was not an actual member of ERM (the European Exchange Rate Mechanism), yet it connected its target-zone band into the ECU in order to buy credibility for its fixed exchange rate regime. (For the performance of the Finnish exchange rate regime, see e.g. Lehmussaari, Suvanto, & Vajanne, 1994.) The deregulation of the capital flows gradually led to the classic situation of the Mundell-Fleming model, which proposes the inefficiency of monetary policy with fixed exchange rates and free capital flows. Whenever the central bank tried to curb the boom with an interest rate hike, it led to a widening of the interest rate differential between Germany and Finland. This, in turn, increased the capital inflow and neutralized the impacts of monetary policy. The Finnish banks also mediated the foreign currency borrowing into to the nontraded sector. Strong and continuously increasing capital inflows strengthened the Finnish *markka*, FIM. In order to curb the boom, the Bank of Finland first widened the target zone band from +–0.75 percentage points and finally revalued the *markka* by 4 per cent in 1989. As a result, the domestic interest rate and interest rate differential increased. This increased the capital inflows and the *markka* became more overvalued, leading to further deterioration of the current account. Several other factors were also boosting the credit expansion. First, regardless of the deregulation of the financial market, no improvements in prudential regulation or bank supervision were made. Second, the tax system favoured debt financing of investments. Third, lending rates were liberated earlier than the deposit rates. All of these factors generated a rapid growth in bank lending, which was directed at real estate, the stock market, and other assets. Although industrial production started to decline from 1990 onwards, total bank lending to the public increased until 1992. As a consequence, this created a massive asset price boom during which the asset prices were doubled.

The boom in asset prices sowed the seeds of the banking crisis. It started when the economy took a downturn. The Finnish economy faced high real interest rates and declining asset prices. The bursting of the bubble halved the price of the assets. As a consequence, the price of the collateral decreased dramatically, causing indebted firms and households and, finally, banks serious problems. Increased numbers of bankruptcies among businesses led to bank credit losses. The loss of the competitiveness in the open sector due to the overvalued Finnish *markka* led to more bankruptcies and unemployment. This caused further unemployment and deteriorated the government balances.

In 1989, investors started to lose confidence in the Finnish economy. The current account deficit increased and the competitiveness of the exports was badly damaged. The poor performance of the Finnish economy called into question the credibility of the target zone. There were continuous devaluation expectations on the Finnish *markka*. The central bank defended the target zone with its foreign currency reserves and by raising the domestic interest rate. The nominal interest rate varied between 12 and 18 per cent and inflation decreased to 2 per cent. This made the real interest rates unprecedentedly high. Extra pressure on the Finnish economy came from the European Monetary System, EMS. Finland connected its target zone unilaterally to the ERM via the ECU connection. The *Deutschmark* (DEM) was the key currency in the system, and all other currencies had devaluation expectations and a positive interest rate differential against the DEM. German reunification prospects in 1989 increased inflation throughout Germany. In order to decrease inflation pressures, the German Bundesbank raised the interest rates. While the devaluation expectations remained constant, interest rates increased in other countries by the same amount. Finally, the interest rates in Finland were so high as to badly erode business activities and private consumption, and they also increased savings and decreased investments. Overindebted households and firms got into trouble and had to start to sell their assets at decreasing asset prices. The financial accelerator mechanism played an important role in the boom and in the start of the decline of the Finnish economy.

Financial accelerator

The economic shocks, such as the collapse of the Soviet trade, hitting the Finnish economy were amplified due to the financial accelerator mechanism, which is related to the agency costs of lending. This adverse shock to the economy was amplified by the worsening credit market conditions which impaired the firms' and households' access to credit at the same time as the need for external funds was rising (Bernanke et al., 1999). That is, the financial friction and investment behaviour had a marked impact on the Finnish boom-bust cycle (Freystätter, 2012).

The financial accelerator mechanism seemed to play an important role in the boom, the recession, and the slow recovery. The collapse of the exchange rate regime also had a major negative impact via the financial accelerator mechanism. The large share of foreign currency debt delayed the recovery. Moreover, the financial accelerator contributed to the severity of the Finnish crisis and made the recovery slower after the bubble burst. During the boom, it greatly increased investments and amplified the upturn. During the subsequent downturn and recession, the financial accelerator mechanism increased the economic contraction.

The sequence of the boom-bust cycle in Finland

As a consequence of the financial liberalization, bank lending expanded rapidly, especially after 1985, and it peaked in 1990, as shown in Figure 8.2. Capital inflows from foreign countries also contributed to the increase of lending booms.

Countries having a boom-bust cycle typically share a common history concerning the timing of financial liberalization and asset price inflation. Financial liberalization itself does not cause the rapid asset price inflation – when the financial markets are deregulated under the monetary easing, the asset price

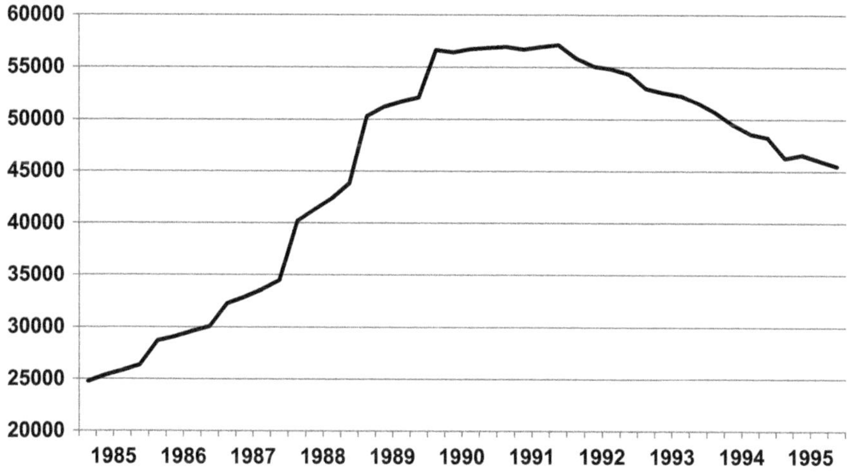

Figure 8.2 Bank lending in Finland (nonbank private, public, government/includes MFIs/mill)

Source: OECD database

increases. Money stock started to increase gradually. The annual growth rate of money stock (M1) reached a peak, 17.7 per cent in the first quarter of 1989. The M2 growth rate also peaked at 18.4 per cent in the first quarter of 1988. Both growth rates declined sharply after their peaks as shown in Figure 8.3.

In Finland, the periods of the bubble formation and the eventual bursting of the bubble are as follows. The bubble period was from 1985 to 1990, while the depression due to the bursting of the bubble took place from 1991 to 1993. The average GDP growth rate from 1985 to 1990 was 3.4 per cent. The factors causing the bubble can be summarized as follows. The first factor was the financial liberalization. The security market developed rapidly, and borrowing from abroad increased substantially because of the abolition of exchange rate controls in the latter half of the 1980s. The liberalization of the bank lending rate and private borrowing from abroad brought about the rapid expansion of bank loans and large capital inflows from foreign countries. The second factor was the sharp improvement in the terms of trade. The decline of oil prices and the rise in the world market prices of forest products promoted Finnish exports. The third factor was the monetary easing. The average growth rate of money was more than 10 per cent in 1986 to 1987, as depicted in Figure 8.3.

The inflation rate gradually began to increase during the boom. Consumer prices rose (DP) from around 2 per cent in 1986 to around 8 per cent in 1990, as reported in Figure 8.4. The rapid rise in the inflation rate weakened the Finnish export competitiveness and caused serious current account problems. Before the deregulation, the firms' loan markets were dominated by indirect bank finance from the domestic banks. Deregulation generated the bond market

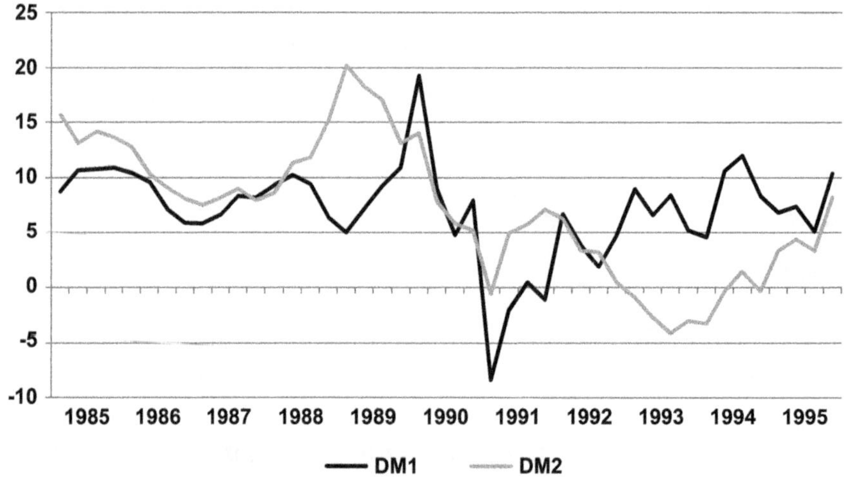

Figure 8.3 Growth of money stock in Finland

Source: OECD database

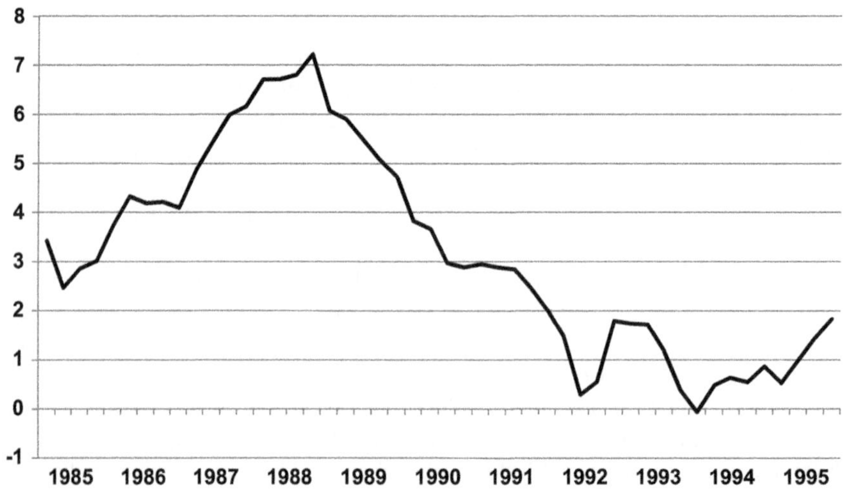

Figure 8.4 Consumer price inflation (DP) in Finland

Source: OECD database

and foreign currency borrowing option for firms. This enhanced the banks' chances of finding new borrowers. The savings banks especially became very aggressive in their risk taking. The banks' profits gradually declined, with the progress of financial liberalization in Finland, too, as reported in Table 8.1. In

Table 8.1 Interest margins of commercial banks, net interest income/assets

	1980	*1984*	*1987*	*1990*	*1991*
Finland	2.28	1.65	1.57	1.60	1.25
Sweden	2.26	2.21	2.49	2.08	2.09
Norway	3.50	3.30	2.78	2.63	2.49
Japan	1.61	1.36	1.20	0.90	1.11

Source: Shigemi, 1995

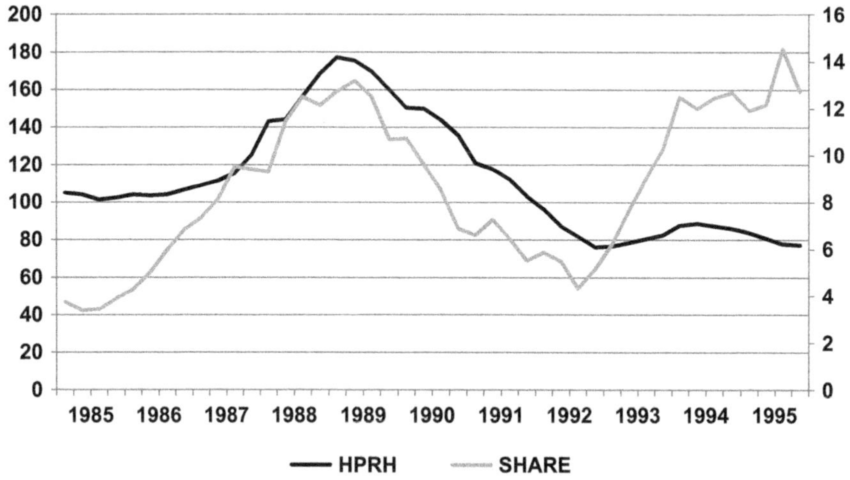

Figure 8.5 Asset prices in Finland

Source: OECD database

Note: HPRH = DWELLING PRICES/HELSINKI/Real price index (1983Y = 100) / FIM
SHARE = SHARE PRICES/ALL SHARES/INDEX PUBLICATION BASE/2000Y = 100

addition, the capital inflows from foreign countries increased rapidly. As a consequence, asset prices and real estate prices increased substantially, as shown in Figure 8.5.

The economic boom had reached its peak in 1990, when the real GDP started to decline. GDP continued to decline until the autumn of 1993. Finnish exports gradually decreased with a decline in price competitiveness and the deterioration of the terms of trade. Moreover, the collapse of the Soviet Union drastically reduced exports to Russia. Finnish exports to and imports from Russia actually dropped by 70 per cent in 1991 (Honkapohja et al., 2009, p. 17). The economic loss caused by the negative demand shock of the collapse of the Soviet

Union, including indirect effects, has been estimated at about 2.5 per cent of GDP (Nyberg & Vihriälä, 1993).

The rise of interest rates in Europe after the German reunification also contributed to the decline of the Finnish economy through the tight monetary policy. Unfortunately, a speculative attack on the *markka* had begun in 1990. The Bank of Finland had to adopt a tight monetary policy to protect the currency. Eventually, this tight monetary policy seriously damaged the Finnish economy.

With the fall in the economy, asset prices started to decline and bankruptcies of firms began to increase. By mid-1991, the number of bankruptcies had increased to a monthly average of circa 600, a significant increase compared to the previous year (see Chart 13 in Nyberg & Vihriälä, 1993). The nonperforming loans in banks accumulated rapidly from FIM 42 billion to FIM 77 billion during 1992. Some 40 per cent of the banks' nonperforming loans were related to construction, real estate, and retail trade (Nyberg & Vihriälä, 1993). The financial crisis had arrived with a vengeance. The savings banks were most severely damaged by the crisis. They had aggressively expanded their loans during the boom and increased their loans to small firms and property-related firms. The nontraded sector was then also badly hit by the crisis. Many firms got into problems due to their currency mismatch. Deregulation had enabled them to take on massive foreign currency loans, although their incomes were denominated in the domestic currency. As a result, the depreciation of the *markka* severely damaged their borrowers. Subsequently, SKOP Bank, a central bank of the saving banks, was the first commercial bank to become insolvent. The banking problems continued and were at their worst in 1992.

The Finnish *markka* was devalued 14 per cent in November 1991, and finally the exchange rate regime was changed from the target-zone system to the floating system in September 1992. Conversion into the floating system devaluated the *markka* 27 per cent with respect to the ECU. In the floating exchange rate regime, the Bank of Finland was relieved of its legal obligation to keep the exchange rate within the decided zone. Under the new currency regime, the Bank of Finland was able to freely implement a monetary policy concentrating on the domestic economy. The Bank of Finland also decided to use the inflation-targeting regime as a signal that the central bank would put a heavy emphasis on inflation. The government injected public funds into the problem banks in the form of preferred capital certificates in early 1992. The Government Guarantee Fund (GGF) was set up in order to prop up the banking system. The public injection scheme continued throughout 1994. The total public funds injected into the financial system reached 7.5 per cent of the GDP in 1992 (Honkapohja et al., 2009, p. 24). The depreciated *markka* also contributed to the rise in exports. As a result, the Finnish economy recovered rapidly after 1994.

Moreover, during the recession, Finland experienced a sharp decrease in asset prices, GDP, the level of employment, and a large fiscal deficit and eventually a sharp increase in the public-debt-to-GDP ratio. The sharp increase in public debt was partly caused by political and institutional factors (Corsetti & Roubini, 1996).

Japanese crises: the sequence of the boom-bust cycle in Japan

Japan's road to the crisis

The roots of the Japanese recession were planted in the deregulation of the Japanese financial market which started in the 1980s. This occurred practically at the same time as the financial liberalization among the Nordic countries. The regulated financial market in Japan had much in common with the financial markets in the Nordic countries. As in the Nordic countries, the Japanese financial system was highly regulated by the government. The interest rate was artificially kept at a low level in order to reduce the fundraising costs of the main industries. It was a kind of subsidy from the households to the industries. The Ministry of Finance exercised strict control over the banks. The securities market was also strictly regulated, and finance mainly depended on indirect financing through financial intermediaries. Firms were heavily dependent on bank credit, and the role of the stock market in acquiring capital for firms was less significant. This was also the case with the Finnish capital market. In Japan, the financial liberalization started in the security markets. The restrictions concerning fundraising in the securities market were relaxed. As a result, large Japanese firms became less dependent on the Japanese banks. At the same time, the liberalization of the deposit interest rates was only gradual and remained at a relatively high level. Consequently, the profits of the banks gradually declined. The banks were finally obliged to seek new lending opportunities among small business and property-related firms. Table 8.1 describes the impacts of financial liberalization on the Scandinavian and Japanese banks' profits. Remarkably, the profitability of the Japanese banks remained constantly at a lower level both before and after the deregulation of the financial market.

The asset price inflation was largely generated due to monetary easing. Together, the capital market liberalization and monetary easing generated rapid asset inflation in Japan. The monetary easing in Japan can be explained as follows. The origin of monetary easing was in trade surplus. The mounting Japanese trade surplus was often condemned by other countries, especially by the United States. The trade balance between Japan and the United States deteriorated year by year. This was even further exacerbated by President Ronald Reagan and Reaganomics. Reaganomics implied a strong monetarist and supply-side policy. Reagan's policy targeted low inflation and a strong dollar. A strong dollar caused considerable problems, the twin deficit, for the US economy. The US trade deficit was especially large with Japan. The US trade deficit with Japan accounted for more than half of the US total trade deficit in the 1980s. This attracted a lot of opposition, and the US Congress took a very hard stance against the Japanese increasing the trade surplus and threatened Japan with retaliatory trade measures.

To halt the appreciation of the US dollar and the twin deficit in the United States, the G5 countries made a Plaza Accord in New York in September 1985.

As a result of the Plaza Agreement, the US dollar depreciated from 1985 to 1987 by 51 per cent against the Yen. The devaluation of the dollar was executed mainly via unsterilized interventions. The Bank of Japan (BOJ) raised the call money rate and the Ministry of Finance executed an extensive sale of US dollars. The Plaza Accord was a turning point for the Japanese economy. The effective real exchange rate of the Yen was 94.3 in August 1985, a month before the Plaza Accord. Previously in April, the effective real exchange of the Yen was at a historically high level, 165.5. After the Plaza Accord, the Yen appreciated altogether by almost 300 per cent. Hamada and Okada (2009) regarded the Plaza Accord as an event which shot the Yen real exchange rate to high levels throughout the next two decades (Hamada & Okada, 2009).

An extra boost to the Japanese output was due to the fall in the price of energy. The Japanese terms of trade improved due to a 50 per cent fall in the dollar price of energy when the Yen appreciated about 50 per cent. Thus, in terms of the Yen, the price of energy dropped in August 1986 to a quarter of the previous levels and caused an approximately 5 per cent transfer of income to the Japanese economy (Hamada & Okada, 2009).

The Plaza Agreement was followed by the Louvre Agreement in February 1987. Due to the Louvre Agreement, Japan was required to cut its trade surplus and to adopt a much easier monetary policy. As a result, the Bank of Japan reduced the official discount rate to 2.5 per cent, then the lowest level, as seen in Figure 8.6. Money growth started to rise already in the first quarter of 1987. It grew more than 10 per cent from the first quarter of 1987 to the first quarter of 1990, as depicted in Figure 8.7. The worldwide decrease in asset prices in October 1987, Black Monday, caused further pressure for lower interest rates.

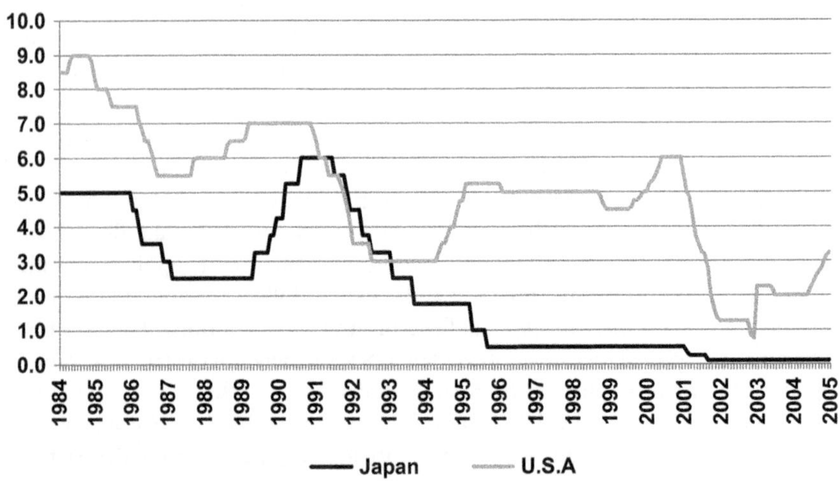

Figure 8.6 Official discount rates: United States and Japan

Source: Bank of Japan

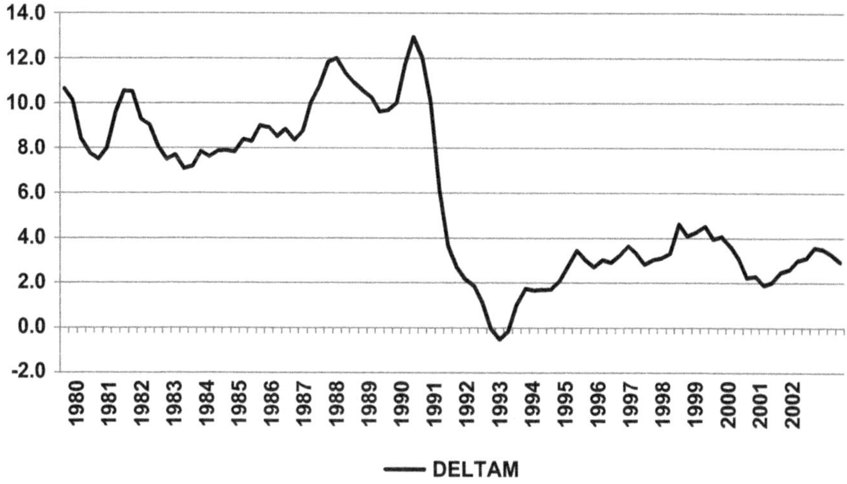

Figure 8.7 Annual growth rate of money

Source: Bank of Japan

This was the beginning of the Japanese bubble economy and, finally, the boom-bust cycle. Under the assumption of unlimited funds available, banks were very aggressive and competitive in their loan business. Anybody could get a loan very easily from the banks if they had land and real assets as collateral. The property prices were believed to increase indefinitely. Accordingly, the Japanese economy was also facing the very same leverage bubble as Finland. Some changes in the structure of bank loans also occurred. Large firms were able to get funds more easily by using 'equity finance'. The banks had to find new demand for their loans. The banks expanded lending to smaller firms and property-related firms. As a result of these changes, both stock and land prices increased rapidly in 1988 and throughout 1989. This expansion cannot be explained by economic fundamentals. The bubble was on its way.

The bursting of the bubble in Japan

The BOJ (Bank of Japan) implemented the third increase in the discount rate from 3.75 to 4.25 per cent in December 1989, when a new BOJ governor, Mr Yasuo Mieno, had taken office. However, the market was still bullish. Land, property, and stock prices continued to rise to levels that could not be rationalized by the fundamentals of the Japanese economy. Mr Yasuo Mieno and the Bank of Japan took a very strong stance on the bullish economy. They implemented a fourth increase in the discount rate from 4.25 to 5.25 per cent.[3] The BOJ took the role of arbitrage of asset prices, unfortunately for the Japanese economy. Furthermore, Governor Mieno had implemented the fifth increase in the discount rate up to 6.0 per cent to avoid homemade inflation caused by the Gulf War in August 1990, as seen in Figure 8.11. In addition to these increases in the interest rate, the Japanese government placed a ceiling on the total amount of financing in the real estate purchases.

Finally, the bubble started to burst. The money stock (M2+CD) declined rapidly. It recorded a negative annual growth in mid-1992; see DELTAM in Figure 8.7 for details. After hitting a record high of 38,915 Yen at the end of 1989, the stock price (Nikkei Dow-Jones Index) began to decline rapidly. In August 1992, stock prices dipped below 15,000 Yen, a 63 per cent plunge from a peak level (see Figure 8.8). Land and property prices began to decrease after hitting a peak in September 1990. This was the start of a decade-long asset price (see Figure 8.8), land price (see Figure 8.9), and price level fall (see Figure 8.11). In response to the asset price decline, the Bank of Japan reduced the discount rate six times from July 1991 to February 1993. The discount rate was ultimately reduced from 6.0 per cent to 2.5 per cent (see Figure 8.6). The government also implemented a fiscal stimulus by spending a total of 29.9 trillion Yen in two years from 1992 to 1993.

Land and stock prices were still expected to decline. In fact, asset prices continued to decline and increased the deflationary pressure. Firms were obliged to continue the adjustment of their balance sheets damaged by the decline of asset prices. The banks were left holding an enormous amount of nonperforming loans (NPL). It was *jusen* which first got the severest damage by the NPLs. Seven *jusen* (*tokutei juutaku kinyuu semmon gasiha*) were mortgage institutions set up by the 21 Japanese major banks in early 1970s. As a result of deregulation, *jusen* banks shifted away from mortgage financing to risky real estate business. *Jusen* were very profitable during the boom but were severely affected by the burst of the bubble. When all seven *jusen* became insolvent after the burst of the bubble, the NPLs were estimated over 6 trillion yen at the time.

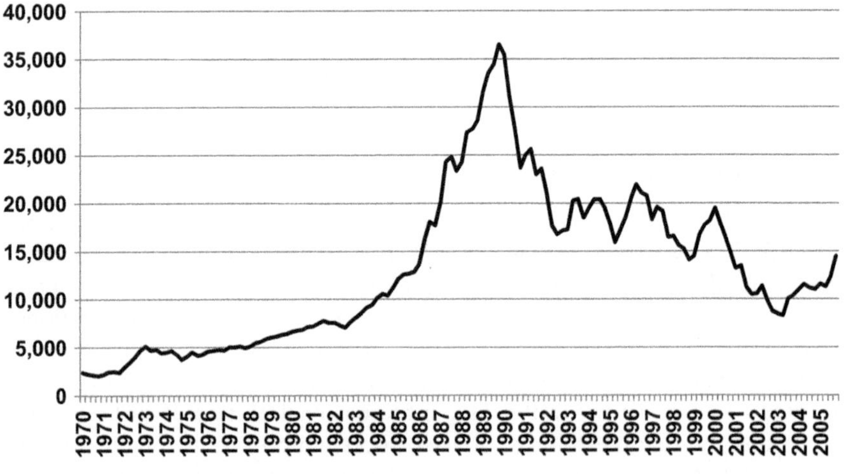

Figure 8.8 Stock price index in Japan (Nikkei Dow-Jones Index)

Source: Tokyo Stock Exchange

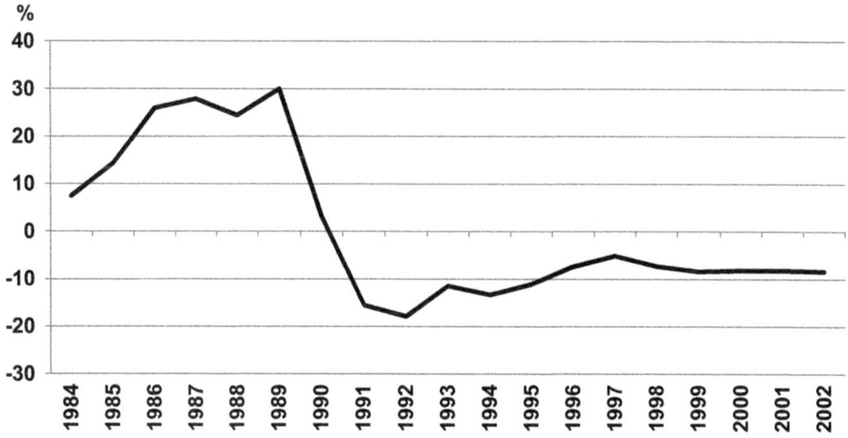

Figure 8.9 Change in land prices in Japan, six large urban areas, average (residential, commercial, and industrial)

Source: Japan Real Estate Institute

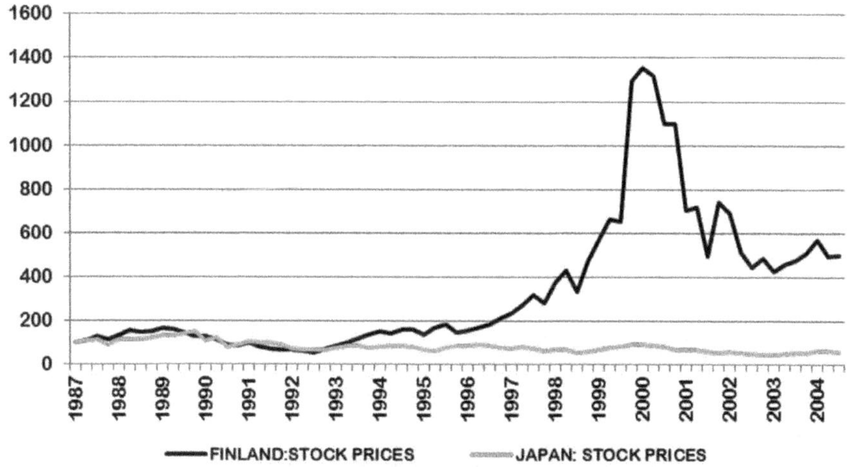

Figure 8.10 Stock prices in Finland and in Japan

Source: Thomson Datastream

Note: Finnish (OMX Helsinki Stock Price Index) and Japanese (TOPIX, Tokyo) stock price indices, normalized 1988 = 100

Figure 8.10 displays the stock market dynamics both in Finland and in Japan in one graph. It clearly points out a nearly simultaneous crash in asset prices both in Finland and in Japan. Overall, the stock market volatility had been slightly higher in Finland than in Japan. The stock market prices also give evidence for the prolonged recovery of the Japanese economy after the crash. The

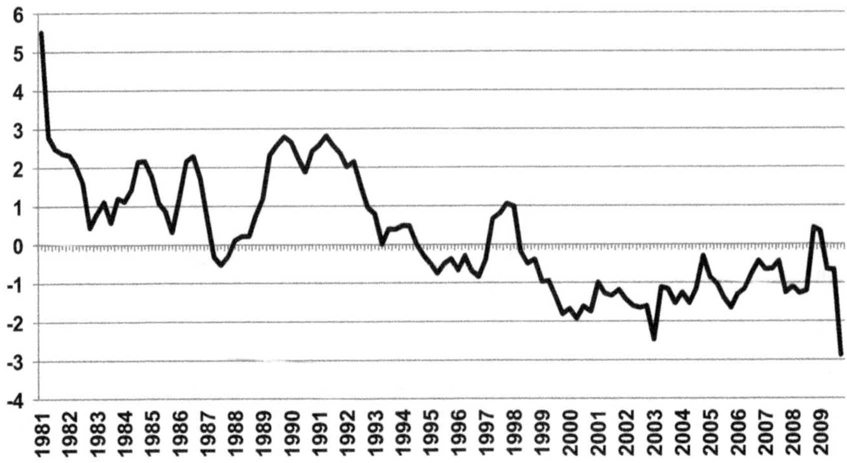

Figure 8.11 Inflation in Japan, GDP deflator

Source: Bank of Japan

stock prices in Finland soon recovered together with the recovery of the real economy after the crash.

Prolonged and difficult recovery

The Japanese economy finally began to show signs of a modest recovery in late 1995, when the real GDP began to increase and the official estimation of NPLs decreased. The Ministry of Finance had issued a report titled 'Reorganizing the Japanese Financial system' (***kinyu shisutemu no kinoukaifuku nituite***) in June 1995, in which they showed a diehard attitude to tackling the NPL problems by officially disclosing the magnitude of bad loans totalling 40 trillion Yen (about 4 per cent of the loans held by depository institutions).

Furthermore, the MOF strongly pledged a complete deposit guarantee by March 2001, with a reform of the Deposit Insurance Corporation and Prompt Corrective Act, which had been already implemented with success in the United States in 1991 after the financial crisis, at the end of the 1980s. As a result, the financial anxieties were dispelled in 1995.

However, Prime Minister Hashimoto was concerned with the future of government finances and implemented measures to reform the financial structures. Fearing that the fiscal conditions would get even worse due to the aging of the population in Japan, he decided to increase the consumption tax from 3 to 5 per cent and abolish the previously introduced special income tax cut in April 1997. These actions amounted to a tax increase of 9 trillion Yen. Consumption had diminished rapidly in response to Hashimoto's tax increase policy. Unfortunately, the East Asian economic crises occurred in July 1997. The fiscal contraction compounded by the Asian crisis decreased the Japanese aggregate demand substantially.

Under such deflationary conditions, a financial panic was a foregone conclusion. Hokkaido Takushoku Bank, one of Japan's city banks (largest 20 banks), and the Yamaichi Securities Company, one of Japan's four largest security companies, failed in November 1997.[4] The failure of two big financial institutions signalled that the government had given up the 'too big to fail' policy. People thought that no financial institutions were immune from failures. Rumours about the other banks' failures spread through the Japanese economy. The stock prices of many financial institutions declined sharply, and the 'Japan premium' in the international money market jumped by circa 100 basis points. Consequently, the Japanese banks were obliged to pay additional basis points for raising funds in the overseas financial markets. The difference between the quoted rates of TIBOR in the Tokyo offshore market and LIBOR in the London offshore market increased. Japanese financial institutions and Japanese government bonds were downgraded in the investment grade ratings by international credit-rating agencies such as Moody's.

In response to the serious situation, the government decided to provide 30 trillion Yen in funds by issuing bonds. The government was not willing at first to inject public funds into the problem banks, given the negative sentiments of the congress and the public. However, the financial panic was so severe that neither the congress nor the public strongly opposed an injection of public funds to assist the problem banks for much longer. The 30 trillion Yen was divided into the following two categories: 13 trillion Yen was allocated for the enforcement of the Deposit Insurance System, while the remaining 17 trillion Yen was intended for the capital injection of the problem financial institutions.

The government actually injected 1.8 trillion yen into the 21 large banks to raise their capital ratios in March 1998. However, this had no significant effect on the banks, because it was insufficient. Long-Term Credit Bank and Nippon Credit Bank had failed in 1998 after the injection of public funds. A further 7.5 trillion yen was injected in March 1999. This time the implementation was quite different from the former injection, and the banks were strictly required to submit a detailed and meaningful restructuring plan (Cargill et al., 2000, pp. 26–7; Hutchinson & McDill, 1999b, p. 66).

The government hesitated to resolve the nonperforming loans and bank problems quickly, which weakened financial institutions and prolonged the recession. The government officially announced in late 1995 that nonperforming loans amounted to 38 trillion Yen, 4 per cent of outstanding loans. In 1998, nonperforming loans increased to 73.1 trillion Yen, 12 per cent of all loans or 10 per cent of GDP. None of the efforts by the government and private banks to reduce the number of nonperforming loans succeeded due to the severe deflationary pressures.

The signs of deflation were apparent. In response to the serious situation, both the BOJ and the government admitted at last that the Japanese economy had fallen into deflation. The Japanese economy was thus caught in a vicious circle, a so-called deflationary spiral as described by Irving Fisher (1933): decline in demand – decline in production and price – decline in employment (decline in consumption), and an increase in real interest rate (decline in investment) – decline in demand. GDP recorded negative growth for five consecutive quarters from the fourth quarter of 1997 onward (for the first time since the start of GDP statistics in 1955). Inflation was heading to zero. Deflation was underway; see Figure 8.11. Finally, the BOJ realized the risky situation in the Japanese economy. The call money rate was reduced to 0.25 per cent in 1998. Eventually, the BOJ also implemented a zero-interest policy by reducing the call money rate to virtually zero per cent in February 1999. Furthermore, the BOJ adopted also the quantitative easing policy measures in March 2001. Owing to the expansionary policy, the financial panic seemed to settle down. The Japanese economy began to show signs of recovery.

Conclusion

In the latter half of the 1980s, a bubble economy emerged not only in Japan but also in many other industrial countries, including the United States, the United Kingdom, Germany, Australia, and the Nordic countries. However, the countries which experienced the biggest fluctuation in asset prices were Japan and the Nordic countries. Both the Japanese and Finnish crises are among the Big Five crises listed by Reinhart and Rogoff (2008). In Finland, asset prices, such as housing prices and share prices, reached a peak in 1989 and then fell sharply towards the end of 1992 (Krugman, 1998; Reinhart & Rogoff, 2008, 2009). In Japan, share prices reached a peak at the end of December 1989 and fell sharply in August 1992, while land prices also declined after peaking in September 1991 and continued to decline for more than 10 years. Both economies underwent an extremely severe recession after the rapid decline of asset prices. There are striking similarities between the boom and the bust cycles of the Japanese and Finnish economies.

The seeds of the crisis in Finland were sown due to the unsuccessful deregulation of the financial market, which started in the 1980s. The availability of funds for borrowers increased rapidly, and monetary policy remained too loose. The deregulation of capital flows together with a fixed exchange rate made it impossible to control the economy via monetary policy. Finally, the loose monetary policy led to credit expansion and asset price inflation. Many different factors were in effect during the boom. The leverage effect in lending boosted lending in both economies. As a result, the impact of the financial accelerator was strong during the boom. The Japanese financial market deregulation had much in common with that of Finland. The deregulation of the Japanese financial market enabled the big firms to give up bank financing. As a response to this, the Japanese banks started to lend to provide loans to new small firms and real estate businesses. This boosted the asset prices, and after the bubble burst, the banks were burdened by nonperforming loans.

The boom in the financial sector was largely self-inflicted. Deregulation of the financial market was unsuccessful in both countries, and a large number of financial risks entered into the balance sheets. However, the start of the bubbles bursting both in Finland and in Japan was related to some extent to exogenous shocks. In Finland, the collapse of trade with the former Soviet Union was decisive in the downturn of the economy. For Japan, the Louvre Accord and requirement for higher interest rates could have been crucial for the downturn. In Finland, the devaluation of the *markka* first exacerbated the crisis. Currency mismatch in assets and loans increased the value of loans. After the bursting of the bubble, the leverage effect started to exacerbate the recession in both countries. The asset market collapse was rapid. Stock market, housing prices, and prices of other assets soared. As a result, the value of collateral decreased, which reduced the lending in recession. In effect, the credit expansion effect started to work the other way round. It contracted the economies. The bursting of the asset market was the start of the banking crises in both countries.

The crisis after the bursting of the bubble was particularly severe for the Finnish aggregate economy. The Finnish crisis was the severest among the industrialized economies since the 1930s. Both Japan and Finland experienced a record decrease in asset prices. The Finnish recovery was closely linked with the devaluation of the Finnish *markka*. Exports started to grow, the current account balance began to improve, and the country started to leave behind the 20 per cent level of unemployment. In Japan, however, the crisis was prolonged. The number of nonperforming loans remained vast in the Japanese economy. The onset of the Japanese crisis marked the start of the lost decade in the Japanese economy. The general malaise over the Japanese economy associated with its episode of banking sector distress was unusually severe. In Finland, public money was widely used to recapitalize the banks. In Japan, there was a long delay in the commitment of public funds to recapitalize the banking sector. This may be one factor behind the differences in the recoveries of these countries from fundamentally very similar financial crises in the 1990s.

Notes

1. A substantial part of this chapter is based on Miyagawa and Morita (2009), who also examine the financial crises in Sweden and Norway.
2. The reasons and consequences of the Finnish crises have been extensively discussed, for example, in Kalela and colleagues (2002), Nyberg and Vihriälä (1993), and Honkapohja and colleagues (2009). This early literature stresses the role of the deregulation of the Finnish financial market as a key reason for crises, whereas some more recent studies stress the role of other factors as well. Among these, Gorodnichenko and colleagues (2012) stress the role of the real economy shock and the collapse of trade with the former Soviet Union, whereas Freystätter (2012) points out the significant role of the financial accelerator mechanism in credit expansion and contraction.
3. New governor Mieno was hailed as an 'Onihei of the Heisei era', a famous police leader, who had strongly fought against the gangs in the Edo era more than 200 years ago. The bubble was mainly discussed from the viewpoint of income and asset distribution. This Mieno episode reflects well the public feeling that 'bubble bursting' was right minded from an ethical viewpoint.
4. The first bank failure since the Second World War was the Tokyo-based Cosmo Credit Corporation, Japan's fifth-largest credit union, in July 1995.

Part IV

Trade and industry

9 Finnish–Japanese trade relations from protectionism to free trade, 1919–2010

Juha Sahi and Kazuhiro Igawa

Introduction

The tradition of Finnish–Japanese trade relations has already lasted for more than 90 years. During this period, the world and the international economy have gone through changes which have also left their mark on Finnish–Japanese trade relations. Trade between the two countries was interrupted during the period 1942 to 1947 due to expansion and the aftermath of the Second World War. In both countries, defeat in the war with all its consequences was followed by an era of intense economic and social development. As of the 1960s, Finland and Japan modified their protectionist trade policies, thus contributing to the development of freer trade in the global economy. In the twenty-first century, connections between Finland and Japan emphasize active trade, science, culture, and political relations.

From the Finnish perspective, trade relations with Japan have been especially significant, for Japan has been one of the most important trade partners of Finland outside Europe both before and after the Second World War. On the other hand, Finland's place in Japan's foreign trade has not been quite so significant. Nevertheless, bilateral relations have offered both countries a fruitful foundation for business activities, such as the export of Finnish pulp and paper to Japan and the export of Japanese textiles and cars to Finland. Finnish exports to Japan have traditionally been products of the forestry industry, while Japanese exports to Finland have been more varied, with distribution of products from numerous fields of industry. Since the 1980s, Finnish–Japanese trade relations have moved towards a more multilateral or global basis. This shows that both countries have adapted to the development experienced in the global trade system. It signifies the movement from restricted trade to freer trade under the General Agreements on Tariffs and Trade (GATT) and the World Trade Organization (WTO).

This chapter is divided into three analytical sections. The first and second sections present a historical review of bilateral trade relations, namely an outline of Finnish–Japanese trade relations starting from the interwar period and continuing to the post-war era until the early 1980s. Questions on how and why trade relations have developed during these seven decades and what significance these relations had will be answered accordingly within the sections. The role of foreign direct investments (FDI) in Finnish–Japanese trade relations is also briefly considered in the period starting from the 1970s. The documents used in these chapters were mainly retrieved from the Archives of the Ministry for Foreign Affairs, Finland. Although the sources emphasize the Finnish point of view, it can be argued that up to a point, they also convey the Japanese perspective on the development of trade relations. A growing surplus of Japanese exports to Finland has been characteristic of post-war trade relations, and this has aroused considerable interest and a need for Finnish trade policy actors to balance trade between the two countries, especially prior to the 1990s. This problematic situation in trade relations supports also the use of this particular source material.

The third section is concerned with the examination of Finnish–Japanese trade relations from the 1980s until the end of the first decade of the twenty-first century in terms of new international trade theories. The source material used is OECD commodity trade data. Trade relations in this period focused on three aspects: bilateral trade imbalances, commodity concentrations in exports or imports, and the extent of intra-industry trade. These aspects show dramatic changes in the pattern of trade between Finland and Japan and a similarity to recent world trade trends. The trade imbalance, the large trade surplus of Japan, is moving toward equilibrium. Extreme concentrations of exports in the products of the Finnish forestry industry and the Japanese automobile industry are changing to become more diversified exports of industrial outputs and manufactured goods. A traditional trade pattern of interindustry trade, reciprocal exchanges in the products of different industries' products, is now changing to a pattern of intra-industry trade, with exchanges of products within the same industry. These changes can be explained using a new international trade theory of increasing returns, product differentiation, and division of labour in intermediate products or production processes.

Trade under protectionism, 1919 to 1962

Trade relations before the Second World War

Finland won her independence from Russia in 1917. Since then, the country has sought to establish her own foreign relations with neighbouring countries while also turning to the East and especially to Japan, the most powerful nation in Asia. Imperial Japan recognized the Republic of Finland on 23 May 1919, and the Treaty of Commerce and Navigation between the two countries was signed in 1924. By concluding this treaty, Finland and Japan undertook to place commerce, navigation, and industry on the footing of the most favoured nation (MFN; Momose, 1973, pp. 7–10; Paasivirta, 1968, pp. 185–6; Sahi, 2008, p. 11).[1] This laid the foundations of Finnish–Japanese trade right up to the present day.

From the beginning, Finland's exports to Japan more or less rested on products of the forestry industry. In 2009, the share of products of the forestry industry still accounted for 38 per cent of Finnish exports to Japan (Finpro,

2010, p. 17). During the interwar period, pulp and paper became the main Finnish export articles to the Japanese market. This was because the Finnish forestry industry was able to become a major player in international markets after being organized in 1918 into export unions through which the sales of products were arranged on a shared basis. The Finnish Cellulose Union (Finncell) exported pulp and the Finnish Paper Mills' Association (Finnpap) sold paper abroad. The Finnish forestry industry provided an exceptionally consistent and close collaboration system which enabled the creation of worldwide sales networks. This allowed the aforementioned sales cartels to develop into giants on the global markets (Häggman, 2006, pp. 156–7; Jensen-Eriksen, 2007, pp. 29–31; Lamberg, Ojala, Peltoniemi, & Särkkä, 2012; Sajasalo & Igawa, 2015). Finncell and Finnpap were closed down in the aftermath of structural changes in the Finnish forestry industry and Finland's entry into the EU in the mid-1990s (Heikkinen, 2000).

Sales of Finnish pulp to Japan increased during the 1920s and especially in the 1930s. This development was due to the Japanese paper industry's need for wood pulp from abroad, but the rapidly growing Japanese textile industry also required foreign rayon pulp. In the early 1920s, exporters of pulp from Canada, Sweden, Norway, and the United States had established their positions on Japan's pulp market (Lintulahti, 1963, p. 57).[2] Finnish paper, especially newsprint, was also in demand in Japan, but its export did not continue to increase after the favourable years of the early 1920s. On the other hand, Finnish pulp gained a strong foothold on the Japanese market to such an extent that in the 1930s, annual total Finnish exports to Japan were almost completely due to the sales of pulp. This dependence on pulp came close to putting Finnish–Japanese trade relations in a risky position if Japan had ever decided to impose restrictions on its import.

Imports to Finland from Japan mainly consisted of products of the textile industry, which had a higher manufacture grade than the Finnish main export. Japan's exports to Finland were not as dependent on one single product as was the case of Finnish pulp. However, one Japanese article rose above others; imports of Japanese cotton fabric increased significantly during the period 1934 through 1937, and it became the main Japanese export to Finland in terms of value and volume. In 1934, Japanese exports to Finland amounted to 15.9 million Finnish Marks, with cotton fabric accounting for 3.9 million (24.5 per cent). By 1937, Japanese exports had increased five and a half fold, thus being valued at 90.3 million, of which the share of cotton fabric was 42.4 million (47 per cent).[3]

Japan was deemed to have started a massive export expansion, especially in the case of textile products. This caused counterreactions in some European countries. For example, the UK, the Netherlands, Belgium, France, and Germany adopted measures to protect the domestic industry from the threat posed by the Japanese products. It was also debated in Finland whether to resort to protective measures like those in Western European countries.[4] The Finnish forestry industry had no interest in restricting trade with Japan, because the exports of Finnish pulp were increasing year after year. However, the Ministry

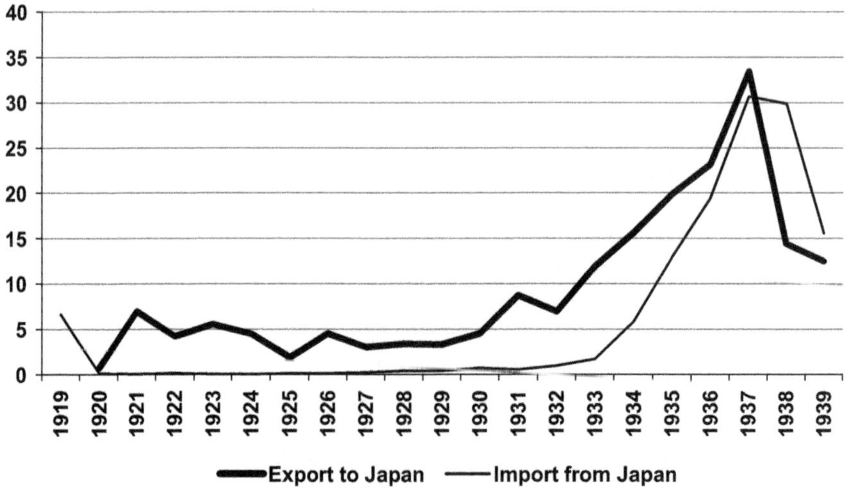

Figure 9.1 Trade between Finland and Japan, 1919–1939 (million Euros in 2010)

Source: SVT, 1919–1986, 2002–2003

Note: Export according to country of sale (before 1935) and country of consumption (since 1935). Import according to country of purchase (before 1935) and country of origin (since 1935).

for Foreign Affairs was interested in starting consultations with Japan on setting limitations to the MFN status.[5]

By the summer of 1938, Japan had been at war with China for a year, and because of the war effort, Japan had imposed restrictions on the importation of pulp. From the Finnish point of view, this action gave a justifiable reason to abandon the treaty.[6] These differences in trade were not solved overnight, for the negotiations between Finland and Japan, conducted in Tokyo from the summer of 1938 onwards, lasted for 9 months. In May 1939, a trade agreement was signed allowing Finland at least a 20 per cent share of rayon pulp imports to Japan for the rest of the year.[7] In 1938, Finland was given a 9 per cent quota for rayon pulp imports, but the quota for Finnish imports amounted to double this amount. In exchange, the Finns agreed not to impose restrictions on Japanese exports to Finland (Fält, 1982, p. 254; Kohvakka, 1996, pp. 108–9).[8] In spite of this favourable agreement, 1938 was a turning point in the reciprocal trade relations. For the first time after 1919, trade with Japan showed a deficit in favour of Finland.

Resumption of trade relations after the war

The outbreak of the Second World War cut short Finnish–Japanese trade in 1941. In accordance with UK requirements, Finland broke off all relations with Japan on 22 September 1944. This took place shortly after Finland had accepted the conditions of armistice with the Soviet Union and the UK. Since official relations were broken off, trade was likewise no longer permissible between the two countries.[9] For Japan, the war ended in surrender in August 1945, to be followed by the occupation of Japan by the Allied Powers. During the next 7-year period, Japan's foreign trade was under the strict control of the occupation force. The authorities directed the country's exports and imports. Furthermore, the Japanese companies were initially not permitted to contact their foreign trade partners independently. The textile industry was afflicted with the war damages and the occupation authorities' decision to dismantle the companies and production units (Opas, 2007, pp. 45–6, 58–9). The forestry industry had also suffered from the war and the loss of territories in the north. Japan's pre-war decision to reach self-sufficiency in the production of wood pulp had not materialized. This meant that there was a demand for foreign-produced pulp in occupied Japan (Kurosawa & Hashino, 2012; Sajasalo & Igawa, 2015).[10]

After the war, Finnish pulp was first exported to Japan in 1948.[11] This became possible after the United States had agreed to allow limited direct trade contacts between foreign and Japanese companies as of 15 August 1947.[12] Finncell was interested in returning officially to the Japanese market after being advised to do so by its sales agent in Osaka.[13] Beginning trade negotiations between Finland and occupied Japan was considered to be essential in order to preserve the pre-war market for Finnish pulp, or rather to resume trading as soon as possible.[14]

The negotiations were eventually started in May 1949, and at once the occupation authorities made it clear that they would not recognize the pre-war treaties concluded by the Japanese government and that they had no interest in intervening in such matters. From the Finnish point of view, too, the Treaty of Commerce and Navigation between Finland and Japan of 1924, for the time being, was not valid.[15] A trade agreement between Finland and occupied Japan was signed in Tokyo on 21 June 1949. This was accompanied by a financial arrangement under which all trade would be conducted on an open-account basis and in terms of US dollars.[16]

The trade agreement covered the period from 1 July 1949 to 30 June 1950, and the value of exports and imports between the two countries comprised around 2.5 million dollars each.[17] According to the trade agreement, Finnish exports to Japan were estimated mainly to consist of pulp for the Japanese rayon industry and kraft paper, whereas Japan's estimated exports to Finland were composed of steel strips, hardened whale oil, textile fabrics, yarns, and fishing nets.[18] However, at the request of the Supreme Commander for the Allied Powers (SCAP), the trade agreement was formulated in such a way that it constituted a development plan or an estimate for trade between Finland and occupied Japan rather than a firmly binding contract.[19] In regards to the trade articles, the trade between the two countries mainly followed the pre-war pattern but now on a more restricted scale.

In light of these agreements, Finland enjoyed unofficial MFN status in occupied Japan.[20] Ultimately, the question of MFN status was resolved when the pre-war Treaty of Commerce and Navigation was brought into effect by an exchange of notes between Finland and sovereign Japan on 28 April 1952. After this, the memorandum concerning trade and payments between Japan and Finland was adopted by an exchange of letters on 24 December 1952. Payments were disbursed using clearing dollars according to the clearing principle (Fält, 1985, p. 44; Lintulahti, 1963, p. 56).[21]

During the 1950s, Finland and Japan regulated their foreign trade by using export and import licenses, and Finnish–Japanese trade was conducted on the basis of parallel trade (Pihkala, 1988, pp. 28–9).[22] On Japan's initiative, in autumn 1956, the valid payments agreement of 1952 and the clearing arrangement described therein were to be discontinued. The Japanese government argued that its intention was to get rid of the clearing arrangement and instead to conduct foreign trade payments using free currencies – in this case, in transferable pounds sterling. As the result of the ensuing negotiations, the new payment arrangement was signed in Tokyo on 10 December 1956 and came into force on 1 April 1957.[23]

Gradual breakdown of trade barriers

Official trade relations normalized gradually during the 1950s, but in terms of annual trade between the two countries, the pre-war level of trade was not reached until the 1960s. During the Korean War (1950–1953), demand for raw materials increased globally. However, the export of Finnish pulp to Japan did not immediately increase. As the world market price of pulp rose, Finncell concentrated on shipping pulp to its biggest clients in the UK, the United States, and France. This boom lasted until 1952, when the production of pulp became unprofitable. As sales of pulp declined in Europe and the United States, the pulp shipments to Japan began to increase (Jensen-Eriksen, 2007, pp. 49–50, 62–3).[24] According to Finncell's invoicing in 1953, in that year, more Finnish pulp was exported to Japan than in any other year during the whole decade. This was due to a short-lived and temporary increase in sales (see Figure 9.4).

In 1954, Japan introduced a global quota allocation system for the import of rayon pulp. This caused a continuous threat for the exports of Finnish pulp to Japan. Thereafter, Canadian and American pulp, which was cheaper than north European pulp, got more easily onto the Japanese market on the basis of free competition. In order to preserve the remaining market position, the price of Finnish pulp had to be reduced by consenting to substitute licencing, which provided that Japanese goods, such as textiles, products of precision mechanics, and optics, were to be given import licences in fixed proportion to the export of Finnish pulp. In 1956, the share of this sort of Japanese imports was 50 per cent of the export value of Finnish pulp. This price levelling of Finnish pulp caused the prices of Japanese imports to rise (Lintulahti, 1963, p. 59).[25]

Japan tightened the granting of import licences in autumn 1957. This was due to Japan's continuously weakening balance of foreign payments. Stocks of

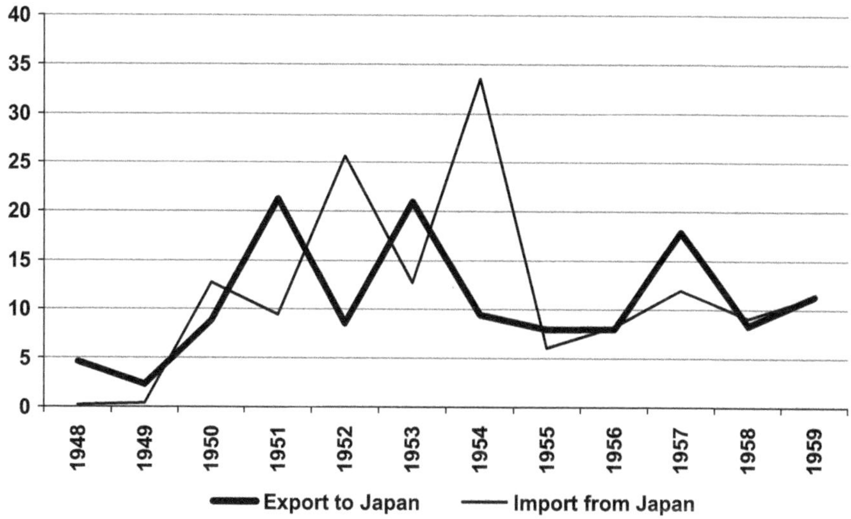

Figure 9.2 Trade between Finland and Japan, 1948–1959 (million euros in 2010)
Source: SVT, 1919–1986, 2002–2003
Note: Export according to country of consumption. Import according to country of origin.

pulp in Japan had become bigger because of the decrease in the export of textiles, which naturally had an effect on the demand for foreign pulp. At the same time, the substitute import of Japanese goods, which was connected to the export of Finnish pulp, faced difficulties in Finland due to the liberation of imports from the West and the devaluation of the Finnish Mark.[26] This situation upset importers and exporters in both countries. In the opinion of Finncell and its agent, Finland Japan Trading Co. Ltd. in Osaka, it was necessary to continue the export of pulp on the basis of substitute trade. Otherwise Finnish pulp would not be able to remain on the Japanese market because of its higher freight charges compared to North American pulp.[27] There was a risk that trade between Finland and Japan would cease completely.

In September 1958, the parallel trade between Finland and Japan ended. By this time, however, the competitiveness of Finnish pulp in Japan had improved thanks to the favourable development of prices. Various restrictions on imports in both countries still impeded the progress of Finnish–Japanese trade.[28] The Finns were interested in starting trade negotiations in Tokyo because Japan had, for instance, already imposed restrictions on the importation of paper pulp in 1952 in order to protect domestic production. The Foreign Ministry of Japan did not consider it necessary to start negotiations because no changes in the restriction on the import of paper pulp were anticipated in the near future (Lintulahti, 1963, p. 59).[29] Import of rayon pulp to Japan was still conducted on the basis of a global quota allocation system.[30]

By the beginning of the 1960s, Finnish exports to Japan were structurally the same, but the imports of Japanese textiles to Finland had decreased. Imports of textiles were more and more replaced by the imports of machines, chemicals, and metal industry products. The Finns were interested in expanding the range of exports to Japan with products of the food industry and the metal industry. The results of marketing these products to Japan were quite modest in spite of frequent efforts. However, a slight improvement in these efforts occurred when the Finns managed to make a long-range deal over the sale of pine oil[31] to Japan. An even more significant change in the development of Finnish–Japanese trade relations ensued from Japan's decision to deregulate the imports of rayon pulp starting 1 April 1962 and paper pulp on 1 October 1962.[32] This was linked to Japan's overall decision to remove restrictions on imports. At the same time, Finland also modified its long-term protectionist foreign trade policies as it took steps towards economic integration with Western European countries (Paavonen, 1998, pp. 296–7).

A big step in the development of Finnish–Japanese trade relations was taken on 22 December 1961, when Finland and Japan agreed to deregulate bilateral trade by exchanging notes in Tokyo. In practice, this meant that Finland would give Japan the benefits of imports based on multilateral treatment, and Japan for its part would give Finland the liberal import treatment of the moment as well as all forthcoming alleviations on import restrictions. A representative of the Foreign Ministry of Japan mentioned during the negotiations that from now on, the imports of Finnish pulp would be made much easier by the granting of import licences in a liberal manner.[33]

In the following years, the exports of Finnish pulp to Japan increased considerably. In addition to this noteworthy improvement in Finnish exports, 1962 witnessed another event which had a profound impact on Finnish–Japanese trade relations in the years to come. This was the beginning of the importation of Japanese cars to Finland. A Finnish car distributor, Autokeskus Oy in Helsinki, made a deal with Nissan Motor Co., Ltd. to buy around 700 Datsun Bluebird cars. By concluding this contract, Autokeskus became the first distributor to start regular importation of Nissan passenger cars to Europe.[34] Another Finnish distributor, Korpivaara Oy, started the importation of Toyota cars in 1964. Toyota, as well as Datsun, became a popular car brand on the Finnish market. In the years 1966, 1969, and 1970, Finland was the biggest importer of Toyota cars in Europe. Korpivaara Oy did not only settle for importing cars from Japan but also started exporting a variety of Finnish goods, ranging from furniture and design products to complete log houses, to Japan in 1972. In the same year, Toyota became the third-biggest car manufacturer in the world, and its share of all Japanese cars sold in Finland was more than 50 per cent (Kuch & Uotinen, 2005, pp. 250–62; Kynnös & Räsänen, 1992, pp. 47–8; Toyota, 1988, pp. 220–1).

The success of Japanese cars in Finland was an outcome of commitment and hard work on the part of the distributors and manufacturers. Initially the Nordic countries were the target market for Japanese cars in Europe. Among the Nordic countries, Finland's market was initially the most important. Not until the 1970s did the other Nordic countries catch up with Finland in the number of Japanese cars imported annually. This was due to the openness of the Finnish market, the high price of fuel, and a tariff policy which favoured the importation of small cars (Koskimies, 1982, pp. 34–6).

Growth and imbalance, 1963 to 1983

Diversification of trade and transportation

In the 1960s, Finland's exports to Japan were still based on pulp, a semifinished product of the forestry industry, whereas Japan's exports to Finland centred on ready-made goods. Since 1962, the number of Japanese textiles (free from import licences) and cars imported to Finland increased significantly, but Finnish pulp and pine oil also reached the Japanese market in bigger shipments. Japan's exports to Finland exceeded by far Finland's exports to Japan. This imbalance of trade was not the only concern for the Finns. The structure of trade also caused anxiety, because the Japanese exports consisted of 600 to 700 articles, while the Finnish exports consisted of a considerably smaller number of articles.[35]

Finland also had to compete with the other Nordic countries for the same market. The value of Sweden's, Norway's, and Denmark's respective trade with Japan exceeded the Finnish–Japanese trade. In regard to the number of sales representatives, the Swedes and the Danes were positioned on the Japanese market on a larger scale than the Finns. Finncell, the biggest player in Finnish exports to Japan until the early 1970s, had given sole rights for the sales of pulp to the Finland Japan Trading Co. Ltd., which also had acted as a representative of Finnpap and Valio, a producer of dairy products.[36]

The geographical distance between the two countries has traditionally impeded the expansion of trade. During 1967 and 1968, a development took place which left a mark on Finnish–Japanese trade in regard to the issue of transportation of goods. In the summer of 1967, a crisis broke out in the Middle East, which resulted to the closing of the Suez Canal. The closing of an important shipping lane was a serious setback for the trade between Asia and Europe. Because of this difficult situation, Japan started negotiations with the Soviet Union in order to open a new sea route from Japan through the north to Europe. The agreement was concluded and the Soviet Arctic Steamship Line started operating in the shipping lane in the Arctic Ocean, the North-East Passage. With the assistance of icebreakers, it was possible for cargo ships to navigate the lane from July 25 to November 1, or as long as the ice conditions permitted. Thanks to the northern shipping lane, it was possible to achieve significant reductions in transportation costs and time. Furthermore, the Japanese were interested in the use of transportation routes through Siberia. In April 1968, the Japanese Yamashita-Shinnihon Steamship Co. Ltd. and Soviet Aeroflot started cooperation on the route by land, sea, and, for the most part, by air between Japan and Europe through Siberia.[37]

In addition to the introduction of the aforementioned new transportation routes, in the beginning of the 1970s, it became possible to use the Trans-Siberian railway for European-Japanese trade on an extensive scale. The Swiss transport and forwarding agency MAT Transport AG introduced containers in the Siberian traffic in cooperation with V/O Sojuzvneshtrans, the official forwarding agency of the Soviet Union. For the Finnish–Japanese trade, the Trans-Siberian railway offered in most cases lower freight charges and shorter transportation time compared to maritime traffic. The Trans-Siberian railway served the Finnish–Japanese trade well, also because of the fact that the railways in Finland and the Soviet Union had the same width of tracks. This made it possible to avoid reloading the cargo and multiple bookings of wagons, unlike in the traffic between Central Europe and the Soviet Union. According to MAT Transport, by the beginning of 1973, the time record in the Siberian container traffic between Finland and Japan was 18 days for transportation to Finland and 19 days for transportation to Japan.[38] The Siberian container traffic was especially suitable for the transportation of machines, furniture, and foodstuffs, whereas the products of the forestry industry were still for the most part exported to Japan by sea.[39]

In spite of these alternative transportation routes, the long geographical distance between Finland and Japan is an unchanging fact. Thus the Finnish companies were interested, for example, in purchasing patents and manufacturing under a licence. In the late 1960s, the structure of Finnish–Japanese trade

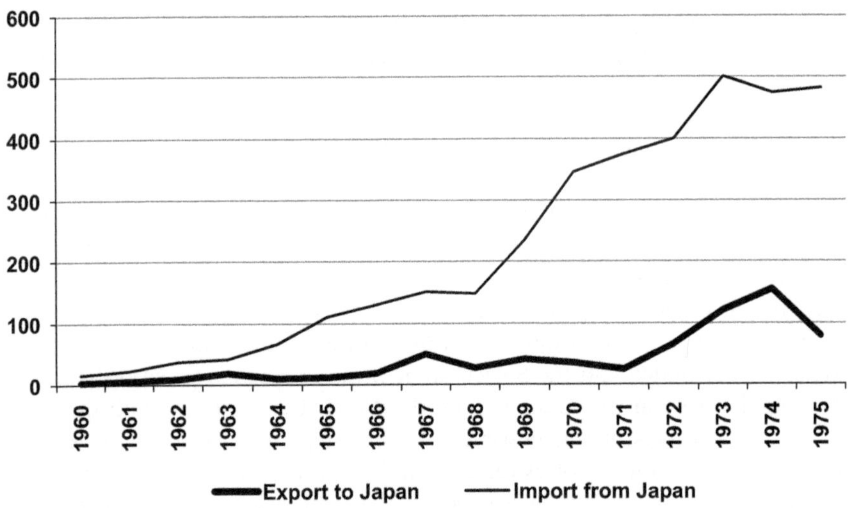

Figure 9.3 Trade between Finland and Japan, 1960–1975 (million euros in 2010)

Source: see previous figures

Note: Export according to country of consumption. Import according to country of origin.

went through changes, when pulp was beginning to lose ground as the biggest Finnish export item to Japan, and in 1968 Finland was no longer the biggest importer of Japanese cars in Europe, even though their imports continued to increase rapidly.[40] In 1972, paper and cardboard surpassed pulp as the main Finnish export articles to Japan.[41]

Closer trade contacts and an even greater imbalance

For decades, the Japanese textile industry had kept up the demand for Finnish rayon pulp in the Japanese market. Restrictions imposed on foreign trade by Japan in the 1950s led to the textile industry's need to secure a steady supply of imported rayon pulp by acquiring the material from a Japanese enterprise called Alaska Pulp Co., which opened a pulp mill in Alaska at the turn of the 1960s. This naturally had a direct impact on the need for imported rayon pulp from other countries.[42] Exports of Finnish rayon pulp to Japan decreased considerably during the 1960s; however, it was replaced by the increasing exports of paper pulp.[43] Japan's foreign trade, which in the 1960s was still characterized by the so-called low-priced exports of textile products, was changing its emphasis towards a more capital- and high-technology–based trend in accordance with the plans of Japan's public and private sectors.[44] The intention of Japan's pulp and paper industry was to secure the supply of foreign raw material by concluding procurement agreements with suppliers in Asian and North American countries, and also with the Soviet Union.[45]

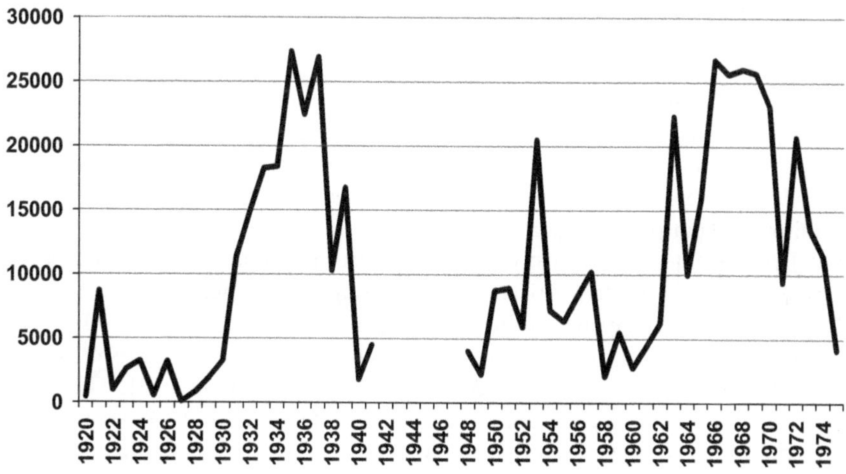

Figure 9.4 Export of Finnish pulp to Japan according to Finncell's invoicing, 1920–1975 (tons in dry weight)

Source: Finncell's annual reports of 1920–1975. The Finncell Archives.

The Finnish paper industry took an interest in the Japanese market in the early 1970s, because the demand for paper was expected to increase there in the near future.[46] As a result of the Oil Crisis in the Middle East, the world market price for paper doubled in the period 1974 to 1975. Even before this, the demand for paper products had considerably increased in Japan due to the rise in the price of plastic and the environmental problems caused by the disposal of plastic waste.[47] Apart from the fact that there was already demonstrable oversupply of paper on the Japanese market in 1974, Japan became the biggest buyer of Finnish paper in Asia in the 1970s and in the early 1980s. The establishment of Finnpap's agency in Tokyo in 1975 and the cooperation between Finnpap and the Japanese trading houses DaiEi Papers Ltd. and Marubeni Corporation promoted the success of Finnish paper in Japan. As a result of their joint project, a sales office called Nippon Finnpap Ltd. was opened in 1980 (Heikkinen, 2000).

Before the early 1970s, Japan had already started carrying out its liberalization programme for imports. This was believed to afford new export opportunities, for instance, for Finnish interior design and leisure products.[48] Finnish companies intending to get into the Japanese consumer market in most cases had no effective marketing system at their disposal. This led to a situation in which competitors' well-known products were more likely to arouse the interest of Japanese importers. The importance of personal connections between business partners has traditionally been significant, especially from the standpoint of the Japanese corporations. This fact was also noticed by Finnish businesses, and in order to enhance the prospects for Finnish exports to Japan, it became relevant to create a fast and easy travelling route between the two countries which could also benefit business contacts. For this reason, in 1971, Finland had already put forward a proposal to start negotiations with Japan over an air traffic convention.[49]

Finnair, the major Finnish airline, was particularly interested in opening a flight path to Japan, and in their view, Finnish officials ought to use 'all possible means of commercial policy and other kind in order to get the negotiations in question started with the Japanese'.[50] The Foreign Ministry of Japan and the Ministry of Transport of Japan were willing to grant Finnair the air route licence, but Japan Airlines was against it.[51] In this situation, Finnair decided to seek the support of the Japanese politicians, which brought out a negative view towards Finnair among the Japanese officials dealing with the issue (Opas, 2003). The problematic question of an air route was finally settled after 10 years of trying, when Finland and Japan concluded an air traffic convention in 1981. The opening of the nonstop flight connection between Helsinki and Tokyo in 1983 introduced a faster and more convenient way of travel, and in that way also more intensive contacts between the two countries.

From the standpoint of Finnish business, the most effective way to diminish the imbalance of trade was thought to be by increasing the presence of Finnish companies on the Japanese market. Gradually the realization of their own shortcomings in export promotion was increasing among the Finnish businesses.

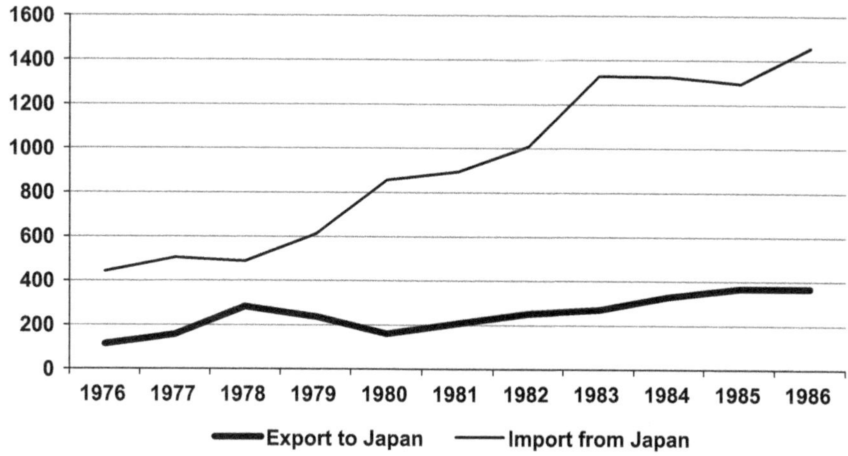

Figure 9.5 Trade between Finland and Japan, 1976–1986 (million euros in 2010)

Source: See Figure 9.1.

Note: Export to Japan according to country of consumption (before 1980) and country of destination (since 1980). Import from Japan according to country of origin.

Besides, dissatisfaction with the unequal trade balance was also growing. The imports of Japanese cars increasing year after year especially came in for harsh criticism by some Finnish foreign trade policy players (Koskimies, 1982, pp. 34–6, 79). In the late 1970s, approximately one quarter of the annual imports from Japan consisted of motor vehicles. In 1979, the market share of the Japanese motor vehicles in Finland was 24 per cent. A year later, they gained a market share of 35.4 per cent. Therefore, in Finland all eyes were on the possibility of restricting the import of Japanese cars, while for example in England and Italy, this action had already been taken. According to a survey conducted by the Ministry for Foreign Affairs, Finland, at the end of 1980, there were, however, not sufficient legitimate or commercial policy grounds for directing restrictions solely at the importation of Japanese cars.[52]

In May 1981, a Finnish delegation started talks in Tokyo with Japanese officials and representatives of the Japanese car industry on possible measures to limit the importation of Japanese cars. In the talks, representatives of the Japanese car industry took a negative attitude towards any measures which would lead to import restrictions based on voluntary actions or concluded agreements. However, on the grounds of the completed talks, the Ministry for Foreign Affairs, Finland, decided to put forward a proposal to subject the importation of Japanese cars immediately to licensing control.[53]

The proposal of the Foreign Ministry was put into practice starting on 1 July 1981. For the next 12 months, the imports of Japanese cars were under licencing control, which, however, did not mean that the importation was restricted *per se*. In August 1980, prices of imported Japanese cars had risen because of a rise in the value of the yen. This development led to a 2 per cent drop in the

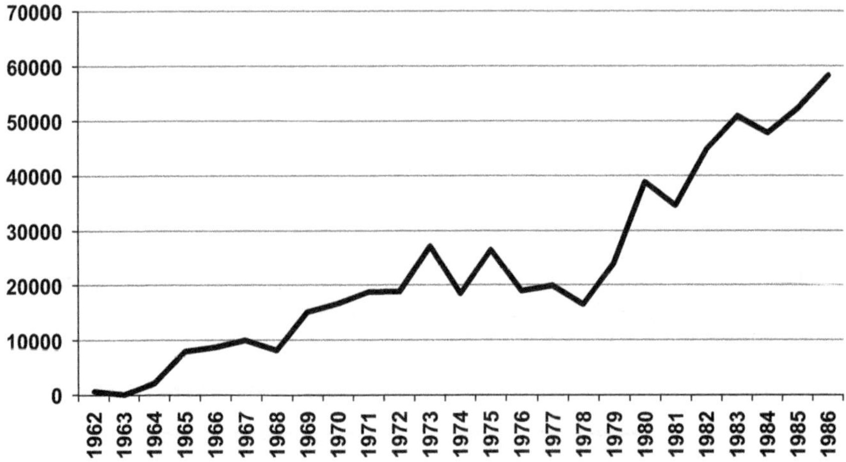

Figure 9.6 Import of new Japanese cars to Finland, 1962–1986 (number of cars)

Source: See Figure 9.1.

Note: Since 1974, the number of passenger cars has included 'cars with a combined possibility of transportation of people and goods'.

market share of Japanese cars by the end of 1981. Changes in the market share of different car classes did not always lead to losses for Japanese cars. From the standpoint of the Ministry of Trade and Industry, Finland, the most important issue was that the domestic car industry was able to maintain its market share and that no increase in the market share of Japanese cars could be expected in the near future.[54] As shown in Figure 9.6, the import of Japanese cars continued to increase in the forthcoming years, and trade between the two countries also continued to show a substantial deficit for Finland.

Significance of bilateral and multilateral trade relations

Throughout the 1960s, the increase in Finnish–Japanese trade exceeded the average annual growth of the Finnish foreign trade (Koskimies, 1982, p. 28). By the 1970s, Japan became Finland's second-biggest non-European trade partner, the United States being the biggest.[55] From Japan's point of view, trade with Finland remained quite insignificant, because according to the Japanese trade statistics, exports to Finland accounted for 1.8 per cent of total exports, while imports from Finland accounted for 1.1 per cent of Japan's total imports in 1974. In comparison with the other Nordic countries, Finland's trade with Japan has been less extensive; in 1974, Finland's exports to Japan were approximately 72 per cent of Norway's, 54 per cent of Denmark's, and 25 per cent of Sweden's exports to Japan.[56] It should nevertheless be noted that Finland's position in Japan's foreign trade has intermittently been quite significant in terms of the importation of pulp and paper.

In the early 1970s, the structure of Finnish–Japanese trade was still decidedly unequal, because for decades Finnish exports to Japan had rested on the sales of pulp, a semifinished product of the forest industry, whereas Japan's exports largely consisted of ready-made consumer goods. Because of its structure, Finnish–Japanese trade resembled a conventional relation between a developing country and an industrialized country in the opinion of the Finnish Embassy in Tokyo.[57]

This characterization is appropriate to describe Finnish export in its entirety from the 1950s until the 1970s. Not until the 1970s did the Finnish forestry industry shift the emphasis of production from the manufacture of semifinished products and raw materials to the manufacture of paper and cardboard. This was related to the removal of commercial policy barriers on the Western European markets (Jensen-Eriksen, 2007, p. 9). Also, the emphasis of Finnish exports to Japan changed from pulp to paper and cardboard. The increasing export of Finnish paper and cardboard was linked to the direct investments of the Finnish paper industry in the form of established sales agencies in Japan. This commitment to the Japanese market attracted Finnish companies, for instance, because the Japanese authorities modified their restrictive approach to foreign direct investments after the late 1960s (Koskimies, 1982, p. 79).

At the beginning of the 1980s, Finnish companies which had established subsidiaries or joint venture types of sales agencies in Japan included Eurocan Enso Far East Co. Ltd. (marketing of paper and cardboard), Nissin Fructose Co. (sale of fructose), and Lappset Japan Ltd. (sale of wooden playground equipment), in addition to the earlier-mentioned Nippon Finnpap Ltd. and Finnair. Kone Oy, which had previously exported laboratory and hospital electronic equipment, was also then planning to establish a subsidiary to Japan (Koskimies, 1982, p. 78). Three decades later, in 2009, almost all internationally oriented major Finnish corporations (excluding Nokia) were present on the Japanese market. Due to the high costs, these corporations have practically no production in Japan.[58] However, since the 1970s, some Japanese enterprises have shown interest in investing in manufacturing companies in the Nordic countries. One of these is a paper company Jujo Thermal, which has a factory in Kauttua, Finland. In 2011, the company was owned by Nippon Paper Industries, Ahlstrom Oyj, and Mitsui & Co.[59]

Closer trade relations between governments and business enterprises have not only required management of bilateral relations. Since the 1950s, Finland and Japan have worked for the opening of world trade within the General Agreements on Tariffs and Trade. Finland joined GATT in 1950, as did Japan 5 years later. During the entry negotiations in 1955, Finland took an open approach to Japan's admission to GATT, although some countries like the UK and France at the time decided not to apply the General Agreements to Japan (Paavonen, 1998, pp. 257–8). As result of multilateral talks within GATT after the 1950s, tariffs on industrial products were reduced significantly (Aunesluoma, 2011, pp. 222–6). This development naturally promoted Finnish–Japanese trade as well as international trade as a whole. The European Union, of which Finland has been a member since 1995, has no bilateral trade treaty with Japan. EU–Japan trade relations are conducted through the mechanisms of the World Trade Organization, the successor to GATT.

Trade under globalism, 1988 to 2010

Trade relations of Finland and Japan in a global world

Before examining trade relations between Finland and Japan, it is interesting to see the trade relations of these countries with the world as a reference. The recession of the Finnish economy in the early 1990s and the collapse of the Soviet Union in 1991, which had been an important trade partner, encouraged a structural change in the Finnish economy from being resource dependent to being knowledge dependent. The success of this change has been reflected in the trade structures of Finland with the world in the 1990s and 2000s.

The exports and imports of Finland increased more than four times in the 20 years from 1988 to 2008. Imports of SITC 2 (Crude materials, inedible, except fuels), SITC 3 (Mineral fuels, lubricants, and related materials), and SITC 4 (Animal and vegetable oils, fats, and waxes) increased 6, 8, and 7 times, respectively, and exports of SITC 3, SITC 4, and SITC 5 (Chemicals and related products), and SITC 7 (Machinery and transport equipment) increased more than 18, 8, 6, and 7 times, respectively. This reflects the structural change in the Finnish economy in the period. The respective shares of imports of SITC 5, SITC 6 (Manufactured goods), SITC 7, and SITC 8 (Miscellaneous manufactured articles) changed from 10.8 per cent to 10.4 per cent, from 15.9 per cent to 12.3 per cent, from 39.2 per cent to 34.9, and from 12.7 per cent to 8.4 per cent in the period. The respective shares of exports of SITC 2, 6, and 7 changed from 12.3 per cent to 4.9 per cent, from 42.6 per cent to 27.9 per cent, and from 27.4 per cent to 43.9 per cent in the period. Finland depends more than 70 per cent on exports of SITC 6 and 7. However, the growth rate of SITC 6 (Manufactured goods) was less than average and of SITC 7 (Machinery and transport equipment) was much higher than average. The Finnish economy now depends on exports of machinery to the world.

The Japanese economy shifted from high growth to steady growth, about 3 per cent annually, in the period of the Oil Crises of the 1970s. Then Japan tried to change its economic structure into an energy-saving and knowledge-intensive (high-tech–based) economy. Japan expanded exports of electrical appliances, machinery, and motor vehicles. The bubble economy in the latter half of the 1980s burst in the early 1990s. The Japanese economy sank into a depression, the so-called lost decade (actually more than 10 years). Japan experienced appreciation of its currency, and this hastened structural changes of its economy. Japanese Yen (¥) was fixed at 1$ = 360¥ until 1971; it was about 120¥ in the late 1980s and reached a high rate of 80¥ in 1995. Many Japanese export-oriented companies outsourced their labour-intensive production processes to East Asian countries. Japanese companies increased exports of core

Table 9.1 Finland (value of exports and imports are billions of US dollars)

	1988		2008		*Change 1988–2008*		*1988 Imports share*	*2008 Imports share*	*1988 Exports share*	*2008 Exports share*
	Imports	*Exports*	*Imports*	*Exports*	*Imports* %	*Exports*	%	%	%	%
All Commodities	20.92	20.81	92.16	96.89	341.00	365.52	100.00	100.00	100.00	100.00
SITC 0: Food and live animals	1.03	0.34	3.82	1.73	270.00	402.40	5.00	4.00	2.00	2.00
SITC 2: Crude materials, inedible, except fuels	1.32	2.57	7.94	4.79	503.00	86.44	6.00	9.00	12.00	5.00
SITC 3: Mineral fuels, lubricants, and related materials	2.00	0.35	16.20	6.63	709.00	1768.84	10.00	18.00	2.00	7.00
SITC 4: Animal and vegetable oils, fats, and waxes	0.02	0.02	0.17	0.19	607.00	734.72	0.00	0.00	0.00	0.00
SITC 5: Chemicals and related products, n.e.s.	2.26	1.19	9.55	7.88	322.00	564.44	11.00	10.00	6.00	8.00
SITC 6: Manufactured goods	3.32	8.86	11.37	27.04	243.00	205.13	16.00	12.00	43.00	28.00

(*Continued*)

Table 9.1 (Continued)

	1988		*2008*		*Change 1988–2008*		*1988 Imports share*	*2008 Imports share*	*1988 Exports share*	*2008 Exports share*
					Imports	*Exports*				
	Imports	*Exports*	*Imports*	*Exports*	%		%	%	%	%
SITC 7: Machinery and transport equipment	8.21	5.71	32.16	42.56	292.00	645.15	39.00	35.00	27.00	44.00
SITC 8: Miscellaneous manufactured articles	2.66	1.71	7.72	4.82	190.00	182.54	13.00	8.00	8.00	5.00
SITC 9: Commodities and transactions, n.e.s.	0.01	0.02	2.44	1.05	32,503.00	5,358.50	0.00	3.00	0.00	1.00

Source: OECD 2011–2012

Table 9.2 Japan (value of exports and imports are billions of US dollars)

	1988		*2008*		*Change 1988–2008*		*1988 Imports share*	*2008 Imports share*	*1988 Exports share*	*2008 Exports share*
	Imports	*Exports*	*Imports*	*Exports*	*Imports*	*Exports*				
					%		%	%	%	%
All Commodities	187.35	264.92	762.53	781.41	307.01	194.97	100.00	100.00	100.00	100.00
SITC 0: Food and live animals	26.96	1.52	53.71	3.33	99.23	118.73	14.39	7.04	0.57	0.43
SITC 1: Beverages and tobacco	2.16	0.13	6.22	0.54	188.75	319.22	1.15	0.82	0.05	0.07
SITC 2: Crude materials, inedible, except fuels	28.79	1.88	54.84	10.23	90.52	444.45	15.36	7.19	0.71	1.31
SITC 3: Mineral fuels, lubricants, and related materials	38.87	0.58	267.78	18.78	588.89	3155.97	20.75	35.12	0.22	2.40
SITC 4: Animal and vegetable oils, fats, and waxes	0.36	0.15	1.74	0.11	378.44	–28.51	0.19	0.23	0.06	0.01
SITC 5: Chemicals and related products, n.e.s.	14.19	13.90	54.54	69.14	284.33	397.36	7.58	7.15	5.25	8.85
SITC 6: Manufactured goods	26.26	35.02	67.69	97.63	157.76	178.81	14.02	8.88	13.22	12.49

(*Continued*)

Table 9.2 (Continued)

	1988		*2008*		*Change 1988–2008*		*1988 Imports share*	*2008 Imports share*	*1988 Exports share*	*2008 Exports share*
	Imports	*Exports*	*Imports*	*Exports*	*Imports* %	*Exports*	%	%	%	%
SITC 7: Machinery and transport equipment	23.14	185.79	158.86	484.40	586.57	160.72	12.35	20.83	70.13	61.99
SITC 8: Miscellaneous manufactured articles	20.50	22.37	83.95	55.19	309.53	146.74	10.94	11.01	8.44	7.06
SITC 9: Commodities and transactions, n.e.s.	6.13	3.58	13.20	42.08	115.43	1074.44	3.27	1.73	1.35	5.39

Source: OECD 2011–2012

Table 9.3 Trade balance of Japan and Finland (billions of US dollars)

	1988	*1990*	*1995*	*2000*	*2005*	*2008*	*2010*
Japan	77.57	52.15	107.11	99.56	79.07	18.88	75.71
Finland	–0.11	–0.37	10.89	11.66	6.77	4.73	1.16

Source: OECD 2011–2012

(high-tech, R&D–intensive) parts of the products to their subsidiaries in Asia, which exports the final products to the world. Japanese imports from the world increased 4.1 times and exports to the world increased 2.9 times in 20 years, from 1988 to 2008. Japanese international trade structure changed from 'resource-import and final-output-export' to 'labour-intensive-products-import and high-value-added-products-export' in this period. For this change, overseas direct investments were important. The share of imports of SITC 2, 3, 6, 7, and 8 in Japan changed from 15.4 per cent (in 1988) to 7.2 per cent (in 2008), from 20.7 per cent to 35.1 per cent (the value increased 6.9 times), from 14.0 per cent to 8.9 per cent, from 12.4 per cent to 20.8 per cent (the value became 6.8 times), and from 10.9 per cent to 11.0 per cent (the value increased 4.1 times), respectively, in the same period. Japan now mainly imports not only mineral fuels but also machinery equipment and manufactured articles. Exports are concentrated on SITC 6 and SITC 7, and their respective shares changed from 13.2 per cent (in 1988) to 12.5 per cent (in 2008), and from 70.1 per cent (in 1988) to 62.0 per cent (in 2008). However, increases in these were less than average, 2.8 times and 2.6 times, respectively. Japanese exports are still concentrated on machinery and transport equipment but are now more diversified, and SITC 5 and SITC 9 are expanding.

The trade balance of Finland to the world showed a deficit in the late 1980s but changed to a surplus in the early 1990s and continues to be in surplus in the 2000s. The Japanese trade surplus to the world was a big issue and caused trade conflicts with the United States in the 1980s. However, Japan had trade deficits with the oil-exporting countries. The direction of exports from Japan diversified from United States–EU to East Asia in the 1990s, and Japan maintained a trade surplus until the 2000s. However, the value of the surplus decreased in the 2000s and showed a deficit in 2011 (the last trade deficit of Japan was in 1980 after the second Oil Crisis).

Trade relations between Finland and Japan

We are now in a position to evaluate the recent trade relations between Finland and Japan and to investigate how the problems mentioned in the previous sections have changed or been removed. In the 1990s, the Finnish economy on the one hand was more deeply integrated with the EU and expanded its multilateral (global) relations with the world. On the other hand, Japan was also

Table 9.4 Trade balance between Japan and Finland (millions of US dollars)

	1988	*1990*	*1995*	*2000*	*2005*	*2008*	*2010*
Japanese trade balance to Finland	770.5	605.4	231.6	382.3	656.0	448.4	–574.2
Finnish trade balance to Japan	–1,171.5	–1,365.9	–853.5	–1,035.4	–998.9	–696.1	–336.5
Japanese exports-Finnish exports	848.2	671.8	366.0	463.1	969.3	1201.9	147.7

Source: OECD 2011–2012

integrated into the regional (East Asia) sphere and extended its global economic activities. In the meantime, the economic relations between Finland and Japan changed from being bilateral (or historical) to become based on a market mechanism or on a multilateral (or global) economy. This is reflected in the trade structure between the two countries and can be found in their trade data.

First of all, it is interesting to see the bilateral trade imbalance, because the trade deficit with Japan had been a big trade issue for Finland. It is now moving towards balance.

In using exports and imports values, it should be noted that an export value of Japan to Finland is not an import value of Finland from Japan. The import value of c.i.f. (cost, insurance, and freight) is normally larger than the export value of f.o.b. (free on board). The Japanese trade balance to Finland was \$770.5 million surplus in 1988 and decreased to \$448.4 million surplus in 2008, and an interesting point is the deficit of \$57.4 million in 2010. The export value of road vehicles in 2008 was extremely high and returned to its former level in 2010; thus the change into a Japanese deficit to Finland might imply a new stage of their trade relations. The main reasons may lie with the Japanese economy, which experienced a trade deficit to the world after 30 years of surplus. The balance of trade of Finland to the world was in surplus after the 1990s, but the Finnish trade deficit to Japan was a problem from a bilateral aspect. However, exports from Finland to Japan increased more rapidly than imports to Finland from Japan, and the Finnish trade deficit became quite small in 2010. In the 20 years from 1988 to 2008, Finnish exports increased 3.1 times and imports increased only 1.2 times; Japanese imports increased 4.2 times and exports only 1.9 times. To investigate export and import structures in international trade between Finland and Japan, the value of exports is mainly used to avoid problems of transaction and transportation costs.

Next, the changes in the export and import structure are investigated using commodity trade data, and movement from mono-culture type (small-number commodity export-import type) to many (diversified) commodities export-import type can be found in the data.

Exports from Japan to Finland concentrated on SITC 7 and mostly on SITC 78 (Road vehicles), and the share was about 87 per cent, both in 1988

Table 9.5 Japanese exports and imports to Finland (millions of US dollars in 2010)

	1988		*2008*		*Change 1988–2008*		*1988 Imports share*	*2008 Imports share*	*1988 Exports share*	*2008 Exports share*
	Imports	*Exports*	*Imports*	*Exports*	*Imports*	*Exports*				
					%		%	%	%	%
All Commodities	452.60	1,223.09	1,902.90	2351.26	320.40	92.20	100.00	100.00	100.00	100.00
SITC 0: Food and live animals	17.06	0.09	22.51	2.31	32.00	2575.00	0.00	0.00	0.01	3.00
SITC 1: Beverages and tobacco	18.29	0.04	0.26	0.05	–98.60	15.80	0.00	0.00	0.00	0.00
SITC 2: Crude materials, inedible, except fuels	66.05	3.63	289.28	4.31	338.00	18.70	0.00	0.00	0.30	24.00
SITC 3: Mineral fuels, lubricants, and related materials	0.16	0.04	1.12	0.31	592.60	669.70	0.00	0.00	0.00	0.00
SITC 4: Animal and vegetable oils, fats, and waxes	0.00	0.02	0.07	0.02	#	6.00	0.00	0.00	0.00	0.00
SITC 5: Chemicals and related products, n.e.s.	18.57	26.04	220.15	53.82	1,085.20	106.70	2.00	5.00	2.13	4.00
SITC 6: Manufactured goods	243.86	49.41	743.38	113.73	204.80	130.20	5.00	4.00	4.04	20.00

(*Continued*)

Table 9.5 (Continued)

	1988		*2008*		*Change 1988–2008*		*1988 Imports share*	*2008 Imports share*	*1988 Exports share*	*2008 Exports share*
	Imports	*Exports*	*Imports*	*Exports*	*Imports* %	*Exports*	%	%	%	%
SITC 7: Machinery and transport equipment	57.23	1,065.41	529.65	2,041.68	825.50	91.60	83.00	82.00	87.11	41.00
SITC 8: Miscellaneous manufactured articles	30.20	73.44	89.95	100.03	197.90	36.20	9.00	9.00	6.00	8.00
SITC 9: Commodities and transactions, n.e.s.	1.19	4.96	6.53	35.010	448.80	605.20	0.00	0.00	0.41	0.00

Sources: OECD 2011–2012

and in 2008, and the increase in export value was the same at 1.9 times as the increase of total exports. The share of SITC8 was 6.0 per cent in 1988 and 4.3 per cent in 2008, and the increase was less than average, 1.4 times. The share of SITC 6 (mainly SITC 62: Rubber manufactures) was 4.0 per cent in 1988 and 4.8 per cent in 2008, and the increase was more than average, 2.3 times. The development of Japanese exports to Finland depends on the export of cars and related products.

Finnish exports of all commodities to Japan increased rapidly (3.1 times) and were rather diversified into different commodities. The main exports of SITC 2, 6, 7, and 8 increased 5.6 times, 1.1 times, 9.0 times, and 3.9 times, respectively, in the 20 years from 1988 to 2008. The share of SITC 2, 6, 7, and 8, was 13.1 per cent, 57.7 per cent, 13.9 per cent, and 5.9 per cent, respectively, in 1988, changing to 24.1 per cent, 20.3 per cent, 41.1 per cent, and 7.6 per cent, respectively, in 2008. Exports of SITC 2 were mainly composed of SITC 24 (Cork and wood) and SITC 25 (Pulp and waste paper), almost 100 per cent together. However, the share of SITC 25 was 80 to 90 per cent before 1990, yet SITC 24 was about 90 per cent after 1995. This implies that Japan endeavoured to import lower-value–added products such as wood-related products. Exports of SITC 6 were composed of SITC 63 (Cork and wood manufactures, excluding furniture) and SITC 64 (Paper and paper manufactures), around 80 per cent together in 1990s and about 90 per cent in the 2000s. The share of SITC 63 in SITC 6 increased rapidly from less than 5 per cent in 1995 to more than 40 per cent in 2008, and the share of SITC 64 in SITC 6 decreased to the level of SITC 63 in 2008. Finnish exports of paper and paper manufactures in SITC 6 stagnated in the period because of Japanese economic stagnation and its oligopolistic competition among Japanese paper companies. Finland expanded cork-wood manufactures and reduced paper-paper manufactures, adapting to the international trade strategy and oligopolistic competition in Japanese paper companies.

Among others, the expansion of Finnish exports of SITC 7 was remarkable in the period and appeared promising for the future. SITC 71 (Power-generating machinery and equipment), SITC 72 (Specialized machinery), SITC 74 (Other industrial machinery), SITC 76 (Telecommunication and sound recording apparatus), and SITC 77 (Electrical machinery, apparatus, and appliances) had important shares in SITC 7, and the export values of these increased 4.5 times, 13.4 times, 8.9 times, 36.6 times, and 7.2 times, respectively, in the 20 years from 1988 to 2008. Promising exports in SITC 8 are SITC 81 (Prefabricated buildings, sanitary, heating, and lighting fixtures) and SITC 87 (Professional and scientific instruments), for which export values increased 4.1 times and 8.9 times, respectively, from 1988 to 2008.

Specific features of Finnish–Japanese trade

Properties of trade structure can be illustrated using some indices, the RCA (revealed comparative advantage) Index, the RCD (revealed comparative

Table 9.6 Finnish exports and imports to Japan (million US dollars in 2010)

	1988		*2008*		*Change 1988–2008*		*1988 Imports share*	*2008 Imports share*	*1988 Exports share*	*2008 Exports share*
	Imports	*Exports*	*Imports*	*Exports*	*Imports* %	*Exports*	%	%	%	%
All Commodities	1,546.44	374.91	1,845.47	1,149.34	19.30	206.60	100.00	100.00	100.00	100.00
SITC 0: Food and live animals	0.77	11.00	1.08	29.84	39.90	171.10	0.05	0.06	2.94	2.60
SITC 1: Beverages and tobacco	0.02	8.64	0.20	0.14	884.70	–98.30	0.00	0.01	2.30	0.01
SITC 2: Crude materials, inedible, except fuels	4.74	49.22	6.23	276.85	31.40	462.50	0.31	0.34	13.13	24.09
SITC 3: Mineral fuels, lubricants, and related materials	0.13	0.22	0.54	0.74	321.00	231.90	0.01	0.03	0.06	0.06
SITC 4: Animal and vegetable oils, fats, and waxes	0.01	0.00	0.02	0.22	154.70	n/a	0.00	0.00	0.00	0.02
SITC 5: Chemicals and related products. n.e.s.	37.67	15.28	86.76	48.16	130.30	215.10	2.44	4.70	4.08	4.19

SITC 6: Manufactured goods	75.24	216.14	77.37	233.54	2.80	8.10	4.87	4.19	57.65	20.32
SITC 7: Machinery and transport equipment	1,290.57	52.19	1,508.21	472.17	16.90	804.70	83.45	81.72	13.92	41.08
SITC 8: Miscellaneous manufactured articles	137.30	22.22	163.97	87.67	19.40	294.60	8.88	8.88	5.93	7.63
SITC 9: Commodities and transactions. n.e.s.	0.00	0.00	1.09	0.00	n/a	0.00	0.00	0.06	0.00	0.00

Source: OECD 2011–2012

disadvantage) Index, and the IIT (intra-industry trade) Index. As explained in the following subsections, RCA and RCD show export and import commodity concentration to Finland or to Japan relative to the world, and IIT shows mutual export-import in a same-commodity classification (industry) of the two countries.

Export and import structures between Finland and Japan can be illustrated clearly by the RCA Index. The Finnish revealed comparative advantage to Japan in commodities is shown as RCA_{fjs}, which is $(EX_{fjs}/EX_{fja})/(EX_{fws}/EX_{fwa})$ where EX_{fjs} expresses exports of suffixes f, j, s, that is from country-f (Finland), to country-j (Japan), and of commodity-s (SITC number-s). When the suffix number is a, suffix-a, the index is of all commodities, and when the suffix country is w, suffix-w, the index is of the world. In the same way, RCA_{jfs} is a Japanese revealed comparative advantage to Finland in commodity-s. If the share of commodity-s in Finnish exports to Japan is the same as to the world, the RCA_{fjs} Index becomes 1. Therefore, when an index is greater than 1, the value of Finnish exports to Japan is more concentrated on the commodity concerned (Finland reveals comparative advantage to Japan in the commodity). If the values of imports are used instead of the value of exports, then we get the RCD Index, the level of concentration on imports of the commodity concerned, and RCD_{fjs} or RCD_{jfs} will be similarly obtained as the case of RCA_{fjs} and RCA_{jfs}.

Now let us look at the RCA index of Japanese exports to Finland and the RCD index of Finnish imports from Japan. First, the share of Japanese exports to Finland in SITC 7 (mainly road vehicles) was 87 per cent of all commodities in 1988 and 2008; however, the Japanese share of exports to the world was also high and RCA_{jf7} was 1.24 (in 1988) and 1.40 (in 2008). This means Japanese exports of SITC 7 were more concentrated to Finland relative to the world.

Table 9.7 Japanese RCA to Finland

	1988	*1990*	*1995*	*2000*	*2005*	*2008*	*2010*
SITC 0	0.012	0.051	5.107	0.202	0.044	0.230	0.251
SITC 1	0.075	0.084	0.446	0.000	0.007	0.032	0.146
SITC 2	0.418	0.323	23.052	0.334	0.124	0.140	0.111
SITC 3	0.015	0.005	0.161	0.000	0.002	0.006	0.074
SITC 4	0.032	0.035	0.000	0.000	0.188	0.073	0.228
SITC 5	0.406	0.597	0.593	0.381	0.211	0.259	0.577
SITC 6	0.306	0.395	3.437	0.383	0.293	0.387	0.607
SITC 7	1.242	1.196	0.452	1.182	1.344	1.401	1.259
SITC 8	0.711	0.803	0.940	1.055	0.685	0.602	0.587
SITC 9	0.300	0.224	0.291	0.640	0.541	0.277	1.069

Source: OECD 2011–2012

Among Finnish imports, RCD_{fj7} was 2.13 (in 1988) and 2.34 (in 2008). This means the share of imports of SITC 7 was twice as concentrated on imports from Japan relative to the share in Finnish imports from the world. The Finns may have wanted to reduce imports of cars for their trade balance and the Japanese may have wanted to increase their exports of machinery in SITC 7. Second, for SITC 8, RCA_{jf8} was 0.71 (in 1988) and 1.05 (in 2000) but fell to 0.60 (in 2008). This means that Japan had competitiveness in miscellaneous manufactured articles in SITC 8 and succeeded in exports to Finland around 2000 but was less competitive in the 2000s. The export share of SITC 8 of Japanese exports to Finland (EX_{jf8}/EX_{jfa}) fell to half the level of the share of Japanese exports to the world (EX_{fws}/EX_{fwa}) in 2010. This shows that Japan has reduced its comparative advantage over Finland in SITC 8. In regards to the Finnish imports side, RCD_{fj8} was 0.70 (in 1988) and increased to 1.11 (in 2010). That is, Finland increased Japanese share more than imports from the world in SITC 8. Finland increased her comparative disadvantage to Japan in SITC 8. Both Japan and Finland are discontented with this situation regarding SITC 8. Third, regarding SITC 6, RCA_{jf6}, Japanese exports to Finland of mainly rubber manufactures, was 0.31 (in 1988), 0.39 (in 2008), and increased to 0.61 (in 2010). As far as the Finnish imports are concerned, RCD_{fj6} was 0.31 (in 1988), 0.34 (in 2008), and 0.32 (in 2010). This shows that Finland (and Japan) are not important partners in Japanese exports (and in Finnish imports) of SITC 6.

In the same way, the comparative advantage or disadvantage of Finnish exports or Japanese imports can be investigated. First regarding SITC 2, RCA_{fj2} was 1.06 in 1988 and increased to 4.03 in 2010, and this shows that Finnish exports of SITC 2 to Japan were similar to the share of exports to the world in 1988 but

Table 9.8 Finnish RCA to Japan

	1988	*1990*	*1995*	*2000*	*2005*	*2008*	*2010*
SITC 0	1.7740	2.2303	0.8258	1.5266	1.7963	1.4539	1.2026
SITC 1	11.6747	6.2700	1.1539	0.1190	0.0927	0.0568	0.0537
SITC 2	1.0637	1.1387	1.6728	3.6044	5.6058	4.8735	4.0267
SITC 3	0.0348	0.0406	0.0332	0.0272	0.0154	0.0094	0.0092
SITC 4	0.0000	0.0000	0.0000	0.0781	0.0095	0.0986	0.0205
SITC 5	0.7155	0.8924	0.6818	0.9497	0.5800	0.5153	0.6935
SITC 6	1.3542	0.9766	0.8393	1.1848	0.9672	0.7282	0.9782
SITC 7	0.5073	0.8225	1.1231	0.4503	0.4592	0.9353	0.6355
SITC 8	0.7234	1.4804	1.1494	1.9673	2.0356	1.5340	1.9280
SITC 9	0.0000	0.0000	0.0000	0.0002	0.0024	0.0003	0.0018

Source: OECD 2011–2012

increased to about five times in 2008. As mentioned, the main contents of SITC 2 changed from pulp and waste paper to cork and wood. However, RCD_{jf2} was not stable in the period, being 0.95 in 1988, 4.26 in 2005, 0.03 in 2008, and 1.90 in 2010. This may reflect changes in the economic conditions and strategy of the Japanese paper industry. Regarding SITC 6, RCA_{fj6} was 1.35 in 1988 and 0.98 in 2010. The main share of SITC 6 changed from paper and paper manufactures to cork and wood manufactures; Finnish export concentration on Japan was not much different from that to the world. RCD_{jf6} was 3.84 in 1988 and 3.82 in 2010, although the index was not stable. In imports of SITC 6, Japan concentrated on Finnish imports about four times from the world.

Third, Finnish exports of SITC 7 to Japan increased nine times from 1988 to 2008; however, RCA_{fj7} changed from 0.51 in 1988 to 0.93 in 2008 and 0.63 in 2010. This shows that the pace of the increase in Finnish exports of machinery to Japan was a little faster relative to its exports to the world. RCD_{jf7} was 1.02 in 1988, 4.17 in 2008, and 1.22 in 2010, and its fluctuation was wide. This implies that the Japanese comparative disadvantage in exporting machinery to Finland increased in the period. It is interesting that Japanese imports of machinery and exports of transport equipment are both in SITC 7. (This point will be discussed more in the discussion on the following intra-industry trade index.) Fourth, regarding SITC 8, RCA_{fj8} was 0.72 in 1988 and increased to 1.48 in 1990 and was 1.93 in 2010. In commodities SITC 8, Finland had a comparative advantage and increased export concentration to Japan. Conversely for Japanese imports of SITC 8, RCD_{jf8} was 0.61 in 1988 and 0.49 in 2010; thus, Japan was not concentrated in Finnish imports of SITC 8. SITC 8, including many diversified commodities, might be promising Finnish exports to Japan in future.

When two countries differ in the developmental stages of their economies, natural resource endowments, climates, and populations, then international trade between these countries will be exchanges of products in different industries – that is, interindustry trade. Of course, this depends on how to aggregate or disaggregate commodities and industries. However, it is significant that between similarly developed countries, reciprocal exports and imports of similar commodities (products of same industry), especially of industrial products, have been increasing. Finland and Japan differ in population and natural resource endowments but are similar and high in per-capita income levels. The differences produced, historically, Finnish export of wood-related products and Japanese export of labour-intensive products, but recently the similarity increased mutual export and import of industrial products.

This can be checked by using the IIT index, defined as follows. IIT_{jfs} (Japan–Finland intra-industry trade index of SITC number s), that is (Ex_{jfs} minus EX_{fjs})/(Ex_{jfs} plus EX_{fjs}). If the index of IIT_{jfs} is 1, only Japanese commodities in SITC number-s are exported (if it is –1, only Finnish commodities are exported), and the index is zero when reciprocal exports are equal. The changes of IIT_{jfs}, (s = 1, 2, 3, 5, 6, 7, 8), can be found in the diagram. For SITC 2, IIT_{jf2} was –0.86

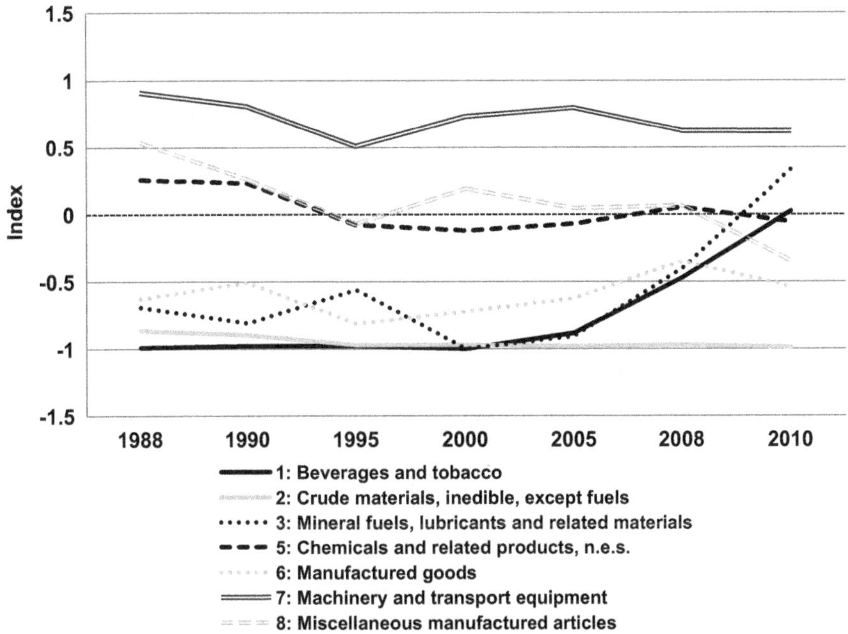

Figure 9.7 IIT between Japan and Finland (SITC 0-9, in exports value) (J – F/J + F)

Source: OECD 2011–2012

in 1988 and –0.99 in 2010; the index was about –1 throughout the period. This reflects a natural-resources – (wood-related-products–) dependent export pattern of Finland and a natural resource scarcity in Japan. For SITC 1, IIT_{jf1} was –0.99 in 1988, changed to –0.47 in 2008, and became 0.02 in 2010. The main Finnish exports were tobacco and tobacco manufactures until 1995 but stopped thereafter, and the index showed mutual export of beverages. Japan gradually expanded its exports of beverages to Finland, and mutual export became almost equal now. Regarding SITC 3, IIT_{jf3} was –0.69 in 1988, –0.41 in 2008, and changed to 0.33 in 2010. Finnish exports of coal and coke dominated until recent years, but Japanese exports of petroleum products increased after 2005 and dominated the index in 2010. Regarding SITC 5, IIT_{jf5} was 0.26 in 1988 and –0.05 in 2010; thus, intra-industry trade between Japan and Finland has been very high in chemicals and related products in SITC 5. For SITC 6, IIT_{jf6} was –0.63 in 1988 and –0.54 in 2010. Finnish exports of wood and paper manufactures dominated Japanese exports of rubber manufactures, both commodities are in SITC 6, and thus the index was negative. The index of intra-industry trade seems to be increasing, but the natural resource factor dominates in SITC 6. Regarding SITC 8, IIT_{jf8} was 0.54 in 1988, and –0.35

in 2010, although it fluctuated in the period. Japan–Finland intra-industry trade in SITC 8 increased in the period, but Finnish exports increased, concentrating on Japan, but Japanese exports did not concentrate on Finland, and thus the index changed from positive to negative. Regarding SITC 7, IIT_{jf7} was 0.91 in 1988 and 0.62 in 2010, showing the dominance of Japanese car exports in SITC 7. This trade pattern could be explained by a production factor, namely abundance of efficient labour and human capital in Japan. However, the index was reduced in the period, reflecting an increase of intra-industry trade in SITC 7. By and large, intra-industry trade between Finland and Japan increased in many industrial products in the period and is expected to increase more in the future.

Conclusions

During the past 90 years, trade relations between Finland and Japan have developed considerably in terms of value and volume. The changes, progress, and downturns of these relations reflect transformation of the economy, industry, and society experienced in both countries as well as globally. After the Second World War, both countries continued to regulate their foreign trade, which also disrupted the bilateral trade until the early 1960s. At the same time, however, both countries concentrated on strengthening their foundations for economic growth, especially in industrial products. Finland and Japan joined GATT in the 1950s, thus making their contribution to the opening of world trade. The increase in post-war Finnish–Japanese trade was ultimately an outcome of the liberalization of bilateral and multilateral trade, which in turn enhanced closer connections between Finnish and Japanese companies.

During the early stage of the post-war period in Finnish–Japanese trade, the goal was to regain the pre-war trade levels, and trade patterns at the time were traditional resource oriented or production factor abundance oriented – that is, Finland exported wood-related products to Japan and the Japanese mainly exported textiles and later cars to Finland. At a later stage, trade patterns moved toward patterns explained by the new trade theory of the reciprocal export-import of similar commodities in capital- and technology-intensive industries. Bilateral trade volumes depend positively on the economic activity levels of the countries concerned and negatively on the distance (transportation and transaction costs) between the countries. As a positive factor, both Finland and Japan have developed and increased human capital and succeeded in technology-dependent industrialization and thus increased reciprocal trade. As to the negative factor of distance, development of transportation – for instance, through the establishment of new transportation routes – helped to increase trade between Finland and Japan in the post-war period.

From the 1960s to the end of the 1990s, trade increased almost annually, thus raising its importance, especially from the standpoint of Finnish foreign trade. In the 2000s, the value of bilateral trade has not increased as in earlier decades. In fact, it has decreased in relative terms during the past 10 years. Bilateral trade balance has experienced a change, for Finland's 'traditional' post-war trade deficit with Japan has now markedly decreased. In 2011, Finland's exports to Japan exceeded Japan's exports to Finland for the first time since 1959.[60] Time will tell if this indicates a new development in the Finnish–Japanese trade.

Archival sources

OECD commodity trade data

Archive sources

The Archives of the Finnish Legation in Tokyo (FLT), placed at the Provincial Archives of Oulu, Finland.

Fc Correspondence relating to the Finnish Legation in Tokyo 1924–1943.

The Archives of the Ministry for Foreign Affairs of Finland (MFA), Helsinki, Finland.

UM 5 G 15 a: The Finnish Legation in Tokyo, foundation and management 1937–1945

UM 53 Japan Osaka: The Finnish Consulates

UM 53 O 4 Japan

UM 56 A Japan: Economic reports

UM 58 B1, B2 Japan: Foreign trade and foreign trade policy of Finland

The Archives of the Finnish Cellulose Union (Finncell), placed at the Central Archives for Finnish Business Records (ELKA), Mikkeli, Finland.

Circulars 1948–1949

Annual Reports 1920–1975

Printed sources

Suomen sopimukset vieraitten valtioitten kanssa 1926. Suomen ulkoasiainministeriön julkaisut. Helsinki 1927. Valtioneuvoston Kirjapaino.

Internet sources

'Jujo Thermal in brief'. Homepage of Jujo Thermal. www.jujothermal.com/about_us/ (Accessed October 4, 2011.)

'Kauppavaihto maaryhmittäin ja maittain; tuonti alkuperämaittain ja vienti määrämaittain. Tammi-joulukuu 2011'. Source: Finnish Customs. Foreign trade statistics of Finland. January-December 2011. www.tulli.fi/fi/suomen_tulli/ulkomaankauppatilastot/tilastoja/maatilastoja/vuodet/index.jsp (Accessed July 16, 2013).

'Maatiedosto Japani. Kahdenväliset suhteet'. Homepage of the Finnish Embassy in Tokyo www.finland.or.jp/public/default.aspx?nodeid=44381&contentlan=1&culture=fi-FI (Accessed October 4, 2011.)

Interview

President Kazuki Yamamoto of Finland Japan Trading Co. Ltd.
Interviewer: Juha Sahi
Time and place: 5.11.2010. Osaka, Japan

Notes

1. The treaty came into force in 1926. Treaty of Commerce and Navigation between Finland and Japan. Suomen sopimukset vieraitten valtioitten kanssa 1926.
2. 'Aineistoa Japanin-Suomen kauppa-sopimusta varten'. Addition B. Chargé d'affaires G.J. Ramstedt's report No 403. Tokyo 23.12.1922. UM 58 B 1 Japan. MFA.
3. Trade negotiations between Finland and Japan. 1938. Statistics. UM 58 B 1 Japan. MFA.
4. 'P.M. Japanilaisten tavarain tuonnista'. Memorandum by J.A. Tamminen. 8.3.1934. Helsinki. UM 58 B 1 Japan. MFA.
5. 'Japanilaisten tavarain polkumyynti'. Letter signed by head of department K.R. Savolahti for the Finnish Legation in Tokyo. Helsinki 24.4.1934. UM 58 B 1 Japan. MFA.
6. 'P.M. Japanin kaupasta ja polkumyynnistä'. 7/9 Kaila. Helsinki 6.10.1938. UM 58 B 1 Japan. MFA. Letter addressed to Minister V. Tanner from managing director V.M.J. Viljanen of the Confederation of Finnish Industries. Helsinki 3.10.1938. UM 58 B 1 Japan. MFA.
7. Quotas on rayon pulp received by other countries: USA 27,3 per cent, Canada 23,6 per cent, Norway 18,2 per cent and Sweden 9,1 per cent.
8. 'Suomen-Japanin kauppaneuvottelut. XIV'. Minister Valvanne's economic report No 20. Tokyo 11.5.1939. UM 58 B 1 Japan. MFA. 'Monsieur le Ministre'. Tokyo 1.5.1939. Enclosure to report: 'Suomen-Japanin kauppaneuvottelut. XV'. Minister Valvanne's economic report No 22. Tokyo 2.5.1939. UM 58 B 1 Japan. MFA. 'Tokion-lähetystön toimintakertomus vuodelta 1939'. Minister Idman. Tokyo 22.1.1940. Fc:15 Annual Report of the Finnish Legation in Tokyo 1939. Fc Correspondence relating to the Finnish Legation in Tokyo 1924–1943. FLT.
9. Copy of a classified telegram No C 69. 22.9.1944. FINLANDIA Ankara Bern Lisboa Madrid FENNIA Cittadelvaticano. UM 5 G 15 a. MFA. Communiqué for Licence Commission and Customs Administration. Helsinki 26.9.1944. Minister A. Martola. UM 58 B 1 Japan. MFA.
10. 'Suomen kauppa Japanin kanssa'. Memorandum by Ragnar Smedslund. Ministry for Foreign Affairs of Finland 14.2.1949. UM 58 B 1 Japan. MFA.
11. SVT I A. Annual publication of foreign trade 1948.
12. 'Japanin kauppa'. Commercial attaché Artturi Lehtinen. Brief No 4000/663. Washington 8.7.1947. Appendix to the brief 'Foreign trade letter. United States Department of Commerce. Trade with Japan resumes August 15'. UM 58 B 2 Japan. MFA.
13. 'The Finnish-Japanese Trade Mission'. Ouchterlony & Co. LTD. sgd. Managing Director. No 63. Osaka Oct. 12, 1948. UM 58 B 1 Japan. MFA.
14. 'Suomen kauppa Japanin kanssa'. Memorandum by Ragnar Smedslund. In the Ministry for Foreign Affairs of Finland 14.2.1949. UM 58 B 1 Japan. MFA.
15. Assistant head of department Ragnar Smedslund's letter to Consul General Rafael Seppälä 22.4.1949. UM 58 B 1 Japan. MFA. 'Suosituimmuus

suomalais-japanilaisessa kaupankäynnissä'. Consul General Rafael Seppälä's memorandum. Helsinki 27.6.1951. UM 58 B 1 Japan. MFA.

16. Financial arrangement was formulated to a standard clearing contract.
17. 'Japanin kanssa tehdyt kauppa- ja maksusopimukset'. Memorandum. Helsinki 2.6.1949. UM 58 B 1 Japan. MFA. Press release for the STT. 21.6.1949. UM 58 B 1 Japan. MFA. 'Kauppa ja maksusopimuksia koskeva sanomalehtikommunikea'. Brief No 4 to the Ministry for Foreign Affairs of Finland. Signed by Consul General Rafael Seppälä. Tokyo, 21.6.1949. UM 58 B 1 Japan. MFA.
18. 'General Headquarters Supreme Commander for the Allied Powers APO 500'. AG o91. 31(23 Apr 49) ESS/FTC. Revised Final Draft 3 June 1949. Finland – Occupied Japan Trade Plan. Estimate of Purchases by Finland from Occupied Japan. Estimate of Sales by Finland to Occupied Japan. UM 58 B 1 Japan. MFA.
19. Consul General Rafael Seppälä's letter to secretary of department Veikko Rutanen of the Ministry for the Foreign Affairs of Finland. New York 30.11.1949. UM 58 B 2 Japan. MFA.
20. 'Suosituimmuus suomalais-japanilaisessa kaupankäynnissä'. Consul General Rafael Seppälä's memorandum. Helsinki 27.6.1951. UM 58 B 1 Japan. MFA.
21. 'Suomen ja Japanin väliset kauppasuhteet'. Envoy C.A. Gripenberg's brief No 1248/463. Stockholm 26.3.1952. UM 58 B 1 Japan. MFA. 'Kaupalliset neuvottelut Japanin kanssa'. Jorma Vanamo's brief No 1643/606. Stockholm 29.4.1952. UM 58 B 1 Japan. MFA. 'Maksusopimus Japanin kanssa'. Pentti Talvitie's report for the Trade Committee.12.12.1956. UM 58 B 1 Japan. MFA.
22. Parallel trade is a foreign trade operation, in which designated export and import transactions constitute one another. 'Japanin ulkomaankauppasäännöstely'. Consul General Ragnar Smedslund's economic report No 1. Tokyo 20.10.1952. UM 56 A Japan. MFA.
23. Before concluding the new payments arrangement with Finland, Japan had ended the use of clearing accounts for instance with Sweden, West Germany, and Italy. 'Suomen – Japanin maksusopimus'. Consul General Ragnar Smedslund's brief No 322/95. Tokyo 2.8.1956. UM 58 B 1 Japan. MFA. 'Maksusopimus Japanin kanssa'. Pentti Talvitie's report for the Trade Committee. 12.12.1956. UM 58 B 1 Japan. MFA.
24. 'P.M. Suomen kauppa Japanin kanssa'. Ragnar Smedslund's memorandum. Helsinki 8.5.1950. UM 58 B 1 Japan. MFA. 'Koskee Suomen-Japanin kauppaa'. Letter by Central Association of Finnish Wood-working Industries to the Department for External Economic Relations of the Ministry for the Foreign Affairs of Finland. Helsinki 11.5.1950. UM 58 B 1 Japan. MFA.
25. 'Suomen ja Japanin välisestä kauppavaihdosta'. Ossi Sunelli's report at the meeting of the Trade Committee 12.11.1956. Helsinki 10.11.1956. UM 58 B 2 Japan. MFA. 'Annual Report for 1955'. Honorary Consul for Finland Masami Yamamoto's annual report on activities of honorary consulate in Osaka and Kobe in 1955. Osaka 14.2.1956. UM 53 Japan Osaka. MFA.
26. 'Selluloosan vienti Japaniin'. Envoy Ragnar Smedslund's brief No 568/145. Tokyo 4.9.1957. UM 58 B 2 Japan. MFA. 'P.M. Selluloosan viennin vastiketuonti Japanista'. Memorandum by acting head of department Pentti Talvitie. Helsinki 7.10.1957. UM 58 B 2 Japan. MFA.
27. 'Suomen selluloosavienti Japaniin'. Envoy Ragnar Smedslund's brief No 25/15. Tokyo 20.1.1958. UM 58 B 2 Japan. MFA. 'Selluloosantoimitukset Japaniin'. Finncell's letter addressed to the Department for External Economic Relations of the Ministry for Foreign Affairs of Finland. 10.12.1957. UM 58 B 2 Japan. MFA.

28. 'Muistio Suomen ja Japanin välisistä kauppasuhteista'. T.M. 2.10.1958. UM 58 B 2 Japan. MFA.
29. 'Suomen ja Japanin välinen kauppa'. First Secretary Martti Lintulahti's brief No 263/74. Tokyo 10.3.1959. UM 58 B 2 Japan. MFA. 'Suomen ja Japanin taloudelliset suhteet vuonna 1958'. First Secretary Martti Lintulahti's economic report No 6. Tokyo 4.3.1959. UM 56 A Japan. MFA.
30. 'P. M'. Memorandum by Osmo Lares 31.3.1959. UM 58 B 2 Japan. MFA.
31. Pine oil (tall oil) is a side product of the manufacture of sulphate pulp. 'Kiertokirje No 6 sulfaattitehtaille'. Circular by Finncell 5.2.1948. 'Kiertokirje No 5 sulfaattitehtaille'. Circular by Finncell 26.4.1949. The Archives of Finncell.
32. 'Suomen ja Japanin taloudelliset suhteet vuonna 1960'. First Secretary Martti Lintulahti's economic report No 3. Tokyo 10.4.1961. UM 56 A Japan. MFA. 'Katsaus Suomen ja Japanin välisiin kaupallisiin suhteisiin'. First Secretary Martti Lintulahti's economic report No 5. Tokyo 26.6.1926 (1963). UM 56 A Japan. MFA.
33. 'Multilateraalinen tuontikohtelu Japanille 1.1.1962 lukien'. Acting chargé d'affaires Martti Lintulahti's brief No 800/301. Tokyo 23.12.1961. UM 58 B 2 Japan. MFA.
34. 'Suomen kauppa Japanin kanssa; auto-ostot Japanista'. Acting chargé d'affaires Martti Lintulahti's brief No 678/222. Tokyo 8.8.1962. UM 58 B 2 Japan. MFA.
35. 'Suomen ja Japanin välinen kauppavaihto ulkomaankauppatilastojen valossa'. Memorandum by the Trade Department of the Ministry of Trade and Industry of Finland. Helsinki 28.10.1963. UM 58 B 2 Japan. MFA. 'Japanin ulkomaankauppa 1965'. First Secretary Erkki Hedmanson's economic report No 7/66. Tokyo 28.3.1966. UM 56 A Japan. MFA.
36. 'Yleisselostus Japanin talouselämästä suomalaisten viejien tarpeita silmälläpitäen'. First Secretary Erkki Hedmanson's economic report No 13. Tokyo 27.4.1966. UM 56 A Japan. MFA. 'Ehdotus konsuli M. Yamamoton nimittämisestä pääkonsuliksi'. Ragnar Smedslund's brief No 720/208. Tokyo 10.10.1960. UM 53 O 4 Japan. MFA.
37. 'Suomen ja Japanin välisestä kaupasta 1967'. Acting chargé d'affaires Heikki Kalha's economic report No 2/68. Tokyo 13.3.1968. UM 56 A Japan. MFA.
38. 'Kontaineriliikenne Siperian halki'. Secretary for trade C-E. Ullner's economic report No 2. Tokyo 16.2.1971. UM 56 A Japan. MFA. 'Japanin kauppa'. Memorandum by MD Aarne Kaivola of M.A.T. Transport Oy to Minister Pentti Uusivirta. Helsinki 17.1.1973. UM 58 B 2 Japan. MFA.
39. Secretary for trade Kari Vainio's part in the article for a Finnish weekly news magazine *Suomen Kuvalehti* on trade with Japan edited by Jouni Lompola. The Finnish Embassy in Tokyo, brief No 744. Signed by Osmo Lares. UM 58 B 2 Japan. MFA.
40. 'Suomen ja Japanin välisestä kaupasta 1967'. Acting chargé d'affaires Heikki Kalha's economic report No 2/68. Tokyo 13.3.1968. UM 56 A Japan. MFA.
41. 'Japanin viennin kehitys v. 1974 tammi-elokuussa ja näkemyksiä vientimahdollisuuksista lähitulevaisuudessa'. Secretary for trade C-E. Ullner's review for the Ministry for Foreign Affairs of Finland. Tokyo 13.11.1974. UM 58 B 2 Japan. MFA.
42. 'Suomen selluloosavienti Japaniin'. Envoy Ragnar Smedslund's brief No 317/102. Tokyo 26.4.1960. UM 58 B 2 Japan. MFA. 'Annual Report for 1960'. Honorary consul general for Finland Masami Yamamoto's annual report on the activities of honorary consulate in Osaka in 1960. Osaka 23.2.1961. UM 53

Japan Osaka. MFA. Interview of President Kazuki Yamamoto of Finland Japan Trading Co. Osaka 5.11.2010.

43. Finncell's annual reports 1960–1970. The Archives of Finncell.
44. 'Vaikutelmia Japanin taloudesta'. Ambassador Osmo Lares's economic report No 11. Tokyo 6.6.1973. UM 56 A Japan. MFA. 'Japani siirtymässä tekstiilien vientimaasta tuontimaaksi'. Acting chargé d'affaires Bo Ådahl's economic report No 14. Tokyo 23.7.1973. UM 56 A Japan. MFA.
45. 'Japanin selluloosa- ja paperiteollisuuden nykynäkymiä'. Acting aide Osmo Lipponen's economic report No 8. Tokyo 20.9.1974. UM 56 A Japan. MFA.
46. 'Suomen ja Japanin välinen kauppa'. Attaché Kari Härkönen's economic report No 14. Tokyo 1.9.1971. UM 56 A Japan. MFA.
47. Heikkinen 2000, p. 331. 'Japanin selluloosa- ja paperiteollisuuden nykynäkymiä'. Acting aide Osmo Lipponen's economic report No 8. Tokyo 20.9.1974. UM 56 A Japan. MFA.
48. 'Suomen ja Japanin välinen kauppa'. Attaché Kari Härkönen's economic report No 14. Tokyo 1.9.1971. UM 56 A Japan. MFA.
49. 'Suomen ja Japanin välinen kauppa v. 1975; lopulliset kauppatilastot'. Acting chargé d'affaires Markku Heiskanen's economic report No 7. Tokyo 3.9.1976. UM 56 A Japan. MFA. 'Suomen ja Japanin välinen kauppa sekä ajankohtaiset kauppapoliittiset kysymykset'. Aide Frank Edman's memorandum. Department for External Economic Relations of the Ministry for Foreign Affairs of Finland 17.8.1977. UM 58 B 2 Japan. MFA.
50. 'Japanin lentoliikenne'. Marketing director Risto Ojanen's letter to Under-Secretary of State Arvo Rytkönen of the Ministry for Foreign Affairs of Finland. Helsinki 22.6.1977. UM 58 B 2 Japan. MFA.
51. 'Japanin suurlähetystön näkemyksiä Finnairin Tokion reitistä, jäämurtajan myyntimahdollisuuksista Japaniin sekä japanilaisen kauppavaltuuskunnan vierailusta Suomeen syksyllä 1978'. Memorandum by head of department Pertti A.O. Kärkkäinen. Department for External Economic Relations of the Ministry for Foreign Affairs of Finland 27.4.1978. UM 58 B 2 Japan. MFA.
52. 'Suomen ja Japanin väliset taloudelliset suhteet'. Memorandum by Second Secretary Leif Fagernäs. Department for External Economic Relations of the Ministry for Foreign Affairs of Finland 25.8.1980. UM 58 B 2 Japan. MFA. 'Japanilaisten autojen tuonti Suomeen'. Memorandum by acting head of department Matti Liukkonen No 616. Department for External Economic Relations of the Ministry for Foreign Affairs of Finland 4.9.1980. Appendix to memorandum: 'P.M. Selvitys mahdollisista Japanista peräisin olevien H-autojen tuontiin vaikuttavista toimenpiteistä'. Memorandum by Marita Eerikäinen 26.7.1980. UM 58 B 2 Japan. MFA. 'Suomen ja Japanin kaupasta'. Memorandum by head of department V.H. Lumme No 893. Department for External Economic Relations of the Ministry for Foreign Affairs of Finland 12.12.1980. UM 58 B 2 Japan. MFA. 'Suomen ja Japanin välinen kauppa; Henkilöautojen tuonnin valvontalisensioinnin käyttöönotto'. Memorandum by head of department Pauli Opas for the Ministry of Trade and Industry of Finland 18.5.1981. UM 58 B 2 Japan. MFA.
53. 'Suomen ja Japanin välinen kauppa; Henkilöautojen tuonnin valvontalisensioinnin käyttöönotto'. Memorandum by head of department Pauli Opas for the Ministry of Trade and Industry of Finland 18.5.1981. UM 58 B 2 Japan. MFA.
54. 'Mahdollinen japanilaisautojen seurantalisensiointi'. Letter signed by the importers of Japanese cars for chief director Kalervo Hentilä of the Ministry of Trade and Industry of Finland. Helsinki 9.6.1981. UM 58 B 2 Japan. MFA. 'Japanilaisten henkilöautojen tuonti ja kilpailu Suomen autoteollisuuden kanssa'. Memorandum by presenter Olli Laitinen. The Ministry of Trade and Industry's

Trade Department's Office of Multilateral Trade. 21.12.1981. UM 58 B 2 Japan. MFA. Koskimies 1982, p. 65.

55. In 2003, China surpassed Japan as Finland's second biggest trade partner outside Europe. SVT I A. Annual publications of foreign trade 2002–2003. 'Suomen ja Japanin välinen kauppa -74'. Aide Osmo Lipponen's economic report No 12/75. Tokyo 8.4.1975. UM 56 A Japan. MFA.
56. 'Japanin viennin kehitys v. 1974 tammi-elokuussa ja näkemyksiä vientimahdollisuuksista lähitulevaisuudessa'. Secretary for trade C-E. Ullner's review for the Ministry for Foreign Affairs of Finland. Tokyo 13.11.1974. UM 58 B 2 Japan. MFA. 'Suomen ja Japanin välinen kauppa -74'. Aide Osmo Lipponen's economic report No 12/75. Tokyo 8.4.1975. UM 56 A Japan. MFA. 'Suomen ja Japanin välinen kauppa v. 1975; lopulliset kauppatilastot'. Acting chargé d'affaires Markku Heiskanen's economic report No 7. Tokyo 3.9.1976. UM 56 A Japan. MFA.
57. 'Japanin ulkomaantalous vuonna 1973'. Acting aide Osmo Lipponen's economic report No 4. Tokyo 17.6.1974. UM 56 A Japan. MFA.
58. 'Maatiedosto Japani. Kahdenväliset suhteet'. Homepage of the Finnish Embassy in Tokyo www.finland.or.jp/public/default.aspx?nodeid=44381&contentlan=1&culture=fi-FI (Accessed October 4, 2011).
59. 'Jujo Thermal in brief'. Homepage of Jujo Thermal. www.jujothermal.com/about_us/ (Accessed October 4, 2011).
60. 'Kauppavaihto maaryhmittäin ja maittain; tuonti alkuperämaittain ja vienti määrämaittain. Tammi-joulukuu 2011'. Source: Finnish Customs. Foreign trade statistics of Finland. January-December 2011. www.tulli.fi/fi/suomen_tulli/ulkomaankauppatilastot/tilastoja/maatilastoja/vuodet/index.jsp (Accessed July 16, 2013).

10 Growth of an industry

A comparison of paper industry in Japan and Finland

Pasi Sajasalo and Kazuhiro Igawa

Introduction

In this chapter we are concerned with understanding the evolution – and, more specifically, the growth – of industries. To do this, we will examine an internationally competitive industry, the paper industry, as the vehicle of our discussion. While the analysis is mostly concerned with industry-level developments, individual firms in both countries will be mentioned in passing, because the development of any industry inevitably has close connections to developments taking place at the firm level; thus, total separation of the two entities in description and analysis would be artificial and counterproductive to our effort at understanding the evolutionary processes involved. Thus, to achieve a better understanding of the overall development of the paper industry in the two countries, alternating between the industry and firm level is required to build up the overall picture of the development.

The papermaking industry is taken as an illustrative case of the processes involved in transforming an industry from modest, almost solely domestic origins to one with far-reaching cross-border operations. As the history of papermaking extends back over several centuries in both Japan and Finland, analysing the paper industry offers valuable insights on the overall industrial development of the two countries from a particular industry viewpoint, thereby shedding some additional light on the development of Japanese and Finnish societies, the focus of the present volume.

The study of the Japanese and Finnish paper industries' growth makes an interesting comparison, as firms originating in these two countries have traditionally been strong in their respective geographical regions – let alone their home countries. Japanese firms have dominated in Southeast Asia and Finnish firms in Europe. At the same time, firms originating in these two countries have played important roles in the global forest industry as well, while the regional character of the industry has remained a persistent feature throughout its history (Lamberg & Ojala, 2006, p. 216; Sajasalo, 2003).

Curiously enough, at present, two firms from both countries rank in the World Top Ten forest products companies (FFIF, 2010a), thereby making the study of the growth of the industry in Japan and Finland a worthwhile endeavour. In this chapter, a comparative case study is conducted to identify some striking similarities and differences in how paper industry firms based in Japan and Finland have been able to achieve their current status – which we take to reflect the overall growth of the industry in the two countries. Emphasis is placed on exploring how the Japanese and Finnish paper industries have been able to benefit from various governmental policies, factor endowment conditions, market characteristics, institutional arrangements, and historical developments of their home bases to reach their current positions within the global forest-based industry.

A striking similarity between Japan and Finland – apart from both being somewhat remotely located in their respective geographic regions – is that both countries are heavily dependent on exports. The relative indicator of share of exports to GDP may be somewhat misleading; it was around 10 per cent in Japan and nearly 40 per cent in Finland in 1997 (MOF, 2010; Savela, 2009), suggesting that Finland is more export dependent than Japan. However, the absolute figures are more informative: in 2010, the value of exports was 765.2 billion USD for Japan and 73.5 billion USD for Finland, making Japan the 5th-largest exporter nation in the world, while Finland is in 40th place (CIA, 2011a). Moreover, in Japan, the paper industry accounted for 1.4 per cent of GDP in 2005 (JPA, 2010a), while in Finland, the corresponding figure in 2005 was 2.6 per cent (FFIF, 2010b), giving the industry quite a different role in the economic well-being of the country and also as a concern of governmental policy making for the industry's well-being.

While the paper industry has been important in Japan, over time, however, its relative weight has not been great in the Japanese industrial structure,[1] and overall, the paper industry has never enjoyed a comparative advantage in Japan. Competitively priced domestic raw material is scarce due to the challenging logging conditions, instabilities in supply, and fragmented land ownership, forcing the industry to resort to imported raw material on a major scale quite early in its development (Iwai, 2002). Furthermore, the production technology was outdated in the early days of the industry, so new technology had to be introduced from abroad in order to be able to compete against foreign producers to protect the large Japanese home market.

Unlike Japan, Finland has relied heavily on forest-based industry throughout her history. Since the sixteenth century, forest-based products have been the dominant export of Finland (Kuisma, 1993). In the late 1920s, the forest products industry accounted for nine tenths of total exports (Kuisma, 2008: 18; Saari, 1928), a figure demonstrating the heavy dependence of Finland on its major industry. The reliance on forest-based industry is understandable, as 86 per cent of Finland is covered by forests, with coniferous forests accounting for the majority (METLA, 2011). While Finland is the most forested country in Europe, it contains only 1 per cent of coniferous forest resources globally. Yet the Finnish paper industry managed to grow to a position where it accounted for one sixth of global paper and (paper)board exports and an overwhelming one fourth of global exports of printing and writing grades (Jensen-Eriksen, 2008a, p. 186).

At face value, there seems to be no basis for comparison between the two countries: in absolute terms, the sheer size of the Japanese economy compared to that of Finland is staggering. However, taking GDP per capita as an indicator, the two countries are relatively close to one another: in Japan 34,000 USD and in Finland 35,400 USD, according to recent statistics (CIA, 2011b). Moreover, the governments of the two countries have historically pursued active export-promotion policies to support their major export industries, and various country-specific institutionalized organizational arrangements have been utilised to promote exports. While the paper industries of the two countries have historically played quite different roles in governmental policy making, the comparison between the two countries will reveal interesting parallels in the development of the industry in Japan and Finland.

The chapter will take a closer look at the growth of the paper industry in the two countries by analysing some of the key institutional and organizational arrangements that the Japanese and Finnish firms were able to utilize after World War II in order to gain a foothold in international markets: namely the *keiretsu* and their role in Japan and the jointly owned sales associations in Finland. Furthermore, we will examine the market characteristics and the policies adopted by governments in supporting their forest product industries. In analysing the growth of the paper industry, attention will also be paid to the differing factor endowments of the two countries, setting them in very different positions during the industry's growth.

While the starting points and subsequent development of the paper industry in the two countries have differed, the result is clear today. Both Japan and Finland are counted among the few major paper-producing countries in the world – Japan being ranked third and Finland eighth by overall production volume (FFIF, 2011). This chapter serves to enhance our knowledge of how this was achieved over time. Analysing the development of the paper industry also affords us an opportunity to shed some further light on the overall industrial development of the two countries, thus making a valuable contribution to furthering our knowledge.

Theoretical framework

Our analysis and discussion are loosely guided by ideas derived from two seemingly disparate but, at closer scrutiny, compatible theoretical lenses supporting one another. We will base our discussion and analysis on Michael Porter's (1990) diamond framework of national competitiveness, supported by John Dunning's (2001) eclectic paradigm of international production, better known as OLI (ownership, location, and internalization advantages) framework. While neither of the frameworks is very recent, they, however, serve our analytical purposes well. The chosen theoretical frameworks enable us to take better and more extensive note of important factors in play in the development of the paper industry in Japan and Finland than would be possible utilising any single theoretical framework.

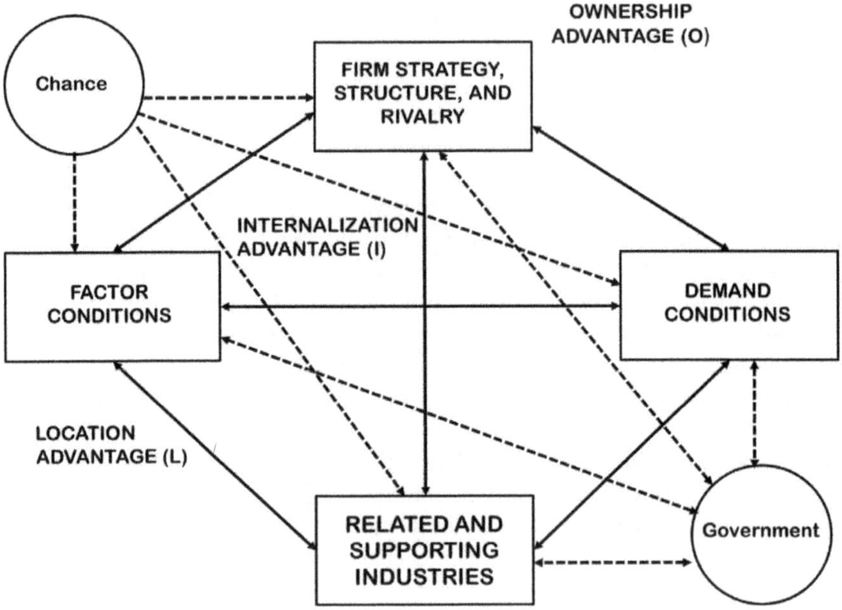

Figure 10.1 Framework for the description and analysis

Source: adapted from Porter, 1990, p. 127

By adopting the chosen theoretical lenses, we are able to better understand the drivers of the evolution of the paper industry in Japan and Finland – the overall process transforming it from a domestic orientation to a regional orientation and, later on, to an increasingly international orientation – and to incorporate into our analysis important aspects of home base–related institutional arrangements supporting the growth of the paper industry in the two countries. Figure 10.1 outlines the framework guiding our discussion and analysis.

Early development of the industry in Finland and Japan

While the focus of this chapter and indeed the whole volume is on developments *after* World War II, a brief outline of the earlier history is in order to set the stage. Both Japan and Finland have a long history in paper production; the Japanese history of papermaking extends to the seventh century, when the technology of traditional Japanese paper (*washi*) production was introduced from Korea (see e.g. Kurosawa & Hashino, 2012). Later paper production expanded in Japan, and a monopolisation system for its production was initiated by a local government during the Edo (Tokugawa) national isolation era of 1600 through 1868. The opening up of Japan to the rest of the world after 1868 had two major impacts on the paper industry. One was the quality improvement of *washi* and the other was the introduction of technology for factory-scale manufacturing of Western paper (*yoshi*) to protect the domestic market from imported paper products (Noda, 2002, p. 216).

The Finnish forest-based industry was heavily downstream oriented and driven by production factors in the early days of the modern paper industry (in the second half of the nineteenth century). The vast raw material resources and readily available cheap labour were favourable prerequisites for large-scale production and the incipient industrialization of a country taking off relatively late compared with the rest of Western Europe (Hjerppe, 1988; Myllyntaus, 1989). Finnish pulp and paper production was internationally oriented early on (Ojainmaa, 1994; Sajasalo, 1999), as the majority of production was exported to the markets of imperial Russia prior to and during World War I. The Russian market subsequently offered a favourable setting for future development and building competitive advantage for the Finnish forest-based industry elsewhere (Sajasalo, 2002). In contrast to Finland, the development of the Japanese paper industry mainly aimed at safeguarding the Japanese home market. This feature has persisted over time (Kurosawa & Hashino, 2012, p. 136).

World War I meant a major breakthrough in the Japanese paper industry, as imports from Germany and Austria diminished to half of the pre–World War I levels due to the war effort assuming priority in Continental Europe (Arisawa, 1966, p. 175). During the period, Japan became self-sufficient in paper production while exporting still higher-quality grades (Noda, 2002, p. 216; Shinomiya, 1995). In 1921, Japan's total production volume was the fifth largest in the world after the United States, Germany, England, and Canada (Arisawa, 1966, p. 175; Okawa, 1981). The turmoil of World War I and its aftermath proved to be a decisive period for the development and growth of the Finnish forest-based industry as well. When Finland gained independence in 1917, the forest-based industries had already established a secure position supported by the large Russian market. The Russian Revolution, nevertheless, changed everything almost overnight, ending nearly all trade between Finland and Russia. The need to penetrate Western European markets arose suddenly, and to be better equipped for the challenges, the Finnish pulp and paper producers joined forces in 1918 by establishing two jointly owned sales associations (in effect cartels): the Finnish Paper Mills' Association, Finnpap, and the Finnish Pulp Mills' Association, Finncell (Heikkinen, 2000; Ojainmaa, 1994). The advent and subsequent role of the newly established sales cartels would prove paramount for the future growth of the industry in Finland, as we will discuss later.

Growth of the paper industry after the Second World War in Japan

Recovery after World War II was controlled by General Headquarters of the United States of America, and the dissolution of the *zaibatsu* industrial conglomerates, including the monopolistic Oji Paper Company, took place in 1949 (Kurosawa & Hashino, 2012, p. 151; Noda, 2002, p. 216). The Oji Paper

Company was the result of a 1933 merger among Oji, Fuji, and Karafuto, and it controlled 80 per cent of paper output and 95 per cent of pulp output in the 1930s (Noda, 2002, p. 216). After the dissolution of the Oji Paper Company, a number of small and medium-sized paper and pulp firms entered the Japanese paper market, intensifying competition. Just after World War II, Oji Paper accounted for 67.5 per cent of total paper production in Japan, but its dominant position was lost, however, as the company was broken up into three separate entities through the dissolution carried out on the orders of the US General Headquarters (Kurosawa & Hashino, 2012, p. 151). Initially, the market share of Oji Paper dropped to 37.7 per cent and further to 27.7 per cent of total volume by 1955. The second half of the decade after World War II was the period of return to normal development, and by 1953, the production level already exceeded the pre-war level (Arisawa, 1967, p. 98).

However, in the 1950s, high raw material costs and low price of paper products became a poignant problem for the Japanese paper industry. Due to the loss of Sakhalin and reckless wartime cuts, the price increase in coniferous lumber far exceeded the wholesale price increase. As a result, the Japanese paper industry had to rethink its raw material base and the focus shifted to the use of a new raw material, hardwood lumber, to tackle availability problems in coniferous lumber (Iwai, 2002, p. xvii).

The abolition of post-war restrictions in 1951 marked the formation of a highly competitive paper market and plummeting paper prices. The increased competition compelled firms to improve their efficiency but, at the same time, the efficiency-seeking investments increasingly jeopardised profitability. However, the *keiretsu* system in Japan internalised some transactions within the *keiretsu* organization and reduced risks, thereby improving the combined competitiveness of the firms operating within given keiretsu boundaries. The *keiretsu* system was characterised by long-term relationships with particular partners based on trust, providing a cushion of support, mutual risk sharing, and joint development of know-how and other resources to be used between partners (Hundley & Jacobson, 1998; Itagaki, 2002).

From the late 1950s, Japan enjoyed high economic growth, which turned into a period of stable economic growth in the 1970s. A demand increase was projected for paper products, and accordingly, firms increased investments significantly and introduced technological innovations to meet the anticipated demand growth. New technologies were imported to Japan, and these technologies were further improved domestically for subsequent application by Japanese firms. This trend of modification and further improvement of imported technology typifies a long-standing Japanese tradition and brought with it a technology ownership advantage for Japanese firms (Ozawa, 1974; Pohl, 2005; Watanabe & Honda, 1991).

In 1959, Japan grew to be the third-largest paper producer in the world, after the United States and Canada. However, the market share of Japanese top paper manufacturers (about 30th in sales in the world) was only 8.3 per cent in 1964, reflecting the fragmented industry structure, and many of the major paper firms fought to survive (Arisawa, 1967, pp. 210–11). A cooperative meeting between the government and private enterprises was set up to regulate competition and to increase international competitiveness in quality (Arisawa, 1967, pp. 212). This was a widely used method of MITI (then Ministry of International Trade and Industry; currently METI, Ministry of Economy, Trade and Industry) to regulate industries in Japan in order to alleviate what was considered unhealthy competition and the unwanted repercussions of competitive pressures (Frenkel, 1984; Kurosawa & Hashino, 2012).

However, notwithstanding the MITI's and private enterprises' efforts, the persistent trend of high raw material costs combined with the low price of paper products even strengthened in 1960s, and administrative guidance for investments was introduced in 1962 when the liberalization of imports of paper and pulp began (Iwai, 2002, pp. xvi–xviii). During much of the 1960s, Japan was considered the target market of North American, Scandinavian, and European producers for their excess production, exacerbating price erosion in the Japanese market (Waitt, 1994). Overcapacity accompanied by intense competition within the industry created a need for product innovations as well as for finding new production locations.

In the 1960s, the liberalization of trade and deregulation of capital movement promoted a merger-and-acquisitions movement in many industries in Japan. As a result, a wave of mergers and acquisitions also commenced within the paper industry, and the three major companies, which formerly made up Oji Paper, wished to join forces. The Fair Trade Commission, however, was opposed to the planned merger in 1968 and the plan was not realized (Kurosawa & Hashino, 2012, p. 160; Takamura & Koyama, 1994, pp. 52–4). In 1970, Japan had already become the second-largest producer of paper after the United States, but the Oil Crisis of 1973 reduced demand and greatly increased the cost of energy for the industry (Shinomiya, 1995). Furthermore, pollution-reduction investments made necessary by tightening environmental legislation impaired the profitability of the companies (MITI, 1994). To reduce raw material costs, the focus of pulp production shifted from coniferous pulp to hardwood pulp even more pronouncedly than before (Iwai, 2002). At the same time, log imports were replaced by wood chip imports and the focus of raw material imports in general shifted towards the USSR, Southeast Asia, and Australia (Shinomiya, 1997).

In 1972, two big pulp companies (also producing paper) merged into Sanyo-Kokusaku-Pulp, and the newly formed company became a major rival of the three companies formerly part of Oji Paper. Cartels were formed before the Oil Crisis to cope with excessive competition and the deregulation of capital movements. During the Oil Crisis, the paper industry in Japan experienced a bubble prosperity and expansion of plants, only to see mergers and acquisitions increase and cartels formed to jointly reduce production levels thereafter. Furthermore, closures of plants and equipment were assisted by governmental planning and the legislation on structural reform within the paper industry (Takamura & Koyama, 1994, p. 54). In 1979, Oji Paper and Japan-Pulp merged, and this merger consolidated Oji Paper's leading position in the Japanese paper industry.

The trend for mergers and acquisitions in the reorganization struggle within the paper industry continued until the mid-1980s.

After the so-called Chip Shock of 1980 (significant increase in the prices of imported wood chips from the United States), recycled paper appeared in a new light as a raw material. Several investments took place after 1980 as a result to increase recycled paper usage. Recycling of paper was expanded and the recycling ratio increased to more than 50 per cent in the 1990s, which was an unprecedented effort in Japan (Noda, 2002, p. 219). In the mid-1980s, the paper industry in Japan emerged from the major recession it had entered in the 1960s.

In 1991, the production capacity had grown to be 30 to 60 per cent higher than the 1987 level, depending on grade. However, this turned out to be a bubble in Japan. After the bubble burst, a chronic recession, the worst since World War II, started, and a new wave of mergers and acquisitions of large companies commenced (Kurosawa & Hashino, 2012, p. 162). In 1993, Jujo Paper and Sanyo Kokusaku Pulp merged to form a new company called the Nippon Paper Industries Company. Furthermore, Oji Paper and Kanzaki Paper merged to form a new corporate entity, the New Oji Paper Company. These two big mergers created two Japanese paper companies to join the World Top Ten paper producers, and five large companies dominated the Japanese paper market in the 1990s, reflecting a strong consolidation development within the industry over the three preceding decades (Noda, 2002, pp. 225–6). The newly created New Oji Paper Company further merged with the Honsyu Paper Company and, in 1996, retook its original name, Oji Paper Company (Kurosawa & Hashino, 2012, p. 163).

In 2001, Nippon Paper merged with Daishowa Paper and the newly merged company assumed the name Nippon Paper Group in 2004. Mergers and acquisitions were called for to achieve even more economies of scale than before and, more generally, to survive in the oligopolistic competition of the Japanese paper industry (JPA, 2010b). The drive for further mergers and acquisitions has continued right to the present day in order to survive in the globally competitive landscape of the paper industry (see e.g. Lamberg et al., 2012). Mergers and acquisitions have not been sought only for economies of scale and with cost reduction in recent years but also due to pressure to diversify to meet the needs of new customers and different end uses for paper-based products (JPA, 2010c, 2012).

The increased international involvement of Japanese paper companies resulted from the need to secure raw materials and from the appreciation of the Japanese Yen. Internationalization after World War II started by importation of logs and pulp around 1965 to 1975, and development-imports of pulp and lower-grade paper became popular around 1975 to 1985. Foreign direct investments in production and exports of final products increased after the 1985 Plaza Agreement (Noda, 2002). For instance, Canada and Indonesia were targeted as suppliers of raw material, for the most part softwood pulp, which was earlier supplied domestically from Sakhalin, but as Sakhalin was lost as a result of World

War II, the domestic production orientation shifted towards the utilisation of hardwood pulp, which was available in the rest of Japan (Noda, 2002).

In addition to the resource-seeking motives for increased international involvement, to some extent paper products are imported to Japan from production sites abroad where various production factors are favourable. Prior to the 1985 Plaza Agreement, only eight major foreign direct investments by Japanese paper industry companies were launched, but reflecting the importance of growth and further regional integration needs, the FDI activity increased dramatically. In total, after 1985, the Japanese paper industry companies made a total of 135 foreign direct investments abroad in afforestation and chip and pulp manufacturing as well as paper and (paper)board manufacturing and converting thereof (JPA, 2010e, 2012). After 1996, however, no investments in pulp production were made (JPA, 2010d). For international activities, the *keiretsu* trading companies, *syosyas*, played an important role.

Growth of the paper industry after the Second World War in Finland

The growth of the forest-based industries in Finland is closely tied to the development of jointly owned sales associations. The issue cannot really be discussed without including the role of the sales associations, the use of which was made possible by the tolerant attitude of Finnish governments toward cartelization within the industry. Sales associations handled the international connections of the paper industry but also worked inside Finland: for example, the paper sales association Finnpap's domestic sales accounted for one fifth of its total sales (Heikkinen, 2000; Sajasalo, 1999). In many respects, the state of affairs in Finland closely resembled the Japanese governments' tolerance of or even highly supportive attitude toward similar arrangements in Japan.

The sales associations were nonprofit organizations set up and owned by their member firms, with the mission of selling products of the same grade at uniform prices (Sajasalo, 1999). In effect, the associations were sales cartels and their role was to control the pricing of all Finnish forest-based products both internationally and domestically. The associations were also important in determining production levels and, thus, governed not only the pricing of products but also their supply. The associations provided a global sales network for their members and helped reduce the cost of maintaining an international presence for individual firms and, by so doing, considerably fostered their growth (Heikkinen, 2000).

The associations promoted their member firms' expansion of international operations, enabling them to maintain an international presence by merely being involved in the joint financing of the associations. This made engaging in wide-scale international business a viable option for even the smallest Finnish producers, who, without the associations, would not have been able to do so. In effect, the members of the associations were able to operate in the international markets at a cost substantially lower than that of operating in international markets on their own and, at the same time, benefit from the resulting economies of scale. Thus the associations' members were able to concentrate solely on production, as sales were handled by the sales associations (Sajasalo, 1999). In addition to Finnpap (paper) and Finncell (pulp), there were two other associations; Finnboard, the Finnish Board Mills' Association (est. 1942 – paperboard), and Converta, the Finnish Paper and Board Converters' Association (est. 1944 – paper- and paperboard-based converted products; Karske, Koskinen, & Moisio, 1993).

The growth of the paper industry in Finland being export led, it is obvious that World War II caused severe problems parallel to those experienced in Japan. During World War II, exports from Finland to the important UK and US markets diminished substantially as the shipping lanes were blocked by German naval forces (Heikkinen, 2000, pp. 168–75). However, by the early 1950s, the exports to the UK and the US picked up and returned to their pre-war level, as did production (Aunesluoma, 2007, p. 263). Similarly to Japan, the recovery from the war was fast, although Finland also lost territory and production sites. In fact, the relative importance of the US market actually grew after the Finnish paper manufacturers' contributions to war indemnities to the Soviet Union had been paid (Heikkinen, 2000, pp. 210–30, 240–2). While the war indemnities placed a strain on the industry, they also provided a means for the firms to operate to their full capacity, thereby helping the industry to regain its 'normal' production level faster than would have otherwise been possible. This meant that efficient export outlets were needed to help the industry handle the increasing production volumes.

The early 1960s witnessed a significant rise in the output of the Finnish paper industry: in 1961 alone, eight state-of-the-art paper machines started up in Finland. Overall, between 1960 and 1972, the production capacity of the Finnish paper industry increased five and a half fold (Jensen-Eriksen, 2008b, p. 198). The investment boom continued into the 1980s, and as a result, a total of 28 big, technologically cutting-edge paper machines commenced production in Finland. During this period, the Finnish paper industry gained a technology leadership position within the global paper industry and was able to derive full benefit from economies of scale in production due to technologically advanced facilities (Ojala, 2008, pp. 196–7).

The rapid upgrading of manufacturing technology was greatly aided by close connections between the paper industry and the leading (Finnish) technology provider, Valmet (see e.g. Alajoutsijärvi, 1993, 1996). However, the downside of the efficiency upgrading and rapid growth of the industry was a heavy burden of debt. Between 1982 and 1992, the debt ratio of Finnish paper manufacturers was 83 per cent (Ojala, 2008, p. 194).

Prior to the liberalization of the Finnish financial sector in the mid-1980s, a system of industrial investment control was in effect. Under the investment-control regime, in addition to the sales associations, the Central Association of Finnish Forest Industries together with the Finnish Central Bank had to jointly approve any planned investments within the paper industry, as there were genuine concerns about the ability of the firms to carry their debt. Furthermore, availability of raw material for the industry was a concern (Ojala, 2008, p. 198). As the debt ratio figure indicates, the investment-control system was not very efficient: with the institutional arrangement in place, the Finnish paper firms still managed to go deep into debt.

The investment controls were lifted in 1988, but they continued for some time as a voluntary arrangement agreed to by the majority of the Finnish paper firms (Ojala, 2008, pp. 201–2). The system used in Finland closely resembles the arrangement in Japan, where METI together with the Japan Paper Association controlled investments. Thus it appears that concern about overinvestment was shared within the industry, and for good reason. The feature of big lump-sum investments to large-scale production machinery has remained a major challenge for the paper industry, and investment frenzies have caused repeated shocks with oversupply eroding price levels, which eventually led to profitability problems, as noted by Noda (2002, p. 225) in the case of the Japanese paper industry.

The Finnish paper industry structure evolved through two major merger-and-acquisition waves after World War II. The so-called Spheres played a central role: banks and insurance companies acted as the main financiers and equity holders of major industrial enterprises, the paper industry firms being the most notable among them (see e.g. Näsi, Lamberg, Ojala, & Sajasalo, 2001; Näsi, Ranta, & Sajasalo, 1998; Näsi, Sajasalo, & Sierilä, 2001; Sajasalo, Ojala, & Lamberg, 2001), and were active in promoting structural reforms. The Spheres closely resembled the *keiretsus* of Japan, and they acted in a similar way as the driving force in the structural arrangements for firms under their influence as the *keiretsus* did in Japan (Näsi et al., 1998; Sajasalo et al., 2001).

The first wave took place in the mid-1980s, when a number of paper industry firms were involved in a series of mergers and acquisitions in which the industry was forced into a new constellation promoted by the spheres controlling the companies. The mid-1980s marked the advent of the predecessors of the surviving Finnish paper manufacturers. The first restructuring wave may be seen as a repercussion of the oil crises of the early 1970s, which set in motion an industrywide restructuring wave, first in the United States and later in other paper-producing countries, only to arrive in Finland almost a decade later. One of the events precipitating the industry restructuring in Finland was similar developments in Sweden, the home base of the closest rivals to Finnish firms, which had to be matched in order to meet the competitive pressure created by the Swedish rivals' growth (Sajasalo, 2007; Sajasalo et al., 2001).

The second restructuring wave took place only a decade later in the mid-1990s. It started with the merger of Kymmene and United Paper Mills (Repola) in 1995 to form a new dominant player in the Finnish paper industry: UPM-Kymmene. This merger was generally considered an impossibility, as the two merging companies were the prominent members of two rival Spheres with a long history of struggle for dominance in the Finnish economy (Näsi et al., 1998). The merger was made possible by the merging of two dominant commercial banks after the Finnish banking crisis of the early 1990s. The advent of UPM-Kymmene prompted another merger between Enso (formerly Enso-Gutzeit) and Stora of Sweden, which, again, had been considered an impossibility (Sajasalo, Ojala, & Lamberg, 2001). This was the first international merger between Nordic paper industry firms and, as such, took the international expansion of the Finnish paper industry to a whole new level (Sajasalo, 2007). As a result of the two major restructuring waves, the industry reorganized itself from nearly 30 companies into a new constellation in which only three major companies – Stora Enso, UPM-Kymmene (currently UPM), and M-real (currently Metsä Group) – remained (Ojala, 2008, p. 214).

The two merger waves marked a shift in orientation towards traditional cooperation through jointly owned sales associations. While the joint operations of the companies remained the dominant mode of operation until as late as the mid-1980s, in 1987, Finnpap was the single largest paper exporter in the world, handling close to 80 per cent of all Finnish paper product exports (Paper and Timber 2/1988) – the growth of the companies through mergers and acquisitions eventually diminished the importance of cooperation through sales associations (Heikkinen, 2000; Sajasalo, 2003). An era of sales cooperation lasting almost eight decades within the Finnish forest products industry came to an end on 1 April 1996. Finnpap was then subsumed under UPM-Kymmene's worldwide marketing organization, and Finnboard was transformed into Metsä-Serla Sales (Finnboard, 1996; Finnpap, 1996), and the traditional associations ceased to operate.

Consequently, the growth and restructuring of the Finnish paper industry had run its course and the remaining firms relied on their own sales organizations in international markets to gain increased strategic freedom. Changes in the institutional environment also played an important role in the development: the European Union's competition legislation made such cooperative arrangements between rival firms impossible, and the long-standing system had to be abandoned (Heikkinen, 2000; Sajasalo, 2003).

In the new prevailing reality, the means of growth had to be rethought. As the domestic growth avenues had already been exhausted by the mid-1980s and, at the very least, by the merger wave of the mid-1990s, the industry's sights were first set on Europe and later increasingly on Southeast Asia and North America at the turn of the millennium. Southeast Asia especially was seen as a tempting growth area by the Finnish paper manufacturers. As a result, both Stora Enso and UPM-Kymmene entered the markets through acquisitive and alliance strategies to gain access to the fastest-growing markets for paper products and cheaper raw material resources. In addition to Southeast Asia, both Stora Enso and UPM-Kymmene entered North America through major acquisitions that quite soon proved ill conceived, resulting in both Stora Enso and UPM-Kymmene divesting themselves of these acquisitions, turning their attention to South America instead in search of cheaper raw materials for pulp production in the form of joint ventures in Uruguay and Brazil (Ojala, 2008, pp. 226–7).

Findings and discussion

In light of the preceding description of the development of the paper industry in Japan and Finland, we will next present our main findings. To structure our discussion, we utilize the framework presented in Figure 10.1 and discuss our findings in relation to the similarities and dissimilarities in the growth of the industries in the two countries.

Some basic similarities may be inferred in the development taking place in Japan and Finland. For one, both countries are relative latecomers in the paper industry, and the rapid catching-up process constitutes an interesting parallel; in both Japan and in Finland, the start of modern papermaking took place at quite the same time in the 1870s. Subsequently, wood-based fibre replaced the use of rag fibre and other sources of fibre (e.g. rice straw) very early in the process of modern Japanese paper manufacturing. By the late 1880s, pulping was based on coniferous (softwood) lumber (Myllyntaus, 1989, for Finland; Noda, 2002, for Japan). Also, in both countries, the industry suffered major setbacks, in terms of both the raw material base as well as production facilities, as a result of World War II (Sakhalin for Japan, the Karelian Isthmus for Finland), yet the industry in both countries recovered surprisingly quickly after the war and, in a matter of only a few years, resumed pre-war production levels.

Another similarity between the countries relates to their overall industrialization processes. Findings in economic history suggest that late industrialisers typically develop a financial system that relies on either bank finance or government intervention and regulation (Pedersen & Thomsen, 1997, 1999). Both Finland and Japan, being late to industrialize, developed a financial system in which the banks assumed a dominant role. In Finland, the banks became substantial equity holders of Finnish enterprises due to extensive financing, and this situation formed the foundation of the Finnish Sphere Economy in which the banks played an important role in the business ownership structure by controlling a number of large Finnish corporations through strategic long-term investments (Näsi, Sajasalo, et al., 2001).

The Japanese *keiretsu*-based approach, in which industry groupings were formed around a major bank, closely resembles the situation prevailing in Finland for several decades to an even greater degree, as bank-centred financing of firms has historically been more important in Japan than elsewhere (McCormick, 2004; Pohl, 2005) and the ties within *keiretsus* are especially lasting. However, the financial *keiretsu*, in which banks play an important role as financiers of companies under their influence (following the *zaibatsu* system), is just one manifestation of the *keiretsu* system in Japan. In addition, vertical *keiretsus*, in which subcontractor groups are closely linked to their major partner, are important in the present context, likewise distribution *keiretsus* (McCormick, 2004).

The situation in both Japan and Finland could be reflected through the '*keiretsu* typology' described. In fact, not only did the financial-type *keiretsu* in Japan and spheres in Finland resemble one another quite closely, but the distribution *keiretsu* also has close parallels in the Finnish paper industry; the jointly owned sales associations served much the same purpose as the distribution *keiretsus* in Japan, as the interlinkages between partners were close and long-lasting in the Finnish case, and the goal of the organizations was to match demand with supply of Finnish paper, wherever in the world that demand might have arisen.

Furthermore, in Japan, the trading companies, *syosyas*, played a very important role for the industry in that these organizations were the international trading arms of their respective *keiretsus*, but their role was the opposite of the Finnish sales associations; the *syosyas* supplied much of the imported inputs, such as lumber, chips, pulp, and other related materials, for the paper industry for them to utilize in their domestic production.[2] However, over time, the role of the *syosyas* evolved similarly to that of the sales associations: their importance for the daily operations of the firms served diminished over time as the firms themselves became more experienced in international operations, be they outward directed as in Finland or inward directed as in Japan. The dissolution of the former association between *syosya* and the paper and pulp companies or non–*keiretsu syosya* specialized in paper and pulp products are to be found, and the development resembles the changing role of the associations for the Finnish paper producers.

Judging from a geographical perspective, the two countries are situated, as noted, on the 'periphery' of their geographic regions. As a result, both the Finnish and Japanese paper industries may be seen to have benefited from their remoteness from the most important players in the early years of the industry (Kuisma, 1993, on Finland; Kurosawa & Hashino, 2012, on Japan). In this respect, their remoteness served as buffer for competition but was also a major obstacle to overcome in later years. As a result, both the Japanese and the Finnish papermaking industry had to actively combat the location diseconomies through constant efficiency improvements. In Japan, that meant mainly efficiency-driven sourcing strategies and domestic development of imported technology, the latter applying also to Finland. The Finnish paper industry, in cooperation with the local technology providers, formed such a strong cluster that a leading paper manufacturing technology provider, Metso Corporation (preceded by Valmet), emerged as a result, likewise several other leading firms in their respective fields of pulping and papermaking technology.

Moreover, Finland has historically suffered from an additional diseconomy related to her location. As most final products had to be exported relatively long distances to reach the main markets – even Central Europe is rather far from the Finnish ports – and shipping has accounted for (and indeed still accounts for) a major proportion in the price of end products, this created a challenge in terms of cost competitiveness. This clearly also applies to present-day Japan, to an even greater extent to its major export industries. To tackle this challenge, the united approach of Finnish paper manufacturers was to rely on the very latest technology in order to improve efficiency and productivity, to remain cost competitive, and to overcome the diseconomies related to their location. In all, it may be inferred that location had its disadvantages but also advantages (Dunning, 2001) for the paper industry, the advantages, regardless of the discussion, being still more pronounced in both the Finnish and the Japanese case. In Finland, the location advantages were related especially to the raw material base, in Japan to market-related issues. In conclusion, the location advantage was related to opposite ends of the industry value chain, but nevertheless, it existed in both countries.

The logical next step in our discussion (after the prelude mentioned earlier), given the industry context, is to address the factor endowment issue. Both Finland and Japan are heavily forested countries. The total forest coverage of Finland and Japan is roughly equal; 23,200 and 24,900 hectares of forest, or 69 per cent and 67 per cent forest coverage, respectively (FAO, 2010). While the countries are very similar in this respect, the strategies of domestic forest resource utilization of the paper industry differed radically. Whereas Finnish industry has historically utilised domestic lumber resources to the fullest, Japanese industry resorted to imported raw material quite early, already to some extent since World War I, to meet the growing demand (Iwai, 2002; Noda, 2002) led by increasing paper consumption.

The choice of the Japanese paper industry to utilise imported raw material may be attributed to several factors. The geographical location of the coniferous forest resources in the northern parts of Japan (Hokkaido, Sakhalin) – while production moved there in the early 1900s – posed challenges in terms of logistics, although shipping was highly developed. Topography, the mountainous landscape, increased the cost of harvesting in the north (and indeed throughout the country), and the forest ownership structure, with nearly 60 per cent of forest privately owned, affected availability and caused fluctuations in the supply of raw material (Iwai, 2002). The most important factor, nevertheless, was the rapid growth of production volume to meet the increasing demand, and as a result, during the interwar period, the imports of logs already increased steadily (Iwai, 2002, p. xv). Thus, while in relative terms Japan was and is a forest-rich country, in reality, it was unable to meet the raw material needs of the paper industry from its domestic raw material base, apart from the early years of modern production. Thus, the paper industry had to resort to importing raw material as the volume of production increased overall.

While the Finnish forest ownership structure closely resembles that of Japan, with large private forest ownership, the logging conditions in Finland may be considered somewhat less challenging. In addition, there has been a deeply rooted culture of cooperation among the industry, the forest owners, and, to some extent, semigovernmental agencies, creating together a centralized price negotiations system. The system, in spite of its challenges, worked well for nearly four decades since the 1960s, building predictability in the supply and pricing of pulpwood especially, so that the domestic raw material base was secure enough, and used to more or less full capacity for the industry, to base plans on domestic raw material, especially coniferous roundwood (Toppinen, 1998, pp. 27–9).

Apart from lumber, the supply of energy (mainly electricity) plays an important role in energy-intensive industries, such as papermaking and pulping. Both in

Japan and in Finland, the early energy needs of the paper industry were met by the hydro-power readily available in both countries. For early location decisions, availability of waterways for energy generation was an important consideration, in addition to their role as shipping routes for end products (on energy, see further discussion in Park & Ruuskanen, 2015). Later, as the paper industry grew in Japan, it became more reliant on imported energy sources, mainly oil, while in the Finnish papermaking industry, a more domestic approach to energy supply was maintained. The factor endowment issue is closely related to location advantage, especially in the Finnish case. However, the growth of the Japanese paper industry could be said to have taken place *despite* the lack of successful factor conditions, making Japan an interesting anomaly in most of the global forest-based industry.

Further considerations in the growth of the industry in Japan and Finland are the demand conditions and their importance for the development and resulting focus of operations which cannot be ignored. While both Finland and Japan were relative latecomers to the industry, they were remarkably fast to catch up with country-specific drivers for the process. Taking into consideration the market size and population base driving the demand for paper products in addition to GNP, which has been an extremely important factor in paper consumption (Noda, 2002; Subramanian, 1988), it is clear that the growth of the industry in Finland and Japan would have different drivers.

In Japan, the development of the paper industry was heavily geared towards serving domestic demand and the substitution of imports, first in those grades which projected the highest demand and later on in higher-value-added paper grades (Kurosawa & Hashino, 2012; Noda, 2002). As newspaper readership has historically been high in Japan, it is only logical that attention was first directed towards developing the domestic capacity in newsprint production to replace imports and take control of the Japanese market. Therefore, the most important driver for the growth of the Japanese paper industry was domestic market pull, which remained the main fuel feeding the growth of the industry until the late 1980s due to population growth and the ever-growing per-capita consumption of paper products (Kurosawa & Hashino, 2012). Thus, in the Japanese case, the location advantage was most closely related to the market proximity of the industry, or rather, being embedded in it, which effectively compensated for the resource endowment deficit.

In Finland, the logic of operations was clearly geared towards markets beyond Finnish borders, with the possible exception of the very early years of operation. Since the late nineteenth century, however, the growth of the Finnish paper industry was driven first by exports through intermediaries, most importantly the jointly owned sales associations, and organic expansion within Finland, later followed by organic expansion mostly in Europe, and, more recently, by cross-border mergers and acquisitions further away from the traditional home base.

The factors behind international orientation are fairly obvious: demand in the small domestic market was quickly met as production increased in the early twentieth century, and competing only for the domestic market was not an option offering opportunities for further growth. Thus, the smallness of the home market was a push factor for the Finnish paper industry to internationalize, and with the burgeoning market of imperial Russia so close, the decision to export for further growth was obvious (Sajasalo, 2003). Early in its development, the Finnish paper industry therefore also benefited from being close to the market, and, in that respect, the location advantage related to markets was present in the Finnish industry as well (Kuisma, 1993).

Both the factor endowment and market conditions discussed clearly connect with firm strategy, industry structure, and rivalry. As strategy serves the purpose of connecting the external and internal context of an organization, and as firms carry out actions based on their strategy, they act between factor and product markets to produce goods that meet demand, and by doing so, they simultaneously affect the industry structure and are affected by it (Murmann, 2003). The connection of strategy, industry structure, and rivalry within the industry and the resulting industry dynamics are reflected in several ways in the development of the paper industry in both countries. Next, our discussion will touch on a small number of issues we consider revealing of the important parallels and differences between Japan and Finland.

Paper industry features common to both countries are close connections between rival firms, oligopolistic competitive setting, and influence of owner groupings on the industry growth and consolidation. In addition, members of the paper industry formed an association/federation that served similar functions and enabled close cooperation even between otherwise competing firms in both countries. While the openly stated objective of these cooperative bodies was to safeguard the interests of the paper industry domestically and to some extent also internationally through directives and lobbying, the operations frequently resulted in a more hands-on approach and even intervention in issues that otherwise could be thought to belong to the managerial realm and be best left to the firms themselves.

The cooperative bodies of the two countries were involved in investment control as well as output control and pricing issues. Until the later 1980s in Finland, especially the Federation of Finnish Forest Industries together with the sales associations Finnpap, Finncell, and the Finnish Central Bank were in decisive positions when investments in the pulp and paper industry were considered. This control was motivated by concern not only for market sustainability but also for the availability of raw material for the growing industry, which – in hindsight – proved to be an ill-judged concern. In Japan, the local association took even more drastic measures in times of trouble in the industry in cooperation with the government to support terminating capacity, as was the case, for instance, in the late 1970s.

While there was close cooperation at various levels of the paper industry in the two countries, that did not mean that the individual firms did not compete, at times even fiercely (Heikkinen, 2000; McMillan, 1991). Competition within the paper industry between domestic companies was about not only market share but also control of capacity, and as a result, attempts to affect the pricing of final products for the domestic market (Japan) and internationally (Finland, especially the European market). In Finland as well as in Japan, the firms competed among themselves and also with international competitors, while in both countries foreign direct investment (FDI) in the industry was virtually nonexistent. The competitive jockeying for position within the paper industry among domestic competitors set the firms on a path of continuous development and improvement to match the competitive moves of domestic peers, and as a result – while sometimes resulting in near catastrophe – built experience of operation, updated technology, and ultimately created competitive advantage for the companies so that they were able to take the next steps to be competitive in the international arena as well.

In terms of overall strategy, the growth aspirations of the paper manufacturers in both countries have driven the industry-level development, and thus, some general inferences may be drawn on the basis of the description linking to the issues already discussed. In terms of technology, the strategy orientations of the Finnish and Japanese paper industries were rather similar. The Finns were aiming at updating technology so that the production would commence with cutting-edge technology to boost efficiency and to lower unit costs (Ojala, Lamberg, Ahola, & Melander, 2006). The same applies to Japanese firms, which had to operate largely with imported raw materials ever since World War II, and therefore efficiency was a major concern (Kurosawa & Hashino, 2012). The control and further development of technology in cooperation with local technology providers provided the individual companies with an ownership advantage (Dunning, 2001) over the technology in use and related know-how.

Moreover, a clear similarity between the Japanese and Finnish paper industries is their orientation towards vertical integration. Control over the whole value chain from raw material (logs, chips) to intermediate products (pulp, bulk paper grades) and to final products (high-value-added grades, converted paper, and paperboard products) and finally their delivery to customer was the norm in both countries. Full vertical integration still typifying the modern Japanese paper industry (Kurosawa & Hashino, 2012, p. 137) may be seen to have resulted from the conditions prevailing in the early years of the twentieth century, when the Japanese paper industry transferred from straw pulp to wood pulp and relocated many of its mills to the north (Hokkaido, Sakhalin), where coniferous lumber was readily available for the needs of the growing industry. This feature has persisted ever since, regardless of the need to rely increasingly on imported wood, as noted by Kurosawa and Hashino (2012, pp. 158–9). While the delivery systems in the countries differed, in effect both industries internalized the whole value chain and were able to utilize transfer pricing and other benefits of an internalized market in contrast to operating in the markets. In Japan, the *keiretsu* system with close linkages between different actors in the value chain basically formed an even larger internalized market, so it may be inferred that internalization advantage existed throughout the industry value chain and even well beyond it.

Furthermore, the paper industry restructuring in the two countries followed very similar paths, although the timing of the consolidation waves differed somewhat. In both countries, an initial consolidation commenced after World War I, followed by different logics in the two countries but taking place, nevertheless, at roughly the same time. In Japan, the first wave of consolidation was due to the recession following World War I and consequent problems within the industry for which a remedy was sought by joining forces, the most pronounced being the birth of Oji Paper (Kurosawa & Hashino, 2012). In Finland, the events were more immediately connected to the Russian Revolution and its aftermath and resulted in the mergers of a number of small one-paper-machine firms into slightly larger entities (Kuisma, 1993; Sajasalo et al., 2001).

The next major consolidation wave was related to the oil crises of the 1970s, to which Japanese industry responded almost immediately due to the rapidly rising energy prices with a dire effect on the prospects of an industry already quite heavily dependent on imported raw material and energy. The oil dependence of the industry had increased as a result of its growth. While prior to World War II, much of the energy needs were met through hydro-power, and after the war until the late 1950s by domestic coal, after that, the energy policy was heavily geared towards oil as main energy source (Kurosawa & Hashino, 2012).

While the Japanese paper industry was quick to react, the results of the oil crises took nearly a decade to materialize within the Finnish paper industry, as Finland was able to compensate to some extent the rising oil prices by utilizing integrated pulp and energy production as well as ownership in the energy sector. In addition, the Finnish government's role in keeping energy costs relatively low through taxation of energy-intensive industries, such as pulp and paper, was important (Sajasalo, 2002). While the impacts were to some extent postponed, in the mid-1980s, the Finnish paper industry reorganized itself – often under considerable pressure from the bank-centred spheres – forming several dozen companies into roughly 20 larger entities, which over the following decade were reorganized once more, as a result of the recession of the early 1990s, into the three major remaining firms in the Finnish pulp and paper industry (see e.g. Sajasalo et al., 2001).

The development in Japan took a similar route from the mid-1990s onward as the once-dissolved Oji Paper Company regrouped, and at the same time, Nippon Paper Industries Company (later Nippon Paper Group) emerged (Kurosawa & Hashino, 2012; Noda, 2002). The consolidation ran its course in both countries, and as a result, only very few major paper firms remained. The development in both countries may be attributed to the realization within the global pulp and paper industry that to stay in the game, growth through consolidation of national industries was required, and similar developments took place all over the world (Lamberg & Ojala, 2006; Ojala et al., 2006; Sajasalo, 2003), not only in Japan and Finland.

To conclude our discussion, we may draw some general inferences about the development patterns. At the most general level, the development of the paper industries in Japan and Finland reflects a typical industry life cycle from introduction through growth and, more recently, maturity (see e.g. Porter, 1980). As this process has unfolded at the national level, a similar development has occurred globally within the forest products industry, and in some markets there are already clear signs of decline (Lamberg et al., 2012).

As maturity has been reached in most developed countries, the competitive setting of the paper industry has tightened: struggle over market share, the search for economies of scale, and further growth have really taken off in most markets, where the 'major-league players' recurrently face each other. Currently the most tempting growth area appears to be China, and that is where Japanese and Finnish paper manufacturers have also established a presence. Increased focus on China represents a clear departure for the Japanese paper industry from its traditional home base–oriented strategy. While intensified involvement in foreign production by Japanese paper firms abroad is visible, the internationalization of the Japanese paper industry depends quite heavily on domestic demand and is still mostly driven by resource-seeking motives to maintain the status quo in the Japanese market controlled by incumbents. It appears that for further growth, it is necessary for the Japanese paper industry to tap into new markets, especially in Southeast Asia and China, where consumption of paper products is still in the growth stage, unlike in Japan. However, instead of a sole orientation of resource-seeking internationalization alone, the Japanese industry is now seeking further growth and cost savings by supplying final products back to Japan but also serving local markets in China.

Growth-oriented internationalization has driven the Finnish paper industry ever since its early days, but it may be inferred that the Finnish industry is at a crossroads in terms of the future importance of the former home base, Finland, and more generally Europe. It appears that within the global forest products industry, two underlying interconnected logics are fundamentally changing the future strategies of firms operating within the industry: the decoupling or fragmentation of the traditional integrated value chain and, as a result, the gravitation of the industry towards Asia (most notably China) and South America (e.g. Brazil, Chile, Uruguay). This may be seen as a natural evolution of the papermaking industry, as these regions have a comparative advantage in the form of favourable factor endowment conditions. However, the challenge of these emerging regions is to transform the comparative advantage into competitive advantage.

To conclude, in the future, it will be increasingly irrelevant what the home base of the giants operating within the paper industry is; what counts is how the firms are able to operate and control the ever-fragmenting value chain and internalize the parts of the value chain that offer the best return on investment.

Notes

1. Currently the five largest Japanese industries include (in order of product shipments): transportation equipment, chemicals, food, iron and steel, electronic devices. Pulp, paper, and processing resides in fifteenth position in the ranking (METI, 2009).
2. For a description of relations of *syosya* to paper and pulp companies, see *Nikkei Map of Industries 2013*, 112–113, 149.

Part V

Concluding remarks

11 Concluding thoughts on the Finnish–Japanese comparison

Christopher Lloyd

The comparative historical analysis in this volume, which at first glance compares two very different societies that may not obviously be comparable to casual observers, shows the potential for such work to illuminate each case within the light of the other. This illumination depends on certain methodological factors being observed if the potential is to be realised. The chapters in this volume, written, as they are, by international collaborations between Finnish and Japanese scholars, ensure that the comparisons are actually made in detail rather than just through hand-waving or juxtaposition. And of course comparisons enable contrasts as well as similarities to be revealed. Questions about why processes and events occurred in each case and what their consequences were can always be better understood through comparison.

Foundations of comparison

Comparison is essential in human understanding and explanation. All understanding and assessment in common sense and in social understanding and explanation involves making at least implicit comparisons. Human brains and social relations have evolved the necessity and capacity to make comparisons in order to survive and prosper. Even in the very small-scale and techno-socially undeveloped societies of hunters and gatherers, which everywhere were the initial socio-economic state of humanity for hundreds of thousands of Pleistocene years, there was the constant necessity to compare natural environments, natural products, potential mates, and potential social groups in order to make choices and decisions about foods and social relations. The capacity to make conscious comparative assessments and choices seems to be an initial condition of human existence. However, even though it's a large, implicated step from that basic human socio-biological substratum to the methodology of comparative historical analysis and explanation, there is a continuity across time and intellectual development. The nature of the social world and the nature of human intelligence are coevolutionary and codevelopmental. It is essential, therefore, for socio-historical analysis to take comparison seriously and to understand its possibilities and limits. The place of comparison within the wider problematic of socio-historical explanation is a basic issue for socio-historical methodology.

An extensive literature has explored why and how comparative research should be done (e.g. Goldstone, 2003; Kocka, 2003; McMichael, 1990; Weber, 2007), some of which is discussed in Chapter 2 by Osinsky and Eloranta. The most important question concerns the relationship of comparison to explanation. Must all explanations, at least implicitly, be comparative? Perhaps so, but before comparison can be made, certain important prior and ongoing elements in explanation have to be developed. In particular, description, categorization, conceptualisation, and theorisation are required. In constructing explanations, then, we have to define the scale of comparison and describe the processes in basic units or structures or systems that we want to compare. There is a mutually implicated relationship between description, categorization, conceptualisation, and theorisation. In this book, the scale is international – Japan and Finland – but comparison can be made on many scales from local to global. Such pairwise international comparisons are common in social science history, but they at least imply wider scales, such as the process of economic development and modernization over recent centuries. This wider perspective is necessary, in fact, for a conceptualisation and theorisation of the processes and cannot be confined to just two countries, for they are actually transnational and global. The Finnish and Japanese cases have to be contextualised in a worldwide framework. Comparative explanation on a worldwide scale is actually a central part of contextual/causal explanation, as reiterated in a masterful chapter by Jack Goldstone (2003) on the comparative explanation of revolutions and as later further reiterated by Charles Tilly (2006) and Tilly and Goodin (2006) in their defence of contextualised history.

Finland and Japan as two late-industrialising and -modernising countries: perspectives on a fruitful comparison in a global framework

Finland and Japan have not often been compared directly. This book corrects that absence and shows why we can learn much from the comparison about the wider paths and causation of economic and social development over the long run. What we learn can be viewed through a wider perspective on socio-economic development.

Finland is a small country and Japan is a large country, but this is not very significant when examining and comparing their economic and social development. They are both industrialised, economically developed, modern countries with very egalitarian socio-cultural norms and structures. These fundamental facts are more than sufficient to get comparison going on a firm foundation. And they belong to a certain (OECD) group of countries which collectively are the subject of much comparison as a group these days. The two countries have experienced contrasting and similar processes and events over the long run of their industrialisation and modernization – historical trajectories that have produced certain significant structural convergences in the twenty-first century as well as very significant and interesting divergences. Like some other OECD countries, in the nineteenth century, both were agricultural and 'backward' compared with the leading industrial countries of Northern Europe and North America at the time. Significant development did not begin until the late nineteenth and early twentieth centuries, which means that they were among the first wave of 'late industrialisers', a group of countries (including Australia, Canada, Italy, Spain) that were the first outside the industrial heartland to experience rapid industrial development. (On late industrialisation, see the canonical statement by Gerschenkron, 1962; see also Amsden, 2001; Hikino & Amsden, 1984; Pierson, 2004; Thompson, 1996.) They were therefore compelled or 'required', in a sense, to catch up rapidly in a manner that has become much more familiar with the second wave of late industrialisers in the post-war years (such as the 'Asian Tigers', Ireland, Portugal) and even more so with the third wave of the post-1990 era (such as China, Brazil, and Thailand). And now perhaps we are beginning to see a fourth wave just emerging in Africa, Latin America, and Asia. Of course, the compulsion to catch up of late industrialisers is not always successful, resulting in the so-called 'middle-income trap', a trap that Finland and Japan both avoided even though they both experienced severe shocks from wars and depressions during their early industrialisation phases that might have stymied their transformations. On the contrary, they have presented outcomes of 'economic miracles' in the post-1945 era.

Late industrialisation and modernization and 'economic miracles' have been topics of interest to economic and socio-political historians for more than a century. Indeed, it could be argued that the topic is even much older, being at the heart, in a certain sense, of Adam Smith's theory of stages of development and of the problems that arise when countries pursue policies of development that seek to avoid a fundamental 'logic of developmental stages'. This issue of relative backwardness became a very significant topic in Germany in the mid-nineteenth century when it became clear that German development was very uneven both economically and politically and the pressure for reform became very great, resulting in the great revolutionary upheaval of 1848. How to achieve catch-up has been a perennial theme in economic policy and political economy. One issue that has been a focus of both scholarly and political interest has been the role of the state as both economic actor and policy framer. The connection between economic catch-up processes and socio-political modernization, including democratization, has been much discussed since the post-war era of transformation became extended into the three-decade-long boom of 1945 to 1974 (cf Moore, 1966, for a still highly pertinent treatment of this issue).

One perspective would argue that Finland and Japan are somewhat unusual cases of *successful* commodity-export-led industrialisation. This is a process more usually understood as having occurred in certain settler societies in the twentieth century such as Australia, Canada, New Zealand, and the western United States, but from an economic and political background quite different from Finland and Japan. In the last half century, resource-based development of undeveloped or emerging countries has been fraught with problems that have resulted in many cases of resource-cursed outcomes of stunted development.

In order to understand this context of development of Finland and Japan, we have to see that a fundamental issue about industrial development and economic and social transformation concerns the sources and scale of capital accumulation and investment. Industrialisation requires a high level of new investment, usually reckoned to be at least 35 per cent of GDP. In the case of commodity-export economies, capital accumulation typically arises out of the commodity export sector and becomes available for investment in new manufacturing, a process usually occurring through close linkages to the commodity-producing sector. Such a process was and is also dependent on export markets, which became greatly enlarged through the emergence of a world economy from about the mid-nineteenth century. This was due to earlier, endogenously induced, and more gradual industrial development in the 'original' industrial core of the world economy in northwest Europe and the northeast of the United States, which was also accompanied by rapid population growth in those regions. The export-dependent settler economies were able to experience the onset of industrial development from the late nineteenth century through a combination of capital imports (especially from Britain), labour imports, and protectionist policies.

Japan, among the first wave of late industrialisers, was not a significant capital importer nor a labour importer. Finland did import a significant capital requirement but not a labour supply. In both cases, labour was available from the labour-intensive primary sector, which contained large reserves of underemployed labour, especially once technical change began to penetrate primary industries. Capital was accumulated out of the commodity-export sector and other domestic sources for reinvestment in raw material processing and associated manufacturing. But the two cases are not completely similar, of course, for their size does make some important differences. Japan, being so much larger, was able to mobilise significantly greater sources of domestic capital from surpluses in the domestic economy as well as from trade and had a much longer history of proto-industrialisation than Finland did. Of course, Finland did have a small industrial base in ironworking and textiles in the nineteenth century, but market expansion within the Russian imperial context, although favourable for a limited range of goods, was always framed by the colonial context.

Thus another perspective concerns the place of governing constitutions in enabling or hindering development. It is interesting to speculate what might have happened to the industrial development of the two countries if crucial constitutional changes had not occurred in the late nineteenth and early twentieth centuries, changes that were essential for economic development. The Meiji Restoration opened the Japanese state to constitutional, institutional, and economic change, which led to industrialisation and modernization. Finland's continuing place in the Russian Empire until 1917 determined the formation of the local state structure and framed the economic policies of the Grand Duchy in a way that other Nordic countries did not have to contend with; and in the aftermath of independence, a bloody civil war broke out that had significant long-term effects on political economy, arguably until the 1960s.

While the early decades of the twentieth century were ones of great political and institutional contrast between Finland and Japan, the role of the state in the era since 1945 has shown how different state structures and policy regimes can converge on somewhat similar broad outcomes in terms of catch-up, modernization, and societal stability and prosperity. The cases of Finland and Japan show how contrasting developmental states can play key roles in the economic and social transformation process. They both succeeded in recovering and catching up despite the great socio-economic and political traumas of war, depression, and destruction in the early twentieth century. In each case, the state was at the centre of the industrialization process, but the two cases epitomise the very different but equally successful, in macroeconomic outcomes, East Asian and Nordic regimes of capitalist development. That is, in the wider sense of the interconnection between political and governance systems, social structure, culture, and business organisation, these two cases, as revealed in the chapters of this book, show that socio-economic transformation can have many paths or regimes of development, an important fact that has became increasingly obvious as the era since the great turning point of 1945 has gone on. This is at variance with the earlier theory of backwardness and catch-up of Gerschenkron and going back much earlier to Smith and Marx. Whereas in the 1950s it seemed to many commentators that the advanced countries should and would converge on economic and social policies and outcomes, in fact various developmental and modernization paths persisted and succeeded. The East Asian path and the Nordic path, which these two cases exemplify in particular ways with local complexities, show the significance that developmental states can have (on developmental states see Jäntti & Vartiainen, 2009; Thompson, 1996; Vartiainen, 1999; Woo-Cummings, 1999).

A further perspective, related to the previous point about the role of the state, concerns the way in which welfare systems have developed, as examined in Chapter 3. All advanced (OECD) countries developed extensive welfare states in the post-war decades within Keynesian social democratic and/or liberal frameworks of macroeconomic management. But there are very significant differences between the advanced countries. A central aspect of the Nordic (including Finnish) model of development has been the large and comprehensive nature of the state welfare system. In contrast, the formal state welfare system in Japan is much smaller as a proportion of GDP and so much less formally redistributive. But the informal welfare system is much more extensive through family structures and nonstate welfare institutions such as charities (Estévez-Abe, 2008). Persistent very egalitarian socio-cultural orders have been a striking feature of both Finland and Japan in the era since 1945, and the contrasting welfare and macroeconomic management systems, combined with a long-existing socio-cultural structure of equality, have preserved this persistent feature in different ways.

A final perspective of comparison worth mentioning here and which the book succeeds in highlighting is the response by the governance and social regimes of the two countries to the growth of economic volatility and effects of crises and shocks in the domestic and global contexts in recent decades. Like most advanced countries, Finland and Japan have suffered from significant demand and supply shocks, especially from 1989 onwards. These shocks, such as the collapse of the Japanese property bubble and subsequent 'long stagnation', the collapse of the communist bloc at the same time as the collapse of the property bubble in Finland in 1989 to 1990, resulting in the Finnish depression of the early 1990s, and the global financial crisis and subsequent great recession of 2008, had to be dealt with by state action but were so in very different ways. Furthermore, the stability that both societies have exhibited through these crises, so very different from the pre-1945 decades, reveals a fundamental fact about their modernization process since 1945: the growth of socio-political 'maturity'. The governance and welfare systems have been more or less adequate to the task of social amelioration, stabilisation, and peaceful adjustment. In 2014, both countries exhibit a high degree of stability yet also policy responsiveness to the global economic crisis of the capitalist system. This stability and responsiveness will surely be tested in coming years as the Great Recession lingers and the global environmental deterioration requires greater responsiveness.

Bibliography

Aamulehti (2013, November 20) [Newspaper].

Abelshauser, W. (2000) 'Germany: guns, butter, and economic miracles', in M. Harrison (ed.), *The economics of World War II. Six great powers in international comparison,* Cambridge: Cambridge University Press.

Adams, J., Clemens, E.S., & Orloff, A.S. (2005) 'Introduction: social theory, modernity, and the three waves of historical sociology', in J. Adams, E.S. Clemens, & A.S. Orloff (eds.), *Remaking modernity: Politics, history, and sociology,* Durham, NC: Duke University Press.

Ahola, S. (1995) *Eliitin yliopistosta massojen korkeakoulutukseen: Korkeakoulujen muuttuva asema yhteiskunnallisen valikoinnin järjestelmänä,* Turku: Turun yliopisto.

Alajoutsijärvi, K. (1993) *Asiakas-myyjä-suhteen muutoksista ja niiden syistä: tulkintaa Kymmenen ja Valmetin suhteen kehityksestä vuosina 1948–90,* Jyväskylä: Jyväskylän yliopisto.

Alajoutsijärvi, K. (1996) *Rautainen pari: Kymmenen ja Valmetin suhde, lähiverkosto ja makrovoimat 1948–90,* Jyväskylä: Jyväskylän yliopisto.

Albrecht, J., & Arts, B. (2005) 'Climate policy convergence in Europe: an assessment based on National Communications to the UNFCCC', *Journal of European Public Policy,* 12: 885–902.

Alestalo, M. (2000) 'The Finnish welfare state in the 1990s: a long-term perspective', in S. Kuhnle (ed.), *Survival of the European welfare state,* London: Routledge.

Alestalo, M., & Uusitalo, H. (1986) 'Finland', in P. Flora (ed.), *Growth to limits. The western European welfare states since World War II,* Berlin: W. de Gruyter.

Amsden, A.H. (2001) *The rise of "the rest": challenges to the West from late-industrializing economies,* Oxford: Oxford University Press.

Anderson, P. (1974a) *Lineages of the absolutist state,* New York: NLB Press.

Anderson, P. (1974b) *Passages from antiquity to feudalism,* London: NLB Press.

Antikainen, A., Rinne, R., & Koski, L. (2006) *Kasvatussosiologia* (3rd ed.), Helsinki: WSOY.

Anttonen, A., & Sipilä, J. (2011) *Suomalaista sosiaalipolitiikkaa* (3rd ed.), Tampere: Vastapaino.

Arisawa, H. (ed.) (1966) *A 100-year history of Japanese Industry. Vol. 1.,* Tokyo: Nihonkeizai-shinbun.

Arisawa, H. (ed.) (1967) *A 100-year history of Japanese Industry. Vol. 2.,* Tokyo: Nihonkeizai-shinbun.

Aspalter, C. (2001) 'Identifying variations of conservative social policy in North East Asia: the welfare state in Japan, South Korea and Mainland China', Australia National University, Graduate Public Policy Programme, Discussion Paper.

Association of Finnish Local Authorities. (2013) Funding of polytechnics. Retrieved 20 November, 2013, from www.kunnat.net/fi/asiantuntijapalvelut/opeku/opetus/amk/amkrahoitus/amkrahoitus/Sivut/default.aspx

Aunesluoma, J. (2007) *Paperipatruunat: Metsäteollisuus sodassa ja jälleenrakentamisessa 1939–1950,* Helsinki: Suomalaisen Kirjallisuuden Seura.

Aunesluoma, J. (2011) *Vapaakaupan tiellä: Suomen kauppa- ja integraatiopolitiikka maailmansodista EU-aikaan,* Helsinki: Suomalaisen Kirjallisuuden Seura.

Averyt, W. (1975) 'Eurogroups, clientela, and the European Community', *International Organization,* 29: 949–972.

Backhouse, R.E., & Bateman, B.W. (2011) *Capitalist revolutionary: John Maynard Keynes,* London: Harvard University Press.

Backhouse, R.E., & Bateman, B.W. (2012) "The right kind of an economist': Friedman's view of Keynes', in T. Cate (ed.), *Keynes's general theory: seventy-five years later,* Cheltenham: Edward Elgar.

Balassa, B. (1964) 'The purchasing-power parity doctrine, a reappraisal', *Journal of Political Economy,* 72: 584–596.

Bendix, R. (1964) *Nation-building and citizenship: studies of our changing social order,* Berkeley: University of California Press.

Bendix, R. (1978) *Kings or people: power and the mandate to rule,* Berkeley: University of California Press.

Bennett, C.J. (1991) 'What is policy convergence and what causes it?', *British Journal of Political Science,* 21: 215–233.

Bergholm, T. (2009) 'The making of the Finnish model: the qualitative change in Finnish corporatism in early 1960s', *Scandinavian Journal of History,* 34: 29–48.

Bernanke, B.S., Gertler, M., & Gilchrist, S. (1999) 'The financial accelerator in a quantitative business cycle framework', in J.B. Taylor & M. Woodford (eds.), *Handbook of macroeconomics vol.1, part C,* Amsterdam: North Holland/Elsevier.

Berry, W.D., & Lowery, D. (1990) 'An alternative approach to understanding budgetary trade-offs', *American Journal of Political Science,* 34: 671–705.

Bonney, R. (ed.) (1999) *The rise of the fiscal state in Europe c. 1200–1815,* Oxford: Oxford University Press.

Bradshaw, J., & Tokoro, M. (2013) 'Child benefit packages in the United Kingdom and Japan', *Social Policy and Society,* 13: 119–128.

Braudel, F. (1982) *Civilization and capitalism 15th–18th century vol. 2: the wheels of commerce,* London: William Collins.

Broadberry, S., & Harrison, M. (2005) 'The economics of World War I: an overview', in S. Broadberry & M. Harrison (eds.), *The economics of World War I,* Cambridge: Cambridge University Press.

Brossard, D., Shanahan, J., & McComas, K. (2004) 'Are issue-cycles culturally constructed? A comparison of French and American coverage of global climate change', *Mass Communication & Society,* 7: 359–377.

Buchardt, M., Markkola, P., & Valtonen, H. (eds.) (2013) *Education, state and citizenship,* Helsinki: Nordic Centre of Excellence NordWel.

Busch, P.-O., & Jörgens, H. (2005) 'The international sources of policy convergence: explaining the spread of environmental policy innovations', *Journal of European Public Policy,* 12: 860–884.

Böckerman, P., & Uusitalo, R. (2006) 'Union membership and the erosion of the Ghent system: lessons from Finland', *British Journal of Industrial Relations*, 44: 283–303.

Calder, K.E. (1988) *Crisis and compensation: public policy and political stability in Japan, 1949–1986*, Princeton, NJ: Princeton University Press.

Calhoun, C. (1996) 'The rise and domestication of historical sociology', in T.J. McDonald (ed.), *The historic turn in the human sciences*, Ann Arbor: University of Michigan Press.

Cameron, R., & Neal, L. (2003) *A Concise Economic History of the World. From Paleolithic Times to the Present* (4th ed.), Oxford: Oxford University Press.

Campbell, J.C., & Ikegami, N. (2000) 'Long-term care insurance comes to Japan', *Health Affairs*, 19: 26–39.

Cargill, T.F., Hutchison, M.M., & Itō, T. (2000) *Financial policy and central banking in Japan*, Cambridge: MIT Press.

Cate, T. (ed.) (2012) *Keynes's general theory seventy-five years later*, Cheltenham: Edward Elgar.

Cato, M.S. (2011) *Environment and economy*, Abingdon: Routledge

Chan, S. (1995) 'Grasping the peace dividend: some propositions on the conversion of swords into plowshares', *Mershon International Studies Review*, 39: 53–95.

Christensen, T.J. (1999) 'China, the US–Japan alliance, and the security dilemma in East Asia', *International Security*, 23: 49–80.

Christensen, T.J. (2006) 'Fostering stability or creating a monster? The rise of China and US policy toward East Asia', *International Security*, 31: 81–126.

Christiansen, N.-F., & Markkola, P. (2006) 'Introduction', *The Nordic model of welfare: a historical reappraisal*, Copenhagen: Museum Tusculanum Press.

CIA. (2011a) Country comparisons: export. *World Fact Book*. Retrieved August 8, 2011, from https://www.cia.gov/library/publications/the-world-factbook/rankorder/2078rank.html.

CIA. (2011b) Country comparisons: GDP – per capita. *World Fact Book*. Retrieved August 8, 2011, from www.cia.gov/library/publications/the-world-factbook/rankorder/2004rank.html.

Clarke, P. (2009) *Keynes: the rise, fall, and return of the 20th century's most influential economist*, New York: Bloomsbury Publishing USA.

Clarke, R., & Edwards, T.H. (1998) 'Deregulation of the Japanese oil products market', *Energy Policy*, 26: 129–141.

Corsetti, G., & Roubini, N. (1996) 'Budget deficits, sector solvency and political biases in fiscal policy: a case study of Finland', *Finnish Economic Papers*, 9: 18–36.

De Vos, G. (1984) *Institutions for change in Japanese society*, Berkeley: University of California.

Demirgüc-Kunt, A., & Detragiache, E. (1998) 'The determinants of banking crises in developing and developed countries', *IMF Staff Papers*, 45: 81–109.

Denzau, A.T., & North, D.C. (1994) 'Shared mental models: ideologies and institutions', *Kyklos*, 47: 3–31.

Domke, W.K., Eichenberg, R.C., & Kelleher, C.M. (1983) 'The illusion of choice: defense and welfare in advanced industrial democracies, 1948–1978', *The American Political Science Review*, 77: 19–35.

Dostaler, G. (2012) 'The general theory, Marx, Marxism and the Soviet Union', in T. Cate (ed.), *Keynes's General Theory: Seventy-Five Years Later*, Cheltenham: Edward Elgar Publishing.

Dunning, J.H. (2001) 'The eclectic (OLI) paradigm of international production: past, present and future', *International Journal of the Economics of Business,* 8: 173–190.

Durkheim, E. (1912/2008) *The elementary forms of religious life,* Oxford: Oxford University Press.

Economic White Paper. (1947). Tokyo: Keizai Antei Honbu.

Edgren, G., Faxén, K., & Odhner, C. (1969) 'Wages, growth and the distribution of income', *The Scandinavian Journal of Economics,* 71: 134–160.

EDMC. (2012) *Energy Keizai Toukei Youran 2012* (*Handbook of energy and economic statistics of Japan 2012*), Tokyo: The Institute of Energy Economics in Japan.

Eloranta, J. (2002) *External security by domestic choices: military spending as an impure public good among eleven European states, 1920–1938.* Ph.D., European University Institute, Florence.

Eloranta, J. (2003) 'National defense', in J. Mokyr (ed.), *The Oxford encyclopedia of economic history,* Oxford: Oxford University Press.

Eloranta, J. (2004) *Warfare and welfare? Understanding 19th and 20th century central government spending.* Coventry: University of Warwick, Department of Economics.

Eloranta, J. (2005) Military spending patterns in history. *EH.Net Encyclopedia.* Retrieved 27 September 2005, from http://eh.net/encyclopedia/article/eloranta.military.

Eloranta, J. (2006a) 'Small state in a changing institutional environment: the impact of interest groups and constraints on Finnish military expenditures and shipbuilding, 1918–1985', in A.-M. Kuijlaars, K. Prudon, & J. Visser (eds.), *Business and society. entrepreneurs, politics and networks in historical perspective,* Rotterdam: Centre for Business History.

Eloranta, J. (2006b) 'Sotien taakka: Makrotalouden ongelmat ja julkisen talouden kipupisteet maailmansotien jälkeen [The burden of wars: the problems of macro economy and public sector after the World Wars]', in P. Karonen & K. Tarjamo (eds.), *Kun sota on ohi,* Helsinki: SKS.

Eloranta, J. (2007) 'From the great illusion to the Great War: military spending behaviour of the Great Powers, 1870–1913', *European Review of Economic History,* 2: 255–283.

Eloranta, J., & Kauppila, J. (2006) 'Guns and butter: Finnish central government spending in the 20th century', in J. Ojala, J. Eloranta, & J. Jalava (eds.), *The road to prosperity: an economic history of Finland,* Helsinki: Suomalaisen Kirjallisuuden Seura.

Eloranta, J., & Kauppila, J. (2007) 'Maanpuolustuksesta hyvinvointivaltioon: valtion menot Suomessa itsenäisyydestä 1990-luvun lamaan', in J. Jalava, J. Eloranta, & J. Ojala (eds.), *Muutoksen merkit. Kvantitatiivisia perspektiivejä Suomen taloushistoriaan,* Helsinki: Tilastokeskus.

Eloranta, J., & Nummela, I. (2014) 'Unequal partners: Germany and Finland during the Second World War', in E. White & J. Scherner (eds.), *Paying for Hitler's war: the consequences of Nazi hegemony for Europe,* New York: Cambridge University Press.

Eloranta, J., & Ojala, J. (2005) 'Converta. A Finnish conduit in the East-West trade', in J. Eloranta & J. Ojala (eds.), *East-West trade and cold war,* Jyväskylä: University of Jyväskylä.

Eloranta, J., Ojala, J., & Valtonen, H. (2010) 'Quantitative methods in business history: an impossible equation?', *Management & Organizational History,* 5: 79–107.
Eloranta, J., & Tanaka, Y. (2015) 'Military spending in Japan and Finland: from warfare to welfare state', in Y. Tanaka, T. Tamaki, J. Ojala, & J. Eloranta (eds.), *Comparing post war Japanese and Finnish economies and societies,* Abingdon: Routledge.
Esping-Andersen, G. (1990) *The three worlds of welfare capitalism,* Princeton, NJ: Princeton University Press.
Esping-Andersen, G. (1997) 'Hybrid or unique? The Japanese welfare state between Europe and America', *Journal of European Social Policy,* 7: 179–189.
Estévez-Abe, M. (2008) *Welfare and capitalism in postwar Japan: party, bureaucracy, and business,* Cambridge: Cambridge University Press.
EVA, & Doyukai, K. (eds.) (2006) *Creative and aging societies: views from Japan and Finland,* Helsinki: Taloustieto.
FAO (2010). *Global Forest Resources Assessment 2010. Main report.* FAO Forestry Paper 163. Rome: FAO.
FEPC. (2011) *FEPC infobase 2011,* Tokyo: Federation of Electric Power Companies of Japan.
Ferguson, N. (2001) *The cash nexus: money and power in the modern world, 1700–2000,* New York: Basic Books.
FFIF. (2010a) Main global forest industry companies. Retrieved September 29, 2010 from www.forestindustries.fi/tilastopalvelu/Tilastokuviot/Basics/Julkinen-EN/a30FinnishForestIndustryCompaniesGlobally_003.ppt.
FFIF. (2010b) Share of forest industry in the Finnish economy. Retrieved September 29, 2010 from www.forestindustries.fi/tilastopalvelu/Tilastokuviot/Basics/Julkinen-EN/a20ImportanceOfForestIndustryInFinland_001.ppt.
FFIF. (2011) Major paper and paperboard producing countries. Retrieved August 8, 2011, from www.forestindustries.fi/statistics/tilastokuviot/Pulp/Forms/DispForm.aspx?ID=19&RootFolder=%2fstatistics%2ftilastokuviot%2fPulp%2fJulkinen%2dEN&Source=http%3A%2F%2Fwww%2Eforestindustries%2Efi%2Fstatistics%2Ftilastokuviot%2FPulp%2FForms%2FAllItems%2Easpx.
Finnboard. (1996) *Finnboard news 1/1996,* Helsinki: Finnboard.
Finnish Ministry of Education and Culture. (2009a) Minister Henna Virkkunen: The Universities Act promulgated. Retrieved 20 November 2013, from www.minedu.fi/OPM/Tiedotteet/2009/06/Yliopistolaki.html?lang=enMinister%20Henna%20Virkkunen:%20The%20Universities%20Act%20promulgated.
Finnish Ministry of Education and Culture. (2009b) *Opetusministeriön strategia 2020,* Helsinki: Opetusministeriö.
Finnish Ministry of Education and Culture. (2013a) Basic education. Retrieved 19 November 2013, from www.minedu.fi/OPM/Koulutus/perusopetus/?lang=en.
Finnish Ministry of Education and Culture. (2013b) Education system in Finland. Retrieved 4 November 2013, from www.minedu.fi/export/sites/default/OPM/Koulutus/koulutusjaerjestelmae/liitteet/finnish_education.pdf.
Finnish Ministry of Education and Culture. (2013c) Financing of education. Retrieved 18 November 2013, from www.minedu.fi/OPM/Koulutus/koulutuspolitiikka/rahoitus/?lang=en.
Finnish Ministry of Education and Culture. (2013d) University education: administration. Retrieved 20 November 2013, from www.minedu.fi/OPM/Koulutus/yliopistokoulutus/hallinto_ohjaus_ja_rahoitus/?lang=en.

Finnish National Board of Education. (2013a) Education system. Retrieved 14 November 2013, from www.oph.fi/english/education_system.
Finnish National Board of Education. (2013b) Universities. Retrieved 20 November 2013, from www.oph.fi/koulutus_ja_tutkinnot/ammattikorkeakoulut_ja_yliopistot/yliopistot.
Finnish Parliament. (2009) *Universities Act,* Helsinki: Finnish Parliament.
Finnpap. (1996) *Finnpap News 1/1996,* Helsinki: Finnpap.
Finpro. (2010) *Country Report, Japan,* Helsinki: Finpro.
Frenkel, O. (1984) 'Flying high: a case study of Japanese industrial policy', *Journal of Policy Analysis and Management,* 3: 406–420.
Freystätter, H. (2012) *Essays on small open macroeconomics,* Helsinki: Bank of Finland.
Fujii, N. (2012) *Ikeda Hayato: Shotoku Baizou de Ikunda,* Kyoto: Minerva Press.
Fujimura, M. (2000) 'The welfare state, the middle class, and the welfare society', *Review of Population and Social Policy,* 9: 1–23.
Fujita, Y. (2009) 'Dengen toshiteno Genshiryoku to Gunji toshiteno Genshiryoku', *Entropy,* 66: 2–10.
Fält, O.K. (1982) *From exotism to realism: the traditional image of Japan in Finland in the transition years of the 1930's,* Rovaniemi: Pohjois-Suomen Historiallinen Yhdistys.
Fält, O. K. (1985) 'Japanin ja Suomen suhteet kansainvälisen politiikan ristiaallokossa 1935–1985', in T. Kinnunen-Härmälä (ed.), *Suomalais-japanilaisia suhteita 1935–1985.* Helsinki: Suomalais-japanilainen yhdistys.
Garand, J.C., & Hendrick, R.M. (1991) 'Expenditure tradeoffs in the American states: a longitudinal test, 1948–1984', *The Western Political Quarterly,* 44: 915–940.
García-Iglesias, C., & Kilponen, J. (2006) 'Monetary aspects of a changing economy', in J. Ojala, J. Eloranta, & J. Jalava (eds.), *The road to prosperity. an economic history of Finland,* Helsinki: SKS.
Garside, W. (2005) 'A very British phenomenon? Industrial politics and the decline of the Japanese coal mining industry since the 1950s', *Australian Economic History Review,* 45: 186–203.
Geanakoplos, J. (2010) 'The leverage cycle', *NBER Macroeconomics Annual,* 24: 1–65.
George, A.L., & Bennett, A. (2005) *Case studies and theory development in the social sciences,* Cambridge: MIT Press.
Gerschenkron, A. (1962) *Economic backwardness in historical perspective,* Cambridge, MA: Harvard University Press.
Glachant, J.-M., & Finon, D. (eds.) (2003) *Competition in European electricity markets,* Cheltenham: Edward Elgar Publishing Ltd.
Goldin, C.D., & Katz, L.F. (2008) *The race between education and technology,* Cambridge, MA: Harvard University Press.
Goldstone, J. (2003) 'Comparative historical analysis and knowledge accumulation in the study of revolutions', in J. Mahoney & D. Rueschemeyer (eds.), *Comparative historical analysis in the social sciences,* Cambridge: Cambridge University Press.
Goldthorpe, J.H. (1991) 'The uses of history in sociology: reflections on some recent tendencies', *British Journal of Sociology,* 42: 211–230.

Goldthorpe, J.H. (1997) 'Current issues in comparative macrosociology: a debate on methodological issues', *Comparative Social Research*, 16: 1–26.

Goodspeed, T.B. (2012) *Rethinking the Keynesian revolution. Keynesian, Hayek, and the Wicksell connection*, Oxford: Oxford University Press.

Gorodnichenko, Y., Mendoza, E.G., & Tesar, L.L. (2012) 'The Finnish great depression: from Russia with love', *American Economic Review*, 102: 1619–1643.

Goto, M., & Sueyoshi, T. (2009) 'Productivity growth and deregulation of Japanese electricity distribution', *Energy Policy*, 37: 3130–3138.

Green, M. (1995) *Arming Japan: alliance politics, defense production and the postwar search for autonomy*, New York: Columbia University Press.

Grossman, H.I., & Mendoza, J. (2003) 'Butter *and* guns: complementarity between economic and military competition', in A. Glazer and K. A. Konrad (eds.) *Conflict and governance*, Berlin Heidelberg: Springer.

GWEC. (2010) *Global wind report 2010*. Brussels: GWEC.

Hamada, K., & Okada, Y. (2009) 'Monetary and international factors behind Japan's lost decade', *Journal of the Japanese and International Economics*, 23: 200–219.

Hannikainen, M., & Heikkinen, S. (2006) 'The labour market, 1850–2000', in J. Ojala, J. Eloranta, & J. Jalava (eds.), *The road to prosperity. an economic history of Finland*, Helsinki: SKS.

Hanska, J., & Vainio-Korhonen, K. (eds.) (2010) *Huoneentaulun maailma. Kasvatus ja koulutus Suomessa keskiajalta 1860-luvulle*, Helsinki: Suomalaisen Kirjallisuuden Seura.

Hanska, J., Vainio-Korhonen, K., & Rahikainen, M. (2010) 'Säädynmukaisen kasvatuksen ja koulutuksen aika', in J. Hanska & K. Vainio-Korhonen (eds.), *Huoneentaulun maailma: Kasvatus ja koulutus Suomessa keskiajalta 1860-luvulle*, Helsinki: Suomalaisen Kirjallisuuden Seura.

Hara, A. (2000) 'Japan: guns before rice', in M. Harrison (ed.), *The economics of World War II. Six great powers in international comparison*, Cambridge: Cambridge University Press.

Harrison, M. (1988) 'Resource mobilization for World War II: the USA, UK, USSR, and Germany, 1938–1945', *Economic History Review*, 41: 171–92.

Harrison, M. (1996) *Accounting for war: Soviet production, employment, and the defence burden, 1940–1945*, Cambridge: Cambridge University Press.

Harrison, M. (ed.) (1998) *The economics of World War II. Six great powers in international comparisons*, Cambridge, UK: Cambridge University Press.

Harrod, R.F. (1972 [1951]) *John Maynard Keynes*, Harmondsworth: Pelican Books.

Hausman, W.J., Hertner, P., & Wilkins, M. (2008) *Global electrification: multinational enterprise and international finance in the history of light and power, 1878–2007*, Cambridge: Cambridge University Press.

Heikkinen, S. (2000) *Paper for the world: the Finnish Paper Mill's Association-Finnpap 1918–1996*, Helsinki: Otava.

Heimonen, K., Miyagawa, S., & Morita, Y. (2015) 'The financial crisis of the 1990s in Finland and Japan', in Y. Tanaka, T. Tamaki, J. Ojala, & J. Eloranta (eds.), *Comparing post war Japanese and Finnish economies and societies*, Abingdon: Routledge.

Heurlin, L.O. a. (1946) 'John Maynard Keynes', *Kansantaloudellinen Aikakauskirja*, 42: 317–324.

Heurlin, L. O. a. (1952) 'Review of Työllisyys, korko ja raha by John Maynard Keynes', *Kansantaloudellinen Aikakauskirja,* 48: 61–62.

Heurlin, L. O. a., & Korpisaari, P. (1940) 'Työllisyyden yleinen teoria', *Kansantaloudellinen Aikakauskirja,* 36: 190–201.

Hikino, T., & Amsden, A. H. (1984) 'Staying behind, stumbling back, sneaking up, soaring ahead: late industrialization in historical perspective', in W. J. Baumol (ed.), *Convergence of productivity: cross-national studies and historical evidence,* Oxford: Oxford University Press.

Hjerppe, R. (1988) *Suomen talous 1860–1985. Kasvu ja rakennemuutos* (Vol. XIII), Helsinki: Suomen Pankki.

Hjerppe, R. (1997) 'Jos ei voi ottaa, täytyy lainata – Suomen valtion velka sotien välisenä aikana', *Kansantaloudellinen aikakauskirja,* 93: 11–20.

Hjerppe, R., & Jalava, J. (2006) 'Economic growth and structural change: A century and a half of catching-up', in J. Ojala, J. Eloranta, & J. Jalava (eds.), *The road to prosperity: an economic history of Finland,* Helsinki: Suomalaisen Kirjallisuuden Seura.

Hobson, J. M. (1993) 'The military-extraction gap and the wary titan: the fiscal sociology of British defence policy 1870–1914', *Journal of European Economic History,* 22: 466–507.

Honkapohja, S. E. K., Leibfritz, W., & Uusitalo, R. (2009) *Economic prosperity recaptured. the Finnish path from crisis to rapid growth,* Cambridge: MIT Press.

Honkapohja, S., & Koskela, E. (1999) 'The economic crises of the 1990s in Finland', *Economic Policy,* 14: 399–436.

Honkapohja, S., Koskela, E., & Paunio, J. (1996) 'The depression of the 1990's in Finland: an analytic view', *The Finnish Economic Papers,* 9: 37–54.

Hook, G. D. (1988) 'The erosion of anti-militaristic principles in contemporary Japan', *Journal of Peace Research,* 25: 381–394.

Horiuchi, T. (2008) *Finland – Yutakasa no Mesoddo 2008. Finland – an affluent society and how did they become so affluent,* Tokyo: Shueisha.

Hoshi, T., & Kashyap, A. (2000) 'The Japanese banking crisis: where did it come from and how will it end?', *The NBER Macroeconomics Annual,* 14: 130–212.

Howard, M. (1972) *Studies in war and peace,* New York: Viking Press.

Huber, E., Ragin, C., & Stephens, J. D. (1993) 'Social democracy, Christian democracy, constitutional structure, and the welfare state', *American Journal of Sociology,* 99: 711–749.

Huber, E., & Stephens, J. D. (2001) 'Welfare state and production regimes in the era of retrenchment', in P. Pierson (ed.), *The new politics of the welfare state,* Oxford: Oxford University Press.

Hundley, G., & Jacobson, C. K. (1998) 'The effects of the keiretsu on the export performance of Japanese companies: help or hindrance?', *Strategic Management Journal,* 19: 927–937.

Hutchinson, M., & McDill, K. (1999a) 'Are all banking crises alike? The Japanese experience in international comparison', *Journal of the Japanese and International Economies,* 13: 155–180.

Hutchison, M., & McDill, K. (1999b) 'Empirical determinants of banking crisis: Japan's experience in international perspective', in C. Freeman (ed.), *Why did Japan stumble? Causes and cures,* Cheltenham: Edward Elgar.

Häggman, K. (2006) *Metsän tasavalta: suomalainen metsäteollisuus politiikan ja markkinoiden ristiaallokossa 1920–1939,* Helsinki: Suomalaisen Kirjallisuuden Seura.

Högselius, P. (2009) 'Spent nuclear fuel policies in historical perspective: an international comparison', *Energy Policy,* 37: 254–263.

Höhne, N., den Elzen, M., & Weiss, M. (2006) 'Common but differentiated convergence (CDC): a new conceptual approach to long-term climate policy', *Climate Policy,* 6: 181–199.

Hölttä, S., Jansson, T., & Kivistö, J. (2011) 'Emerging markets in the Finnish system', in R. Brown (ed.), *Higher education and the market,* New York: Routledge.

IEA. (2010) *Key world energy statistics 2010,* Paris: IEA.

IEA-PVPS. (2010) *Preliminary trends report 2010,* Paris: IEA-PVPS.

IEEJ. (ed.) (1986) *Sengo Energy Sangyoshi,* Tokyo: Toyo Keizai Inc.

Iggers, G. G. (1984) *New directions in European historiography* (rev. ed.), Middletown, CT: Wesleyan University Press.

Iisalo, T. (1988) *Kouluopetuksen vaiheita keskiajan katedraalikoulusta nykyisiin kouluihin,* Helsinki: Otava.

Ishi, H. (2001) *The Japanese tax system* (3rd ed.), Oxford: Oxford University Press.

Ishi, H. (2009) *Syouhizei no Seiji-Keizaigaku [Political economics on the Japanese consumption tax],* Tokyo: Nihon Keizai Shimbun.

Isosaari, J. (1973) *Suomen koululaitoksen rakenne ja kehitys,* Helsinki: Otava.

Itagaki, H. (2002) 'Japanese multinational enterprises: the paradox of high efficiency and low profitability', *Asian Business & Management,* 1: 101–124.

Ito, M. (1981) 'Shogen Kodoseichoki no Nihon – Ito Masaya', *Economist in Japan,* 59: 84–91.

Iwai, Y. (2002) 'Introduction', in Y. Iwai (ed.), *Forestry and the forest industry in Japan,* Vancouver: British Columbia Press.

Jahn, D. (1998) 'Environmental performance and policy regimes: explaining variations in 18 OECD countries', *Policy Sciences,* 31: 107–131.

JAIF (2006) *Sekaino Genshiryokuhatsuden Kaihatsu no Doko 2006,* Tokyo: Japan Atomic Industrial Forum.

Jalonen, O.-P., & Vesa, U. (1992) 'Something old, something new, something borrowed, something blue: Finland's defence policy in a changing security environment', *Cooperation and Conflict,* 27: 377–395.

Jenkins, H. (2006) *Convergence culture: where old and new media collide:* New York: NYU Press.

Jensen-Eriksen, N. (2007) *Läpimurto: Metsäteollisuus kasvun, integraation ja kylmän sodan Euroopassa 1950–1973,* Helsinki: Suomalaisen Kirjallisuuden Seura.

Jensen-Eriksen, N. (2008a) 'Lama ja uusi nousu', in M. Kuisma (ed.), *Kriisi ja kumous: Metsäteollisuus ja maailmantalouden murros 1973–2008,* Helsinki: Suomalaisen Kirjallisuuden Seura.

Jensen-Eriksen, N. (2008b) 'Tuotanto, yritykset ja rahoittajat', in N. Jensen-Eriksen (ed.), *Läpimurto: Metsäteollisuus kasvun, integraation ja kylmän sodan Euroopassa,* Helsinki: Suomalaisen Kirjallisuuden Seura.

Jonung, L., Kiander, J., & Vartia, P. (2009) *The great financial crisis in Finland and Sweden. The Nordic experience of financial liberalization,* Cheltenham: Edward Elgar.

Jonung, L., Söderström, H. T., & Stymne, J. (1996) 'Depression in the north. Boom and burst in Sweden and Finland, 1985–1993', *Finnish Economic Papers,* 9: 55–71.

Jordan, A. J., & Liefferink, D. (2004) *Environmental policy in Europe: the Europeanization of national environmental policy,* Abingdon: Routledge.

Joutsivuo, T. (2010) 'Papeiksi ja virkamiehiksi', in J. Hanska & K. Vainio-Korhonen (eds.), *Huoneentaulun maailma: Kasvatus ja koulutus Suomessa keskiajalta*, Helsinki: Suomalaisen Kirjallisuuden Seura.

JPA. (2010a) Position of the pulp and paper industry within the manufacturing, from www.jpa.gr.jp/en/industry/data01/

JPA. (2010b) *The present condition of paper and pulp industry*, Tokyo: Japan Paper Association.

JPA. (2010c) *Pulp & paper statistics 2010*, Tokyo: Japan Paper Association.

JPA. (2010d) *Pulp STATISTICS 2009*, Tokyo: Japan Paper Association.

JPA. (2010e) *Paper and cardboard annual statistics 2009*, Tokyo: Japan Paper Association.

JPA. (2012) *Pulp and paper statistics 2012*, Tokyo: Japan Paper Association.

Julkunen, R. (1990) 'Women in the welfare state', in M. Manninen & P. Setälä (eds.), *The LADY WITH THE BOW*, Helsinki: Otava.

Julkunen, R. (2001) *Suunnanmuutos: 1990-luvun sosiaalipoliittinen reformi Suomessa*, Tampere: Vastapaino.

Jäntti, M., & Vartiainen, J. (2009) 'The Finnish developmental state and its growth regime', *Research Paper No 2009/35*, Helsinki: UNU-WIDER, United Nations University.

Kahl, S. (2005) 'The religious roots of modern poverty policy: Catholic, Lutheran, and Reformed Protestant traditions compared', *Archives européennes de sociologie*, 46: 91–126.

Kajaste, I. (1992) 'Soviet trade and the Finnish economy', *Ministry of Finance of Finland, Discussion Paper*, 33.

Kalela, J., Kiander, J., Kivikuru, U., Loikkanen, H., & Simpura, J. (eds.) (2002) *Down from the heavens, up from the ashes*, Helsinki: Government Institute for Economic Research, Academy of Finland.

Kamikubo, S. (2008) *Hyoden Nihon no Keizai Shiso Shimomura Osamu: Nihon Keizaigaku no Jissensha*, Tokyo: Nihon Keizai Hyoronsha.

Kaminsky, G., & Reinhart, C. (1996) 'The twin crises: the causes of banking and balance-of-payments problems, board of governors of the federal reserve system', *International Finance Discussion Papers. Board of Governors of Federal Reserve System*, 544.

Kansallinen ilmastostrategia. (2001) *Valtioneuvoston selonteko eduskunnalle*, Helsinki: Kauppa- ja teollisuusministeriö.

Karjalainen, A. (1954) 'Review of *De ekonomiska ideernas historia* by Philip Ch. Newman', *Kansantaloudellinen Aikakauskirja*, 50: 58–61.

Karske, M., Koskinen, T., & Moisio, J. (1993) *A world of paper*, Helsinki: Finnpap.

Kauhanen, M. (2007) 'Eriytymiskehitys työmarkkinoilla jatkunut 2000-luvulla', in H. Taimio (ed.), *Talouskasvun hedelmät–kuka sai ja kuka jäi ilman*, Helsinki: Työväen sivistysliitto.

Kauhanen, M. (2008) 'Part-time work and involuntary part-time work in the private sector', *Economic and Industrial Democracy*, 29: 217–248.

Kautto, M. (1999) 'Changes in age structure, family stability and dependency', in M. Kautto, M. Heikkilä, B. Hvinden, S. Marklund, & N. Ploug (eds.), *Nordic social policy: changing welfare states*. London and New York: Routledge.

Keane, W. (2005) 'Estrangement, intimacy, and the objects of anthropology', in G. Steinmetz (ed.), *The politics of method in the human sciences: positivism and its epistemological others*, Durham, NC: Duke University Press.

Kela. (2011) *Opintolainan suosio on hiipunut parissa vuosikymmenessä,* Helsinki: Kelan tilastoryhmä.

Kersbergen, K. v. (2000) 'The declining resistance of welfare states to change?', in S. Kuhnle (ed.), *Survival of the European welfare state,* London: Routledge.

Kettunen, P. (2001) 'The Nordic welfare state in Finland', *Scandinavian Journal of History,* 26: 225–247.

Kettunen, P. (2006) 'The tension between the social and the economic. A historical perspective on a welfare state', in J. Ojala, J. Eloranta, & J. Jalava (eds.), *The road to prosperity: an economic history of Finland,* Helsinki: Suomalaisen Kirjallisuuden Seura.

Kettunen, P. (2011) 'The transnational construction of national challenges: the ambiguous Nordic model of welfare and competitiveness', in P. Kettunen & K. Petersen (eds.), *Beyond welfare state models: transnational historical perspectives on social policy,* Cheltenham: Edward Elgar.

Kettunen, P., & Petersen, K. (2011) 'Introduction: rethinking welfare state models', in P. Kettunen & K. Petersen (eds.), *Beyond welfare state models: transnational historical perspectives on social policy,* Cheltenham: Edward Elgar.

Keynes, J.M. (1951) *Työllisyys, korko ja raha: yleinen teoria,* Porvoo: WSOY.

Keynes, J.M. (1957) *The general theory of employment, interest and money,* London: Macmillan.

Kiander, J., & Lönnqvist, H. (2002) *Hyvinvointivaltio, sosiaalipolitiikka ja taloudellinen kasvu,* Helsinki: Sosiaali-ja terveysministeriö.

Kibune, H., & Kudo, H. (1996) 'Structural changes in Japan's economy and society and outlook for long-term energy supply and demand', *Energy Policy,* 24: 1119–1125.

Kim, P.H. (2010) 'The East Asian welfare state debate and surrogate social policy: an exploratory study on Japan and South Korea', *Socio-Economic Review,* 8: 411–435.

Kindleberger, C.P., & Aliber, R.Z. (2011) *Manias, panics and crashes. A history of financial crises* (6th ed.), Basingstoke: Palgrave Macmillan

King, J.E. (2002) *A history of post Keynesian economics since 1936,* Cheltenham: Edward Elgar Publishing.

Kingston, J. (2004) *Japan's quiet transformation: social change and civil society in 21st century Japan,* London: Routledge.

Kingston, J. (2011) *Contemporary Japan: history, politics, and social change since the 1980s,* Chichester: Wiley-Blackwell.

Kinmonth, E.H. (2005) 'From selection to seduction: the impact of demographic change on private higher education in Japan', in J.S. Eades, R. Goodman, & Y. Hada (eds.), *The 'big bang' in Japanese higher education: the 2004 reforms and the dynamics of change,* Melbourne: Trans Pacific Press.

Kiser, E., & Hechter, M. (1991) 'The role of general theory in comparative-historical sociology', *American Journal of Sociology,* 97: 1–30.

Kiser, E., & Hechter, M. (1998) 'The debate on historical sociology: rational choice theory and its critics 1', *American Journal of Sociology,* 104: 785–816.

Kivinen, P. (1949) 'Review of *The Keynesian revolution* by Lawrence R. Klein', *Kansantaloudellinen Aikakauskirja,* 45: 94–97.

Kivinen, P. (1950) 'Review of *The new economics. Keynes' influence on theory and policy* by Seymour E. Harris ed.', *Kansantaloudellinen Aikakauskirja,* 46: 281–285.

Kivinen, P. (1952) 'Täystyöllisyys ja inflaatiovaara', *Kansantaloudellinen Aikakauskirja,* 48: 171–201.

Klein, L. R. (1966) *The Keynesian revolution, Macmillan Paperbacks Ed.* (2nd ed.), New York: Macmillan.

Klinge, M. (2010) *A European university: the University of Helsinki 1640–2010,* Helsinki: Otava.

Klinge, M., Knapas, R., Leikola, A., Strömberg, J., Kolbe, L., Klinge, M., & Velling, R. (1987) *Helsingin yliopisto 1640–1990: Kuninkaallinen Turun akatemia 1640–1808,* Helsinki: Otava.

Kocka, J. (2003) 'Comparison and beyond', *History and Theory,* 42: 39–44.

Kohno, M. (1997) *Japan's postwar party politics,* Princeton, NJ: Princeton University Press.

Kohvakka, M. (1996) *Etabloituminen Itä-Aasiaan: Suomen ja Japanin kaupalliset suhteet maailmansotien välillä,* Jyväskylä.

Koivisto, J. V. (1998) *Cultural heritages and cross-cultural management: cross-cultural synergy and friction in Finno-Japanese management,* Helsinki: Helsinki School of Economics and Business Administration.

Kokkinen, A. (2012) *On Finland's economic growth and convergence with Sweden and the EU15 in the 20th century,* Helsinki: Tilastokeskus.

Koskimies, I. (1982) *Japani Suomen viennin kohdemaana.* Master's thesis, Turku School of Economics, Turku.

Kosonen, P. (1978) 'Keynesiläisyys ja Suomen talouspolitiikka', in P. Kosonen, T. Koste, J. Pekkarinen, & J. Willner (eds.), *Keynesiläisyys ja Suomen talouspolitiikka,* Helsinki: Tutkijaliitto.

Kronlund, J. (1989) *Suomen puolustuslaitos 1918–1939. Puolustusvoimien rauhan ajan historia,* Porvoo: WSOY.

Krugman, P. (1998) 'It's baaack: Japan's slump and the return of the liquidity trap', *Brookings Papers on Economic Activity,* 2: 137–205.

Kröger, T., Anttonen, A., & Sipilä, J. (2003) 'Social care in Finland: stronger and weaker forms of universalism', in A. Anttonen, J. Baldock, & J. Sipilä (eds.), *The young the old and the state: social care systems in five industrial nations,* Cheltenham: Edward Elgar.

Kuch, J., & Uotinen, K. (2005) *Toyota vuodesta 1936,* Helsinki: Alfamer.

Kuikka, M. (2009) 'Zur Entwicklung des finnischen Schulsystems', in A. Matthies & E. Skiera (eds.), *In Das Bildungswesen in Finnland: Geschichte, Struktur, Institutionen und pädagogisch-didaktische Konzeptionen, bildungs- und sozialpolitische perspektiven,* Bad Heilbronn: Julius Klinkhardt.

Kuisma, M. (1993) *Metsäteollisuuden maa. Suomi, metsät ja kansainvälinen järjestelmä 1620–1920,* Helsinki: SKS.

Kuisma, M. (1997) *Kylmä sota, kuuma öljy,* Porvoo: WSOY.

Kuisma, M. (2008) 'Mikä kriisi, mikä kumous', in M. Kuisma (ed.), *Kriisi ja kumous. Metsäteollisuus ja maailmantalouden murros,* Helsinki: Suomalaisen Kirjallisuuden Seura.

Kurokawa, K., & Ikki, O. (2001) 'The Japanese experiences with national PV system programmes', *Solar Energy,* 70: 457–466.

Kurosawa, T., & Hashino, T. (2012) 'From the non-European tradition to a variation on the Japanese competitiveness model: the modern Japanese paper industry since the 1870s', in J.-A. Lamberg, J. Ojala, M. Peltoniemi, & T. Särkkä (eds.), *The evolution of global paper industry 1800–2050,* Dordrecht: Springer.

Kuusi, P. (1961) *60-luvun sosiaalipolitiikka,* Porvoo: WSOY.

Kynnös, P., & Räsänen, A. (1992) *Itsenäisen Suomen ikäinen Korpivaara 1917–1992,* Vantaa: Korpivaara.

Kyoto Protocol. (2008) The cabinet of Japan, Kyoto Protocol target achievement plan, totally revised March 28, 2008. Retrieved August 14, 2012, from www.kantei.go.jp/foreign/policy/ondanka/KP_Achievement_Plan_Text.pdf

Laine, E.M., & Laine, T. (2010) 'Kirkollinen kansanopetus', in J. Hanska & K. Vainio-Korhonen (eds.), *Huoneentaulun maailma: Kasvatus ja koulutus Suomessa keskiajalta,* Helsinki: Suomalaisen Kirjallisuuden Seura.

Lamberg, J.-A., & Ojala, J. (2006) 'Evolution of competitive strategies in global forestry industries: introduction', in J.-A. Lamberg, J. Näsi, J. Ojala, & P. Sajasalo (eds.), *The evolution of competitive strategies in global forestry industries,* Dordrecht: Springer.

Lamberg, J.-A., Ojala, J., & Eloranta, J. (1997) *Uusi Institutionaalinen Taloushistoria: Johdanto Tutkimukseen,* Jyväskylä: Atena.

Lamberg, J.-A., Ojala, J., Peltoniemi, M., & Särkkä, T. (eds.) (2012) *The evolution of global paper industry 1800–2050: a comparative analysis,* Dordrecht: Springer.

Lampinen, O. (1998/2000) *Suomen koulujärjestelmän kehitys* (2nd ed.), Helsinki: Gaudeamus.

Landes, D.S. (1999) *The wealth and poverty of nations: Why some are so rich and some so poor,* New York: W.W. Norton & Company.

Lange, M. (2013) *Comparative-historical methods,* Thousand Oaks, CA: Sage Publications.

Laratta, R. (2009) 'Hand in hand or under the thumb? A new perspective on social welfare in Japan', *Social Policy and Society,* 8: 307–317.

Laurent, H. (2012) 'War and the emerging social state: social policy, public health and citizenship in wartime Finland', in T. Kinnunen & V. Kivimäki (eds.), *Finland in World War II. History, memory, interpretations,* Leiden: Brill.

Lehmussaari, O.-P., Suvanto, A., & Vajanne, L. (1994) 'The currency band and credibility: the Finnish experience', in J. Åkerholm & A. Giovannini (eds.), *Exchange rate policies in the Nordic countries,* London: CEPR.

Lévy, P. (1999) *Collective intelligence: mankind's emerging world in cyberspace,* Cambridge: Perseus Publishing.

Lieberson, S. (1991) 'Small *N*'s and big conclusions: an examination of the reasoning in comparative studies based on a small number of cases', *Social Forces,* 70: 307–230.

Lieberson, S. (1994) 'More on the uneasy case for using mill-type methods in small-*N* comparative studies', *Social Forces,* 72: 1225–1237.

Liebowitz, S.J., & Margolis, S.E. (1990) 'The fable of the keys', *Journal of Law and Economics,* 33: 1–25.

Lilja, R., & Mäkilä, A. (eds.) (1996) *Koulutuksen talous nyky-Suomessa [English summary: Economics of education in today's Finland],* Helsinki: Taloustieto.

Lin, K., & Rantalaiho, M. (2003) 'Family policy and social order: comparing the dynamics of family policy-making in Scandinavia and Confucian Asia', *International Journal of Social Welfare,* 12: 2–13.

Lindbeck, A. (2002) 'Changing tides for the welfare state: an essay', in S. Cnossen & H.W. Sinn (eds.), *Public finance and public policy in the new century,* Cambridge: MIT Press.

Lindert, P.H. (1994) 'The rise of social spending, 1880–1930', *Explorations in Economic History,* 31: 1–37.

Lindert, P.H. (2004) *Growing public. Social spending and economic growth since the eighteenth century* (Vol. 1), Cambridge: Cambridge University Press.

Linnamo, J. (1957) 'Mitä on talouspolitiikan teoria?', *Kansantaloudellinen Aikakauskirja*, 53: 272–285.

Linnamo, J. (1966) 'Keynes ja kolmekymmentä vuotta', *Kansantaloudellinen Aikakauskirja*, 62: 134–156.

Lintulahti, M. (1963) *Finland to tainichikankei no enkaku: A treatise of the Finno-Japanese relations from the early contacts to the present*, Tokyo: Hosei University.

Lustick, I.S. (2006) 'History, historiography, and political science: multiple historical records and the problem of selection bias', *American Political Science Review*, 90: 507–548.

Luukkanen, J., Vehmas, J., Karjalainen, A., & Panula-Ontto, J. (2009) 'Energiaskenaarioita vuoteen 2050', *Katsaus energia-alan haasteisiin, mahdollisuuksiin ja vaikutuskeinoihin*, Turku: Tulevaisuuden tutkimuskeskus ja Turun kauppakorkeakoulu.

Maddison, A. (2001) *The world economy: a millennial perspective*, Paris: OECD.

Maddison, A. (2003) *The world economy. Historical statistics*, Paris: OECD.

Maddison, A. (2011) *The world economy: a millennium perspective*, Paris: OECD.

Mahoney, J. (2006) 'On the second wave of historical sociology', *International Journal of Comparative Sociology*, 47: 371–377.

Mahoney, J., & Rueschemeyer, D. (2003) 'Comparative historical analysis: achievements and agendas', in J. Mahoney & D. Rueschemeyer (eds.), *Comparative historical analysis in the social sciences*, Cambridge: Cambridge University Press.

Mahoney, J., & Villegas, C.M. (2007) 'Historical inquiry and comparative politics', in C. Boix & S.C. Stokes (eds.), *The Oxford handbook of comparative politics*, Oxford: Oxford University Press.

Mann, M. (1994) 'In praise of macro-sociology: a reply to Goldthorpe', *The British Journal of Sociology*, 45: 37–54.

Markkola, P. (2011) 'The Lutheran Nordic welfare states', in P. Kettunen & K. Petersen (eds.), *Beyond welfare state models: transnational historical perspectives on social policy*, Cheltenham: Edward Elgar.

Markkola, P., & Ojala, J. (2012) 'Seguridad social y bienestar en Finlandia', *Istor*, 12: 95–128.

Marriott, M. (1990) 'Constructing an Indian ethnosociology', in M. Marriott (ed.), *India through Hindu categories*, New Delhi: Sage Publications.

Marshall, M. (1996) 'The changing face of Swedish corporatism: the disintegration of consensus', *Journal of Economic Issues*, 30: 843–588.

Marx, K. (1852/2008) *The 18th brumaire of Louis Bonaparte*, London: Wildside Press.

Marx, K. (1867/1992) *Capital: volume 1: a critique of political economy*, New York: Penguin.

Marx, K. (1871/2012) *The civil war in France*, London: GreatSpace.

McCloskey, D.N. (1987) *Econometric history. Studies in economic and social history*, Basingstoke: Macmillan Education.

McCormick, K. (2004) 'Whatever happened to the 'Japanese model'?', *Asian Business & Management*, 3: 371–393.

McMichael, P. (1990) 'Incorporating comparison within a world-historical perspective: an alternative comparative method', *American Sociological Review*, 55: 385–397.

McMillan, C.J. (1991) 'Going global: Japanese science-based strategies in the 1990s', *Managerial and Decision Economics*, 12: 171–181.

McNeill, W. (1990) 'The rise of the West after twenty-five years', *Journal of World History*, 1: 1–21.

Melby, K., Ravn, A.-B., & Carlsson Wetterberg, C. (2008) 'A Nordic model of gender equality? Introduction', in K. Melby, A.-B. Ravn, & C. Carlsson Wetterberg (eds.), *Gender equality and welfare politics in Scandinavia. The limits of political ambition?* Bristol: Policy Press.

Meltzer, A.H., & Richard, S.F. (1981) 'A rational theory of the size of government', *The Journal of Political Economy*, 89: 914–927.

METI. (2009) *The census of manufacture*. Tokyo: The Research and Statistics Department, Economic and Industrial Policy Bureau, Ministry of Economy, Trade and Industry.

METLA. (2011) Finnish forests, from www.metla.fi/metla/finland/finland-forests.htm.

MEXT. (1962) *Growth and education in Japan*, Tokyo: Ministry of Education, Culture, Sports, Science and Technology in Japan (MEXT).

MEXT. (2004) *Biannual student living survey*, Tokyo: Ministry of Education, Culture, Sports, Science and Technology in Japan (MEXT).

MEXT. (2005) *School basic survey 1955–2005*, Tokyo: Ministry of Education, Culture, Sports, Science and Technology in Japan (MEXT).

MEXT. (2008) *Educational statistics 2008*, Tokyo: Ministry of Education, Culture, Sports, Science and Technology in Japan (MEXT).

MEXT. (2009) *School basic survey*, Tokyo: Ministry of Education, Culture, Sports, Science and Technology in Japan (MEXT).

MEXT. (2013) Principles guide Japan's educational system. Retrieved 4 November, 2013, from www.mext.go.jp/english/introduction/1303952.htm.

Michelsen, K.-E., & Särkikoski, T. (2005) *Suomalainen ydinvoimalaitos*, Helsinki: Edita.

Milward, A.S. (1977) *War, economy and society 1939–1945*, London: Allen Lane.

Minsky, H.P. (1975) *John Maynard Keynes*, New York: Columbia University Press.

Mintz, A. (1989) 'Guns versus butter: a disaggregated analysis', *The American Political Science Review*, 83: 1285–1293.

Mintz, A., & Huang, C. (1991) 'Guns versus butter: the indirect link', *American Journal of Political Science*, 35: 738–757.

Mintz, A., & Stevenson, R.T. (1995) 'Defense expenditures, economic growth, and the "peace dividend": a longitudinal analysis of 103 countries', *Journal of Conflict Resolution*, 39: 283–305.

Mitchell, B.R. (2003) *International historical statistics: Africa, Asia & Oceania, 1750–2000*, New York: Palgrave Macmillan.

MITI. (1994) *Paper and pulp industry in greening and internationalization*, Tokyo: MITI.

Miyagawa, S., & Morita, Y. (2009) 'Financial crises of Finland, Sweden, Norway and Japan', *Journal of Faculty of Economics, KGU*, 19: 45–77.

Miyagawa, S., Morita, Y., & Sawada, Y. (2008) *Financial crisis and money demand: in the case of Japan and Finland*, Turku: University of Turku.

Miyamoto, T. (2003) 'Dynamics of the Japanese welfare state in comparative perspective: between "three worlds" and the developmental state', *The Japanese Journal of Social Security Policy*, 2: 12–24.

Mizuki, Y. (1999) *Ekonomisuto Sangohusi: Sengo Keizaiwo Tsukutta Otokotachi*, Tokyo: Bungei Shunju.

Momose, H. (1973) 'Japan's relations with Finland 1919–1944: as reflected by Japanese source materials', *Slavic Studies,* 17: 1–39.

Momose, H., & Ishino, Y. (eds.) (2008) *Finlando wo Shiru Tameno 44 Shou (44 chapters on how we can know about Finland),* Tokyo: Akashi Shoten.

Monstadt, J. (2004) *Die Modernisierung Der Stromversorgung: Regionale Energie Und Klimapolitik Im Liberalisierungs Und Privatisierungsprozess,* Wiesbaden: Vs Verlag Fur Sozialwissenschaften.

Moore, B. J. (1966) *Social origins of dictatorship and democracy: lord and peasant in making of the modern world,* Harmondsworth: Penguin Books.

Mosk, C. (1983) Patriarchy and fertility: Japan and Sweden, 1880–1960. From http://ssrn.com/abstract=1807370.

Mosk, C. (2000) 'Secular improvement in well-being: Britain and Japan compared', *Jahrbuch für Wirtschafts Geschichte,* 11: 113–128.

Murmann, J. P. (2003) *Knowledge and competitive advantage: the coevolution of firms, technology, and national institutions,* Cambridge: Cambridge University Press.

Murray, W., & Millett, A. R. (2009) *A war to be won: fighting the Second World War,* Cambridge MA: Harvard University Press.

Myllyntaus, T. (1989) *Finnish industries in transition 1885–1920: responding to technological challenges, Tekniikan museon julkaisuja 4,* Helsinki: The Museum of Technology.

Myrskylä, P. (2012) 'Alueellisten työmarkkinoiden muutos', *Työ ja yrittäjyys. Työ ja elinkeinoministeriön julkaisuja,* 1.

Narizny, K. (2003) 'Both guns and butter, or neither: class interests in the political economy of rearmament', *American Political Science Review,* 97: 203–220.

Nevala, A. (1999) *Korkeakoulutuksen kasvu, lohkoutuminen ja eriarvoisuus Suomessa,* Helsinki: Suomen historiallinen seura.

Niemelä, H., & Salminen, K. (2006) *Social security in Finland,* Helsinki: Social Insurance Institution.

Noda, H. (2002) 'The Japanese pulp and paper industry and its wood use', in Y. Iwai (ed.), *Forestry and the forest industry in Japan,* Vancouver: University of British Columbia.

Noguchi, Y. (2010) *Shin Taisei: Saraba Sengo Keizai Zouho Ban,* Tokyo: Tokyokeizai Shinposha.

Norpoth, H. (1987) 'Guns and butter and government popularity in Britain', *The American Political Science Review,* 81: 949–959.

North, D.C. (1990) *Institutions, institutional change, and economic performance,* New York: Cambridge University Press.

Nyberg, P., & Vihriälä, V. (1993) 'The Finnish banking crisis and its handling', *Bank of Finland Discussion Papers,* 8/93.

Nygård, F. (1989a) 'Lifetime incomes in Finland: desk calculations based on civil servant salaries 1985', in R. Hagfors & P. Vartia (eds.), *Essays on income distribution, economic welfare and personal taxation,* Helsinki: Elinkeinoelämän tutkimuslaitos.

Nygård, F. (1989b) 'Relative income differences in Finland 1971–1981', in R. Hagfors & P. Vartia (eds.), *Essays on income distribution, economic welfare and personal taxation,* Helsinki: Elinkeinoelämän tutkimuslaitos.

Näsi, J., Lamberg, J.-A., Ojala, J., & Sajasalo, P. (eds.) (2001) *Metsäteollisuuden strategiset kehityspolut: Kilpailu, keskittyminen ja kasvu pitkällä aikavälillä,* Helsinki: WoodWisdom/Tekes.

Näsi, J., Ranta, P., & Sajasalo, P. (1998) *Metsäteollisuuden megamuutos: pelinäkökulmainen analyysi suomalaisen metsäteollisuuden kehkeytymisprosesseista vuosina 1985–1996,* Jyväskylä: Jyväskylän yliopisto.

Näsi, J., Sajasalo, P., & Sierilä, P. (2001) *A game-playing perspective on industry level megachange: an analysis of concentration in the Finnish forest sector 1985–1995: paper presented at the 18th Annual Conference of the Strategic Management Society,* Orlando, FL.

O'Brien, P. (2006) 'Historiographical traditions and modern imperatives for the restoration of global history', *Journal of Global History,* 1: 3–39.

OECD. (1981) *The welfare state in crisis,* Paris: OECD.

OECD. (2010a) Education at glance 2010: indicator A7: what are the economic benefits of education? Retrieved 30 March, 2011, from http://dx.doi.org/10.1787/888932310206.

OECD. (2010b) *Factbook 2010: economic, environmental and social studies,* Vienna: OECD.

OECD. (2011) *Economic policy reforms 2011: going for growth,* Paris: OECD.

OECD. (2011–2012) *Commodity Trade Data,* Paris: OECD.

OECD. (2012) *Education at glance 2012,* Paris: OECD.

OECD. (2013) *OECD skills outlook 2013: first results from survey of adult skills,* Paris: OECD.

Ojainmaa, K. (1994) *International competitive advantage of the Finnish chemical forest industry,* Helsinki: Taloustaito.

Ojala, A., Tanaka, Y., & Turunen, O. (2015) 'Higher education systems and labour market outcomes in Japan and Finland, 1950–2010', in Y. Tanaka, T. Tamaki, J. Ojala, & J. Eloranta (eds.), *Comparing post war Japanese and Finnish economies and societies,* Abingdon: Routledge.

Ojala, J. (2008) 'Pankkileireistä kansainvälisiin jättiyhtiöihin', in M. Kuisma (ed.), *Kriisi ja kumous,* Suomalaisen Kirjallisuuden Seura: Helsinki.

Ojala, J., Lamberg, J.-A., Ahola, A., & Melander, A. (2006) 'The ephemera of success: strategy, structure and performance in the forestry industries', in J.-A. Lamberg, J. Näsi, J. Ojala, & P. Sajasalo (eds.), *The evolution of competitive strategies in global forestry industries,* Dordrecht: Springer.

Okamoto, D. (2011) 'Revisiting Japanese lifetime employment system: financial performance analysis using artificial neural networks', *Keio Business Review,* 46: 1–23.

Okawa, K. (1981) *Paper and pulp industry: Kyouikusya-shinsyo,* Tokyo: Kyoikusha.

Okita, S. (1981) 'Shogen Kodoseichoki Okita Saburo', *Economist in Japan,* 59: 84–91.

Olábarri, I. (1995) 'A 'new' new history: a longue duree structure', *History and Theory,* 34: 1–29.

Opas, P. (2003, October 28) 'Japani kauppapolitiikkamme ongelmana', *Kauppapolitiikka.* Retrieved from http://www.kauppapolitiikka.fi/public/default.aspx?contentid=158251&nodeid=41404&contentlan=1&culture=fi-FI

Opas, P. (2007) *Japani: Aasian todellinen talousmahti,* Oulu: Metavisual.

Oshima, K. (2010) *Saisei Kanou Energy no Seiji Keizaigaku,* Tokyo: Tokyo Keizai Inc.

Osinsky, P., & Eloranta, J. (2015) 'Longitudinal comparative historical analysis: challenges and possibilities', in Y. Tanaka, T. Tamaki, J. Ojala, & J. Eloranta (eds.), *Comparing post war Japanese and Finnish economies and societies,* Abingdon: Routledge.

Ozawa, T. (1974) *Japan's technological challenge to the West, 1950–1974: motivation and accomplishment,* Cambridge: MIT Press.

Paasivirta, J. (1968) *Suomen diplomaattiedustus ja ulkopolitiikan hoito itsenäistymisestä talvisotaan,* Porvoo: WSOY.

Paavonen, T. (1998) *Suomalaisen protektionismin viimeinen vaihe: Suomen ulkomaankauppa- ja integraatiopolitiikka 1945–1961,* Helsinki: Suomen historiallinen seura.

Pajunen, K. (2008) 'Institutions and inflows of foreign direct investment: a fuzzy-set analysis', *Journal of International Business Studies,* 39: 652–669.

Palmer, G. (1990) 'NATO, social and defense spending, and coalitions', *The Western Political Quarterly,* 43: 479–493.

Paloheimo, M., Sugahara, K., Fukui, T., & Uotila, M. (2015) 'Two paths to building a welfare society: the development of work and family-related policies in post-war Finland and Japan', in Y. Tanaka, T. Tamaki, J. Ojala, & J. Eloranta (eds.), *Comparing post war Japanese and Finnish economies and societies,* Abingdon: Routledge.

Paret, P. (1992) *Understanding war. Essays on Clausewitz and the history of military power,* Princeton, NJ: Princeton University Press.

Park, S.-J., & Ruuskanen, E. (2015) 'Energy supply and regulation', in Y. Tanaka, T. Tamaki, J. Ojala, & J. Eloranta (eds.), *Comparing post war Japanese and Finnish economies and societies,* Abingdon: Routledge.

Paunio, J.J. (1959a) 'Review of *The Keynesian theory of economic development* by Kenneth K. Kurihara', *Kansantaloudellinen Aikakauskirja,* 55: 274–276.

Paunio, J.J. (1959b) 'Talousteoria ja talouspolitiikka', *Kansantaloudellinen Aikakauskirja,* 55: 129–134.

Pedersen, T., & Thomsen, S. (1997) 'European patterns of corporate ownership: a twelve-country study', *Journal of International Business Studies,* 28: 759–778.

Pedersen, T., & Thomsen, S. (1999) 'Business systems and corporate governance', *International Studies of Management and Organization,* 29: 43–59.

Pekkarinen, J. (1984) 'Kansantaloudellinen Yhdistys ja taloudellinen keskustelu Suomessa' *Sata vuotta suomalaista kansantaloustiedettä: Kansantaloudellinen Yhdistys 1884–1984,* Helsinki: Kansantaloudellinen Yhdistys.

Pekkarinen, J. (1986) *Keynesianism and the Finnish model of economic policy in a comparative perspective,* Helsinki: Työväen taloudellinen tutkimuslaitos.

Pekkarinen, J. (1988) *Keynesianism and the Scandinavian models of economic policy,* Helsinki: World Institute for Development Economics Research.

Pickett, S.E. (2002) 'Japan's nuclear energy policy: from firm commitment to difficult dilemma addressing growing stocks of plutonium, program delays, domestic opposition and international pressure', *Energy Policy,* 30: 1337–1355.

Pierson, C. (2004) 'Late industrializers and the development of the welfare state', *Social Policy and Development Programme Paper Number 16,* Geneva: United Nations Research Institute for Social Development.

Pieterse, J.N. (2009) *Globalization and culture: global mélange,* New York: Rowman & Littlefield.

Pihkala, E. (1988) 'Kauppapolitiikka ja ulkomaankauppa 1945–1986', in Y. Kaukiainen (ed.), *Sotakorvauksista vapaakauppaan. Kauppa- ja teollisuusministeriön satavuotisjuhlakirja,* Helsinki: Kauppa-ja teollisuusministeriö.

Piore, M.J. (1987) 'Historical perspectives and the interpretation of unemployment', *Journal of Economic Literature,* 25: 1834–1850.

Pohjola, M. (1996) *Tehoton pääoma. Uusi näkökulma talouden ongelmiin,* Porvoo: WSOY.

Pohl, N. (2005) 'Industrial revitalization in Japan: the role of the government vs the market', *Asian Business & Management,* 4: 45–65.

Pomeranz, K. (2000) *The great divergence: China, Europe, and the making of the modern world economy,* Princeton, NJ: Princeton University Press.

Porter, M.E. (1980) *Competitive strategies: Techniques for analyzing industries and competitors,* New York: Free Press.

Porter, M.E. (1990) *The competitive advantage of nations,* New York: Free Press.

Povinelli, E.A. (2001) 'Radical worlds: the anthropology of incommensurability and inconceivability', *Annual Review of Anthropology,* 30: 319–334.

Puikkonen, I. (2010) 'Cooperative Mankala companies: the acceptability of the company form in EC Competition Law,' *Helsinki Law Review,* 1: 139–156.

Ragin, C.C. (1987) *The comparative method,* Berkeley: University of California Press.

Ragin, C.C. (2000) *Fuzzy-set social science,* Chicago: University of Chicago Press.

Ránki, G. (1993) *The economics of the Second World War,* Vienna: Böhlau.

Reinhart, C.M., & Rogoff, K. (2008) 'Is the 2007 US sub-prime financial crisis so different? An international historical comparison', *American Economic Review,* 98: 339–344.

Reinhart, C.M., & Rogoff, K. (2009) *This time is different: eight centuries of financial folly,* Princeton, NJ: Princeton University Press.

Ringius, L., Torvanger, A., & Underdal, A. (2002) 'Burden sharing and fairness principles in international climate policy', *International Environmental Agreements,* 2: 1–22.

Robson, W.A. (1976) *Welfare state and welfare society: illusion and reality,* Crows Nest, Australia: Allen and Unwin.

Russett, B. (1982) 'Defense expenditures and national well-being', *The American Political Science Review,* 76: 767–777.

Ruuskanen, E. (2010) *Suosta voimaa ja lämpöä: Turve Suomen energiapolitiikassa. With English summaries,* Jyväskylä: Vapo Oy.

Räisänen, H., & Heinonen, E. (2005) *Comparative analysis on the job-broking market in Japan and Finland,* Helsinki: Valtion taloudellinen tutkimuskeskus.

Räisänen, H., & Hori, H. (2008) *Employment policies in two ageing societies: Japan and Finland compared,* Helsinki: Government Institute for Economic Research.

Rønsen, M., & Sundström, M. (2002) 'Family policy and after-birth employment among new mothers: a comparison of Finland, Norway and Sweden', *European Journal of Population,* 18: 121–152.

Saari, E. (1928) 'Suomen metsien taloudellinen merkitys', in L. Ilvessalo (ed.), *Maa ja metsä IV: Metsätalous, 1,* Porvoo: WSOY.

Sahi, J. (2008) *Salasähkeitä Tokiosta: Suomen Tokion-lähetystön toiminta ja suomalais-japanilaiset suhteet lähetystön perspektiivistä toisen maailmansodan aikana.* Master's thesis, University of Tampere, Tampere.

Sahi, J., & Igawa, K. (2015) 'Finnish-Japanese trade relations from protectionism to free trade 1919–2010', in Y. Tanaka, T. Tamaki, J. Ojala, & J. Eloranta (eds.), *Comparing post war Japanese and Finnish economies and societies,* Abingdon: Routledge.

Sainsbury, D. (1994) *Gendering welfare states,* London: Sage.

Sajasalo, P. (1999) 'Effects of substantial operating environment changes on mode of international operations', *Academy of Marketing Studies Journal,* 3: 20–42.

Sajasalo, P. (2002) 'Internationalization of a key industry: implications for a business and society relationship's development – case Finland', *Journal of International Business Research*, 1: 45–61.

Sajasalo, P. (2003) *Strategies in transition-the internationalization of Finnish forest industry companies (Diss.)* (Vol. 23/2003), Jyväskylä: Jyväskylän yliopisto.

Sajasalo, P. (2007) 'Analysis of internationalization strategy choices of firms through the metaphor of game', in G.R.G. Benito & H.R. Greve (eds.), *Progress in international business research*, Amsterdam: JAI Press/Elsevier.

Sajasalo, P., & Igawa, K. (2015) 'Growth of and industry: a comparison of paper industry in Japan and Finland', in Y. Tanaka, T. Tamaki, J. Ojala, & J. Eloranta (eds.), *Comparing post war Japanese and Finnish economies and societies*, Abingdon: Routledge.

Sajasalo, P., Ojala, J., & Lamberg, J.-A. (2001) 'Muutoksia suomalaisen metsäteollisuuden peliympäristössä', in P. Sajasalo, J. Ojala, & J.-A. Lamberg (eds.), *Metsäteollisuusyritysten strategiset kehityspolut: Kilpailu, keskittyminen ja kasvu pitkällä aikavälillä*, Helsinki: WoodWisdom.

Salomaa, T. (1999) *Japanai 2001*, Helsinki: Suomen yrityslehdet.

Samuelson, P. (1964) 'Theoretical notes on trade problems', *The Review of Economics and Statistics*, 46: 145–154.

Sandler, T., & Hartley, K. (1995) *The economics of defense*, Cambridge: Cambridge University Press.

Savela, O. (2009) Viennin romahdus ei lupaa hyvää: Tieto & trendit, 3/2009. From www.stat.fi/artikkelit/2009/art_2009-06-01_001.html.

Savolainen, J. (1994) 'The rationality of drawing big conclusions based on small cases: in defense of Mill's methods', *Social Forces*, 72: 1217–1230.

Schneider, M., Froggatt, A., & Thomas, S. (2011) *Nuclear power in a post-Fukushima world*, Washington, DC: Worldwatch Institute.

Sewell, W.H. (1996) 'Three temporalities: toward an eventful sociology', in T.J. McDonald (ed.), *The historic turn in the human sciences*, Ann Arbor: University of Michigan Press.

Shibata, T., & Tomokiyo, H. (1999) *Genpatsu Kokumin Seron – Seronchō̄sha ni miru Genshiryoku ishiki no hensen (Citizens' public opinion on nuclear power: changes in attitudes toward nuclear power seen through public opinion surveys)*, Tokyo: ERC Publishing Centre.

Shigemi, Y. (1995) 'Asset inflation in selected countries', *Monetary and Economic Studies: Bank of Japan*, 13: 89–130.

Shimomura, O. (1952) *Keizai Hendou no Josu Bunseki*, Tokyo: Toyokeizai-shinposya.

Shimomura, O. (1981a) 'Shogen Kodoseichoki no Nihon-Shimomura Osamu Jou', *Economist in Japan*, 59: 80–85.

Shimomura, O. (1981b 'Shogen Kodoseichoki no Nihon-Shimomura Osamu Ge', *Economist in Japan*, 59: 82–87.

Shinomiya, T. (1995) 'Paper and pulp industry', in O.K. (ed.), *History of Japanese industry after WW II*, Tokyo: Toyokeizai-shinposya.

Shinomiya, T. (1997) *Competition and cooperation in modern Japanese paper industry*, Tokyo: Nihonkeizai-hyoronsya.

Shionoya, T. (1941) *Koyou Rishi oyobi Kahei no Ippan Riron (Translation of J.M. Keynes, The general theory of employment, interest and money)*, Tokyo: Toyokeizai-shinposya.

Singer, J.D., & Small, M. (1993) *National material capabilities data, 1816–1985, 2001*, University of Michigan: Inter-university Consortium for Political and Social Research.

Sipilä, J., Anttonen, A., & Baldock, J. (2003) 'The importance of social care', in A. Anttonen, J. Baldock, & J. Sipilä (eds.), *The young, the old and the state. Social care systems in five industrial nations*, Cheltenham: Edward Elgar.

Skaperdas, S., & Syropoulos, C. (2001) 'Guns, butter, and openness: on the relationship between security and trade', *The American Economic Review*, 91: 353–357.

Skocpol, T. (1979) *States and social revolutions*, Cambridge, UK: Cambridge University Press.

Skocpol, T. (1987) 'Social history and historical sociology: contrasts and complementarities', *Social Science History*, 11: 17–30.

Skocpol, T., & Somers, M. (1980) 'The uses of comparative history in macrosocial inquiry', *Comparative Studies in Society and History*, 22: 174–197.

Slater, D., & Ziblatt, D. (2013) 'The enduring indispensability of the controlled comparison', *Comparative Political Studies*, 46: 1301–1327.

Somers, M. (1998) 'We're no angels: realism, rational choice, and relationality in social science', *American Journal of Sociology*, 4: 722–784.

Statistics Finland. (2011a) Employment of students. Retrieved 28 November 2013, from www.stat.fi/til/opty/2011/opty_2011_2013-03-20_tie_001_en.html.

Statistics Finland. (2011b) Official statistics of Finland (OSF): households' assets. Retrieved 22 November 2013, from www.tilastokeskus.fi/til/vtutk/tau.html.

Statistics Finland. (2012a) Official statistics of Finland (OSF): educational structure of population. Retrieved 30 October 2013, from http://tilastokeskus.fi/til/vkour/tau.html.

Statistics Finland. (2012b) Official statistics of Finland (OSF): entrance to education. Retrieved 14 November 2013, from www.tilastokeskus.fi/til/khak/2011/khak_2011_2012-12-13_tie_001_en.html.

Statistics Finland. (2012c) Official statistics of Finland (OSF): population structure. Retrieved 30 October 2013, from http://tilastokeskus.fi/til/vaerak/tau.html.

Statistics Finland. (2012d) Official statistics of Finland (OSF): providers of education and educational institutions. Retrieved 22 November 2013, from www.tilastokeskus.fi/til/kjarj/2012/kjarj_2012_2013-02-19_tau_001_en.html.

Statistics Finland. (2013) Official statistics of Finland (OSF): students and qualifications of educational institutions. Retrieved 22 November 2013, from http://stat.fi/til/opiskt/tau_en.html.

Statistics Japan. (2006) *Population census*, Tokyo: The Statistics Bureau, Ministry of Internal Affairs and Communications.

Stearns, P.N. (2003) 'Social history present and future', *Journal of Social History*, 37: 9–19.

Steinmetz, G. (2004) 'Odious comparisons: incommensurability, the case study, and "small *N*'s" in sociology', *Sociological Theory*, 22: 371–400.

Steinmetz, G. (2005) 'Positivism and its others in social sciences', in G. Steinmetz (ed.), *The politics of method in the human sciences: positivism and its epistemological others*, Durham, NC: Duke University Press.

Stinchcombe, A. L. (1991) 'The conditions of fruitfulness of theorizing about mechanisms in social sciences', in A. B. Sorensen & S. Spilerman (eds.), *Social theory and social policy: essays in honor of James S. Coleman*, Westport, CT: Praeger.
Subramanian, A. (1988) 'The paper industry: consumption trends and projections up to 2000 AD', *Economic and Political Weekly*, 23: M47–M52.
Suviranta, B. (1951) 'John Maynard Keynes. 5.6.1883–21.4.1946', in J. M. Keynes (ed.), *Työllisyys, korko ja raha*, Porvoo: WSOY.
SVT. (1919–1986, 2002–2003) [Official Statistics of Finland]. *Annual publications of foreign trade 1919–1986, 2002–2003*. Helsinki: Statistics Finland.
Takahashi, M. (1995) *Japanese welfare society: analysing the Japanese welfare discourses*, Tampere: University of Tampere.
Takahashi, M. (2003) 'Care for children and older people in Japan: modernizing the traditional', in A. Anttonen, J. Baldock, & J. Sipilä (eds.), *The young, the old and the state: social care systems in five industrial nations*, Cheltenham: Edward Elgar.
Takahashi, M. (2010) 'Risk, family, and gender justice in contemporary Japan', in M. Folkerts, R. K. H. Chan, & M. Takahashi (eds.), *Risk and public policy in East Asia*, Farnham: Ashgate Publishing Group.
Takamura, J., & Koyama, H. (1994) *History of Japanese industry 3*, Tokyo: Nihonnkeizai-shinbun.
Takegawa, S. (2009) 'International circumstances as factors in building a welfare state: welfare regimes in Europe, Japan and Korea', *International Journal of Japanese Sociology*, 18: 79–96.
Talouselämä (2013, June 3) [Newspaper].
Tamaki, T., & Särkkä, T. (2015) 'Macroeconomic thinking and policymaking in post-war Japan and Finland: the role of Keynesian macroeconomics', in Y. Tanaka, T. Tamaki, J. Ojala, & J. Eloranta (eds.), *Comparing post war Japanese and Finnish economies and societies*, Abingdon: Routledge.
Tamminen, M. (1951) 'Tämän hetken kansantalaoustiede', *Kansantaloudellinen Aikakauskirja*, 47: 17–30.
Tanzi, V., & Schuknecht, L. (2000) *Public spending in the 20th century. A global perspective*, New York: Cambridge University Press.
Tarjanne, R., & Kivistö, A. (2006) *Arvio Suomen energiatalouden nykytilanteesta ja siihen johtaneesta energiapolitiikasta*. Lappeenranta: Lappeenrannan teknillinen yliopisto.
Tarkka, J. (1988) 'Kahlitun rahan aika. Suomen rahoitusmarkkinoiden säännöstelyn vuosikymmenet', in S. Honkapohja & A. Suvanto (eds.), *Raha, Inflaatio ja Talouspolitiikka*, Helsinki: Valtion painatuskeskus.
Taylor, A. J. P. (1961) *The origins of the Second World War*, London: Hamilton.
Tervasmäki, V., Vuorenmaa, A., & Juutilainen, A. (1977) 'Ylimääräiset kertausharjoitukset – liikekannallepano, joukkojen keskittäminen ja sotavalmius' *Talvisodan historia 1, Suomi joutuu talvisotaan, Sotatieteen laitoksen julkaisuja XVI:1*, Porvoo: Sotatieteen laitos.
Thompson, M. (1996) 'Late industrialisers, late democratisers: developmental states in the Asia-Pacific', *Third World Quarterly*, 17: 625–647.
Tilastokeskus. (2009) CO_2 emissions in Finland. Retrieved May 26, 2012, from http://tilastokeskus.fi/til/khki/2009/khki_2009_2011-04-28_kuv_001_en.html.

Tilly, C. (1963) *The Vandee: a sociological analysis of the counter-revolution of 1793,* Cambridge: Cambridge University Press.

Tilly, C. (1975) 'Reflections on the history of European state-making', in C. Tilly (ed.), *The formation of national states in Western Europe,* Princeton, NJ: Princeton University Press.

Tilly, C. (1984) *Big structures, large processes, huge comparisons,* New York: Russell Sage Foundation.

Tilly, C. (2006) 'Why and how history matters', in R. Goodin & C. Tilly (eds.), *Oxford handbook of contextual political analysis,* Oxford: Oxford University Press.

Tilly, C., & Goodin, R. (2006) 'It depends', in R. Goodin & C. Tilly (eds.), *Oxford handbook of contextual political analysis,* Oxford: Oxford University Press.

Tocqueville, A. d. (1835/2003) *Democracy in America,* New York: Penguin.

Tocqueville, A. d. (1856/2008) *Ancien regime and the French Revolution,* New York: Penguin.

Tokoro, M. (2003) 'Social policy and lone parenthood in Japan: a workfare tradition', *The Japanese Journal of Social Security Policy,* 2: 45–58.

Tokoro, M. (2012) 'Recent policy changes in the Universal Child Benefit in Japan', *Local Economy,* 27: 651–656.

Toppinen, A. (1998) *Econometric models on the Finnish roundwood market* (Vol. 701), Helsinki: METLA.

Toyota. (1988) *Toyota. A history of the first 50 years,* Tokyo: Toyota Motor Corporation.

Turkki, T. (2005) *Kahdeksan pilven takaa: Japanin murros ja uusi nousu,* Helsinki: Edita.

UNESCO. (2008) Gender parity index. Retrieved 22 November 2013, from http://stats.uis.unesco.org/unesco/TableViewer/tableView.aspx?ReportId=3677.

UNESCO. (2010) Education. Retrieved 22 November, 2013, from http://stats.uis.unesco.org.

UNESCO. (2013) Education & public reports: historical data – tertiary education. Retrieved 22 November, 2013, from http://stats.uis.unesco.org/unesco/TableViewer/tableView.aspx?ReportId=3677.

Urponen, K. (1994) 'Huoltoyhteiskunnasta hyvinvointivaltioon', in Jouko Jaakkola et al. (eds.), *Armeliaisuus, yhteisöapu, sosiaaliturva: suomalaisen sosiaalisen turvan historia,* Jyväskylä: Sosiaaliturvan Keskusliitto.

Uusitalo, R. (1999) 'Return to education in Finland', *Labour Economics,* 6: 569–580.

Uzuhashi, T. (2002) 'Fukushi Kokka, Fukushi Zaisei no Kokusai-hikaku', in S. Saito, E. Yamamoto, & M. Ichien (eds.), *Fukushi Zaisei Ron,* Tokyo: Yuhikaku Publishing.

Valaskivi, K. (ed.) (2006) *Vaurauden lapset: Näkökulmia japanilaiseen ja suomalaiseen nykykulttuuriin,* Tampere: Vastapaino.

Valtonen, H. (2013) 'How did popular educators transform into experts of the Finnish welfare state from the 1860's to the 1960's?', in M. Buchardt, P. Markkola, & H. Valtonen (eds.), *Education, state and citizenship,* Helsinki: Nordic Centre of Excellence NordWel.

Vartiainen, J. (1999) 'The economics of successful state intervention in industrial transformation', in M. Woo-Cummings (ed.), *The developmental state,* Ithaca, NY: Cornell University Press.

Veblen, T. (1899/2009) *The theory of the leisure class*, Oxford: Oxford University Press.
Veblen, T. (1915/2006) *Imperial Germany and the Industrial Revolution*, New York: Cosimo Classics.
Vesterinen, I. (1995) *Valkoisen rannan kylä. Tutkimus itäjapanilaisesta pienyhteisöstä*, Helsinki: Yliopistopaino.
Vesterinen, I. (2001) *Geishan maailma. Tarua ja totta*, Hämeenlinna: Karisto.
Vihriälä, V. (1997) *Banks and the Finnish credit cycle 1986–95*, Helsinki: Bank of Finland.
von Fieandt, O. (1951) 'Review of *The Life of John Maynard Keynes* by R.F. Harrod', *Kansantaloudellinen Aikakauskirja*, 47: 240–244.
Vuori, J., & Merviö, M. (2007) *Japanin ja Suomen hyvinvointijärjestelmien vertailtavuus: vertailu- ja arviointimallin konstruointi erityisesti julkisen ja yksityisen käsitteiden näkökulmasta*, Kuopio: Kuopion yliopisto.
Välimaa, J. (2001) 'The changing nature of academic employment in Finnish higher education', in J. Enders (ed.), *Academic staff in Europe: changing contexts and conditions*, Westport, CT: Greenwood Press.
Välimaa, J. (2013) 'Das Bildungwesen und die Entwicklung der Nation', in A. Halmesvirta (ed.), *Lant unter dem Nordlicht. Eine Kulturgeschichte Finnlands*, Darmstadt: WBG.
Waitt, G. (1994) 'Global competition and the nature of trade in the European Community's pulp and paper industry', *Economic Geography*, 1: 60–71.
Wallerstein, I. (1974) *The modern world-system 1: capitalist agriculture and the origins of the European world-economy in the sixteenth century*, Berkeley: University of California Press.
Ward, M.D., & Davis, D.R. (1992) 'Sizing up the peace dividend: economic growth and military spending in the United States, 1948–1996', *The American Political Science Review*: 748–755.
Waris, K. (1958) 'Aktiivinen rahapolitiikka nykysuhdanteessa', *Kansantaloudellinen Aikakauskirja*, 54: 98–111.
Watanabe, C. (1995) 'Identification of the role of renewable energy: a view from Japan's challenge: THE New Sunshine Program', *Renewable Energy*, 6: 237–274.
Watanabe, C., & Honda, Y. (1991) 'Inducing power of Japanese technological innovation-mechanism of Japan's industrial science and technology policy', *Japan and the World Economy*, 3: 361–390.
Webber, C., & Wildavsky, A. (1986) *A history of taxation and expenditure in the Western world*, New York: Simon and Schuster.
Weber, H. (2007) 'A political analysis of the formal comparative method: historicizing the globalization and development debate', *Globalizations*, 4: 559–572.
Weber, M. (1905/2002) *The Protestant ethic and the spirit of capitalism*, New York: Penguin.
Weber, M. (1922/1978) *Economy and society. 2 volumes*, Berkeley: University of California Press.
Wickering, H. (2004) *Umweltziele und Indikatoren: Wissenschaftliche Anforderungen an ihre Festlegung und Fallbeispiele*, Heidelberg: Springer.
Wiener, J.B. (ed.) (2011) *The reality of precaution: comparing risk regulation in the United States and Europe*, London: Routledge.
Wilensky, H.L. (1975) *The welfare state and equality: structural and ideological roots of public expenditures*, Berkeley: University of California Press.

Windolf, P. (1997) *Expansion and structural change: higher education in Germany, the United States, and Japan, 1870–1990,* Boulder, CO: Westview Press.

Woo-Cummings, M. (ed.) (1999) *The developmental state,* Ithaca, NY: Cornell University Press.

Yamaguchi, S. (2009) 'Denki Jigyou' *Keizai Bunya ni okeru Kisei Kaikaku no Eikyou to Taisaku,* Tokyo: National Diet Library.

Yasui, T. (1970–1972) *Yasui Takuma Chosakusyu,* vols. 3. Tokyo: Sogensha.

YLE Uutiset (2013, February 12) [Newspaper].

Yoshikawa, H. (2012) *Kodo Seicho: Nihon wo Kaeta 6000 Nichikan,* Tokyo: Chuo-Koronsha.

Zhang, Y., Song, J., & Hamori, S. (2011) 'Impact of subsidy policies on diffusion of photovoltaic power generation', *Energy Policy,* 39: 1958–1964.

Index